ANCIENT ISRAEL
A Short History from Abraham to the
Roman Destruction of the Temple

On the cover: The silver dome of the Al-Aqsa mosque on Jerusalem's
Temple Mount overlooks extensive excavations of the ancient remains
along the Old City's southern wall. *Photo by Garo Nalbandian.*

ANCIENT ISRAEL

A Short History from Abraham to the Roman Destruction of the Temple

Edited by
Hershel Shanks

PRENTICE HALL

PRENTICE-HALL
ENGLEWOOD CLIFFS, NEW JERSEY

BIBLICAL ARCHAEOLOGY SOCIETY
WASHINGTON, D.C.

Library of Congress Cataloging-in-Publication Data

Ancient Israel : a short history from Abraham to the Roman destruction
of the Temple / edited by Hershel Shanks.
   p.   cm.
Includes index.
   Contents: The Patriarchal Age / P. Kyle McCarter, Jr. -- Israel in
Egypt / Nahum M. Sarna -- The settlement in Canaan / Joseph A.
Callaway -- The united monarchy / André Lemaire -- The divided
monarchy / Siegfried H. Horn -- Exile and return / James D. Purvis -
- The Age of Hellenism / Lee I. A. Levine -- Roman domination /
Shaye J.D. Cohen.
   ISBN 0-13-036435-5 (pbk.) : $15.00
   1. Jews--History--To 70 A.D.   I. Shanks, Hershel.   II. Biblical
Archaeology Society.
DS117.A66   1988b
933--dc19   88-22583
                                                        CIP

Copyright by the Biblical Archaeology Society, 1988
Co-published by: Biblical Archaeology Society
3000 Connecticut Avenue, N.W.
Washington, D.C. 20008
and
Prentice-Hall
A Division of Simon & Schuster
Englewood Cliffs, New Jersey 07632

Design by Auras Design, Washington, D.C.
Library of Congress Catalog Card Number: 88-42996
ISBN #0-9613089-4-X (clothbound)
ISBN #013-036435-5 (paperbound)

Prentice-Hall International (UK) Limited, *London*
Prentice-Hall of Australia Pty. Limited, *Sydney*
Prentice-Hall Canada Inc., *Toronto*
Prentice-Hall Hispanoamerican, S.A., *Mexico*
Prentice-Hall of India Private Limited, *New Delhi*
Prentice-Hall of Japan, Inc., *Tokyo*
Simon & Schuster Asia Pte. Ltd., *Singapore*
Editora Prentice-Hall do Brasil, Ltda., *Rio de Janeiro*

List of Illustrations

List of Color Plates

1 The Sinai peninsula
2 Beni-hassan wall painting
3 Ai (et-Tell)
4 Philistine pottery
5 Ammonite king statue
6 Israelite bull figurine
7 Wall relief of Judeans leaving Lachish
8 Herodium
9 Masada

List of Maps and Charts

Introducing the Authors . . .

P. KYLE McCARTER, JR. is associate dean of the School of Arts and Sciences and William F. Albright Professor of Biblical and Ancient Near Eastern Studies at Johns Hopkins University in Baltimore, Maryland. He was recently elected president of the American Schools of Oriental Research. He has also taught at Harvard, the University of Virginia and Dartmouth. His extensive writings include the volumes on I Samuel and II Samuel in the Anchor Bible series.

NAHUM M. SARNA is Dora Golding Professor Emeritus of Biblical Studies at Brandeis University. He is the author of the widely acclaimed *Understanding Genesis* (New York: Schocken Books, 1970) and *Exploring Exodus* (New York: Schocken Books, 1986). He is the general editor of the forthcoming *Bible Commentary* of the Jewish Publication Society of America. He also served as a principal editor and translator of the new Jewish Publication Society's translation of the Hebrew scriptures. He is the author of hundreds of scholarly articles and encyclopedia entries.

JOSEPH A. CALLAWAY directed the archaeological expedition to Ai between 1964 and 1976. He has also excavated at Jericho, Shechem and Bethel. He served as president of the William F. Albright School of Archaeological Research in Jerusalem and is a trustee of the American Schools of Oriental Research. Until his retirement in 1982, he was professor of biblical archaeology at Southern Baptist Theological Seminary. He is the author or editor of eight books and innumerable articles.

ANDRÉ LEMAIRE is chargé de recherche at the Centre National de la Recherche Scientifique in Paris. He has excavated at Lachish and Tel Keisan in Israel. He is the author of a history of Israel in French. His most important scholarly work involves ancient Hebrew inscriptions. He is the editor of a collection of ancient Hebrew ostraca and is presently preparing a full corpus of Paleo-Hebrew inscriptions from the First Temple period.

SIEGFRIED H. HORN directed the excavation of Hesban from 1968 to 1973 after having dug at Shechem for four seasons in the 1960s. Now dean and professor emeritus at Andrews University, Berrien Springs, Michigan, Horn was honored in 1978 when the university's archaeological museum was renamed for him. The author of 12 books and more than 800 articles, Horn is a former director of the American Center of Oriental Research in Amman, Jordan.

JAMES D. PURVIS is professor of Religion at Boston University; for ten years he served as chairman of the department of religion. He has excavated at Tel Dor and Tel Gezer in Israel and at Idalion in Cyprus. He is the author of "The Samaritans in the Hellenistic Period" in *The Cambridge History of Judaism* and of numerous articles in the new *Harper's Bible Dictionary*, as well as in scholarly journals.

LEE I. A. LEVINE is associate professor of archaeology and history at the Hebrew University in Jerusalem. He has directed the excavation of an ancient synagogue at Horvat Ammudim and has co-directed excavations at Caesarea. His *Excavations at Caesarea Maritima—Final Report*, written with Ehud Netzer, was published in 1987. In 1986-87 he served as research professor of history at Harvard University and as visiting professor of history at Yale University.

SHAYE J. D. COHEN is Jack and Miriam Shenkman Professor of the Post-Biblical Foundations of Western Civilization at the Jewish Theological Seminary of America in New York and dean of the seminary's graduate school. He is the author of two books, most recently *From the Maccabees to the Mishnah: A Profile of Judaism* (Philadelphia: Westminster Press, 1987). He is the author of nearly 50 scholarly articles and reviews.

HERSHEL SHANKS is founder, editor and publisher of *Biblical Archaeology Review* and *Bible Review*. He is the author of *The City of David*, a guide to biblical Jerusalem; and *Judaism in Stone*, tracing the development of ancient synagogues. A graduate of Harvard Law School, he has also published widely on legal topics.

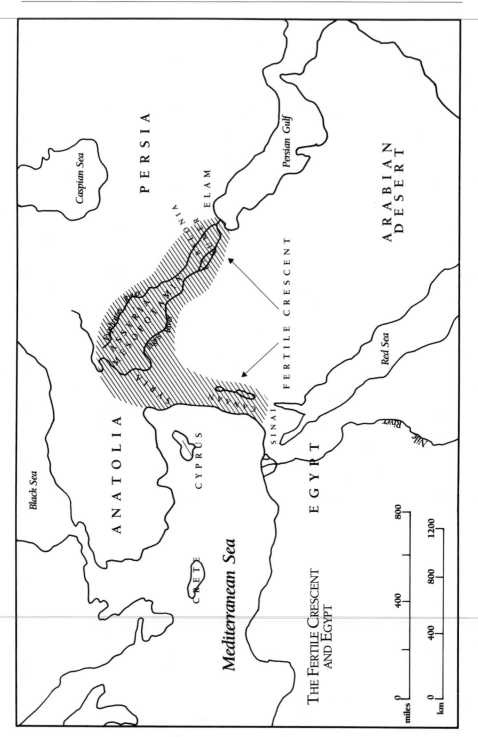

THE FERTILE CRESCENT
AND EGYPT

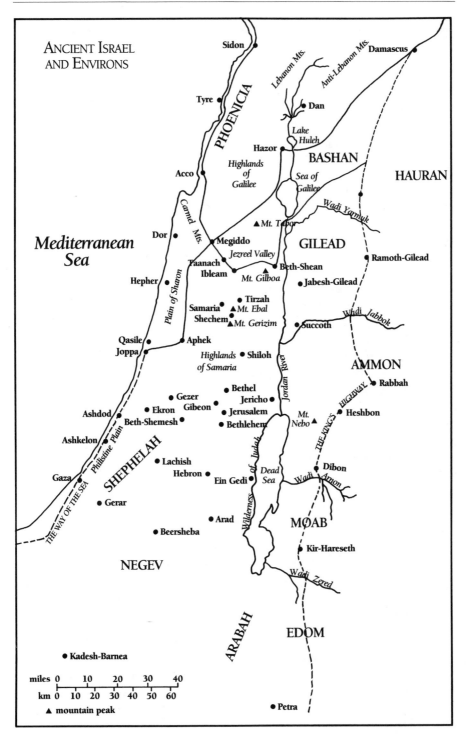

ANCIENT ISRAEL
AND ENVIRONS

Sidon

Damascus

Tyre

PHOENICIA

Lebanon Mts.

Anti-Lebanon Mts.

Dan

Lake Huleh

Hazor

BASHAN

HAURAN

Acco

Highlands of Galilee

Sea of Galilee

Wadi Yarmuk

Carmel Mts.

Dor

▲ Mt. Tabor

Mediterranean Sea

Megiddo

Jezreel Valley

GILEAD

Ramoth-Gilead

Taanach
Ibleam

Beth-Shean

Hepher

▲ Mt. Gilboa

Jabesh-Gilead

Plain of Sharon

Tirzah

Samaria
Shechem

▲ Mt. Ebal
▲ Mt. Gerizim

Succoth

Wadi Jabbok

Qasile
Joppa

Aphek

Highlands of Samaria

Shiloh

Jordan River

AMMON

Rabbah

Bethel

Jericho

Gezer

Gibeon

Jerusalem

Mt. Nebo ▲

Heshbon

Ashdod

Ekron

Beth-Shemesh

Bethlehem

THE KING'S HIGHWAY

Ashkelon

SHEPHELAH

Lachish

Wilderness of Judah

Dead Sea

Dibon

Gaza

Philistine Plain

Hebron

Ein Gedi

Wadi Arnon

Gerar

THE WAY OF THE SEA

Arad

MOAB

Beersheba

Kir-Hareseth

NEGEV

Wadi Zered

ARABAH

EDOM

Kadesh-Barnea

miles 0   10   20   30   40

km 0   10   20   30   40   50   60

▲ mountain peak

Petra

Abbreviations

AJS	Association for Jewish Studies		4 vols. (Nashville, TN: Abingdon Press, 1962; supp. vol., 1976)
ANEP	*Ancient Near East in Pictures*, James B. Pritchard (Princeton, NJ: Princeton Univ. Press, 1954; 2nd ed., 1969)	IEJ	*Israel Exploration Journal*
		IES	Israel Exploration Society
ANET	*Ancient Near Eastern Texts*, ed. James B. Pritchard (Princeton, NJ: Princeton Univ. Press, 3rd ed., 1969)	JAAR	*Journal of the American Academy of Religion*
		JAOS	*Journal of the American Oriental Society*
Antiq.	Josephus, *Antiquities of the Jews*	JBL	*Journal of Biblical Literature*
Apion	Josephus, *Contra Apion*	JCS	*Journal of Cuneiform Studies*
ASAE	*Annales du Service des Antiquités de l'Égypte*	JEA	*Journal of Egyptian Archaeology*
ASOR	American Schools of Oriental Research	JJS	*Journal of Jewish Studies*
AUSS	*Andrews University Seminary Studies*	JNES	*Journal of Near Eastern Studies*
BA	*Biblical Archaeologist*	JNSL	*Journal of Northwest Semitic Languages*
BAR	*Biblical Archaeology Review*	JQR	*Jewish Quarterly Review*
BAS	Biblical Archaeology Society	JR	*Journal of Religion*
BASOR	*Bulletin of the American Schools of Oriental Research*	JSJ	*Journal for the Study of Judaism*
BJRL	*Bulletin of the John Rylands Library*	JSOT	*Journal for the Study of the Old Testament*
BN	*Biblische Notizen*	JSS	*Journal of Semitic Studies*
BR	*Bible Review*	MDOG	*Mitteilungen der deutschen Orient-Gesellschaft*
BS	*Bibliotheca Sacra*	NTS	*New Testament Studies*
BZAW	*Beihefte zur Zeitschrift für die alttestamentliche Wissenschaft*	PAAJR	*Proceedings of the American Academy of Jewish Research*
CAH	*Cambridge Ancient History*, ed. I.E. Edwards (Cambridge, UK: Cambridge Univ. Press, 1981)	PEQ	*Palestine Exploration Quarterly*
CBQ	*Catholic Biblical Quarterly*	RB	*Revue Biblique*
CHJ	*Cambridge History of Judaism*, ed. W.D. Davies and Louis Finkelstein (Cambridge, UK: Cambridge Univ. Press, 1984)	REJ	*Revue des Études Juives*
		SBL	Society of Biblical Literature
		THB	*Tyndale House Bulletin*
EAEHL	*Encyclopedia of Archaeological Excavations in the Holy Land*, 4 vols., ed. Michael Avi-Yonah and Ephraim Stern (Englewood Cliffs, NJ: Prentice-Hall, 1975)	TDOT	*Theological Dictionary of the Old Testament*, 5 vols., ed. G.J. Botterweck and H. Ringgren (Grand Rapids, MI: Eerdmans, 1978)
		VT	*Vetus Testamentum*
HDB	James Hastings, ed., *Dictionary of the Bible* (New York: Scribners, 1963)	War	Josephus, *The Jewish War*
HTR	*Harvard Theological Review*	ZAW	*Zeitschrift für die alttestamentliche Wissenschaft*
HUCA	*Hebrew Union College Annual*	ZDPV	*Zeitschrift des deutschen Palästina-Vereins*
IDB	*Interpreter's Dictionary of the Bible*,		

Acknowledgments

First and foremost, our gratitude goes to the eight authors of the chapters in this book. Each of them is a great scholar absorbed in a dozen different tasks. Each took time out to synthesize and summarize, to speak to the layperson about a particular period in ancient Israelite history in a way that could be easily understood. Each willingly worked with the editor to polish and clarify, to enhance understanding without sacrificing detail or accuracy.

The beautiful color pictures that enhance the text could not be included within the strictures of commercial publishing. To bridge this gap, so that we could have a colorful book as well as a readable text, several foundations and individuals stepped forward. We are deeply grateful to them:

The Joseph Meyerhoff Foundation

The Leopold and Clara M. Fellner Charitable Foundation, Frederick L. Simmons, Trustee

Kathe Weiss Schwartzberg

Milton Gottesman, Esq.

Arnold J. and Amalie M. Flegenheimer

The staff of the Biblical Archaeology Society worked unstintingly, as usual, to make this book a superior product: Wendy Miller copy-edited the text with great care, wrote the captions and prepared the map material; Carol Andrews undertook the painstaking task of editing the endnotes; Susan Laden coordinated the entire production; Robert Sugar designed the book and its cover with the immeasurable assistance of Karol A. Keane.

Thanks also to Barry J. Beitzel, author of *The Moody Atlas of Bible Lands,* who consulted on the maps; Donald Wigal, who prepared the index; and our printer, Alvin Shultzberg of Townhouse Press.

Finally, we thank the staff at Prentice-Hall for their guidance and support: Joseph Heider, Religion Editor, Simon and Schuster Higher Education Group; and Linda Albelli, his assistant.

Hershel Shanks

Introduction

HERSHEL SHANKS

This is a unique history of ancient Israel. Obviously, there are many other histories of ancient Israel, some of them recent, but none like this one. These are the features that make this one unique:

- It is short. The text itself—from Abraham to the Roman destruction of the Temple—is only 235 pages, including pictures, charts and maps.
- The scholarship is absolutely first rate. This is because each of its eight chapters has been written by a world-famous scholar treating his specialty.
- This history reflects the most recent developments and the latest archaeological discoveries. While thinking about producing this book, I asked experts in the field to name a first-rate short history of ancient Israel, and they invariably came up with something 25 or 30 years old and therefore necessarily out-of-date.
- This book is intended for people of all faiths—and for skeptics, too. It reflects no particular religious commitments—nor is it anti-religious. The authors include Protestants, Catholics and Jews. They live in Israel, France and the United States.
- This history of ancient Israel spans the centuries from her patriarchal beginnings to 70 A.D., when the Romans burned Jerusalem and destroyed the Temple. Almost all other histories of ancient Israel either begin later (for example, with the settlement period) or end earlier (for example, with the return to Jerusalem of the Babylonian exiles). By contrast, here the reader will face the full impact of an unparalleled historical sweep.
- This text is highly readable—written to be understood, as we say at

the Biblical Archaeology Society. It has been carefully edited, so that the words of the text are an enticement, not an obstacle. All arcane academese has been purged. I must add that the eminent scholars who wrote the text have been most cooperative during the sometimes arduous editing process; their aim, like the editor's, has been maximum clarity and maximum readability consistent with accuracy.

• Although it is short and readable, the text is fully annotated, so that the interested student has the references with which to explore in greater detail any matter of particular interest. Moreover, despite the brevity of the text, we have tried to give the evidence, or at least examples of the evidence, that lies behind the historical judgments. We hope we have avoided the unsupported assertion: "Trust me; I know the answer." There is enough evidence here to let the reader make his or her own judgment.

• Finally, the text is festooned with beautiful pictures—many of them in full color—that enhance and illuminate the text.

For these reasons, I believe this is the best book available for all those who are taking their first serious look at the history of ancient Israel—religious school students, college students, seminary students, adult study groups and the intellectually curious of all ages. This book also provides a short, but comprehensive and up-to-date refresher course for those who have been here before.

There are many ways to use this book—as many ways as there are teachers, students and interested readers. But for all, I would suggest an initial quick-through reading. Read it like a novel from beginning to end. If you begin to bog down in too many details for this kind of reading, then skip—but keep going.

It is important to get the sweep of things, the big picture. This is a remarkable story, an immensely moving passage through time—about 2,000 years of it, ending nearly 2,000 years ago. I don't mean to suggest that reading this book is like attending a Cecil B. DeMille saga. This is a serious study. But beneath the details is a panorama of historical movement that is spiritually elevating as well as intellectually stimulating. No reader should miss this scope.

Moreover, a quick reading should make the reader comfortable with the overarching structure of ancient Israel's history. The major segments in that history—patriarchal wanderings, the Egyptian sojourn and the Exodus, the settlement of Canaan in the time of the Judges, the institution and development of the monarchy under Saul, David and Solomon, the split-up of the kingdom, the destruction of the northern kingdom by the Assyrians, the destruction of Solomon's Temple and the southern kingdom by the Babylonians, exile in Babylonia and Egypt, the return to the land, the rise of a new Jewish state under the Maccabees, the Hellenization of the Jewish world, the tensions of Roman domination in the Herodian period and, finally, the burning of Jerusalem and destruction of the Second Temple that effectively ended the Jewish revolt against Rome—will be firmly fixed in mind. Then details can be filled in on a slower, more intensive second reading.

A word of explanation may be appropriate to explain why we begin and end where we do. Why we begin with Abraham is simple. According to the Bible, he was the first Hebrew. The first 11 chapters of Genesis, before the introduction of Abraham, are referred to as the Primeval History. They do not purport to cover Israelite history.

Moreover, the first 11 chapters of the Bible, in the judgment of modern critical scholars, are mythic, not historic. This does not diminish the power or meaning of these stories, but it does mean that from a factual viewpoint we must approach them differently. Of course, this judgment sometimes collides with the religious faith of people who are committed to the literal truth of Scripture. This issue, however, need not detain us here because even in the Bible's own terms, the history of Israel begins only with Abraham, the first Hebrew.

For many scholars, the more difficult question will be why we begin so early, rather than so late—with the patriarchs rather than, say, with the Israelite settlement in Canaan. Some scholars will question whether there is any discoverable history in the Bible's stories about the patriarchs Abraham, Isaac and Jacob. There is obviously a historiographic problem here, to which we shall return. Suffice it to say at this point that the fact that the Bible recites the stories of the patriarchs as the earliest chapters of Israelite history is enough to require a consideration of the extent to which, if at all, these stories reflect or contain history of one sort or another. We are not, *a priori*, committed to an answer, but we are committed to asking the question.

At the other end of the time continuum, many scholars will question our decision to end with the Roman destruction of the Temple in 70 A.D. In discussing this project with scholars, I was told several times that it would be more appropriate to continue the story to 135 A.D., when the Romans finally suppressed the second Jewish Revolt, the so-called Bar-Kokhba Revolt.

There is substance to this contention. I nevertheless rejected it for several reasons. First, any cut-off is to some extent arbitrary. The world always goes on, or at least it has until now. And past events always influence the future. Second, the final destruction of the Jewish Temple in Jerusalem in 70 A.D. was such a cataclysmic event that it can lay claim to marking a historic termination and a new beginning. Third, the book was already long enough, especially as a short history. Fourth, and perhaps decisive, we hope to produce a subsequent volume tracing the parallel developments of Christianity and Judaism during the early centuries of the Common Era; in that book, we will cover the events both leading up to and following the Bar-Kokhba revolt.

I have mentioned the sweep of the story and the overarching structure of the historical development. The reader will also notice another development as the story moves along. This development relates to the *nature* and *reliability* of the sources from which this history is constructed.

Let us consider the kinds of sources on which the recovery of our history depends. From the patriarchal period through the Exile (chapters

I through VI), the primary source is the Bible. The biblical account is supplemented by what we loosely call archaeological discoveries. (They may or may not have been recovered in a scientifically controlled excavation.) These archaeological artifacts are of two kinds—the "word" kind and the "non-word" kind. The "word" kind includes inscriptions and texts. The "non-word" kind includes anything from a pollen sample, to a pottery sherd, to the wall of an ancient palace. In addition to the Bible and archaeological discoveries, we occasionally have a late copy of an earlier book whose author refers to or makes use of ancient sources now lost. But this last category is relatively rare.

The reader will notice that archaeological discoveries are more helpful in uncovering the past as we move down the time line. They are least helpful and least specific in the patriarchal period. Gradually they become more helpful and more specific.

There is another kind of development—a development on the continuum of reliability. We are least sure of what happened in the patriarchal period. Gradually, we become more confident of the history we are recounting as time moves on. Where we are least sure of what happened, we are most reliant on the biblical text. This might be thought to lead to the conclusion that archaeological discoveries are what really give reliability to the biblical text. But this is not true. As between the biblical text and archaeological discoveries, the biblical text is overwhelmingly more important than the archaeological discoveries. We would pretty much know what happened from the biblical text even without the archaeological discoveries. The reverse is not at all true.

Why then is the early history of ancient Israel less reliable than the later history? The answer relates not to the illumination archaeology provides but to the nature of the biblical text. The traditional, etiological stories of the patriarchal period present far different historiographic problems than the account of, for example, the Divided Kingdom, which the biblical writers took largely from royal annals.

As a result, the reader will notice another kind of development. In the early chapters of this book, the authors devote major attention to the reliability of the biblical account and to the ways they can penetrate the text to discover what in fact happened. In the earlier periods, we are more concerned with how to deal with the biblical text than with how to interpret the history recounted. Gradually, the emphasis shifts. By the time we reach the Divided Kingdom, we can pretty much rely on the facts given in the Bible, and the historian's task is chiefly to present and interpret those facts to create a modern history. By contrast, in the patriarchal age we confront a basic question of biblical historicity: Were the patriarchs real people who lived at a particular time in history?

In the period of the Egyptian sojourn and the Exodus, we are still at an early time when we must ask whether there was an Egyptian enslavement and an Exodus, but it seems relatively clear that something like that in fact occurred. We are more concerned with placing events in a particular period and with assessing the reliability of details.

By the time we reach the period of the settlement and the Judges, we are on firm, datable historical ground. But here we are faced with a fundamental question. Did the Israelites possess the land by military conquest, by peaceful infiltration into uninhabited areas, or was there perhaps an internal revolt of the underclass that led to Israel's emergence in Canaan? This is obviously a different kind of historiographic problem than the authors of the previous chapters were required to face.

In the period of the United Kingdom, the question of factual historicity begins to fade into the background. The major historical problem is to redress the biases reflected in the text, so that we can arrive at a more objective history of the period.

When we deal with the period of the Divided Kingdom, and the Babylonian Exile and return, less attention is paid to historiography or the question of reliability, although these questions never disappear.

For the history recounted in the last two chapters of the book, dealing with the Hasmonean period and Roman rule, only a few late books of the Bible are relevant. Equally, if not more important, is a host of classical authors, especially the first-century Jewish historian Josephus. So-called intertestamental texts, pseudepigrapha and apocrypha, such as Maccabees, as well as later rabbinic writings and the New Testament also provide evidence. The amount of archaeological materials that shed light on this period is enormous. Pride of place, of course, goes to the famous Dead Sea Scrolls, many of which are only now becoming available to scholars. But scholars must also absorb a host of other religious and non-religious texts, as well as archaeological artifacts ranging from buildings to coins.

Another contrast: In the earlier period described in this book the relevant evidence is sparse, and we must squeeze it in a dozen different ways to get what we reliably can from it. In the later periods, on the other hand, the amount of evidence is truly overwhelming, beyond the capacity of any human being to command. Here the task is to find meaningful strands, overarching trends in a sea of material.

The differences in the various chapters of the book reflect the differences outlined above—in the nature and reliability of the sources; in the historiographic problems; in the light archaeology sheds on the particular period and in the sheer quantity of material that must be taken into account. The result is a fascinating variety. Reading this story will be a richer experience if these differences are kept in mind.

Ancient Israel was, in the end, defeated; but it was not destroyed. It survived. And it continued to shape the world, as the Bible says, "to this day." To understand this history is to discern why its influence endured. And only in terms of this history can we truly appreciate the scriptural treasures it left us. It is a history that is at once intellectually penetrating and spiritually uplifting. Now, in the words attributed to the great first-century sage Hillel, "Go and study!"

June 1988, Washington, D.C.   *Hershel Shanks*

O N E

The Patriarchal Age

Abraham, Isaac and Jacob

P. KYLE McCARTER, JR.

THE HISTORY OF ISRAEL BEFORE THE EXODUS FROM EGYPT IS, AS the Bible presents it, a family history. The story begins with the departure of Abram, son of Terah, from Ur, his ancestral homeland in southern Mesopotamia. He journeys to Haran, a city in northwestern Mesopotamia, and from there to the land of Canaan (Genesis 11:31-12:5). In Canaan, Abram's son Isaac is born, and Isaac, in turn, becomes the father of Jacob, also called Israel (Genesis 32:28). During a famine Jacob and his 12 sons, the ancestors of the 12 tribes of Israel, leave Canaan and settle in Egypt, where their descendants become slaves.

This segment of Israel's history, therefore, is the story of the patriarchs: Abram or Abraham (Genesis 17:5), Isaac, Jacob/Israel and the 12 sons of Jacob.

The biblical description of the patriarchal period is concerned largely with private affairs, as one might expect in the story of an individual family. There are only a few references to public events, and none of these corresponds to a known event of general history. Genesis 14, for example, describes a war in which the kings of the five Cities of the Plain (Sodom, Gomorrah, Admah, Zeboiim and Bela or Zoar) are arrayed against an alliance of four kings led by Chedorlaomer, king of Elam, a country that lay east of Mesopotamia. Chedorlaomer is said to have ruled over the Cities of the Plain before they rebelled (Genesis 14:4). There is no surviving extra-biblical record of these events, and neither the name of Chedorlaomer nor that of his ally Amraphel, king of Shinar (Babylonia), has been found in Mesopotamian records. Despite numerous attempts, no scholar has succeeded in identifying any of the nine kings involved in the war. The same is true of the other public figures mentioned in the patriarchal history: None can be identified from extra-biblical sources. Thus, we know nothing of Melchizedek, king of Salem, apart from what we read in Genesis 14, or of Abimelech, king of Gerar, apart from what is said in Genesis 20 and 26. There is no mention in external sources of the Egyptian officer Potiphar (Genesis 39), of Hamor, apparently a ruler of Shechem (Genesis 35), or of Ephron the Hittite, a prominent citizen of Hebron (Genesis 23). The early kings of Edom listed in Genesis 36:31-39 are known only from the Bible. We might expect to be able to identify the pharaoh of Genesis 12:10-20 or the pharaoh of the Joseph story, but neither pharaoh is called by name in the Bible.

When did the patriarchs live?   In the absence of references to persons or events of general history, it is very difficult to determine the historical context to which the stories in Genesis 12-50 belong. The initial question, then, is a simple one. When did the patriarchs live?

At first glance, an answer to this question seems to be available from chronological indications in the biblical narrative itself. We are told that Abraham was 75 years old when he set out for Canaan (Genesis 12:4) and 100 when Isaac was born (Genesis 21:5). According to Genesis 25:26, Isaac was 60 years old when Jacob was born. Then, if Jacob was 130 when he descended into Egypt, as we read in Genesis 47:9, the full time the patriarchs spent in Canaan before going to Egypt was 215 years. Subsequently, we are told that the period of slavery in Egypt lasted 430 years (Exodus 12:40), and that the time from the Exodus from Egypt to the beginning of the construction of the Temple in the fourth year of Solomon's reign was 480 years (1 Kings 6:1). This brings us close to the period where we have secure chronological information: Scholars agree that Solomon died within a decade or so of 930 B.C. According to 1 Kings 11:42 he reigned 40 years. It follows that his fourth year, the year work began on the Temple, was about 966 B.C. Reckoning backward from this date and using the numbers cited above, we arrive at the following scheme.

2091 B.C. Abram's departure for Canaan
1876 B.C. The descent of Jacob's family into Egypt
1446 B.C. The Exodus from Egypt
966 B.C. The beginning of the construction of Solomon's Temple

According to these calculations, the patriarchal period (the time of the sojournings of Abraham, Isaac and Jacob in Canaan) was between 2091 and 1876 B.C., and the time of the enslavement of the Israelites in Egypt was between 1876 and 1446 B.C.

Unfortunately, there are serious problems with this scheme. First, it accepts the impossibly long lifespans assigned the patriarchs.*

Second, it is internally inconsistent. Moses and Aaron were fourth generation descendants of Jacob's son Levi (1 Chronicles 5:27-29). The 430 years assigned the slavery in Egypt is too much for the three generations from Levi to Moses and Aaron, an average of about 143 years. In any event, this is inconsistent with the notice that Joshua, a younger contemporary of Moses and Aaron, was a 12th-generation descendant of Levi's brother Joseph (1 Chronicles 7:20-27). If this were true, the 11 generations from Joseph to Joshua would average about 39 years each.

Third, the dates produced by this chronology for the Exodus and settlement do not correspond well with the evidence of history and archaeology. If the Exodus occurred about 1446 B.C., then by the same chronology the conquest of Canaan must have begun 40 years later, about 1406 B.C. There is, however, no archaeological evidence of a widespread destruction or change of population at the end of the 15th century. On the contrary, the changes in material culture that archaeologists associate with the appearance of the Israelites in Canaan took place, in general, in the 13th or 12th century B.C., and the first clear historical evidence for the presence of Israel in Canaan is in the so-called Israel stele of the Egyptian pharaoh Merneptah, dating about 1207 B.C. (see chapter 3).

The Bible's own chronological scheme, therefore, does not provide intelligible evidence for the dating of the patriarchal period. This fact, combined with the absence of references to events of general history noted above, indicates that the patriarchal narratives in Genesis cannot be utilized as historical resources in any simple or straightforward fashion. They must be interpreted on the basis of an understanding, first, of their distinctive literary history and the purposes for which they were composed and, second, of the development of the traditions upon which they are based.

Scholars are generally agreed that the patriarchal narratives, as we now have them, are composite. They contain at least three written strata, or strands, of which the earliest was composed during the time of the kingdoms of Israel and Judah (tenth to sixth centuries B.C.)** and the latest after the Babylonian destruction of Jerusalem (587 B.C.†). All of these strata were brought together and arranged in approximately their present form at some time in the Second Temple period (after 538 B.C.) or, at the earliest, during the Babylonian Exile (587-538 B.C.). On the surface, therefore, the biblical patriarchal history reflects the political and religious viewpoint of the Judean monarchy and priesthood. Thus, the

---

* Abraham, 175 years (Genesis 21:7); Isaac, 180 years (Genesis 35:28); Jacob, 147 years (Genesis 47:28); Joseph, 110 years (Genesis 50:26).

** This is the earliest period in Israel's history when written historiography could be expected to develop. See chapter 4 by André Lemaire on the period of the United Kingdom.

† Scholars do not agree on the date of the Babylonian destruction of Jerusalem. In this volume, Profs. McCarter, Lemaire and Purvis ascribe a date of 587 B.C., while Profs. Horn, Cohen and Levine use the date 586 B.C.

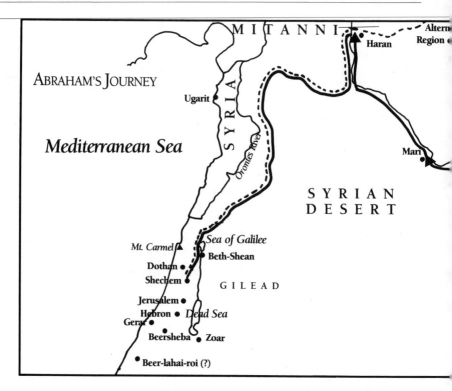

ABRAHAM'S JOURNEY

Mediterranean Sea

MITANNI

Haran

Altern
Region

Ugarit

SYRIA

Orontes River

Mari

SYRIAN
DESERT

Mt. Carmel
Sea of Galilee
Beth-Shean
Dothan
Shechem
GILEAD
Jerusalem
Hebron • Dead Sea
Gerar
Beersheba • Zoar
Beer-lahai-roi (?)

Are the
patriarchs
historical
individuals or
eponyms?

promise made to Abram in Genesis 12:2 is that his descendants will be, not simply a numerous people, but a great "nation."

On this level, the men and women who appear in Genesis 12-50 are less accessible as historical individuals than as typological prefigurations of the later Israelites and their neighbors. In many cases they are eponyms, that is, persons from whom the names of the later groups were supposed to be derived. Thus Jacob is also called "Israel" (the name of the nation in later times), and his 12 sons are the eponymous ancestors of the 12 tribes of Israel. The narratives and genealogies characterize the various peoples of the writers' own times and delineate the relationships among them from an Israelite perspective. Thus, Israel's ancestors are born under auspicious circumstances, whereas the eponymous ancestors of the Moabites and Ammonites, "Moab" and "Ben-ammi," are born of incestuous unions of Lot and his daughters (Genesis 19:30-38). Jacob ("Israel") outwits his brother Esau, who is also called "Edom" (Genesis 25:30, 36:1), and wins Esau's birthright and blessing. Ishmael, the eponymous ancestor of the tribes that inhabited the desert region between Judah and Egypt, is the child of the Judahite patriarch Abram and Sarai's Egyptian maid Hagar (Genesis 16). This kind of material, though of great value in considering the political outlook of later Israel, is very difficult to use for historical purposes in an effort to reconstruct the world of

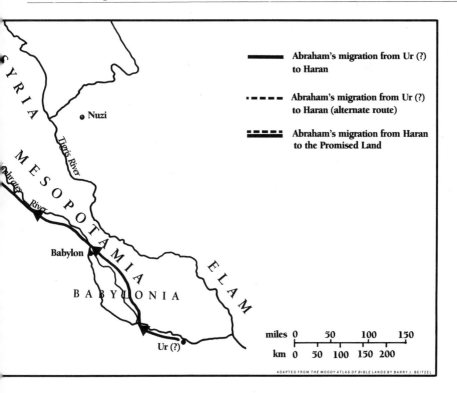

Legend:

━━━━━ Abraham's migration from Ur (?) to Haran

▪ ▪▪ ▪▪ Abraham's migration from Ur (?) to Haran (alternate route)

▬▬▬▬ Abraham's migration from Haran to the Promised Land

miles 0   50   100   150

km 0   50   100   150   200

ADAPTED FROM *THE MOODY ATLAS OF BIBLE LANDS* BY BARRY J. BEITZEL

Israel's ancestors.

If Genesis 12-50 in its present form reflects the time of the biblical writers (that is, the time of the monarchy or later) rather than the time of the patriarchs themselves, is it possible to look behind the present, literary form of the biblical narrative to examine the traditions upon which this material is based? Such a procedure might shed light on the development of the traditions and, ultimately, provide information about the history of the patriarchal age. Modern scholars, therefore, have developed methods for studying the preliterary history of the stories in Genesis.

One such method, which was especially popular in the middle decades of the 20th century, was based largely on archaeology. The scholars associated with this method took a generally positive view of the historical value of Genesis 12-50. They acknowledged that the patriarchal narratives in their present form were composed no earlier than the United Kingdom (tenth century B.C.). Nevertheless, they argued that these materials were based on historically reliable traditions deriving from earlier periods. Excavations had provided extensive new data, including a substantial amount of written material. After studying these texts, many scholars were convinced that the biblical patriarchal stories contained authentic details preserved from the time of their origin. It seemed reasonable, therefore, to suppose that there was a historical patriarchal period and to hope that it might be identified.

This point of view is associated most closely with the work of William F. Albright and his students.[1] It was also developed and promoted by other prominent scholars, especially Ephraim A. Speiser.[2] In brief, the argument of this "school" was as follows: Certain details in the biblical patriarchal stories—including personal names, social customs, legal practices and aspects of life-style—correspond to known features of second-millennium culture in Mesopotamia, Syria and Canaan. Many of the same details, moreover, do not fit into the culture of the Israelite monarchy, the time when the stories were first written down. Thus, in the judgment of Albright and those who shared his viewpoint, it seemed likely that these details preserved authentic elements of the civilization of the patriarchal period and that by studying them and comparing them to surviving second-millennium materials outside the Bible, we can determine the original historical context of the patriarchal traditions. As Albright himself put it,[3]

> "So many corroborations of detail have been discovered in recent years that most competent scholars have given up the old critical theory according to which the stories of the Patriarchs are mostly retrojections from the time of the Dual Monarchy [tenth century B.C. and later]."

He wrote elsewhere,[4]

> "As a whole, the picture in Genesis is historical, and there is no reason to doubt the general accuracy of the biographical details and the sketches of personality which make the patriarchs come alive with a vividness unknown to a single extrabiblical character in the whole vast literature of the ancient Near East."

In general, Albright's students did not express this viewpoint quite so strongly. As they acknowleged, archaeology cannot be expected to corroborate biographical details or specific references to private events. Nevertheless, archaeology might be able to shed light on the general historical context of the patriarchal stories. And this is primarily what was claimed by Albright and his students. They argued that the general cultural milieu of the patriarchal stories—as indicated by the details of social, economic and legal customs mentioned in the Bible—could best be identified with an early period and, more particularly, with the early second millennium B.C. According to G. Ernest Wright:[5]

> "We shall probably never be able to prove that Abram really existed, that he did this or that, said thus and so, but what we can prove is that his life and times, as reflected in the stories about him, fit perfectly within the early second millennium, but imperfectly with any later period."

The reconstruction of patriarchal history achieved by Albright, Speiser and the others has had far-reaching consequences. It remains widely influential today. Recent research, however, has cast substantial doubt on many of its arguments, and the confidence these arguments inspired in scholars a generation ago is gone. To understand why this change has taken place, we must look more closely at the reconstruction and the evidence upon which it was based.

An urban culture flourished in Syria and Canaan during the Early Bronze Age, which spanned much of the third millennium B.C. During the last quarter of the third millennium, however, this civilization collapsed and was replaced by a predominantly nonurban, pastoral culture. The factors that produced this change are not fully known. The third dynasty of the city of Ur held sway in Mesopotamia at the time, and the records of the Ur III rulers complain of chronic trouble with nonurban peoples who were laying claim to lands previously controlled by the city. Scholars long supposed, therefore, that a chief factor in the urban collapse was an invasion—or at least a massive immigration—of nomadic peoples from the desert fringes of the region. These peoples, called *Amurru*—that is, "Westerners" or "Amorites"—in the Mesopotamian sources, gradually gained the ascendancy in the settled portions of both Syria-Canaan and Mesopotamia, so that in the early second millennium they took the leadership in the reestablishment of urban centers.

The theory that an invasion or immigration of Amorites was responsible for the radical cultural changes that characterized the transition from Early to Middle Bronze is sometimes called "the Amorite hypothesis." A corollary of this hypothesis identifies the biblical patriarchs as Amorites. Albright associated Abraham's wanderings with the Amorite movements and dated the Abraham phase of the patriarchal period to the end of the third millennium. He called this period, which he dated to 2100-1900 B.C., Middle Bronze I (MB I), since it represented a break from the preceding Early Bronze Age and it was characterized by the arrival of the people who would assume cultural leadership in the subsequent Middle Bronze Age.

The succeeding period, which Albright called MB II A, was an age of unwalled villages in Syria and Canaan. The strong 12th Dynasty kings of Egypt encouraged the gradual development of a system of city-states in Syria and Canaan. Then, as Egypt began to weaken at the end of this period, the new urban centers entered a period of independence, prosperity and high cultural attainment. Albright thought of this period, which he called MB II B, as the time of the patriarch Jacob. It was the Old Babylonian period in Mesopotamia, when Hammurabi and his successors ruled. In Syria it is sometimes called "the age of Mari," after a city on the upper Euphrates that attained a position of ascendancy in Syria and western Mesopotamia at the time. The life and history of Mari are recorded in a major cuneiform archive found at the site, Tell Hariri on the Syrian side of the Syro-Iraqi frontier. Local leadership for the process of reurbanization came from the previously nomadic Amorite population. We know this because the new ruling dynasties in the city-states of Syria and Mesopotamia have characteristically Amorite names. There remained, however, a substantial nomadic population, which was also Amorite. The royal archives of Mari provide ample illustration of the coexistence of the two groups.

Many scholars—including many of Albright's students—were reluctant to be as precise as Albright himself in his dating of the Abraham phase of the patriarchal period to MB I and the Jacob phase to MB II B. They preferred a more general date, contending "simply that the Patriarchal stories are best understood in the setting of the early second millennium."[6] This position had the advantage of avoiding one of the problems of the Amorite hypothesis in its original form: Although MB I (to which Albright assigned the Abraham phase) was a strictly nonurban period, several cities *are* mentioned in the Abraham narratives in the Bible.* Moreover, none of the archaeological sites associated with these cities has yielded any substantial MB I remains.[7] It seemed better, therefore, to identify the patriarchal age with the subsequent period of reurbanization in MB II and, more particularly, MB II B. Throughout Genesis Abraham, Isaac and Jacob are depicted as living in tents in proximity to urban centers, a situation compared to the coexistence of nomadic and urban peoples at Mari and other cities in MB II B. Thus it was argued that the patriarchal way of life as depicted in the Genesis narratives was especially compatible with what we know of the civilization of the early second millennium.[8]

In addition to general observations of this kind, two arguments were developed to support the association of the patriarchs with the early second millennium. The first was based on analysis of the personal names found in Genesis 12-50; the second, on studies of the social customs and legal practices mentioned in the patriarchal narratives.

Let us consider the personal names first. As indicated above, Amorite names form a distinctive group. They can be identified by a number of peculiar linguistic features. Names of this type are common in materials from the first half of the second millennium. Advocates of a similar date for the patriarchal age pointed out that the names in the patriarchal narratives are largely of the same type. A form of the name "Jacob," for example, occurs several times in early second-millennium materials, and the name "Abram" is said to be attested for the same period.[9] No examples of "Isaac" or "Joseph" have survived, but both of these names are of the Amorite type. By contrast, names of this type are not found in the biblical records of the monarchical period. The argument, therefore, was that the biblical names from the patriarchal period fit well in the historical context of the early second millennium and cannot have originated later, at the time of the biblical writers.

Second, Albright, Speiser and others cited numerous parallels between social and legal practices mentioned in extra-biblical texts from the second millennium and social and legal practices referred to in the biblical patriarchal narratives. Cuneiform texts from Nuzi in upper Mesopotamia were especially prominent in this part of the discussion.[10]

---

* The various cities of the Jordan valley (Genesis 14:12), the Philistine city of Gerar (Genesis 20:1), the fortified city of Hebron (Genesis 23:10), etc.

The Nuzi tablets reflect the practices and customs of the Hurrians, a people who flourished in the eastern Tigris region in the middle of the second millennium. Although no one attempted to associate the patriarchs directly with the Hurrian kingdom of Mitanni, it was well known that Hurrian influence was widespread in Syria and even Canaan in this period. Thus, numerous Hurrian-biblical connections were proposed. According to the terms of a Nuzi marriage contract, for example, a barren wife was required to provide a slave woman to her husband to bear his children.[11] In Genesis 16:1-4 the barren Sarai sends her maid Hagar to Abram for the purpose of bearing children. The parallel is obvious. At Nuzi, if the union produced a son the slave woman's child could not be subsequently expelled; compare Abraham's unwillingness to send away Hagar and Ishmael, her son, in Genesis 21:10-11. Again, as interpreted by Speiser:[12]

"In Hurrian society a wife enjoyed special standing and protection when the law recognized her simultaneously as her husband's sister, regardless of actual blood ties . . . . This dual role conferred on the wife a superior position in society."

According to Speiser, this custom lies in the background of those episodes in Genesis where Abraham (12:10-20, 20:1-18) and later Isaac (26:6-11) introduce their wives as their sisters.

The story of Sarai and Hagar and the wife-sister episodes are only two examples of the numerous details of the patriarchal narratives that were interpreted in light of information drawn from texts of the Middle Bronze Age (about 2000-1500 B.C.). The general argument was that many social and legal customs referred to in Genesis have parallels in middle or early second-millennium practice, while the same customs are without parallel in later times. From this it was concluded that the presence of these references in Genesis was an indication of the early second-millennium origin of the traditions.

Despite its attractions, this reconstruction has proved vulnerable to criticism of various kinds.

A scholarly failure

Doubts about the application of the Amorite hypothesis to the problems of the patriarchal period have led to serious modification or abandonment of many of the positions cited above. It now seems unlikely that an invasion or immigration of nomads was a primary factor in the collapse of urban civilization in the last part of the third millennium.[13] The pastoral peoples so prominent in this period were present in earlier times as well, living alongside the established urban centers. Overpopulation, drought, famine or a combination of such problems may have exhausted the resources necessary to the maintenance of an urban way of life. When the cities disappeared, the nomadic encampments remained. Other nomads, originally living on the fringes of the desert, probably took advantage of the new situation to infiltrate previously settled areas; but there was no widespread immigration, and most of the cultural changes detected by archaeology can best be explained as indigenous, not produced by the arrival of outsiders. The period called MB I by Albright, therefore, was really the last, post-urban phase of the Early Bronze Age, and an emerging consensus of scholarship now prefers to call it Early Bronze IV (EB IV).*

If no invasion or widespread migration is assumed to have taken place in EB IV, there is no reason to associate Abram's wanderings with the events of that period, especially in view of the difficulty, already noted, created by the absence in this period of the urban centers mentioned in Genesis 12-25.

On the other hand, the circumstances of what we now call late MB I (Albright's MB II A) and MB II (MB II B), during which nomads and urban dwellers lived side by side in Syria and Canaan, remain a suitable context for the patriarchal stories.[14] Also, as we have seen, a modified version of the Amorite hypothesis located the patriarchal period more generally in the early second millennium. It is becoming increasingly clear, however, that this "dimorphic" pattern—of city dwellers and tribal peoples (including both pastoralists and villagers) living contiguously— has been typical of the Middle East from ancient until modern times.[15] This pattern prevailed even in the third millennium; after the interruption of EB IV, it resumed in the Middle Bronze Age, as the archives from Mari show.[16] Although we do not have archival evidence for later periods, as we do for the earlier period at Mari, there is no reason to doubt that the pattern persisted throughout the Late Bronze Age and beyond. The archaeological evidence and modern anthropological studies seem to confirm this.[17] Thus, the observation that this dimorphic lifestyle is a fitting background for the stories about the patriarchs provides no basis for locating them in MB I and II in preference to other periods.

The other criteria urged in favor of an early second-millennium date for the patriarchal age have also been challenged. In almost every specific instance, the proposed parallels between details of the patriarchal stories and information found in surviving second-millennium documents have now been disputed.[18] Many of the parallels are no longer regarded as valid. In many other cases, the phenomena in question have been identified in texts from one or more later periods, thus diminishing the importance of the parallels for dating the patriarchal tradition. More particularly, the Nuzi evidence, which figured so prominently in the discussion, has been vitiated by the discovery that the information it provides about private life reflects widespread Mesopotamian practices,

---

* Many scholars also now believe that Albright's dates for this period were about a century too low. Our dating and periodization of the Middle Bronze Age in contrast to the scheme developed by Albright is shown in the following chart. In general, we follow Dever (see endnote 13):

Date	Archaeological Period	Albright's Scheme	Albright's Date
2250-2000	EB IV	MB I	2100-1900
2000-1800	MB I	MB II A	1900-1750
1800-1630	MB II	MB II B	1700-1600
1630-1550	MB III	MB II C	1600-1550

rather than distinctively Hurrian customs that might be assumed to have penetrated into Canaan.[19]

We can no longer argue, for example, that the patriarchal names fit best into the early second millennium. Names similar or identical to the names found in Genesis are attested from a number of different periods. The identification of the name "Abram" or "Abraham" in Middle Bronze materials is uncertain or dubious, whereas forms of this name ("Abram," "Abiram") occur several times in texts from the Late Bronze Age (1550-1200 B.C.) and later.[20] Moreover, names with the same structure are exceedingly common, attested in almost all periods.[21] Similarly, the name type to which "Isaac," "Jacob" and "Joseph" belong is widely distributed across the history of the ancient Near East. It is especially well known from Middle Bronze sources and, in fact, is the most characteristic type of Amorite name.[22] But there is no reason to believe that its use diminished after the Middle Bronze Age; in the Late Bronze Age, it is well attested in Ugaritic and Amarna Canaanite names.[23] Thus, while it is true that the name "Jacob" is very common in the Middle Bronze Age, it is also found in Late Bronze sources,[24] and related names occur in both Elephantine (fifth century B.C.) and Palmyrene (first century B.C. through third century A.D.) Aramaic.[25]

Similar difficulties exist with the proposition that the legal practices and social customs referred to in the stories in Genesis support a Middle Bronze date for the patriarchs. Reexamination of the second-millennium parallels proposed by Albright, Speiser and the others has shown that many cannot be restricted to a single, early period. Thus, for example, the Nuzi parallel to Genesis 16:1-4, in which the barren Sarai provides her husband with her bondwoman, is not unique: The responsibility of a barren wife to provide a slave woman to her husband for the purpose of bearing children is cited in Old Babylonian, Old Assyrian and Nuzi texts (all from the Middle Bronze Age), but also in a 12th-century Egyptian document and a marriage contract from Nimrud, dated 648 B.C.[26] As for the biblical "wife-sister motif," it now seems doubtful that relevant parallel material is to be found in the Nuzi archives. In the contracts cited by Speiser the adopting "brother" is not ordinarily the future husband of the adopted woman.[27] Although in one case a "brother" does subsequently marry his "sister," this is a special case requiring a document of marriage to replace the earlier document of adoption. In the biblical stories, moreover, the designation of the wives of the patriarchs as sisters is a trick to protect the patriarchs from men who might lust after their wives, not a legal procedure intended to confer status. Speiser recognized this, suggesting that the "original" meaning was lost; but Speiser's assumption is highly questionable in view of the inapplicability or at least ambiguity of the Nuzi parallels.[28]

A second and very different attempt to trace the preliterary history of the patriarchal stories—undertaken at about the same time that Albright and the others were investigating the archaeological materials—is

The search for the history of tradition

associated with the names of Martin Noth and his teacher Albrecht Alt. These two scholars sought to penetrate to an early stage in the patriarchal tradition by means of a critical analysis of the biblical literature itself.

On the basis of his study of the biblical materials pertaining to the premonarchical period, Noth was convinced that the larger entity of Israel had been formed by an amalgamation of various clans and tribes, a process that took place gradually during the period of settlement in Canaan.[29] From Noth's point of view, therefore, it seemed impossible that all of these clans and tribes could have known *all* of the traditions about the presettlement period—about the patriarchs, the captivity in Egypt and the Exodus, the wanderings in the wilderness, the revelation at Sinai, and the conquest of Canaan. Instead, individual elements of these traditions must have been passed down within individual tribes or clans. As these groups were absorbed into the larger association of Israel, the various elements of tradition were combined and incorporated into a common heritage.

Drawing on the form-critical method devised by Hermann Gunkel,[30] Noth tried to reconstruct the history of discrete units of tradition from their origin within a particular tribe or clan to their integration into the larger story.[31] This method has been described as the "history of traditions."

A major clue to the origin of a particular element of a tradition is its connection with a region, place or other geographical feature. The narratives about the individual patriarchs have certain clear geographical connections. Abraham is generally associated with southern Canaan, and his principal residence is at the "oaks of Mamre" near Hebron (Genesis 13:18, 14:13, 18:1). Isaac dwells at the oases of Beersheba (Genesis 26:32-33) and Beer-lahai-roi (Genesis 24:62, 25:11). Jacob is most closely identified with Shechem (Genesis 33:18-19) and Bethel (Genesis 28:18-19, 35:1-8), though he also has important associations with Gilead (Genesis 31:43-50, 32:2-3, 32:30, 33:17). Thus, it seemed likely to Noth that the traditions about Abraham come from the Judean Hills, those about Isaac from southwestern Judah and the Negev, and those about Jacob from the central Ephraimite hills. Noting that Jacob—the immediate ancestor of the Israelites, whose name was also Israel—is linked with the heartland of the country, Noth concluded that the Jacob tradition is the oldest component of the patriarchal lore. As Israel expanded southward, absorbing Judah and the northern Negev, Abraham and Isaac entered the tradition and then were linked by genealogy with Jacob. The priority eventually assigned to Abraham (the first patriarch) is an indication of the southern development of the tradition as it has come down to us.

When did this blending of patriarchal traditions take place? That is, when were the stories about Abraham and Isaac combined with those about Jacob? It is obvious that this development was completed during the time when the stories were being transmitted orally, before the composition of the so-called J source,* the earliest of the literary strands in Genesis, in which Abraham, Isaac and Jacob are understood to be members of the same family. The dates biblical scholars assign to J differ widely, however, ranging from the tenth to the sixth centuries B.C. A better clue to the date at which the northern and southern patriarchal traditions were combined, therefore, is the priority that was assigned the southern patriarchs when the combination took place. The fact that a southern patriarch (Abraham) was regarded as the eldest suggests that the combination occurred at a time when Judah was in ascendancy over Israel. Such a political situation cannot have existed, however, before the establishment of the Davidic monarchy. Indeed, it is unlikely that Judah was incorporated into Israel before the reign of David.[32] And even if Judah was a part of Israel when David came to the throne, it had not been so for long, since the earliest tribal list makes no mention of the southern tribes (cf. Judges 5:14-18). It is not likely, therefore, that patriarchal figures from the newly incorporated regions of Hebron and Beersheba would have been accorded priority over the old Israelite patriarch Jacob before the radical realignment of power that took place when David the Judahite became king of Israel. Thus, the combination of traditions that led to the arrangement that has been preserved in the patriarchal stories cannot have been complete before the end of the 11th century. We must not forget, however, that this combination was one of the last phases of a lengthy and complex development, which must have gone on for centuries. Noth believed that the development of the tradition was coeval with the development of Israel itself. That is, the process that shaped the patriarchal tradition was concurrent with the long series of clan and tribal alliances by which Israel grew from the earliest group that bore the name to a larger tribal association and, finally, to a kingdom.

Although the history of traditions allows us to trace the preliterary development of the *traditions* about the patriarchs, it provides only very indirect information about the patriarchs themselves. Noth did not deny that the patriarchs might have actually lived, but he believed that even if they did, they are now inaccessible as historical figures. Because the patriarchal traditions as we know them are products of the settlement period, they cannot be relied upon to preserve authentic historical information about the patriarchal period itself.[33]

Noth assumed that the patriarchal tradition grew from small, originally independent literary units into its present complex pattern. In this assumption he followed Gunkel, who believed that folk literature evolved from short, simple units into extended, discursive complexes. Thus, for Noth, a story with a complex structure was necessarily late, whereas a simple narrative unit was likely to be early. Subsequent improvement in our understanding of oral literatures, however, has exposed the error

Another scholarly failure

---

* According to the documentary hypothesis, the Pentateuch is an amalgam of at least four strands or sources: the J source (the Yahwist); the E source (the Elohist); the P source (Priestly material) and the D source (Deuteronomistic material). J and E were combined before the introduction of D and P. Many scholars now doubt that E had an independent existence apart from J.

of this view.[34] We now know that in the preliterary, oral stage of transmission, long stories with complex structures were routine in most traditional literatures. Homer, for example, was almost certainly an oral poet; the Ugaritic* myths and epics, if they are not actual transcriptions of oral performances, stand very close to the stage of oral composition. Both the Homeric and Ugaritic literatures are characterized by extended narratives with complex structures.

Recent analysis of the patriarchal tradition itself shows that Noth's account of its evolution from isolated units to interconnected patterns requires revision. As we noted at the outset of our discussion, the story of the biblical patriarchs is a family story. The traditional complex that underlies the present narratives of Genesis is, in the last analysis, an elaborate account of kinship relationships that existed (or were believed to exist) between the ancestors of Israel and their neighbors. Modern anthropological research has shown that kinship patterns are very often the central factors in the social structure and self-definition of a community. Drawing upon this research and his own studies of the stories in Genesis 12-36, Robert A. Oden has been able to demonstrate that the tradition complex that underlies the patriarchal narratives constitutes a systematic definition of Israel according to criteria of lineage and marriage alliance commonly found in other societies and traditional literatures.[35]

In general, Oden's conclusions are as follows: Citing Robert Wilson's work on ancient Near Eastern genealogies,[36] he notes that the patriarchal stories represent an elaboration of two types of genealogy. One is a linear genealogy,[37] extending from Abraham** to Jacob, which defines Israel *externally*, that is, in relation to other peoples. The second is a segmented (laterally branched) genealogy, beginning with the 12 sons of Jacob, which defines Israel *internally*, that is, in terms of its own tribes and smaller units. The narrative expresses a special interest in the marriages of the patriarchs, placing stress on the fact that Abraham, Isaac and Jacob all marry within the larger family group. There is some vagueness about the precise preexisting familial relationship between Abraham and Isaac and their wives:[38] In one of the early source strata of the Pentateuch (the so-called E stratum) we are told that Sarah was Abraham's half-sister (Genesis 20:12), but in the other early source (the older J stratum) this relationship is not mentioned. Rebekah was Isaac's first cousin if Bethuel was her father, as indicated in Genesis 24:15 and 24, but his second cousin if Nahor was her father as Genesis 24:48 and 29:5 seem to imply.[39] In the case of Jacob, however, the tradition provides very clear and extensive detail: He marries the two daughters of Laban, his mother's brother. Jacob's marriages, in other words, are of the type anthropologists

---

* Ugarit was the name of a city on the northern coast of Syria, which flourished in the 14th and 13th centuries B.C. A large cuneiform archive has been found at the site, modern Ras Shamra.

** And, we might add, from Shem or even Adam.

refer to as "cross-cousin," a type to which many societies give special preference, probably because it satisfies the requirements of both exogamy (the obligation to marry outside the family group) and endogamy (the obligation to marry within the family group).[40] Thus Oden is able to show that "the relationship which creates and thus defines the descendants of Israel in the patriarchal narratives is the same relationship by which many societies first define themselves culturally through their kinship systems and through myths in which these systems are recounted."[41]

A second important aspect of Jacob's marriages is the relationship thus established with Laban. Like cross-cousin marriages, the avunculate (nephew-uncle) relationship has received considerable attention from anthropologists, who stress its importance in the definition of kinship systems. Oden is able to explain the tradition's extraordinary elaboration of Jacob's dealings with his maternal uncle:[42]

"Only in the generation of Jacob is an adequate and complete system of kinship relations articulated. The capstone of the system is the avunculate relationship. Precisely because of the significance of this relationship for the entire kinship system, Jacob's interaction with Laban demands a long and complex narrative account."

Genealogical structure—a new key?

The implications of this understanding of the patriarchal tradition for tradition-historical analysis are fundamental. It turns out to be the larger structure of the tradition that conveys its primary purpose. It is inconceivable, therefore, that it developed from numerous discrete units of tradition, as Noth suggested. In fact, we must suppose the opposite, namely, that the larger pattern, especially including the relationships that exist among the smaller units, is primary. Thus the tendency of tradition-historical analysis to see the genealogy that links the patriarchs as one of the latest components of the tradition is mistaken. On the contrary, the genealogical structure must have been worked out at the beginning of the development of the tradition. It was this structure that defined Israel from the beginning.

This is not to say, of course, that all or even many of the details of the tradition as it appears in Genesis were there in very early times. As we know from the study of oral composition as well as literary motifs in folklore, the details of peoples and places are subject to change in a story, while the story's basic structure remains the same. Moreover, as Wilson has shown, the same thing is true of oral genealogies: They are characterized by "fluidity," that is, the capacity to change to adjust to altered social conditions.[43] This is what must have happened in the case of the biblical patriarchal tradition, which, as we have noted, is based on an elaborated oral genealogy. The basic structure of this genealogy and many of the complex relationships within it were present at the beginning of the development of the tradition. In the course of this development, the basic structure remained more or less constant. However, many of the details—especially the identities of individuals holding places in the genealogy—must have changed as the historical experiences of the people dictated.

The tradition-historical method is especially useful for the analysis of these changing details in the patriarchal tradition. Take, for example, the relationship between Jacob and Esau. In the present form of the story, Esau is clearly identified with Edom, and the relationship between the two brothers represents the relationship that existed between the brother nations of Israel and Edom in the time of the biblical writers. Noth pointed out, however, that none of the stories about Jacob and Esau is set in Edom.[44] Apart from Beersheba, the home of their parents, central, not southern, Transjordan is the locale for all the interaction between the two sons. From this, Noth concluded that the connection between Esau and Edom is secondary, having arisen in Judah at a time when Edom was naturally thought of as the rival "brother." But originally, according to Noth, the Jacob-Esau traditions were at home in central Transjordan. These traditions derive from an early period when Israelite pastoralists from west of the Jordan were expanding their territory eastward into Gilead, where they came into conflict with indigenous hunter groups (compare Genesis 25:27).

In this case, Noth's analysis illustrates what we are suggesting about the priority of the larger structure of the tradition. At this point we are concerned with only one component of this structure—namely, the relationship that existed between the ancestor of Israel and his brother. This relationship contributes to the favorable presentation of the ancestor (Jacob), especially with regard to his marriages, through the contrasting example of the brother (Esau), whose marriages are conspicuously and exclusively exogamous (see Genesis 26:34, 28:9, 36:2-3). At an early stage in the development of the tradition, the ancestor was Jacob, father of a group of pastoralists living in the hills near Shechem and Bethel; the brother was Esau, who (as Noth argued) probably represented the hunter groups of adjacent Transjordan. Historical developments then altered the identity of the ancestor and his brother. Israel came to include not only people from the Ephraimite hills but other people as well, and eventually the southern, Judean group became dominant. The earlier shepherd-hunter conflict in Gilead was largely forgotten, and Israel's principal sibling rivalry was now the nationalistic antipathy between Judah and Edom. Thus the ancestor, Jacob, came to be thought of chiefly in his role as the ancestor of Judah; and his brother, Esau, was identified with Edom. The basic structure of the story, however, remained the same.

Patriarchal narratives contain a kernel of authentic history

In contrast to the confident scholars of an earlier generation, today's historians of ancient Israel are extremely cautious in their approach to the prehistory of Israel. Most remain convinced that the stories about Abraham, Isaac and Jacob contain a kernel of authentic history. Recognizing the complexity of the oral and literary development of the narratives in Genesis 12-50, however, they are reluctant to designate individual features as historically authentic. The best hope of success probably lies in the selective application of the methods used in the past (archaeology and philology, and tradition history), supplemented or modified according to the results of more recent research, including studies using the methods of sociology and anthropology.

In this effort, we must always be aware that the patriarchal narratives are ideology, not history. They were composed in the first millennium B.C. for the purpose of making political and theological statements about the Israelite nation. They cannot be approached as historiography in anything like the modern sense. If we tried to do so, we would not only arrive at a spurious prehistory of Israel but we would also overlook the authentic information the patriarchal narratives provide about a later period.

It does not follow from this that Genesis 12-50 has no value for the reconstruction of the prehistory of Israel. It is safe to assume that the Israelites, like almost all other peoples, had a tradition about their own past, and it seems likely that the biblical writers set their stories within the framework of this tradition. Using a modified form of the tradition-historical method, therefore, we can hope to separate this traditional framework from its ideological content and hold up its structure for inspection.

As we have seen, Noth and others were able to trace the preliterary history of this tradition—that is, its history before it was written down—with some success. In general, it seems to have developed into its present form during the period when the community was taking shape—from the time of the unification of the forerunners of Israel at the end of the Late Bronze Age (about 1200 B.C.) to the establishment of the Davidic monarchy (about 1000 B.C.). According to Noth, the basic elements in this development were independent stories of ancestors drawn from the lore of the various tribes and groups that became part of Israel; at the end of the process was the fully evolved patriarchal tradition we know from the Bible, with its trigenerational genealogy of Abraham, Isaac and Jacob. As we have seen, however, it now seems likely that the primary component of the tradition was the kinship pattern itself, expressed in a complex narrative with much the same structure as the surviving biblical account. This elaborate story emerged at the very beginning of the history of the community we call Israel; indeed, in one sense, it created that community, inasmuch as it provided it with social boundaries. Israel never existed—and could not exist—apart from the story, which was the basis of its self-understanding and social organization. In short, the story gave the community definition.

Many of the features of the patriarchal narratives are essential to this definition and cannot, therefore, have originated independently. These include the identification of three generations of patriarchs,[45] the stories of their relationships with various kinsmen, and the details of their marriages and the births of their children, as well as the genealogy that links everything together.

This is not to say, however, that these features existed from the beginning in the forms with which we are familiar. It was the structure of the patriarchal narrative that carried its primary meaning; thus the relationships that existed between individuals in the story must have remained more or less constant in the tradition. On the other hand, the concrete details of the story, especially including the identification of people and places, were subject to change, as we have noted.

Thus, to use the example cited earlier, the immediate ancestor of Israel, from whom all the tribes were directly descended by propitious marriages, must have always had a brother who was the ancestor, by unsuitable marriages, of a related but alien group. The character of this sibling relationship, therefore, was a stable factor in the tradition. Esau's particular association with the hunters of central Transjordan, however, was not essential to the relationship. It was subject to change, and, as we know, it was replaced by an association with Edom. It seems safe to assume that such changes in the tradition were responsive to changes in the historical circumstances of the people. In the case of the present example, Esau's association with Gilead arose at a time when Israel was a small tribal group in the process of expanding eastward into Gilead from its home west of the Jordan. At a later time, when Israel was a larger group and Israelite leadership had shifted south to Judah, Esau was identified with Edom, and the older link with Gilead faded into the background.

Patriarchal history represents Israel's self-understanding, about 1000 B.C.

The story of the patriarchs in its final form (with all its present details) reflects the self-understanding of the community at the end of the period of settlement, about 1000 B.C. Israel is represented as a 12-tribe entity with the southern tribes, and notably Judah, in full membership, something that probably did not occur until David's time. This scheme reflects considerable southern development: The eldest patriarch (Abraham) is especially associated with Hebron, the traditional capital of the Judean hill country in the southern part of the country; the second patriarch (Isaac) is at home even farther south, in the northern Negev. The patriarchal stories are not likely to have existed in this form before the institution of the Davidic monarchy about 1000 B.C.[46] The priority of Abraham as the eldest patriarch suggests the intertribal relationship that existed during the reigns of David and Solomon and, in any case, reflects a Judahite point of view.

To a limited extent, the evolution of the tradition can be reconstructed from biblical and extra-biblical evidence. The 12 sons of Israel who appear in the present form of the stories about Jacob and Joseph reflect the tribal roster as it stood at the end of the process. A somewhat different list is preserved in Judges 5:14-18, part of an ancient poem describing the victory of the Israelite tribes over a Canaanite foe. Here there is no mention of the southern tribes, Judah and Simeon, suggesting that southern Canaan had not yet been incorporated into Israel at that time. Moreover, Manasseh and Gad are also missing in this old poem, while two tribes are cited that do not appear in the later list, namely, Machir (Judges 5:14) and Gilead (Judges 5:17).[47] This list in Judges 5 provides us with a glimpse of the tribal association as it stood about the middle of the 12th century, say 1150 B.C.[48] Moreover, we know that a group named Israel already existed, at least in rudimentary form, by about 1207 B.C., when the Egyptian king Merneptah boasts of having defeated a people named "Israel."[49]

It follows that tribal Israel existed in the central hills before about 1150 B.C. and probably as early as 1207 B.C. Though this community may have been newly formed, it already had a sense of ethnic identity: Its members were Israelite or "Hebrew" and not something else.[50] This identity found expression in and, at the same time, derived its authority from the ancestral tradition that is preserved in the patriarchal narratives of the Bible.

The insistence upon ethnic separateness is one of the most conspicuous features of this tradition. The stories uniformly assert that the ancestors of Israel were foreigners, not natives of Canaan. They came from "beyond the River," that is, beyond the Euphrates (cf. Joshua 24:2-3), in the region we call Mesopotamia (modern Iraq and eastern Syria). Whatever the ultimate origin of the term "Hebrews," this was the meaning it came to have in the tradition: The *'ibrîm*, "Hebrews," were those who came from *'ēber*, "beyond," the Euphrates.

As explained in Chapter III, the early Israelites were probably of diverse origin, and many or most seem to have been indigenous to Canaan. The strong insistence in the patriarchal narratives that the ancestors of Israel were *not* Canaanites is a reflection of the process of ethnic boundary-marking by which the early Israelite community was defined and by which its identity was subsequently maintained. This kind of boundary-marking is well known to modern students of the social phenomenon of ethnicity.[51] In the present case, it probably derives from the early conflict between the hill-dwelling people from whom Israel emerged and the population of the cities of the plains and valleys controlled by the Egyptian Empire in the Late Bronze Age. Through the tradition of Mesopotamian origin and in the biblical genealogical materials generally, the Israelites acknowledge ethnic solidarity with the peoples of the east, the Transjordanians and the Arameans, but deny any link with the peoples of the Egypto-Canaanite west.

The basic structure of the patriarchal tradition, therefore, emerged at the end of the Late Bronze Age, contemporary with the early formation of Israel. This conclusion, however, pertains only to the patriarchal tradition, not to the patriarchs themselves. We must now attempt to discover the extent to which the tradition was based on historical people and events.

This is a difficult task. As we have seen, the structure of the tradition came into existence at the same time as the community itself. A careful investigation of this structure and its purposes might help us understand the circumstances under which the community first coalesced in central Canaan, but this structure cannot be expected to shed light on an earlier period.

*Personal
names and
geographical
references
provide clues*

If we cannot look to the structure, we must look to the concrete details—especially personal names and geographical references—that fill out the structure. But, as we have seen, many of these names and references changed as the tradition developed. We cannot assume, therefore, that any given detail was present from the beginning, and we must evaluate all details accordingly.

Moreover, even when we have identified a particular detail as primitive, we have to reckon with the possibility that its basis was fictitious or imaginary rather than historical.

Finally, as I shall explain, the patriarchal narratives are predominantly eponymic in character. For this reason, we cannot easily separate personal names from geographical associations when assessing the historical signficance of the various details in the story.

We might expect that personal names would be among the most tenacious of the details in the patriarchal narratives. And, in fact, none of the names of the primary patriarchs—"Abram," "Abraham," "Isaac," "Jacob," "Israel" or "Joseph"—is likely to have had a late or artificial origin. Each has the form of an authentic Semitic name. None has an obvious thematic signification that would suggest an artificial origin (as, for example, in the case of Adam, "Mankind").* Four of the names ("Jacob," "Israel," "Isaac" and "Joseph") share the same form.[52] This form is found in a large group of *personal* names. But this same form can be detected in numerous *geographical* and *tribal* names. Moreover, "Jacob" and "Israel" are commonly used in the Bible as collective names as well as individual names, and this is sometimes true of "Isaac" and "Joseph" as well. The question then is whether these names originated as geographical or tribal names that were subsequently projected back onto fictitious ancestors.

The invention of such ancestors is a common way of establishing the kinship bonds that are necessary for the cohesion of a community. The practice is known among modern Bedouin, and it is well attested in antiquity. The "Amorite" dynasties of Hammurabi of Babylon and Shamshi-Adad I of Assyria shared a common tradition about their tribal origins, and many of the names of their early ancestors are also known as names of West Semitic tribes.[53]

Similar fictitious heroes are frequently encountered in biblical genealogies, and often their origins can be traced. Jerahmeel, for example, was the name of a non-Israelite tribe living somewhere in the Negev in the time of David (1 Samuel 27:10, 30:29). In the course of time, however, the Jerahmeelites were incorporated into Judah, and the new relationship was expressed genealogically by the identification of Jerahmeel as a great-grandson of Judah in a line collateral to that of David (1 Chronicles 2:9, 25-27).

* The meanings given to "Abraham" in Genesis 17:5, "Isaac" in Genesis 21:6 (cf. Genesis 17:17-19, 18:12-15), and "Jacob" in Genesis 25:26 are all examples of etymological wordplay. They do not reflect the actual origins of the names.

There is no question that the patriarchal genealogies contain the names of many individuals who originated as fictitious eponyms.* Moab and Ben-Ammi, the sons of Lot and ancestors of the Moabites and Ammonites (Genesis 19:37-38), are obvious examples, as is Shechem son of Hamor, the prince of the city of Shechem (Genesis 34:2). There are many others. Sometimes these figures play prominent roles in the story, as in the case of Ishmael, the ancestor of the Ishmaelites (cf. Genesis 16:10-12, 17:20 and 25:12-16). The Edomite genealogy recorded in Genesis 36 contains a mixture of personal and tribal or clan names. Thus, for example, Esau's eldest son bears the name "Eliphaz," which has the form of a personal name. Eliphaz was probably a hero of the past rather than an eponym (cf. Job 2:11), but his sons (Genesis 36:11-12) include eponyms of well-known tribes or places, including Teman, the home of the Eliphaz of the Book of Job. This, then, is what we expect from the early genealogies: a few names of traditional heroes sprinkled among a preponderance of eponymic names derived from clans, tribes, places and regions.

Abraham seems to belong in the former category. His name (in contrast ***Abraham*** to those of Isaac, Jacob, Israel and Joseph) appears only as a personal name in the Bible, never as a tribal or local designation. Thus it seems fairly certain that he was not an eponymous ancestor. He may have been a historical individual before he became a figure of tradition and legend. If so, however, it seems impossible to determine the time period in which he lived. "Abram," at least in the form "Abiram," is a name of a very common type, known in all periods. It is especially well attested in the Late Bronze Age (about 1550-1200 B.C.),[54] though this may be no more than a coincidence. The variants "Abram" and "Abraham" arose in different languages or dialects.[55]

Nor can we determine whether any of the biblical stories told about Abraham has a historical basis. The claim that Abraham came to Canaan from Mesopotamia is not historically implausible. Such a journey could have taken place in more than one historical period. As we have seen, however, the insistence that the Israelites were not Canaanite in origin was so pervasive that the belief that the first patriarch came from a foreign land could have arisen as part of the ethnic boundary-marking that characterized the development of the tradition. Still, the connections between the family of Abraham and the city of Haran in northern Mesopotamia (Eski Harran or "Old Haran" in modern Turkey) are very precise in our earliest narrative source ("J"). Terah, Nahor, and Serug, Abraham's father, grandfather, and great-grandfather (Genesis 11:22-26), seem to be the eponymous ancestors of towns in the basin of the Balikh River, near Haran. All three are mentioned in Assyrian texts from the first half of the first milllennium B.C. as the names of towns or ruined towns in the region of Haran, namely, Til-(sha)-Turakhi ("the ruin of

---

* To repeat, an eponym is a person, real or imaginary, from whom the name of a later group is derived or is supposed to be derived.

Turakh"), Til-Nakhiri ("the ruin of Nakhir"), and Sarugi. Earlier, in the second millennium B.C., Til-Nakhiri had been an important administrative center, called Nakhuru. Abraham's brothers are also eponymous figures with the names Nahor, who shared his grandfather's name, and Haran (Genesis 11:27). Many scholars still believe that Abraham's connection with Haran rests on a firm historical basis. Others think that Abraham's family was originally associated with part of Transjordan, east of the boundary established between Jacob and Abraham's great-nephew Laban in Genesis 31:43-50, and that this association was extended to Haran later, when it became commercially important in the first millennium B.C.

We can no longer suppose, as Noth did in a previous generation, that Abraham was not a primitive part of the patriarchal tradition. Nevertheless, it is unlikely that Abraham was associated with Hebron before the last phase of the development of the tradition, when Judah became the dominant tribe.[56] (Hebron is in Judah.) Originally, Israel's (that is, Jacob's) grandfather, like Israel himself, is likely to have been at home in the central highlands south of the valley of Jezreel. In the earlier form of the tradition, it was here, rather than in the Hebron area (Genesis 13:18), that Abraham settled when he separated from his kinsman, Lot, who settled in Transjordan and became the ancestor of the Moabites and Ammonites (but not, significantly, of the Edomites). Abraham's first son, Ishmael, was the forebear of the northern Arabs who lived "in general to the east of Palestine in the Syrian Desert,"[57] and Ishmael's mother, Hagar, was the eponymous ancestress of the Hagrites of northern Arabia, east of Gilead (1 Chronicles 5:10, 19-20; cf. Psalm 83:6). When historical circumstances prompted the relocation of the Abraham stories in the Judean hills around Hebron, the various geographical associations of the family shifted south to a corresponding degree. Lot's home was located within the so-called cities of the valley, in the vicinity of the Dead Sea,* Hagar was identified as an Egyptian, and Ishmael's descendants were conceived more broadly as the camel nomads in general and especially those of the northern Sinai.[58]

Isaac   As we have noted, the biblical Isaac has clear geographical associations with the northern Negev, and particularly the oases of Beersheba and Beer-lahai-roi (Genesis 24:62, 25:11, 26:32-33). The archaeological record indicates that this area was not settled before the end of the Late Bronze Age. Expansion into the Negev from the north began no earlier than the latter part of the 13th century. Archaeological excavations at Beersheba have shown that a deep well associated with the sanctuary was dug at about this time.[59] Apparently it is the well mentioned in Genesis 21:25 and 26:25. The settlement of the Negev spread southward and was complete by the 11th century.[60] This shows that the attachment of the

---

* It may have been at this point that the account of the destruction of Sodom and Gomorrah, originally an independent story, was attached to the tradition.

HERSHEL SHANKS

Beersheba well. In Genesis 26, we are told that "Isaac dug anew the wells which had been dug in the days of his father Abraham and which the Philistines had stopped up after Abraham's death... From there [Rehoboth] he went up to Beersheba... Isaac pitched his tent there and his servants started digging a well." This well at ancient Beersheba may have been the well the author of this passage had in mind. The excavator of Tel Beersheba, Yohanan Aharoni of Tel Aviv University, dated this well to the late 13th century B.C.

patriarchal tradition to the Beersheba region cannot have preceded the 12th century, and, in fact, may have occurred later as a part of the southern development of the tradition in the time of David and Solomon.

We cannot agree with Noth, however, that Isaac himself was absent from the tradition before this later period. He must have been present from the beginning, both in his role as the favored son of the eldest patriarch and as the father of Israel (Jacob) himself.

Like Abraham, then, Isaac probably had an earlier association with the central hill country, and the evidence of his name gives a good indication of this. As we have noted, "Isaac" is structurally suitable as a personal, tribal or geographical name. We might expect the meaning of the name to indicate which of these possibilities is most likely. Though it is unattested outside the Bible, we assume that "Isaac" is a shortened form of a name like "Isaac-El," which may mean "May [the god] El smile," that is, "May El look favorably upon."[61] If this is correct,* the name then

---

* Our uncertainty about this meaning arises from the fact that the verbal element does not have quite this sense elsewhere; it ordinarily means "laugh, laugh at, sport, jest."

seems equally acceptable as the designation of an individual, group or place. In referring to the northern kingdom in the eighth century, moreover, Amos twice uses the name Isaac in parallel with Israel (Amos 7:9, 16). This usage must reflect a recollection of the name Isaac as a designation for the northern tribal region.[62] I assume, therefore, that the patriarch Isaac arose as an eponym of this group.

Jacob In general, the stories about Jacob were less affected by the southern reorientation of the tradition at the end of its development than were those about Abraham and Isaac. According to the final form of the tradition, the events of Jacob's birth and childhood took place at Beersheba, his father's home, but he remains primarily associated with the central hill country, especially the vicinity of Shechem, and with central Transjordan. It is not surprising that the Jacob stories were able to resist the geographical displacement we see in the rest of the tradition. Jacob *was* Israel, the patriarch from whom all the tribes were descended. The historical association of Israel with the central hills was strong, as its persistence into the time of David and later shows. In contrast to Abraham and Isaac, therefore, Jacob was never thought of in close association with the southern part of the country.

It is generally agreed that the biblical name "Jacob" is a shortened form of "Jacob-El" or something very similar. An early form of "Jacob," constructed with "El" or another divine name, was a common West Semitic personal name of the Middle Bronze Age and the Hyksos period.[63] It is also attested at Ugarit (in Syria) in the Late Bronze Age, but (outside of the biblical patriarchal narratives) not again until the Persian period. "Jacob-El," however, was also a Late Bronze Age place name. It occurs in lists of enemies conquered by Tuthmosis III ([1504] 1483-1450) and other kings of the Egyptian empire.[64] Most of the identifiable names in these documents refer to cities, though some designate districts and even tribal groups. Because of the loose organization of the lists, the precise location of Jacob-El cannot be determined. It is clear, however, that it was in central Canaan,[65] most probably in the general vicinity of Rehob and Beth-Shean, both of which lay north of Shechem.[66] In view of the proximity of both time and place, therefore, it does not seem reckless to conclude that the Jacob-El conquered by Tuthmosis had something to do with the biblical Jacob tradition.

We must ask, then, which had priority, the patriarch Jacob or the place Jacob-El. The name probably means "Let El protect,"* and this seems equally suitable as the name of a person or a place. It is possible that there was an early hero called Jacob-El who gave his name to the town or district mentioned in the Egyptian lists.[67] If so, he must also be the ultimate referent of the biblical Jacob tradition. It is at least equally

---

* The verb is known with this meaning in Ethiopic and Old South Arabic but not biblical Hebrew.

possible, however, that the biblical Jacob arose as a fictitious eponym of Jacob-El, and in view of the preponderance of such eponyms in the patriarchal genealogy this may be the more probable explanation.

In the Bible, however, Jacob has two names. According to the earliest written account, Jacob was given the name Israel after wrestling with a divine being on the bank of the Jabbok River (Genesis 32:28).* In the latter part of Genesis the two names, Jacob and Israel, are used more or less interchangeably. Modern biblical scholars have explained these facts in a variety of ways. Noth concluded that Israel, the collective name of the tribes, was assigned to the patriarch Jacob at a fairly late point in the development of the tradition.[68] I have argued, however, that the elaborated structure of the tradition was itself an early feature and that the purpose of this structure was to give a social definition to Israel. Jacob, the eponym of the people or district of Jacob-El, was the key figure in the genealogical scheme. It is very likely, then, that he was identified as Israel, the eponym of the newly emerging community, when the kinship tradition was devised at the time of the formation of the tribal alliance.

This is not to suggest, however, that the name "Israel" was invented at this time. Several scholars have attempted to identify a distinctive group of traditions around a patriarch Israel, whom they would distinguish from Jacob,[69] and it is possible that there was some kind of early tribal group in the central hills called Israel.[70] In fact, however, our sources give us no hint of the use of the name in Canaan before the time of Merneptah (about 1207 B.C.), which, as we have seen, must have been very close to the time of the formation of the community itself. Since we know that the population of the hill country was growing steadily at this time,[71] we must also consider the possibility that the name "Israel" was brought into the region by one of the arriving peoples.

Joseph

Turning finally to the the sons of Israel, we begin by recalling that the name "Joseph" belongs in the category of "Isaac," "Jacob" and "Israel," as noted earlier. We assume that it is a shorter form of "Joseph-El," which means "May El increase," and this too seems equally suitable as a personal, tribal or geographical designation.** Thus it is possible that Joseph was a hero of the past (like Abraham) or the fictitious eponym of a group or district (like Isaac and Jacob). The latter possibility is suggested by the use of "the house of Joseph" as a collective designation for the northern tribes in the literature of the early monarchy (2 Samuel 19:21) and elsewhere. A strong case can be made, however, that this expression was coined after the unification of Judah and Israel as a parallel term to "the house of Judah."[72] References to a tribe of Joseph, moreover, are rare and appear only in late materials (Numbers

---

* According to the later account in Genesis 35:10, the renaming took place at Bethel.

** That is, it might be a wish for the addition of another child (cf. Genesis 30:24) or for an increase in the fertility or prosperity of the tribe or town.

13:11, 36:5). Thus, it seems more likely that "Joseph" was a personal name belonging to a local hero of the past.[73] During the period of the formation of the Israelite community, he was identified as a son of Jacob and the father of the tribal eponyms Ephraim and Manasseh.

The special prominence of Joseph in the present form of the biblical narrative must be, at least in part, a reflection of the eminence of "the house of Joseph" at the end of settlement period (about 1000 B.C.) and the continuing historical importance of the Manasseh-Ephraim region. Scholars believe that the long story about Joseph and his family in Genesis 37 and 39-47 originated independently of the other patriarchal narratives. This story depicts Joseph as preeminent among his brothers and the favorite of Jacob/Israel. The story was probably passed down orally among the inhabitants of the region around Shechem and Dothan (cf. Genesis 37:12 and 38:18), in the heart of the traditional territory of Ephraim and Manasseh, the two "half-tribes" of Joseph's sons. In an early form, this story may have eulogized Joseph, the tribal patriarch, as a man who went to Egypt as a slave and rose to a position of authority in the Egyptian court.

Many scholars believe that the events described in the story of Joseph have an ultimate basis in historical fact. It has often been supposed, especially by those scholars who believe that Abraham, Isaac and Jacob lived in the Middle Bronze Age (about 2000-1550 B.C.), that Joseph lived during the so-called Hyksos period, when Egypt was ruled by two dynasties of Asiatic princes (about 1674-1567 B.C.). The scholars who hold this view argue that since Joseph was himself an Asiatic, he would be most likely to find a favorable reception from an Asiatic king of Egypt. Moreover, the capital of Egypt during the Hyksos period was located in the eastern Delta, which is generally agreed to have been the site of the biblical "land of Goshen," where the family of Joseph settled (Genesis 45:10, 46:28-29, 47:1).

But even if the general outline of the Joseph story is based on the life of a historical individual, it is unlikely that much of the information found in Genesis 37 and 39-47 is historically factual. The biblical Joseph story has more in common with a historical romance than a work of history. Its carefully planned story line is fashioned from narrative motifs that were widespread in the literature and folklore of the ancient Near East. The episode of Potiphar's wife, who accuses Joseph of attempted rape after she fails to seduce him (Genesis 39:6b-20), has numerous parallels in the literature of the ancient world,[74] including the popular "Tale of Two Brothers" of 19th-Dynasty Egypt (13th century B.C.).[75] The motifs of dreams and dream interpretation are found in literature, folklore and myth throughout antiquity.[76] The convention of the seven lean years is known from Egyptian, Akkadian and Canaanite literature.[77]

The author of the biblical Joseph story displays only a limited knowledge of the life and culture of Egypt.[78] Thinking of the hot wind that blows across the Transjordanian plateau into Israel, he speaks of the *east* wind scorching pharaoh's grain (Genesis 41:23,27), but in Egypt it is the *south* wind that blights crops.[79] The titles and offices the author assigns to various Egyptian officials fit better with known parallels in Syria and Canaan than with Egyptian parallels.[80]

There are a number of authentic Egyptian details in the Joseph story, but these details correspond to the Egyptian way of life of the author's own day, not that of the Hyksos period. The king of Egypt is called "Pharaoh," an Egyptian phrase meaning "great house," which was not used as a title for the king before the reign of Thutmosis III (about 1490-1436 B.C.). In Genesis 47:11, the area in which the family of Joseph settles is called "the land of Rameses," a designation that could not have been used earlier than the reign of Ramesses II (about 1279-1213 B.C.).*

Some of the personal names in the story are Egyptian. Joseph's wife is called Asenath (Genesis 41:45), a name with parallels beginning in the middle of the 20th Dynasty (about 1184-1070 B.C.), thus about 1100 B.C.[81] The name of Asenath's father is Potiphera (Genesis 41:45), and this name has been found on an Egyptian stele dating to the 21st Dynasty (about 1070-945 B.C.) or later.[82] The name of Joseph's Egyptian master, Potiphar (Genesis 37:36), is probably a shorter form of the name Potiphera. Joseph's own Egyptian name, Zaphenath-paneah (Genesis 41:45), has no exact parallel in extant Egyptian records, but names with a similar structure are attested from the 21st Dynasty (about 1070-945 B.C.) and later.[83]

It is unlikely, therefore, that the Joseph story as we know it in the Bible was composed before the establishment of the United Kingdom (that is, before about 1000 B.C.). Many of the elements of the plot of the biblical Joseph story and most of its narrative details are fictional. It does not follow from this, however, that the tradition upon which the story is based is unhistorical. We cannot exclude the possibility that there was a historical Joseph who went to Egypt as a slave and rose to a position of power there.

Egyptian records from the Middle Kingdom (before 1786 B.C.) to the Roman period (after 30 B.C.) cite numerous individuals of Syrian, Canaanite and nomadic origin who rose to high positions in the Egyptian government.[84] An especially interesting parallel to the story of Joseph is that of an Asiatic named Irsu, who seized power in Egypt during a period of hardship (probably famine) at the end of the 19th Dynasty (about 1200 B.C.).[85] Many Egyptologists believe that Irsu was another name for Bay, the powerful chancellor who ruled Egypt during the minority of the last king of the 19th Dynasty and who may have come from Palestine.[86]

Clearly, then, the biblical description of Joseph's career is historically plausible in its general outline. We might surmise that Joseph was the leader of a group of people from the vicinity of Shechem and Dothan who migrated to Egypt seeking pasturage during a time of drought in

---

* It is possible, however, that "in the land of Rameses" in Genesis 47:11 is a scribe's gloss, intended to harmonize the account of the Israelites' entry into Egypt with the statement in Exodus 1:11 that locates the Israelites in "Pithom and Raamses."

Canaan. Such groups are amply attested in Egyptian records. In a text from the reign of Merneptah (about 1212-1200 B.C.), for example, a frontier official reports:[87]

"[We] have finished letting the Bedouin tribes of Edom pass the Fortress [of] Mer-ne-Ptah . . . which is (in) Tjeku*. . . to the pools of Per-Atum**. . . which are (in) Tjeku, to keep them alive and to keep their cattle alive . . . ."

When the Joseph group returned from Egypt to central Canaan, they brought with them the memory of Joseph's success in the service of the Egyptian king. This memory was preserved in the hills around Shechem until the time of the Israelite monarchy, when it became the basis for the embellished Joseph story now found in the Bible. In the meantime, the descendants of Joseph had become part of the people of Israel, and Joseph himself had come to be thought of as one of the sons of Jacob, the progenitor of the Israelites.

The names of most of the other sons of Jacob/Israel do not have the form of personal names. Several are geographical names. "Zebulun," for example, means something like "highland." Originally it must have been the name of the mountainous hinterland of Lower Galilee; the tribe that settled there took the name. "Asher" was a name by which the Egyptians knew the coastal region north of Carmel in the Late Bronze Age.[88] "Judah," "Ephraim"† and "Naphtali" seem first to have been the names of ranges of hills (cf. Joshua 20:7); the people who inhabited the hill country of Judah were called *běnê yěhûdâ*, "the children of Judah" or "Judahites," and so on.[89] The name "Benjamin" probably arose from the location of the tribe's territory; it lay to the south of the other (northern) tribes, so that the people were called *běnê yāmîn*, "the children of the south" or "Benjaminites."[90]

Jacob/Israel's other sons   On the other hand, the names of a few of the sons of Jacob/Israel do have the form of personal names. "Simeon" and "Manasseh,"† for example, are most easily understood this way,[91] and the corresponding tribes may have been named after tribal heroes or even patriarchs. If there was a tribal patriarch Simeon or Manasseh, however, he was not the biblical Simeon or Manasseh. The 12 sons of Israel are fictional eponyms of the 12 tribes of Israel, created in the course of the evolution of the Israelite tradition during the period of settlement. The process of community formation, which began in about 1200 B.C. at the end of the Late Bronze Age, presupposes the existence of the tribes with established names. The origin of the various tribal names—whether derived from geographical associations, ancestral traditions or something else—was already in the remote past. When the tribes were joined

* The Egyptian name for the land called Goshen in the Bible.

** Biblical Pithom (Exodus 1:11).

† Ephraim and Manasseh were sons of Joseph and grandsons of Jacob/Israel. According to Genesis 48:5, however, they were adopted by their grandfather.

together into the larger entity of Israel, their kinship was expressed in terms of brotherhood; and a group of 12 sons, the eponyms of the 12 tribes, was assigned to the patriarch Jacob.

It follows from all of this that the setting of the prehistory of the Israelite community was the central hill country between the valley of Aijalon and the Beth-Shean corridor in the Late Bronze Age. This region was very sparsely populated before 1200 B.C.,[92] suggesting that the people among whom the Israelite tradition germinated were pastoralists, as the patriarchal stories would lead us to expect. They venerated a local hero called Abram or Abraham, who was probably already regarded as a patriarchal figure; that is, he was identified as the ancestor of one or more of the groups in the region. These people (or some of them) were collectively called Isaac. Some lived in the vicinity of Jacob-El.

These proto-Israelites were hill people and shepherds, and they must have seen themselves as distinct from the peoples of the cities, which, in this period, were situated on the coastal plain and in the major valleys.[93] This was the period of the Egyptian empire in Canaan, but the remoteness of the highlands from the population centers and the major trading routes sheltered Israel's forerunners from the full influence of the Egyptian presence. These circumstances were favorable to the creation of a national community larger than the city-states of the Bronze Age,[94] a development that needed only an increase in population to make it possible. This requirement was fulfilled at the end of the Late Bronze Age when new peoples penetrated into the forests of the Ephraimite plateau and the saddle of Benjamin to the south. At this time a larger tribal alliance was formed, and the old relationships were formalized genealogically. Abraham was identified as the father of Isaac and Isaac of Jacob. Jacob became the father of a large group of sons, eponyms of the various groups and districts that made up the new alliance. The basis of this alliance, however, was the recently arrived population of Ephraim and Benjamin. These people (or some of them) brought with them the collective name "Israel." Thus the eponym Israel had an equal claim to the status of tribal father, and he was identified with Jacob.

T W O

Israel in Egypt

The Egyptian Sojourn and the Exodus

N A H U M   M.   S A R N A

A
CCORDING TO THE BIBLE, A FAMINE OF UNUSUAL SEVERITY
and duration in the land of Canaan brought the patriarch
Jacob and his family to Egypt. They settled in the region of
Goshen, in the Nile Delta, through the influence of Joseph, Jacob's son,
who was a high official in the Egyptian administration (Genesis 41:1-
47:12). This Hebrew migration was intended to be temporary (Genesis
46:4, 50:24), but soon extended itself. After the death of Joseph and his
brothers, a change of fortunes occurred when a new pharaoh "who did
not know Joseph" came to the throne (Exodus 1:8). The Israelites'
proliferation and prosperity was perceived as a threat to Egyptian security.
The new pharaoh introduced drastic measures to curb the Hebrews'
population growth: The Israelites were pressed into corvée service
(Exodus 1:9-13). As the biblical text describes it: "They set taskmasters
over them to oppress them with forced labor; and [the Israelites] built
garrison cities for Pharaoh" (Exodus 1:11). The harsh labors to which
they were subjected did not have the anticipated results: "The more they
were oppressed, the more they increased and spread out, so that the
[Egyptians] came to dread the Israelites" (Exodus 1:12). New repressive
measures were instituted. In addition to intensifying the various physical
labors imposed on them, the king ordered midwives to kill the newborn
males at birth. Motivated by compassion, however, the midwives resisted
the infamous decree. Pharaoh then ordained that all male Hebrew babies
were to be abandoned to the Nile (Exodus 1:15-22).

possible, and the mother was forced to yield him to the river. Placing him in a waterproof basket, she set him among the Nile reeds and appointed his sister to keep watch over him. In a short while, the basket was discovered by pharaoh's daughter. At the suggestion of the baby's sister, the princess hired the baby's Hebrew mother to nurse the child. Of course, the relationship was not disclosed. When the boy was sufficiently grown, he was taken to the palace and adopted by pharaoh's daughter, who named him Moses[1] (Exodus 2:1-10).

The Bible relates practically nothing about Moses as a young man. The few incidents that are recorded testify to his hatred of injustice. On one occasion Moses struck down and killed an Egyptian whom he saw beating a Hebrew. Later the deed became known and Moses was forced to flee Egypt. He found refuge in the land of Midian, and there, by a well, he saw another injustice. Male shepherds were unfairly taking advantage of their female counterparts who were waiting their turn at the well. Moses saved the shepherdesses from maltreatment. The upshot of this was that he married one of the women, thereby becoming the son-in-law of Jethro, priest of Midian, who employed him to tend his flocks (Exodus 2:11).

Once, while grazing the sheep deep in the wilderness, Moses caught sight of a bush all aflame, yet the bush remained unaffected[2] (Exodus 3:1-22). Fascinated by the scene, he approached it, only to hear himself addressed by a voice disclosing that he was standing on holy ground. Here Moses experienced his first encounter with God. Moses was informed that the divine promises that had been made to the patriarchs of Israel—Abraham, Isaac and Jacob—were now to be realized. God designated Moses to assume the leadership of Israel and to wage the struggle for liberation from Egyptian bondage. His instinctive reaction was to shrink from the task. "Who am I," he answers, "that I should go to Pharaoh and free the Israelites from Egypt?" (Exodus 3:11). After considerable resistance, Moses finally agreed when his brother Aaron was appointed his spokesman.

Moses returned to Egypt to rally his people and to engage the obdurate monarch. His initial efforts were ineffective. Pharaoh was unyielding. Pharaoh said to Moses: "Who is the Lord that I should heed him and let Israel go? I do not know the Lord, nor will I let Israel go" (Exodus 5:2). Pharaoh imposed even harsher measures on the Israelites, and their situation deteriorated further (Exodus 5:1-22).

A series of ten plagues was then visited upon the land and people of Egypt. Man and beast, the soil and the ecology, were all severely affected. In the course of these plagues, pharaoh repeatedly made concessions, only to withdraw them at the last moment. Finally, his will was broken. He summoned Moses and Aaron in the middle of the night and capitulated. The Israelites assembled at a town called Raamses and marched to Succoth, the first stopping place on their route out of Egypt.

From there they entered the wilderness, headed for the land of Canaan[3] (Exodus 7:14-11:10, 12:29-37).

The shortest route would have taken them up the Mediterranean coastal road, but they deliberately avoided it, following instead a roundabout course that led far into the wilderness. The Egyptians interpreted this to mean that the fleeing Israelites were hopelessly lost. Pharaoh mustered his forces and went after them in hot pursuit. The Israelites suddenly found themselves hemmed in by the Sea of Reeds* on one side and the Egyptian army on the other. At that critical moment, they were told by God to advance into the sea. As they did so, the waters parted, allowing the Israelites to cross over to the other shore. Just as the Egyptian forces were halfway across in pursuit, the waters returned to their normal state. The entire Egyptian infantry and chariotry were drowned and Israel was free at last (Exodus 13:17-14:31). Forever after, the event has been celebrated annually in the Passover festival (Exodus 12:1-28,43-50, 13:1-10).

This narrative, as set forth in the first 15 chapters of Exodus, raises numerous historical problems. It is extremely difficult to fit the events described in the Bible into the framework of known history. No existing Egyptian source even hints at Israel in Egypt. And no synchronism exists to coordinate an event recorded in Genesis and Exodus with a datable occurrence documented in an extra-biblical source.[4]

Given these restrictions, we can nevertheless attempt to place these events into a historical context by other means. For example, we can work forward in time from the patriarchs. Or we can reckon backward from some fixed date in later history. The first approach is unavailing. True, the patriarchal period—from the birth of Abraham to the death of Jacob—may be easily calculated to have lasted 307 years (Genesis 21:5, 25:26, 47:28). But when did it begin? Notwithstanding all the archaeological finds of the past half century or so, no scholarly consensus has emerged concerning the date of the "patriarchal period."[5] Nor do we have any reliable information about how soon after the death of Jacob the oppression of the Israelites began. Another difficulty is that the pentateuchal texts do not agree with one another as to how long the sojourn in Egypt lasted. Various biblically preserved traditions mention four generations (Genesis 15:16), 400 years (Genesis 15:13), and 430 years (Exodus 12:40-41). The first-century Jewish historian Josephus records a tradition of 215 years,[6] and an ancient rabbinic source gives 210 years.[7] How entangled the issue is is reflected in the case of Machir, grandson of Joseph. His sons were born in the lifetime of Joseph, yet they not only participated in the conquest of Canaan, but in the settlement as well (Genesis 50:23; Numbers 32:39-40; Joshua 13:31, 17:1).

Placing the Exodus account in historical context

---

* This is the literal translation of Hebrew *yam suph*. *Suph* is a borrowing from Egyptian *twf*, which means "papyrus/reed thicket." The rendering "Red Sea" goes back to the Greek and Latin translations and is itself a mystery. For a different understanding of the Hebrew name, see Bernard F. Batto, "Red Sea or Reed Sea?" *BAR*, July/August 1984, pp. 56-63.

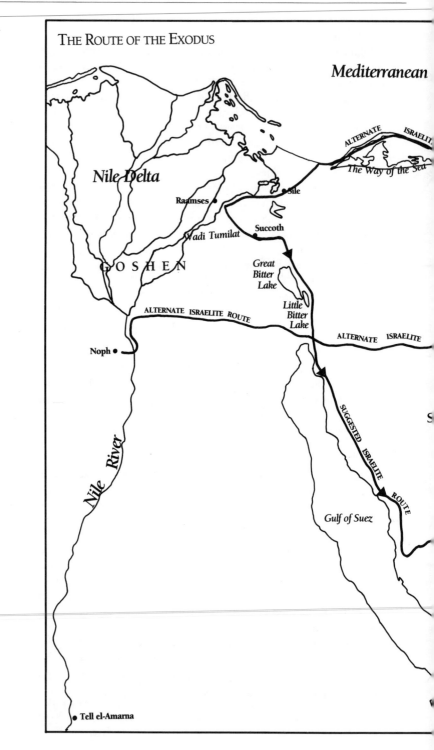

THE ROUTE OF THE EXODUS

Mediterranean

Nile Delta

ALTERNATE

ISRAELIT

The Way of the Sea

Sile

Raamses

Wadi Tumilat

Succoth

GOSHEN

Great
Bitter
Lake

Little
Bitter
Lake

ALTERNATE ISRAELITE ROUTE

ALTERNATE ISRAELITE

Noph

SUGGESTED ISRAELITE ROUTE

S

Nile River

Gulf of Suez

Tell el-Amarna

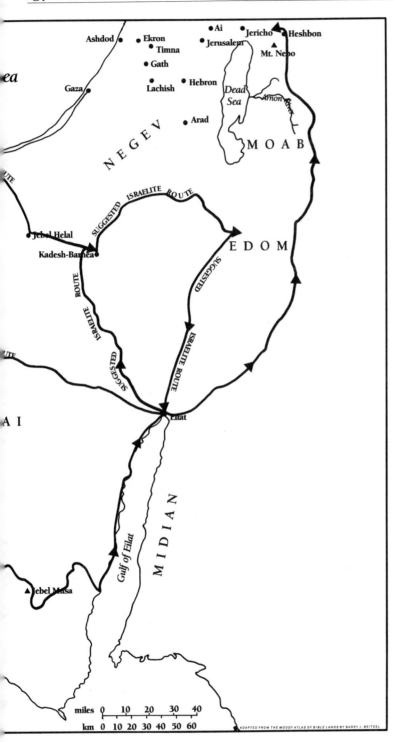

If this was true, then the Hebrew enslavement was limited to one generation. How then could it be that, as the opening words of Exodus declare, the Israelites in Egypt had "multiplied and increased very greatly, so that the land was filled with them"? (Exodus 1:7). Indeed, how could this have occurred in four generations? Working forward from the patriarchal period, then, is not very helpful in fixing the date of the Exodus.[8]

But it is equally unfruitful to calculate back from some recognized date in history. Only once in the Bible do we find the Exodus coordinated with another event in the history of Israel. We are told that: "In the four hundred and eightieth year after the Israelites left the land of Egypt, in the fourth year of his reign over Israel, Solomon began to build the House of the Lord" (1 Kings 6:1). It is generally agreed that Solomon came to the throne in about 962 B.C., so that according to this reckoning the Exodus would have occurred about 1438 B.C. However, most scholars question the accuracy of the number 480. It bears the marks of a symbolic rather than literal number. It is 12 generations of 40 years each, a conventional figure in the Bible. The wilderness wanderings lasted 40 years (Numbers 14:33-34, 32:13; see also Deuteronomy 2:7, 8:2, 29:4; Joshua 5:6; Amos 2:10, 5:25; Psalm 95:10); 40 is used repeatedly in the period of the Judges (Judges 3:11, 5:31, 8:28, 13:1; see also 3:30 [80= twice 40]); and it also determines the incumbency of Eli the priest (1 Samuel 4:18) and the reigns of David (2 Samuel 5:4; 1 Kings 2:11; 1 Chronicles 29:27) and Solomon (1 Kings 11:42; 2 Chronicles 9:30). Exactly 480 years elapsed from the fourth year of Solomon, when he commenced the building of the Temple, to the end of the Babylonian Exile, according to the data given in Kings.[9] All this suggests that we are dealing with a schematized chronology that dates the Temple from the Exodus. The biblical writer wanted to place the Temple at the center of biblical history.

Difficulties with a 15th-century B.C. Exodus

Apart from these considerations, an Exodus in the 15th century B.C. presents other difficulties. In the 15th century, Pharaoh Thutmoses III (1490-1436 B.C.) and his son Amenhotep (Amenophis) II (1438-1412 B.C.) conducted extensive campaigns in Canaan. It would be very unlikely that the Exodus occurred during the reigns of these powerful kings. Egypt is not even mentioned in the biblical accounts of Joshua's conquest of Canaan. This would be most unlikely if the conquest took place in the 15th century.

Another difficulty with a 15th-century Exodus is that it appears to conflict with the archaeological evidence that points to a later date for the Israelite settlement in Canaan (see below). If the Exodus occurred some 40 years earlier than the settlement, this would place the Exodus about 1250 B.C., rather than in the 15th century.

Of course, our inability to fit either the Exodus (or the patriarchs) into an acceptable chronological framework does not necessarily invalidate the historicity of the narrative. Even if it could be positively proven that our scriptural texts are composites, redacted from diverse sources, and that the documents that recount the doings of the patriarchs were fashioned many hundreds of years after the events they purport to describe—a widely held scholarly hypothesis—this would have little bearing on the accuracy and authenticity of the events, questions that are quite independent of the literary issues. The same is true of the Exodus narratives.

It is obvious, however, that the biblical writers were not concerned with the objective recording of details and processes of historical change, as a modern historian would be. The biblical writers were not consciously engaged in what we call historiography. Rather, their concern was with the didactic use of selected historical traditions. Our exclusive concentration on the criterion of literal historicity tends to obscure the purpose and message of the text, which, after all, are the enduring qualities of Scripture. Recognition of this reality, however, raises serious questions about the possibility of ever recovering the true, chronological course of events.

The Egyptian sojourn cannot be fictional

Do we have a simplified, telescoped account in the Bible of what was in fact a very complex situation? Was there a single, united Exodus or did the emigration from Egypt take place in stages. Is it so difficult to delineate the route of the Exodus because it in fact occurred in stages? Is it possible that some Israelite tribes never even left Canaan but were later joined by those who returned from Egypt?[10]

Each of these possibilities has been suggested. But no single theory provides a satisfactory solution to all the problems, and each is itself beset by freshly introduced obscurities. One thing, however, seems certain: The Egyptian oppression of the Israelites cannot possibly be fictional. The sojourn in Egypt provides a theme of paramount and fundamental importance in the historical consciousness and religious development of the people of Israel. No nation would be likely to invent for itself, and faithfully transmit century after century and millennium after millennium, an inglorious and inconvenient tradition of this nature unless it had an authentic core.

Moreover, the historical problem of the Exodus is not entirely invincible. True, the pharaoh of the oppression is simply referred to as "pharaoh" and therefore cannot be identified from the narrative. Nevertheless, embedded in the text are tidbits of information that cumulatively suggest a dating in the 13th century B.C.

The region of Israelite settlement in Egypt is consistently designated as Goshen (Genesis 45:10, 46:28,29,34; 47:1,4,6,27; 50:8; Exodus 8:18, 9:26). This territory surely lay in the eastern Nile Delta. This points to the period of the Hyksos occupation of Egypt. Between the 18th and 16th centuries B.C., an era that Egyptologists call the "Second Intermediate Period," a motley population of Asiatics infiltrated Egypt in increasing numbers, eventually taking control of Lower Egypt. These Asiatics seem to have come mainly from Canaan. The governing class became known as "Hyksos" which means "Rulers of Foreign Lands."[11] Hyksos rulers formed the 15th and 16th Egyptian Dynasties of Egypt (c. 1700-1542). Their chief base was at Avaris, in the eastern Delta. The story of Joseph's rise to power undeniably makes considerable sense in this period. Similarly, the expulsion of the Hyksos about the middle of the 16th century B.C. and the founding of the New Kingdom, with the advent of the 18th Egyptian Dynasty, provide a plausible background for the reversal in the fortunes of the Israelites after "a new king arose over Egypt who did not know Joseph" (Exodus 1:8).

A 13th-century B.C. Exodus?   Another bit of evidence is found in another name of the area of Israelite settlement: "the region of Rameses" (Genesis 47:11). The Israelites are said to have built a city named Raamses (Exodus 1:11), which was the rallying point for them at the time of the Exodus. (Exodus 12:37; Numbers 33:3,5) This strongly suggests a connection with Pharaoh Ramesses II (1290-1224 B.C.), who shifted the administrative center of Egypt to the northeast Delta and named the capital that he built there after himself.[12] This pharaoh was famous for his extensive and massive building program which he executed by conscripting large numbers of civilians, especially foreigners. Two biblical stories indicate that pharaoh's royal palace was situated not too far from the area of Israelite settlement. Miriam, Moses' sister, was able to run home quickly and fetch her mother when the Egyptian princess found the baby Moses in his basket on the river (Exodus 2:5-8). Again, when pharaoh's firstborn son was stricken in the middle of the night, the king summoned Moses and Aaron to his royal residence, and they were able to inform the people in no time of their imminent departure (Exodus 12:29-32).

Known developments in Egyptian history also suggest Ramesses II as the pharaoh of the oppression. Toward the end of Ramesses' long reign, Egyptian national power declined greatly. Apart from a raid into Canaan by his successor Merneptah, the Egyptian hold on Asian lands weakened appreciably. Around 1200 B.C. the 19th Dynasty came to an end amidst anarchy and chaos. The internal and external situations at this time provide the most appropriate background for the events of the Israelite oppression, the liberation, the wars of conquest and the Israelite settlement in Canaan.

Another relevant item is the famous Merneptah Stele, known also as the Israel Stele.[13] Pharaoh Merneptah (1212-1200 B.C.) led a punitive expedition into Canaan, in the course of which he clashed with the Israelites. According to the stele that he set up to commemorate his foray, the Israelites were already in the central highlands of Canaan, though they were not at this time a state with definable borders. Thus in about 1200 B.C. the Israelites had only recently entered the country. The Exodus would therefore have taken place about a half a century earlier.

Finally, we must consider the Amarna letters, Akkadian texts written in cuneiform and found at Tell el-Amarna in Egypt. These letters from the 14th century B.C. vividly expose the disintegration of Egyptian control

Amarna letter. In cuneiform signs on a clay tablet, Abi-milki, king of Tyre, writes to the Egyptian Pharaoh Akhenaten (1353-1335 B.C.) that he is "protecting the city [Tyre]" during a period of rebellion. More than 350 such letters were found in an archive at Akhenaten's capital of Tell el-Amarna, many of them sent to him by his vassal kings in Canaan.

of Canaan toward the end of the Late Bronze Age (c. 1550-1200 B.C.).[14] The Amarna letters paint a picture of internecine warfare, of deteriorating morale and of a breakdown in internal security, with the city-state populations menaced by marauders called Habiru. The chief urban centers are the coastal plains, the Plain of Jezreel and the Jordan Valley. Aside from the towns of Shechem, Jerusalem and Hebron, the hill country was sparsely settled and densely wooded.

Archaeology has been able to reconstruct far-reaching changes that occurred in Canaan around 1200 B.C., with the close of the Late Bronze Age and the beginning of the Iron Age. The landscape of the central highlands underwent transformation. New settlers appeared in sizable numbers. Villages were founded on the hilltops, and extensive deforestation took place. Large-scale terrracing of the slopes was undertaken to create areas for agricultural cultivation so that the needs of the enlarged population could be met. Cisterns were constructed throughout the central highlands, distinguished by waterproof linings of lime plaster that rendered them impermeable.[15]

There is no direct evidence to prove that the new arrivals who were responsible for these changes were the tribes of Israel. But this is a thoroughly reasonable assumption. It also happens to correlate with the destruction of a significant number of important city-states, among them Lachish, Bethel and Hazor, in the second half of the 13th century B.C. Each of these cities is said in the Bible to have been destroyed by Joshua (Joshua 10:31-32, 12:7-16, 11:10-11).

The situation in Transjordan is also relevant. In Numbers 20:14-21 and 21:21-35 we are told that Moses was in contact with the kingdoms of Edom, Moab and Ammon. Archaeological surveys have shown that these settled kingdoms did not exist before the 13th century B.C.[16] This too helps to place the Exodus in a historical context.

In short, the biblical account of the Exodus seems to fit best with a variety of developments that occurred during the 13th century.

The Egyptian coloration of the narrative   There is no question that the biblical narrative exhibits a distinctly Egyptian coloration in many respects. For example, the original motive for the descent of the Hebrews to Egypt was to find relief from famine (Genesis 42:1-2, 43:1-2). When Joseph disclosed his true identity to his brothers, he told them that there were still five years of famine to be expected, and he advised them to migrate to Egypt at once. He promised them: "I will provide for you...that you and your household and all that is yours may not suffer want" (Genesis 45:11). This advice clearly reflects a migratory pattern of seminomads, well illustrated by an extant report of an Egyptian frontier official to his superior in the 13th century. He records that the Bedouin tribes of Edom had been permitted to pass the fortress of Merneptah in the eastern end of Wadi Tumilat (usually identified with biblical Goshen) and to proceed to the pools of Per-Atum (probably biblical Pithom) in order "to keep them alive and to keep their cattle alive."[17]

The biblical narrative lays great stress on the toilsome labor involved in brick making assigned to the Hebrews (Exodus 1:14). We are told that at one point state-supplied straw was withdrawn; the Israelite laborers had to find their own straw while maintaining the same daily output as before (Exodus 5:6-18). The process of manufacturing bricks in Egypt is well documented in papyri and in art. Alluvial Nile mud was mixed with stubble, shaped into a mold and left to dry in the sun. The celebrated paintings from the tomb of the vizier Rekhmire (c. 1460 B.C.) at Thebes portray the varied steps involved in brick making and provide a realistic illustration of the chores to which the Hebrews were subjected. The reason why brick making looms so large in the Exodus story is that brick, not masonry (as in Canaan), was the characteristic building material of ancient Egypt. The brick factories had to turn out huge quantities even in normal times. The frenetic construction activities of Ramesses II all over the country and especially in the Nile Delta required staggering quantities of bricks. A leather roll from the fifth year of Ramesses' reign lists a quota of 2,000 bricks for each of 40 workmen. Since Egyptian towns were generally surrounded by brick walls nearly 60 feet high and 50 feet wide, the incessant demand for bricks and labor can easily be imagined.[18]

Brick making in Pharaonic Egypt. This panel from a wall painting in the tomb of the vizier Rekhmire (c. 1460 B.C.) shows some of the chores involved in brick making. Men with hoes knead clay moistened with water, as other workers carry material to two brick makers. The Hebrews' labors for Pharaoh described in Exodus 1:14 were no doubt similar to these realistic scenes.

In the Bible Egypt is often referred to as "the house of bondage" (Exodus 13:3,14, 20:2; Deuteronomy 5:6, 6:12, 7:8, 8:14, 13:6,11; Joshua 24:17; Judges 6:8; Jeremiah 34:13; Micah 6:4). What the Book of Exodus describes is not domestic slavery of the Israelites but compulsory state labor on public projects. The obvious economic importance of an abundant supply of free labor explains pharaoh's intransigeance in refusing Moses' demands for the release of the Israelites. The corvée system is known to have been practised in Egypt in all periods, but it was Ramesses II especially who conscripted and exploited the foreign population in the country.

There is more: Three times Moses requests the Egyptian administration to give the Israelites time off for a religious observance: "So we must go a distance of three days into the wilderness to sacrifice to the Lord our God as he may command us" (Exodus 8:23; cf. 3:18, 5:3). A leather scroll from the fifth year of the reign of Ramesses II records a feast day of a certain goddess that was a holiday for the corvée conscripts. Similarly, records from a Theban workers' village mention that laborers were idle on certain days because they had gone to make offerings to their gods.[19]

The ten plagues also reflect an authentic Egyptian background. The plagues visited on the Egyptians are presented not only as punitive and coercive measures, but also as "judgments" on Egyptian divinities. God is said to warn: "I will mete out punishments to all the gods of Egypt" (Exodus 12:12). Following the Exodus, we are told retrospectively that "the Lord executed judgment on their gods" (Numbers 33:4). This observation is another way of saying that from the viewpoint of the biblical narrator, at least some of the plagues functioned to expose the impotence and the futility of polytheism. The first and ninth plagues—the Nile turning to blood and the three days of darkness—can, indeed, be so explained against the background of the religious and mythological beliefs of ancient Egypt.

The Nile and the sun constituted the twin underpinnings of Egyptian civilization. Both were deified. Hapi was the Nile god who fructified the fields and personified the powers of fertility and nourishment. Turning the Nile into blood meant the victory of chaos over order. An Egyptian text, "The Admonitions of Ipu-wer," purports to foretell a series of national calamities, and features this motif: "The River is blood. If one drinks of it, one rejects it and thirsts for water."[20]

The ninth plague, three days of darkness, may also be viewed in the context of Egyptian religious thought in which the sun-god assumed primal importance. In one Egyptian myth, the serpent Apophis personifies the powers of evil; he is arrayed against the Sun-god; Apophis symbolizes the darkness that the Sun-god had to defeat anew each morning.[21] Hence, the three days of darkness that the God of Israel visited upon Egypt would signify to local worshippers the defeat of the solar deity, the supreme god of Egypt. Another Egyptian text known as "The Prophecy of Nefer-rohu [Neferti]" foretells that the sun-disc would be covered over and would withhold its light from the earth and the people would be unable to see.[22]

The plague of frogs may also have been interpreted as a judgment on an Egyptian god. The frog-headed goddess Heqt was the consort of Khnum, who created human beings at the potter's wheel. Heqt was appropriately assigned to assist women in childbirth. The plague of frogs that menaced Egypt could well have meant to the biblical narrator retribution for the decree of the pharaoh for ordering the killing of all Israelite male babies.

To sum up: The biblical narrative that describes the experience of Israel in Egypt exhibits many items that genuinely reflect Egyptian background.

The route of the Exodus presents its own set of problems.

Problems with the route of the Exodus

The shortest and most important route from Egypt to Canaan in the second millennium was the international highway known as the "Way of the Sea," which more or less followed the Mediterranean coastline. The biblical account of the Exodus reports that the departing Israelites deliberately avoided this route, however, and instead pursued a circuitous course. The text says:

"God did not lead them by way of the land of the Philistines, although it was nearer; for God said, 'The people may have a change of heart when they see war, and return to Egypt.' So God led them roundabout, by way of the wilderness at the Sea of Reeds" (Exodus 13:17-18).

The Way of the Sea is undoubtedly the route used by Pharaoh Thutmosis III and his army in his campaign against central and northern Canaan in 1468 B.C. In an Egyptian text describing this campaign we are told that the journey from the Egyptian border fortress of Sile to Gaza, a distance of about 150 miles (240 km) took Thutmosis and his army only ten days.[23] The Israelites sensibly avoided this strategic route, however, for the reason that it was heavily fortified because Egypt's northeastern frontier was so highly vulnerable to invasion from Asia. The reliefs carved on the outer wall of the hypostyle hall of the temple of Amun at Karnak display a chain of forts, way stations and wells along this route. Excavations have uncovered ancient Egyptian citadels strung all the way from the Nile Delta to Gaza.[24] In light of these facts, it was certainly the better part of valor for the fleeing Israelites to have taken a different route in their trek to Canaan.

The Bible refers to the Way of the Sea as the Way of the Land of the Philistines. Another passage, Exodus 23:31, refers to the Mediterranean Sea as the Sea of Philistia. Many scholars regard this designation as an anachronism because the Philistines are not mentioned outside the Bible prior to about 1185 B.C., when they first appear in texts from the time of Ramesses III. At any rate, their appearance in the Book of Exodus certainly testifies to the power and importance of that people in biblical times. Actually, the Philistines are not mentioned among Israel's enemies in the accounts of Joshua's wars of conquest. However, toward the end of Joshua's life, the Philistines were organized into a pentapolis comprising Gaza, Ashdod, Ashkelon, Gath and Ekron, each city governed by a *sèren* or a "lord" (Joshua 13:1-3).

The Philistines are first mentioned in an extra-biblical text in connection with an invasion of Egypt by the Sea Peoples in the fifth year of the reign of Ramesses III (1185 B.C.), as recorded in an inscription in the temple of Amun at Medinet Habu near Thebes.[25] One of the Sea Peoples was the Philistines. The Sea Peoples migrated from the Aegean area—most likely having been pushed out by the arrival of the Greeks—but they also had strong ties with Anatolia. The biblical sources have preserved consistent traditions that the Philistines reached the coast of Canaan directly from Crete (Genesis 10:14; 1 Chronicles 1:12; Deuteronomy 2:23; 1 Samuel 30:14; Ezekiel 25:16; Zephaniah 2:5). The prophet Amos has God saying: "I brought Israel up from the land of Egypt, but also the Philistines from Caphtor"(Amos 9:7), which is the biblical term for Crete. The prophet Jeremiah makes the same association: "For the Lord will ravage the Philistines, the remnant from the island of Caphtor" (Jeremiah 47:4). The Sea Peoples, including the Philistines, ravaged and overran much of the eastern Mediterranean countries toward the end of the Late Bronze Age (c. 1550-1200 B.C.). They came in waves and, after being repulsed by the Egyptians, they became mercenaries of the pharaohs, who settled them in their strategic garrisons along the coast of Canaan.

Following the decisive deliverance of Israel at the Sea of Reeds, the Israelites made their way through the wilderness, and headed for Mt. Sinai. The location of this famous site and the entire route of the Exodus have remained an unsolvable scholarly crux.[26] There are several reasons why this is so.

First, some of the place names recorded in the biblical texts were invented by Israel as a consequence of specific events that occurred there during their wanderings. For instance, Marah (Exodus 15:23), which means "bitter," was so named because after three days of thirst the wandering Israelites found the waters at the next oasis, Marah, to be bitter; another station received the name Taberah, "conflagration" (Numbers 11:3), because of a disastrous fire that broke out there; a devastating plague that followed a gluttonous devouring of quails gave rise to the place-name Kibroth-hattaavah, "the graves of craving" (Numbers 11:34). These designations would not have been known or perpetuated by the Bedouin who regularly inhabited the wilderness. Second, a high proportion of the names mentioned in the Israelite itineraries cannot be identified by archaeological investigation. Third, even modern place names that sound similar to those listed in the Pentateuch cannot be proven with certainty to refer to the same location. Fourth, the tradition that associates Mt. Sinai of the Bible with the present-day site of Jebel Musa (Mount of Moses), where there is a monastery and a basilica of St. Catherine, is not earlier than the fourth century A.D.; in other words, 15 centuries separate that tradition from Israel's journey through the wilderness. A tradition whose origins are so late has little credibility.[27]

As if this were not enough, there is the further complication that from the biblical data it is possible to reconstruct both a northern and a southern location for Mt. Sinai and for the route of wanderings within the peninsula now called after it. Based on some biblical passages, even a site in Arabia has been defended as Mt. Sinai.[28]

In short, we simply cannot locate Mt. Sinai or the route to or from it. The Israelite journey from Raamses to Sinai took nearly three months. It was a period of trial and tribulation. After crossing the Sea of Reeds, the Israelites marched three days through an area devoid of water. Then the first source of water they came upon turned out to be bitter and undrinkable. This disappointment engendered widespread discontent among the Israelites until, at the Lord's instruction, Moses was able to make the water potable (Exodus 15:22-25).

By contrast, the next stopping place, Elim, was an oasis with abundant springs and palm trees (Exodus 15:27). Next, in the wilderness of Sin, the food provisions gave out, and hunger led to demoralization. The leadership of Moses and Aaron was challenged. Again, according to the biblical account, divine intervention saved the day (Exodus 16:1-36). Manna and quails were supplied.[29] Manna is believed to be a common sticky, whitish, honeydew excretion produced by certain insects on tamarisk twigs. Quails are migrating birds of the pheasant family. As they travel in large flocks from Europe to Africa in the autumn and back in the spring, they land, exhausted, on the shore of the Mediterranean, where they are easily caught. To this day they are considered a great delicacy.

Moving on from the wilderness of Sin, the Israelites reached Rephidim. Here another water shortage occurred. The situation was explosive. Moses was instructed to strike a certain rock with his rod, and water gushed forth (Exodus 17:1-7). At Rephidim the Israelites were forced to defend themselves against an unexpected assault by a tribe of Amalekites. Most probably, the Amalekite attack was prompted by fear of Israel's encroachment on its control of the oasis and the caravan route along which it lay (Exodus 17:8-16; see also Deuteronomy 25:17-19).[30]

In the third month after the Exodus, the people arrived at Sinai and encamped before the mountain. Here, preparations were made for a great national religious experience—the establishment of a covenant between God and the entire community of Israel. The mountain was cordoned off and placed out of bounds. The people were ordered to refrain from sexual relations and to dress in freshly laundered clothes. On the day of the ceremony, thunder was heard and lightning flashed. A dense cloud hovered over the mountain. Moses led the Israelites out of their camp to the blare of a horn. They assembled at the foot of the mountain. From its summit, fire and smoke issued. Moses alone ascended the mountain. There the divine voice was heard proclaiming the Ten Commandments. This awesome, direct experience terrified the people, who asked Moses to act as an intermediary between themselves and God (Exodus 19:1-20:21).

The Covenant at Sinai

The relationship between Israel and God would henceforth be governed by this covenant, which embraced all aspects of life. The main provisions of criminal, civil and religious law were set forth in a document called the record of the covenant. Moses publicly read this record to the assembled Israelites who affirmed: "All that the Lord has spoken we will faithfully do!" (Exodus 24:7). The covenant was then sealed with a formal ritual ceremony (Exodus 24:4-8).

The covenant ceremony at Sinai, as a national experience, is a unique phenomenon in the history of the world. However the inspiration for the covenant and the particular form it took may be found in the political treaty of vassalage that frequently regulated international relationships at this time. The suzerain (monarch) would make a contract with a vassal state, assuring it of protection in return for the vassal's exclusive and unreserved loyalty. Concededly, the parallel with the Sinai covenant is inexact, but there are enough formal similarities between it and extant Near Eastern treaties to establish a connection beyond doubt. The original model has, however, been subtly transformed: Israel now owed exclusive and absolute fealty to the Lord; a breach of duty constituted an offense of the utmost gravity. Moreover, the definition of fealty was broadened to embrace the entire moral life of the individual and society.[31]

Moses remained on the mountain in seclusion for 40 days. During his prolonged absence, Aaron was besieged with popular demand for a visible, concrete symbol of the continued presence of God in the midst of the Israelite camp. To Aaron's request for donations of gold, the people responded generously. Out of these contributions Aaron fashioned a golden calf, which he set up before the people; in front of it he erected an altar. He then announced a festival of the Lord for the following day. The people arose early next morning, offered sacrifices and engaged in feasting and revelry. When Moses, at divine behest, descended the mountain bearing two tablets of stone on which the Ten Commandments were incised, and witnessed the scene, he smashed the tablets. He then burned the golden calf, ground it to powder, scattered it over the water and forced the Israelites to drink the mixture (Exodus 32:1-20).

The inscribing of treaties on tablets is well attested. One excellent example contains a treaty between the Hittites and Egypt engraved on a silver tablet.[32] In Mesopotamia, agreements and pacts between individuals were also recorded on tablets. The invalidation or repudiation of such agreements was signified by smashing the tablet. Moses' action, therefore was invested with profound symbolic meaning.

By this time, the people were out of control. Moses issued a call for those who, in effect, were willing to fight to maintain the pristine purity of Israel's religion. The tribe of Levi rallied to his side, and a slaughter of thousands ensued. The covenant between God and Israel was then renewed (Exodus 32:25-35, 34:27-28).

The golden calf   The story about the golden calf can be understood on several levels. The parallel with the golden calves that were set up in the northern kingdom of Israel after Solomon's death immediately springs to mind. Following Solomon's death the northern tribes broke away from the south and set up their own kingdom. Their first king, Jeroboam, installed two golden calves at cult centers in Dan and Bethel (1 Kings 12:28-30; 2 Chronicles 11:15). There is an obvious connection between this episode and the golden calf episode at Mt. Sinai. But scholars are divided as to which of the two accounts came first and influenced the other. One school regards the Exodus narrative as a polemic written after Jeroboam's apostasy in order to condemn it as a breach of the covenant that had been severely punished in the past. Other scholars view Jeroboam's cultic installations as having derived their inspiration from an original narrative that ascribed the calf symbolism to Aaron. The Exodus text as it has come down to us is, according to these scholars, a later expansion designed to deny the legitimacy of the northern Israelites' cultic centers.[33]

The golden calf incident at Mt. Sinai exposed the popular need for symbolic representation of the divine Presence. This void was then filled, according to the biblical account, by a mobile sanctuary that would accompany the people as they departed from Sinai in continuation of their trek to the Promised Land. The construction materials were generously donated by the people. A master craftsman named Bezalel was appointed to execute the divinely given instructions for design and organization of the sanctuary. The Tabernacle, as it has come to be called, was completed and thereafter remained the focus of religious life throughout the wilderness wanderings (Exodus 25:1-31:11, 35:4-40:38).

Scholars are skeptical of the historicity of the narrative detailing the construction and establishment of the mobile sanctuary in the wilderness. The precious materials of which it was constructed—metals, gems, fabrics and timber—would be unlikely to have been available to a seminomadic people, erstwhile slaves, in Sinai. It is doubtful that the necessary specialized technical and artistic skills would have been available. Some have even questioned whether the very concept of such a portable shrine reflected ancient reality. Many critical scholars argue that the Tabernacle as described in the Book of Exodus is a late, theoretical, idealized construct of priestly writers based upon Solomon's Temple in Jerusalem and retrojected into the period of the Exodus.[34]

Other scholars, responding to these arguments, point out that prefabricated structures and tent-shrines can be documented from ancient Egypt and Ugarit, among the Phoenicians, and among pre-Islamic and Islamic Arab tribes. At Timna, north of modern Eilat, a Midianite tent-shrine erected over an earlier Egyptian temple has been uncovered.[35] Further, the biblical texts emphasize that the Egyptians furnished their former victims with objects of gold and silver as well as clothing, and that the departing Israelites "stripped the Egyptians" (Exodus 12:36). Finally, since the Israelites had long been employed on massive Egyptian building projects, the skilled craftsmen needed for the Tabernacle construction could easily have been among them. Such arguments obviously do not prove that the wilderness sanctuary is historical; at most they demonstrate that there are no historical objections to the reality of a portable tent-shrine in the wilderness period.[36]

The subsequent history of Israel in the wilderness[37] is for the most part wrapped in obscurity; the biblical sources preserve very few traditions. We are told that in the second year after the Exodus, the people arrived at the wilderness of Paran (Numbers 13:3,26; see also Genesis 14:6-7). Their main objective was the oasis at Kadesh (Numbers 33:36; Deuteronomy 1:19; Judges 11:16-17). The distance between Sinai and Kadesh was covered in 11 days. Kadesh, or Kadesh-Barnea as it is also called, is almost certainly to be identified with Ain el-Qudeirat, about 150 miles (240 km) from the Nile Delta.[38] This is the largest oasis in northern Sinai. It has a perennial spring, and close by is extensive pasturage. It is also strategically located just south of the later Israelite border. It lay at the intersection of two major desert routes; one led down to Egypt from Edom and the Arabah by the the Way of Shur; the other went from Eilat and the central Negev to Arad and Hebron.

38 years at Kadesh-Barnea

Israel stayed at Kadesh for 38 years (Deuteronomy 2:14; see also Deuteronomy 1:46). Kadesh-Barnea, its full name, has been excavated and the ruins of three Iron Age Israelite fortresses have been uncovered. However, nothing earlier than a Solomonic stratum (tenth century B.C.) was found. This makes for a historical puzzle in light of the biblical traditions. It is possible that the partial nature of the excavations, confined to a segment of the mound, may account for the absence of remains from the period of the Exodus.[39] Some of the most significant events recorded in the Pentateuch appear to have occurred there. A disastrous fire broke out in the camp at Kadesh (Numbers 11:1-3). A mass protest erupted against the monotonous, scant and meatless diet. Some even expressed regret at having left Egypt. Suddenly, the air teemed with quails. The people gorged themselves on the delicacy, but a severe epidemic broke out. The site was named Kibroth-hattaavah which means, "the graves of craving" (Numbers 11:4-35).

At the next stopping place, Hazeroth, Miriam and Aaron criticized Moses for having married a Cushite woman (Numbers 12). Cush is the biblical name for Nubia, a region south of Egypt, modern northern Sudan. It is also possible that "Cush" is an ancient name for Midian, the homeland of Zipporah, Moses' wife. (In Habakkuk 3:7 the "tents of Cushan" are parallel to the "pavilions of Midian.") In the Table of Nations in Genesis 10, Cush is one of the "sons" of Ham and a "brother" of Egypt, and the "sons of Cush" are located in the Arabian area (Genesis 10:6-7). Whatever her origin, Moses' Cushite wife was not welcomed by his brother and sister, and they called into question his preeminence. Thereupon, God affirmed Moses' unique status as a prophet. Miriam was punished with a cutaneous infection, but was healed at Moses' behest, though only after a week's quarantine.

An event of major significance occurred when 12 scouts were dispatched to reconnoiter the land of Canaan, especially the Negev and the central highlands of the Hebron region as far as Wadi Eschol (Numbers 13-14). Their report provoked a crisis. They affirmed the fertility of the land and exhibited samples of its fruits to prove it. But ten of the scouts also reported on the great strength of the Canaanite fortifications. They described the physique of the inhabitants in superhuman terms. The scouts' report quickly spread defeatism throughout the Israelite camp. An encouraging minority report by Joshua and Caleb could do nothing to quell the ensuing insurrection. Completely demoralized, the people demanded to return to Egypt and were on the point of stoning Moses and Aaron when the presence of the Lord became manifest in the community. Moses once again interceded on behalf of Israel, thereby averting national catastrophe. But the entire generation that came out of Egypt was now doomed to die in the wilderness—except for Joshua and Caleb, the two scouts who had remained steadfast in their faith and had tried to restore the confidence of the people. Upon hearing this judgment, the people's mood changed from defeatism to foolhardiness. In defiance of Moses' veto, an ill-conceived invasion of the hill country of Canaan was launched from the south, at Hormah. The Israelites suffered a shattering defeat.[40]

Korah's   A rebellion led by Korah presented the next serious challenge to the
rebellion   leadership of Moses and Aaron. Korah, a Levite, was supported by three prominent Reubenites and a cabal of 250 chieftains of high social standing. Their indictment against Moses and Aaron was broad: it included resentment at their domination of all Israel, opposition to Aaron's monoply of the priesthood and, finally, criticism of Moses' and Aaron's failure to lead Israel into the Promised Land. When the rebellion broke out, Moses proposed settling the issue of priestly leadership by a trial involving incense offerings. The conspirators and Aaron each would come to the Tabernacle sanctuary the following morning with a

fire pan of incense. God would decide whose incense offering was acceptable. The right to offer incense had been the exclusive prerogative of the Aaronide priesthood, so this was a critical test. Korah appeared, but his Reubenite collaborators in the rebellion refused to accept the challenge. The entire community assembled to watch the proceedings. The people apparently sympathized with Korah. Moses and Aaron pleaded with God to punish only the active conspirators. The onlookers were then warned to distance themselves from the tents of the Reubenites and Korah. Then an earthquake swallowed up the leaders of the insurrection, and a fire broke out that incinerated the conspirators (Numbers 16; see also Numbers 26:9-10, 27:3; Deuteronomy 11:6; Psalm 106:16-18).

The vindication of Moses and Aaron aroused popular indignation and resentment, but when a plague broke out among the people, Aaron took the fire pan, offered incense, and made expiation for the people, whereupon the plague was checked. To prove the religious preeminence of Aaron and the tribe of Levi, each tribal chief was asked to deposit in the sanctuary a staff with his name inscribed upon it. The divine election of the Levites was proven by the blossoming of Aaron's staff, which was inscribed with the name Levi (Numbers 17).

Hostility to the Israelites east of the Jordan

All these episodes reflect the considerable opposition to Mosaic leadership that surfaced periodically in the course of Israel's wilderness wanderings. Many critical scholars see behind these events as recorded in the text (Numbers 16-17) a lost history describing intra-Levitical struggles for control of the national religious institutions and of rivalry for civil and political leadership.

The story of the wanderings continues with an explanation for the remarkable fact that the great leader Moses was not permitted to enter the Promised Land but instead died in the wilderness. Once, when there had been a shortage of water, the carping and grumbling of the people so exasperated Moses that he violated the divine command to order a rock to release water and instead struck the rock (Numbers 20:2-13; this episode should be distinguished from the one described in Exodus 17:1-7, where Moses was instructed to strike the rock).

The Israelites were now on the border of Edom, east of the Jordan River. Earlier experiences had convinced Moses that the most practical strategy was to try to penetrate Canaan from eastern Transjordan. He sent a friendly request to the king of the Edomites seeking permission to pass through his land. Edom not only refused but threatened military action against the Israelites. So the Israelites chose to make a detour rather than press the issue. As a consequence, they had no option but to trek further through the desert that bordered Moab on the east (Numbers 20:14-21).

Sihon, king of the Amorites, also denied the Israelites permission to cross his land. This time, however, Israel decided to engage the enemy. Israel successfully occupied the important city of Heshbon with its many dependent villages (Numbers 20:21-29). This city has been identified with the modern village of Hisban in Jordan, about 47 miles due east of Jerusalem. Several archaeological campaigns conducted there turned up remains from Iron Age I, but nothing earlier. That is to say, the period of the Exodus and conquest drew a blank. It is possible, of course, that following the destruction of Heshbon by the Israelites, a new city was built on another site and given the name Heshbon, present-day Hisban.

Israel was now in possession of the territory between the Arnon and Jabbok rivers that flow into the Jordan. Having seized this strategic area, Moses turned his attention northward toward the Bashan, a fertile region stretching from just below the Yarmuk River to Mt. Hermon in the north. The Israelites defeated King Og of Bashan at Edrei, his capital, which is most likely modern Dar'a in Syria near the border with Jordan, about 60 miles south of Damascus. At this site, Early Bronze Age potsherds have been uncovered. Evidence for the Israelite conquest, if it exists, must await further excavation (Numbers 21:33-35; Deuteronomy 1:4-5, 3:1-17).[41] All these lands east of the Jordan were then allotted to the Israelite tribes of Reuben, Gad and half the tribe of Manasseh.[42]

The Israelite presence in the Plains of Moab was regarded as a threat by the Moabites. The Moabite king Balak told his Midianite neighbors: "Now this horde will lick clean all that is about us as an ox licks up the grass of the field" (Numbers 22:4). Apparently fearful of resorting to military means, Balak hired Balaam, a famous soothsayer (Joshua 13:22; see also Numbers 22:7), to place a magical curse on Israel. The "Execration Texts"[43] from ancient Egypt provide other examples of such curses. It was believed that, when properly administered, these curses would defeat an enemy. Balaam arrived on the scene at King Balak's request, but blessings rather than curses unaccountably issued from his mouth. In a series of oracles, Balaam predicted Israel's ultimate victory over Moab, Edom and others (Numbers 22-24; Deuteronomy 23:5-6; Joshua 24:9-10; Nehemiah 13:2). Later King David would subjugate these territories (2 Samuel 8:2,13-14).

A curious light on the Balaam episode has been uncovered at Tell Deir 'Alla in Transjordan in the middle Jordan Valley, about one mile north of the River Jabbok. An inscription on a plastered wall mentions "Balaam son of Beor, the one who was seer of the gods." Written in the eighth century B.C. in what seems to be an Old Aramaic dialect, it is a copy of a text hundreds of years older. It contains certain features reminiscent of the biblical narrative about the same personality. The inscription raises the likelihood that traditions about Balaam reached Israel from a Moabite source.[44]

The Israelites then fought a war against the Midianites who inhabited the desert borders east of the Jordan from Moab down to Edom. Midian had earlier cooperated with Moab in hiring Balaam. The tribal rulers of Midian were killed in battle and Balaam too was put to the sword (Numbers 31:8; Joshua 13:22).

Most of the area east of the Jordan was now firmly in Israelite hands. Moses, the great leader, died on Mt. Nebo overlooking Canaan. The mantle of leadership passed to Joshua, his military commander. The Israelites consolidated their positions in the area and prepared themselves for what the Bible describes as the wars of conquest and settlement in Canaan.

Evaluating the historicity of the biblical narrative

It now remains to review and evaluate the results of scholarly investigation. The biblical writings are the only ones available, and they are full of complexities. They do not permit us to fix without question the Exodus events and to place them in a historical framework. Moreover, they contain an inherent limitation that results from the aims and goals of the biblical writers. They were not recording history for its own sake but were making theological-didactic interpretations of selected historical events. The tendencies, slant and emphases of the biblical narratives are shaped to conform to these purposes, and must be read and utilized accordingly. There are no extra-biblical sources, either literary or inscriptional, that refer to the experiences of Israel in Egypt or that unequivocally and directly bear upon them. There is nothing, including the results of archaeological research, that can be described as constituting clear-cut and objective evidence for the historicity of the biblical narrative.

All this, on the other hand, is an argument from silence, and the lack of concrete confirmation of the scriptural account cannot be adduced to undermine its essential veracity. The cumulative effect of several varied lines of approach tend to support the historicity of the slavery in Egypt, the reality of the migration from that country and the actuality of the subsequent Israelite penetration and control of much of Canaan.

Had Israel really arisen in Canaan and never been enslaved in Egypt, a biblical writer would have had no reason to conceal that fact and could surely have devised an appropriate narrative to accommodate that reality were he given to fictional inventiveness. We are at a loss to explain the necessity of fabricating an uncomfortable and disreputable account of Israel's national origins, nor can we conceive how such a falsity could so pervade the national psyche as to eliminate all other traditions and historical memories, let alone become the dominant and controlling theme in the national religion. It will not do, in refutation of this argument, to point to other peoples, such as the Romans, who also reproduced inglorious traditions about their own past.[45] On the contrary, such tales may well reflect historical reality, and in any case did not become a central and formative factor in shaping the religion and culture of their respective bearers over thousands of years.

Scattered data culled from the Joseph narratives and Exodus accounts add up to a consistent picture in respect to the Israelite area of settlement. They also combine to place the main events within the 13th century B.C. if taken against the background of known developments in Egyptian history. It is hardly decisive but it is significant that not only do the narratives feature authentic Egyptian coloration, they also preserve Egyptian names for important personalities: Moses, Hophni, Phinehas and Hur.

A 13th-century B.C. date also correlates with major events that were taking place on the international scene. The end of that century witnessed historic turmoil and social upheaval in both East and West. The Hittite empire collapsed; important city-states like Alalakh, Ugarit and Qatna in Syria were destroyed; the Sea Peoples invaded the east Mediterranean coast; the Trojan wars were taking place; Egypt, greatly weakened, retreated from Asia; and Assyria and Babylonia were wracked by bitter internal dissension.[46] What is more, Canaanite culture had by then become thoroughly decadent, its political system had broken down, major fortified urban centers were violently destroyed and on the ruins of several arose new settlements materially much inferior to those of their predecessors. The new settlements exhibit clear signs of being the work of seminomads.[47]

To sum up: Are the Israelite slavery, liberation and conquest as described in the Bible "proven" in a scientific sense? Defintely not! Does the assumption of their general historicity provide the most reasonable explanation to account for and accommodate the most facts despite the puzzling complexity of the literary sources?[48] Decidedly yes!

T H R E E

The Settlement in Canaan

The Period of the Judges

JOSEPH A. CALLAWAY

H OW THE ISRAELITES ACQUIRED THEIR TERRITORIES IN THE HILL country of Canaan and what their first settlements were like continue to be among the most unsettled issues in Israelite history. A casual reading of the Book of Joshua leaves one with the feeling that there is no problem: Joshua and the Israelites entered the land from east of the Jordan River, captured Jericho with the aid of divine intervention and took the rest of Canaan in a series of lightning military campaigns. The various peoples of Canaan were defeated and, as in the case of the inhabitants at Jericho, were "utterly destroyed . . . both men and women, young and old, oxen, sheep, and asses, with the edge of the sword" (Joshua 6:21). "So Joshua defeated the whole land, the hill country and the Negev and the lowland and the slopes, and all their kings; he left none remaining, but utterly destroyed all that breathed, as the Lord God of Israel commanded" (Joshua 10:40). "There was not a city that made peace with the people of Israel, except the Hivites, the inhabitants of Gibeon; they took all in battle" (Joshua 11:19).

The biblical description is so graphic and direct that many people just never thought of Israel's entry into Canaan in any other way: The land was acquired by military conquest in less than five years of struggle (Joshua 14:7, 10) and was divided among the nine and one-half tribes that had not yet received territorial allotments (Joshua 13:8-19:51).* The

---

* Joshua 13:15-31 states that Moses gave allotments east of the Jordan to the tribes of Reuben, Gad and the half-tribe of Manasseh.

Israelites displaced the various peoples that occupied the towns and villages, and all Israel was involved in taking the land and in settling the portions allotted to the various tribes. A statement in Joshua 21:43 summarizes this view:

> "Thus the Lord gave to Israel all the land which he swore to give to their fathers; and having taken possession of it, they settled there."

Joshua vs. Judges

A quite different view of the "conquest" and settlement in Canaan emerges in the Book of Judges. The events related in that book purportedly come "after the death of Joshua" (Judges 1:1), but the picture of Israel in Canaan is not at all what one would expect after reading the Book of Joshua. For instance, the sequence of "conquest followed by allotment of land" is reversed in Judges; in Judges the sequence is allotment of land and then conquest. Thus, Judah says to Simeon, his brother, "Come up with me into the territory allotted to me, that we may fight against the Canaanites; and I likewise will go with you into the territory allotted to you" (Judges 1:3). Most of Judges 1 describes scattered struggles undertaken by individual tribes, or related tribes, trying to gain a foothold in the hill country of Canaan; here we find no unified effort by "all Israel" to possess the land, as seems to be described in the Book of Joshua.

Furthermore, in contrast to the sweeping statements in Joshua that Israel wiped out the inhabitants of the land, Judges 1 concludes with a list of 20 cities in which the people were not driven out by the newcomers (Judges 1:21, 27-33). Among these cities are Jerusalem, Beth-Shean, Taanach, Dor, Ibleam, Megiddo, Gezer and Beth-Shemesh. These are among the most strategically located and most influential cities in the later history of Israel. By contrast, in the summary of Israel's victories in Joshua 12:7-24, however, it is expressly stated that Jerusalem, Gezer, Taanach, Megiddo and Dor were defeated by "Joshua and the people of Israel."

The Book of Judges, unlike the Book of Joshua, preserves a tradition that the land of Canaan was possessed over a long period of time in operations that involved individual tribes or groups of related tribes acting independently. Also, the land was acquired in various ways. Judah and Simeon, as noted above, fought "against the Canaanites" in small military operations for their allotments. On the other hand, the Kenites, descendants of Moses' father-in-law, "went up with the people of Judah from the city of palms into the wilderness of Judah, which lies in the Negev near Arad; and they went and settled with the people" (Judges 1:16), apparently peacefully. And then, still others coexisted with Canaanite enclaves, such as the Jebusites, who are said to ". . . have dwelt with the people of Benjamin in Jerusalem to this day" (Judges 1:21).

Yigael Yadin, the eminent Israeli archaeologist, consistently maintained that "the main written source" for understanding the Israelite settlement in Canaan is the Bible.[1] We have seen, however, that the traditions in Joshua 1-12 emphasize a "conquest, then settlement" of the land, while the traditions in Judges preserve memories of peaceful intermingling as well as isolated fighting for certain regions. In Judges, we also find coexistence with the inhabitants of some 20 major cities that did not come under Israelite control until much later. So the question arises: What is the biblical view? Or, is there a "biblical view"?

Again, we refer to the late Professor Yadin, and to his colleague of many years at the Hebrew University, Abraham Malamat. The traditional view that Israel inherited the land of Canaan by force, as related in Joshua 1-12, is characterized by both as the "biblical" view.[2] But one qualifier must be added: it is the "biblical" view in the present form of the traditions. Both scholars recognize that Joshua and Judges were given their present form long after the settlement in Canaan took place.

Malamat notes that "the tradition of the conquest that the Bible records crystallized only after generations of complex reworking and, in certain respects, reflects the conceptions . . . of later editors and redactors."[*3] The resulting biblical historiography "explained historical events theologically," which "accentuated the role of the Lord of Israel and submerged the human element."[4] Thus, the canonical, or "official," tradition of the conquest emerged. According to this tradition, all 12 tribes of Israel were involved, acting together in military operations on both sides of the Jordan. "Thus," Malamat says, "the divine pledge to the Patriarchs (as in Deuteronomy 30:20) that Canaan would be occupied in its entirety was redeemed."[5]

The biblical conquest tradition reflects generations of reworking

The biblical tradition itself thus reflects a time much later than the settlement and the conquest it describes. For instance, Joshua 8:28 states that ". . . Joshua burned Ai, and made it forever a heap of ruins, *as it is to this day*." The site of Ai was a village from about 1200 to 1050 B.C., after which it was abandoned and never rebuilt.[6] Joshua 8:28, therefore, reflects a time when the site of Ai was a ruin, after 1050 B.C., probably during the early monarchy, not the time of the conquest some centuries earlier. In Joshua 10:12-13, the Book of Jashar is cited as a source of information about the sun standing still in the battle between Israel and the Amorite alliance at Gibeon. The Book of Jashar has not survived, but it is mentioned again in 2 Samuel 1:18 as containing the lament of David over Saul and Jonathan after their deaths at the battle on Mt. Gilboa. If this Book of Jashar is the same as that mentioned in Joshua 10:12-13, then it dates at least to the time of David. This also would place the present composition of the Book of Joshua hundreds of years after the settlement in Canaan.

What we have, then, in the books of Joshua and Judges is the "official" view, to use Malamat's term, of later editors who had access to traditions and documents that do not exist today. They had theological reasons for selecting only short sections of documents such as the Book of Jashar,

---

* Redactors reorganized, interpreted and modified ancient traditions to make them relevant to needs in later times.

quoted in Joshua 10:12-13, that suited their purposes, and leaving out the rest. This was a common practice in history writing in the biblical period, evident in passages such as 1 Chronicles 29:29. The account of David's rule is concluded in verse 28, and the sources used by the writers, who lived at a later time, are cited in verses 29-30. These sources are ". . . the Chronicles of Samuel the seer . . . the Chronicles of Nathan the prophet . . . and the Chronicles of Gad the seer." None of these sources, which belong to the time of David, exists today, and we have only the parts selected for use by the later editors for their view of David's history.

The "official" view of Israel's history writers who lived hundreds of years after the settlement in Canaan thus became the "biblical" view of a military conquest of Canaan. Evidence in the Book of Judges of a longer process in acquiring the land through isolated fighting, infiltration and coexistence is secondary to the "official" position. Nevertheless, there are some scholars who regard the process of settlement reflected in the Book of Judges as more realistic historically than the lightning military campaigns in the Book of Joshua, and no less biblical than the view in the Book of Joshua. Consequently, there are advocates of various scenarios for the entry of Israel into Canaan and subsequent settlement; all the scenarios are regarded in some sense as biblical, and all differ to some degree from each other.

We shall examine the various ways of looking at the settlement of Israel in Canaan, beginning with the canonical* view in the Book of Joshua that Israel acquired the land by force.

| *Did Israel take the land by conquest?* | Was there a conquest of Canaan? "The fact is," argued Professor Yadin, "that excavation results from the last 50 years or so support in a most amazing way (except in some cases . . .) the basic historicity of the Biblical account."[7] Yadin noted that "the Biblical narrative in broad outline tells us that at a certain period nomadic Israelites attacked the city-state organization of the Holy Land, destroying many cities and setting them on fire. Then, slowly but surely, the Israelites replaced these cities with new, unfortified cities or settlements."[8] He goes on to say that this account "is exactly the picture which the archaeological finds present to us: a complete system of fortified cities collapsed and was replaced by a new culture whose material aspect can be defined as the first efforts of seminomads to settle down."[9] |

Both Malamat and Yadin recognize that the actual events of the conquest and settlement were more complex than they appear in the present "official" or "biblical" tradition in the Book of Joshua. "But at the core," Malamat contends, "a military conquest remains."[10] This is reflected in "an intimate and authentic knowledge of the land, and a

---

* "Canonical" means the accepted, or "official," view of the biblical tradition. The word itself came into use in the early Christian period, signifying an accepted list of books commonly regarded as inspired and authoritative. Before this, the Hebrew Bible was called "the scripture" (John 2:22; Acts 8:32; 2 Timothy 3:16, etc.), meaning essentially the same thing.

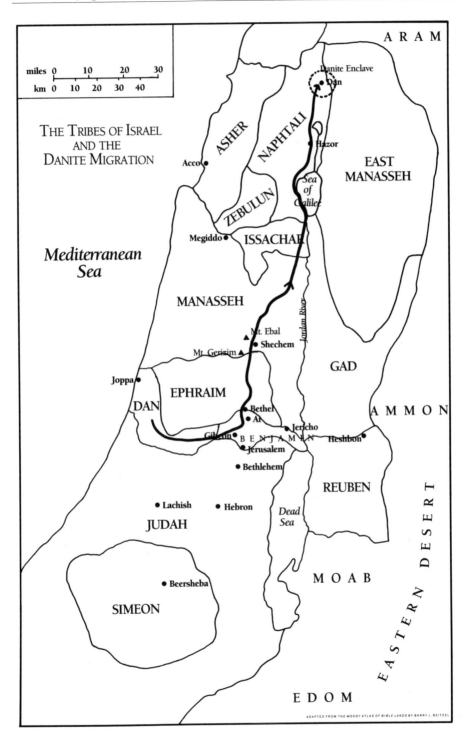

THE TRIBES OF ISRAEL
AND THE
DANITE MIGRATION

Mediterranean
Sea

ARAM

Danite Enclave

Dan

Hazor

ASHER

NAPHTALI

EAST
MANASSEH

Acco

ZEBULUN

Sea
of
Galilee

Megiddo

ISSACHAR

MANASSEH

Mt. Ebal

Shechem

Mt. Gerizim

Jordan River

GAD

AMMON

Joppa

EPHRAIM

DAN

Bethel

Ai

Gibeon

BENJAMIN

Jericho

Heshbon

Jerusalem

Bethlehem

REUBEN

Lachish

Hebron

Dead
Sea

JUDAH

Beersheba

MOAB

EASTERN DESERT

SIMEON

EDOM

ADAPTED FROM THE MOODY ATLAS OF BIBLE LANDS BY BARRY J. BEITZEL

knowledge of its topography . . . as they relate to military strategy."[11]
Yadin likewise would not mount a full-court press on every historical
detail of the accounts in Joshua and Judges, but he insists that the biblical
narrative "in broad outline" is supported by archaeological evidence from
the cities named in the conquest.[12]

Assuming, with Malamat, that the present biblical traditions in Joshua
reflect "a basic element of Israelite consciousness . . . that Canaan was
'inherited' by force,"[13] the question we must still ask is whether the
military strategy, which Malamat uses to support his view of a military
conquest, belongs to 1200 B.C., the time of the settlement in Canaan,
or to a later period, such as the early monarchy when the traditions
apparently began to take shape. As to Yadin's argument that the material
evidence is of cities destroyed by fire and replaced by seminomad
settlements, we must ask whether the archaeological record of the cities
named in the conquest narrative supports, even in broad outline, the
historicity of the narrative, as Yadin maintains.

During the Amarna period,* a century before the settlement of Israel
in Canaan, the land was organized politically into small city-states. This
seems to be the kind of organization reflected in Joshua 1-12 at the time
of the conquest. Jericho, the first city encountered in the conquest (Joshua
2:1ff.), seems to stand alone, not allied with any other city. It is located
on the western edge of the Jordan valley, a few miles south of the Wadi
Makkuk, a deep network of valleys that cuts an opening into the hill
country.[14] The second city, Ai (Joshua 7:2ff.), is on the plateau of the
hill country, about ten miles in distance and 3,500 feet in elevation from
Jericho. Located about two miles east of Bethel, Ai sits on the eastern
limit of cultivated land, at the edge of the wasteland that reaches down
to Jericho. In the biblical account, Ai seems to be allied with Bethel,
because men of Bethel are said in one tradition to have fought with men
of Ai in defense of the city (Joshua 8:17). Whatever the association was,
Bethel and Ai appear in later references together (cf. Nehemiah 7:32; Ezra
2:28), and Bethel is said in Nehemiah 11:31 to have had "its villages,"
which would make it the center of a small city-state.

Shechem, the third city where Joshua appears in the biblical accounts,
is the center of a larger city-state. During the Amarna period, the ruler
of Shechem extended his power as far north as Megiddo, controlling a
large territory of villages that must have reached as far south as Shiloh.
The villages allied with Shechem at the time of the conquest are not
named, but we find in the list of captive kings in Joshua 12:7-24 the
rulers of Tappuah, Hepher, Aphek and Tirzah, all located in the vicinity
of Shechem. A fourth city-state alliance is evident in the negotiations
between Joshua and the Hivites from Gibeon (Joshua 9:3-27). The Hivites

---

* The first half of the 14th century B.C., when Egyptian rule of Canaan under Pharaoh
Akhenaten collapsed. The Amarna period is named for the famous archive of cuneiform
diplomatic correspondence found at Tell el-Amarna in Egypt, describing political conditions
in Egypt and Canaan at the time.

are probably related to the Hittites or Hurrians, whose origins are found to the north of Canaan. They settled four cities named in Joshua 9:17—Gibeon, Chephirah, Beeroth and Kiriath-jearim—and maintained a separate identity from the Amorites who lived south of Gibeon. Gibeon is identified with modern El-Jib, located about five miles north of Jerusalem.

Jerusalem seems to have been the head of an Amorite alliance that included the major cities of the southern hill country. Five cities are named in Joshua 10:5: Jerusalem, Hebron, Jarmuth, Lachish and Eglon. Hebron is the southernmost city, 17 miles from Jerusalem. Lachish guards one of the classic routes from the southwest into the hill country. Jarmuth and Eglon are in the foothill region near Lachish. The Amorites are generally associated with the "Amurru" of extra-biblical texts, a West Semitic people whose origins may be traced to migrations from northeastern Syria.[15]

Hazor, the last major city of the Israelite conquest, was the head of an alliance that included Madon (possibly Merom), Shimron, Achshaph and unnamed villages around southern Galilee and in the hills of northern Galilee (Joshua 11:1ff.). Hazor itself is on the west side of the fertile Huleh valley and on the route that runs north-south on the west side of the Sea of Galilee. It seems to be the leading city of a Canaanite alliance whose origins may be traced to the Phoenician coastal region.

The Israelite conquest of the land of Canaan, therefore involved penetration and settlement: of the hill country, which in the south was occupied by an Amorite alliance of cities; in the region north and west of Jerusalem, where a Hivite alliance united four villages, with Bethel and Ai sitting alone on the east side of the Hivites; in the central hills, known later as Samaria, with Shechem and its allied towns and villages; and in Galilee, where Hazor headed up a league of Canaanite towns and villages. Jericho, not allied with any of the city-states, was alone in the Jordan valley.

The strategy for penetrating the hill country is significant. The Wadi Makkuk, leading up from Jericho to the north side of Ai, was chosen as the point of entry. However, the Wadi Makkuk is very narrow and deep, too rugged in the region near the site of Ai to allow cultivation of even small plots of land. It is lined with caves and small branch wadis, including the Wadi Asas, which defines the steep north side of the site of Ai. Actually, the Wadi Makkuk and the Wadi Asas are more suited to infiltration by small bands rather than by armies of thousands, which would be strung out in such a thin column that superior numbers would not give superiority in fighting ability. In fact, a large army would find the Wadi Farah, beginning some 15 miles north of Jericho and emerging in the hills at Tirzah, east of Shechem, much more suitable. The Wadi Farah is wide and is presently planted in lush banana and citrus groves.

The general lay of the land between Jericho and Ai/Bethel lends itself to the strategy of Joshua and the Israelites described in Joshua 7-8. Ai is "east of Bethel" (Joshua 7:2); also the site is 3,500 feet in elevation above Jericho, or "up" from Jericho (Joshua 7:2-4); and there is a mountain "behind" Ai, between it and Bethel (Joshua 8:2). But the numbers of people involved are too many for the terrain. Three thousand men (Joshua 7:3) in the Wadi Makkuk, and especially in the Wadi Asas, would be strung out half the distance from Jericho to Ai, and 30,000 men (Joshua 8:3) would have to find another route to the Bethel/Ai plateau. This, admittedly, is the kind of detail both Yadin and Malamat would not press, but it does jeopardize the claim of a military operation that involved all Israel and a strategy that placed an army of thousands in a valley too narrow and steep for such an army to operate.

Malamat noted that the Canaanite city-states and ethnic groups described above "had no unified, overall military organization with which to confront the [invading Israelites]. Their [the Canaanites'] absence of political cohesion was matched by the lack of any Canaanite national consciousness."[16] As a result, no effort was made to keep the Israelites from fording the Jordan.

| Israel's military stratagems | Both Yadin and Malamat characterize the Israelites as seminomads, "emerging from the desert fringes,"[17] a view that has support in the "official," or biblical accounts. Facing the strongly fortified cities of Canaan with their chariotry and trained forces, Israel's "unmounted horde" was at a definite disadvantage. However, this disparity was compensated by maximum use of reconnaissance, clever stratagems such as ambush and preemptive strikes, and the convenient recruitment of defectors, such as Rahab the Canaanite harlot of Jericho, who collaborated with Israel against her own people. Furthermore, considerable attention was given to "logistics," the organization of support services for fighting men in the field, and the timing of campaigns to enable the army to live off the land. For instance, before crossing the Jordan, Joshua passed on an order to the people to "prepare your provisions; for within three days you are to pass over this Jordan" (Joshua 1:10-11). The crossing itself occurred on "the tenth day of the first month" (Joshua 4:19), or in early spring, when crops had begun to ripen in the Jordan valley.[18] |

Joshua dispatched two men to spy out Jericho (Joshua 2:1), and they went forthwith and found lodging at the house of Rahab, which was the nearest thing to a hotel one could find in those times. Rahab's friendly reception enabled the spies to escape an effort by the king of Jericho to capture them, and they returned to the camp at Shittim. Jericho itself was placed under siege by the Israelites and its gate was shut (see Joshua 2:5) so that "none went out, and none came in" (Joshua 6:1). In the biblical account, the Israelites marched around the city seven days, and on the seventh day the priests blew their trumpets, the people shouted and the wall of Jericho "fell down flat" (Joshua 6:20). A hint of more military action than this ritualistic account indicates is found in Joshua's farewell address: "And you went over the Jordan and came to Jericho," he said, "and the men of Jericho fought against you" (Joshua 24:11).

The stratagem of marching around besieged cities until the enemy inside relaxed its defenses is known from military annals, as Malamat notes. In one case, Frontinus, a Roman military strategist of the first century A.D., cited a Roman general who "marched his troops regularly around the walls of a well-fortified city in northern Italy, each time returning them to camp; when the vigilance of the defenders waned, he stormed the walls and forced the city's capitulation."[19]

The conquest of Ai, located ten miles west of Jericho on the plateau of the hill country, also involved sound military strategy. Spies were sent from Jericho to assess the strength of the city of Ai (Joshua 7:2), and they returned with a report that the people "are but few" and a large force was not needed. Some local realism stands out in the spies' request: "Do not make the whole people toil up there," because the route to Ai is along the deep, rugged Wadi Makkuk that snakes relentlessly upward from the vicinity of Jericho, 700 feet below sea level, to the hilltop site of Ai, about 2,800 feet above sea level. Based on the spies' report, Joshua sent about 3,000 men from Jericho to Ai, and they were chased back down the valley toward Jericho with a loss of 36 men (Joshua 7:3-5).

Theology then takes over in the account of Ai by attributing the defeat to the sin of Achan, who disobeyed the ḥerem, or command that everything in Jericho was to be destroyed in a kind of sacrifice of the first fruits of the military campaign to the Lord of Israel. When Achan, his household, his possessions and the items he had salvaged from Jericho were destroyed to eradicate the sin, Joshua prepared another expedition to Ai. Nothing is said about the spies underestimating the strength of the defenders at Ai; the defeat of the first expedition is laid to the sin of Achan. However, Joshua sent 30,000 men the second time and instructed them in setting up an elaborate ambush that could close in on the men of Ai when they were drawn out of the city into the deep valley. The second expedition succeeded: the defenders of Ai were drawn into the valley in a feigned retreat by Joshua and his decoy force; 5,000 Israelites lying in ambush rose up and took the city; then they helped destroy the men of Ai trapped between the two Israelite forces (Joshua 8:10-23).

Both Jericho, whose wall "fell down flat" (Joshua 6:20), and Ai, which was burned (Joshua 8:19-21), should have identifiable traces of destruction dating to the time of the conquest. The kidney-shaped mound of ancient Jericho still has about 70 feet of occupation layers intact, dating from the earliest settlement, about 9000 B.C., beside the spring known today as Ain es-Sultan. During the 1930s, John Garstang discovered collapsed mudbrick walls under the ruins of houses that he identified as evidence of the destruction by the Israelites. The walls had fallen outward, down the slope of the mound, and ashes from burned houses lay on top of the mound accumulated in depths up to three feet.[20]

Garstang's conclusions were challenged, however, by Kathleen Kenyon, who excavated the site extensively from 1952 to 1958.[21] Using improved techniques for controlling the removal of layers of ancient remains, she

The archaeology of Jericho

reconstructed the actual phases of occupation from the first crude shrine, built on bedrock, to the last fragmentary corner of a small 14th-century B.C. hut on top of the mound. The prehistoric phases (from 9000 to 3200 B.C.) were dated by radiocarbon (Carbon 14)* analyses of wood, grain and other organic remains, while the phases after 3200 B.C. were placed in their chronological context by comparative studies of finds, in addition to radiocarbon dating.[22]

Kenyon concluded that Garstang's collapsed mudbrick wall, which he dated to about 1400 B.C., actually dated to about 2300 B.C., a thousand years before the Israelite settlement in Canaan. In fact, Kenyon found evidence of many collapses of mudbrick walls at Jericho belonging to the period between 3200 and 2300 B.C., which she attributed mostly to frequent earthquakes in the area. Jericho sits on top of the fault line along the west side of the Jordan valley. Formed in geological ages past by parallel faults on each side of the valley, this fault line allowed the entire valley to settle down almost 3,000 feet below the level of the plateaus on either side.

Kenyon also found a city wall from the Middle Bronze Age (about 1560 B.C.) built on top of the Early Bronze Age walls dating to the third millennium. The city that was enclosed by this Middle Bronze wall had been burned. A substantial portion of the fortifications and the city burned about 1560 B.C. had eroded away—the part of the city on the top of the mound—so it is impossible to reconstruct the city's history after 1560 B.C.

Does this mean that a walled city existed on top of the present ruin in Joshua's time, and that it has eroded away in the past 3,000 years? In my judgment, that's not likely. If a city had existed between 1400 and 1200 B.C., then surely some pottery sherds or other artifacts would be found on the slopes of the mound, washed and blown by the wind off the summit. The only evidence of any occupation in this period is the remnant of one corner of a small mudbrick house on the mound's east side, on top of the ruins of the city destroyed about 1560 B.C. One juglet on the packed earth floor of the three-foot square remnant can be assigned a date of about 1325 B.C.[23] The location of the hut suggests that squatters lived on top of the ruins of the ancient city.

There is no archaeological evidence of a walled city of Jericho dating to the period from about 1400 to 1200 B.C., when most scholars would date the entry into Canaan. Yadin's question in the light of this conclusion is pertinent: "How could the walls of Jericho come tumbling down during the Late Bronze Age (ca. 1560-1200 B.C.) if there was no Late Bronze Age wall around the town?"[24] He has an explanation. "In many cases," he observes, "the Late Bronze Age people did not actually

---

* Living organisms absorb a fixed ratio of Carbon 14 (radioactive carbon), which disintegrates at a known rate after the organism dies. By measuring the rate of disintegration, the length of time since the organism died can be calculated. Carbon 14 dating is useful for dating organic material from about 10,000 B. C. to the end of the Old Testament period, within a possible error margin of plus or minus 100 years.

build new fortifications but, rather, reused Middle Bronze (ca. 1800-1560 B.C.) fortifications, strengthening them where necessary."[25] Thus Yadin allows the possibility that the Late Bronze Age settlement at Jericho reused the earlier fortifications, and the account in Joshua 6 is about these walls. This, in my opinion, is highly unlikely. The houses destroyed about 1560 B.C. were not reoccupied, and no artifacts from the period after this destruction were found, except the three-foot-square remnant of a squatter's hut. And since the squatter's hut was located on an eroded slope unfortified even by the 1560 B.C. city walls, Yadin's view that the Late Bronze Age inhabitants reused the earlier fortifications lacks support. Thus, we are confronted with negative archaeological evidence of a walled city at Jericho, despite the highly descriptive account of a conquest of the city in the biblical tradition.

At Ai (et-Tell) John Garstang excavated eight trenches in 1928. In 1931 he wrote that "a considerable proportion of L.B.A. I [Late Bronze Age I, ending about 1400 B.C.]" wares were found, including "a Cypriote wishbone handle," and that they were left "in the collection of the American School (now the Albright Institute)."[26] This pottery has never been found. Nothing in the one box of material from this excavation now in possession of the Department of Antiquities comes from the Late Bronze Age. Thus none of Garstang's "Late Bronze" evidence is available for a "second opinion" of his interpretation.

Problems with Ai

Judith Marquet-Krause led three seasons of excavation at Ai in 1933-1935, and was preparing for a fourth season when she died in the summer of 1936 at the age of 29. Although she apprenticed to Garstang at Jericho for her first field experience in 1932, she later came under the influence of William F. Albright and Père Louis-Hugues Vincent and concluded that the city at Ai was destroyed and abandoned at the end of the Early Bronze Age, about 2400 B.C. It was not resettled until about 1200 B.C., when an unfortified village of about three acres was built on the acropolis area of the earlier city. Accordingly, Marquet-Krause concluded that the site lay unoccupied from about 2400 B.C. until about 1200 B.C.[27]

The most recent excavations at Ai, nine seasons from 1964 to 1976 led by the writer, confirmed the results of the earlier excavations.[28] There was no walled city at Ai after about 2400 B.C., and the only evidence of occupation afterward was the small unfortified village built over the earlier ruins on the acropolis. This village was constructed about 1200 B.C. and was abandoned about 1050 B.C.—prior to the emergence of the Israelite monarchy under David about 1000 B.C.

The excavations at Jericho and Ai pose problems for reconstructing a military conquest of Canaan. The site of Jericho was occupied only briefly in the 14th century B.C., or about 1325 B.C.; the site of Ai was unoccupied. When Ai was reoccupied as a village about 1200 B.C., there was nothing at Jericho. If we accept the most popular date for the conquest, about 1250 B.C., which is held by both American and Israeli scholars based on destruction levels at other major sites, there was nothing at either Jericho or Ai at the time. And at no time during this period between 1400 B.C. and 1200 B.C. was there any settlement at both sites.

What did Yadin have to say about the negative evidence at Ai? "My own view," he said, "is that here (at Ai) the archaeological evidence contradicts the Biblical narrative and we must interpret the Biblical account as etiological."[29] An "etiological" interpretation would explain how the imposing ruin of ancient Ai came to be. The later biblical writers of Joshua 8:28 believed that "Joshua burned Ai, and made it forever a heap of ruins, as it is to this day." However, the archaeological evidence is that the city was burned and made into a ruin about 2400 B.C.

Malamat also has difficulties with the biblical narrative of the capture of Ai. He notes that the strategem used in the capture of Ai, as described in Joshua 8:1-23, is almost identical to that described in the internecine battle for Gibeah in Judges 20:18-44. In the latter, the people of Israel went up against the Benjaminites at Gibeah twice and were driven back with heavy casualties (Judges 8:18-28). On the third attempt, an ambush was set "round about Gibeah" (Judges 8:29), and the Benjaminites were drawn out of the city and trapped between the main force of the people of Israel and the ambush, which rose up and cut them off from the city. Malamat notes that this similarity of strategems "has led many commentators to believe that one of the two accounts served as the literary model for the other."[30] Malamat yields to the archaeological record at Ai and concludes that "if indeed there was interdependence the capture of Ai (et-Tell) is more likely the copy, for the archaeological evidence there is quite negative, indicating no destruction level during the period of the Israelite conquest and settlement."[31]

The case of Gibeon   Now let us turn to Gibeon and the Israelites' battle with the Amorite alliance. Malamat discusses at length the strategem of surprise used in this battle (Joshua 10:1-14). "So Joshua came upon them [the Amorites] suddenly, having marched all night from Gilgal [to Gibeon]. And the Lord threw them into a panic before Israel, who slew them with a great slaughter at Gibeon and chased them by the way of the ascent of Beth Horon" (Joshua 10:9-10). "Taking advantage of the hours of darkness," Malamat writes, "the Israelites made a lightning march from Gilgal to Gibeon (el-Jib)—a distance of about 20 miles, involving a climb of over 3,000 feet. The attack upon the astonished enemy apparently took place at dawn."[32] This seems to be borne out in the quotation from the Book of Jashar, now lost, about the sun standing still (Joshua 10:12-13). Actually, Joshua commanded the sun to "be silent," or not shine, so that the darkness of the early morning would be extended while Israel followed up the surprise attack in hot pursuit of the fleeing enemy.

Excavations at Gibeon by James B. Pritchard in the 1960s have posed the same problems that we have noted at Jericho and Ai. No evidence of a city dating to the 13th century B.C. has been found, although material from that period was found in some reused tombs.[33] The evidence from Gibeon is thus also negative for the 13th-century B.C. city that seems to be required by Joshua 9-10. An extensive surface survey of Khirbet Kefire, probably biblical Chephirah of Joshua 9:17 (one of the Hivite cities allied with Gibeon), indicates no 13th century B.C. city there.[34] Some pottery from the period after 1200 B.C., however, was found. Only excavation of the site will reveal what kind of village or city belonged to this period after 1200 B.C.

Malamat observes that "utilization of the veil of darkness in achieving surprise was ingrained in Israelite tactical planning, from the days of the Conquest to the beginning of the Monarchy."[35] The strategy of surprise attack at Gibeon is plausible and practical, as narrated in the biblical account. The problem is that we do not have a city for the Gibeonites during the time that both Malamat and Yadin would place the events. This, like the evidence from Jericho and Ai, fails to support their view of a military conquest of Canaan.

Following the defeat of the Amorite alliance and the execution of their kings at Makkedah (Joshua 10:16-27), Joshua led a mop-up operation against the cities of the executed kings: Makkedah, Libnah, Lachish, Eglon, Hebron and Debir. The territory of the tribe of Judah was comprised largely of these principal cities, along with Gezer (Joshua 10:33), and the territory to the south. Alberto Soggin has observed that the itinerary followed by the Israelites is a traditional one; it was followed later by Sennacherib in 701 B.C. (2 Kings 18:13) and by Nebuchadnezzar in 587 B.C. (Jeremiah 34:7).[36] Thus the conquest tradition here too may be a retrojection from a later time.

Other "conquered" cities

Lachish has been excavated extensively, and a massive destruction dated to about 1230 B.C. was found there, which has been attributed to the Israelite conquest.[37] Nearby Tell Beit Mirsim, identified as Debir by Albright, was destroyed about the same time, and its destruction has also been attributed to the Israelites.[38] Debir, however, is more likely to be identified with Khirbet Rabud, which was also destroyed in the Late Bronze Age.[39]

The pattern of destruction in these cities of the Shephelah persuaded Yadin that they must be associated with Joshua and the Israelites. However, as some have observed, the conquerors did not leave calling cards. Other predators known to have been in the region may be responsible. Ramesses II campaigned through the vicinity of Lachish on his way to Syria, as did his son, Merneptah, who claimed to have conquered Ashkelon, Gezer and Yano'am.[40] Also, the Sea Peoples, among whom the Peleset, or Philistines, are named, were active along the coastal region at about this time.[41]

As a result of recent archaeological investigations, Arad, Heshbon, Hormah (that is, the sites that are candidates for Hormah) and apparently Jarmuth, all named in the Israelite conquest accounts, "have taken their place alongside Jericho, Ai, and Gibeon as cities which the Bible

BRITISH MUSEUM

Philistine warrior. The characteristic battle headdress includes a headband and upright strips that may be feathers, reeds, leather strips, horsehair or some bizarre hairdo.

associates with the period of the conquest but which offer little or no evidence of having been occupied during the thirteenth century."[42]

In the campaign related in Joshua 11:1-15, the Israelites fought against Jabin, king of Hazor in Galilee, and an alliance of Canaanite kings. Jabin is also the king of Hazor named in a much later war against the same alliance, recounted in Judges 4:1-5:31. Details of the earlier war, in Joshua 11:1-15 are meager and are obscured by the way it is narrated.

For instance, the cause of Joshua's war against the Hazor alliance is not clear. Jabin, king of Hazor, seems to have been threatened by the successes of Joshua in the south, so he pulls together an army of chariots from the member cities of the alliance. Represented are the northern lowland cities of Hazor, Madon, Shimron and Achshaph (Joshua 11:1). But then the situation is immediately made unreal by introducing contingents from all the foes Israel fought in Canaan, from Jebusites in the south to Hivites at the foot of Mt. Hermon. The great host of troops, "in number like the sand . . . upon the seashore" (Joshua 11:4), gives the account an unreal appearance, apparently to extol the greatness of the Lord in giving the victory to Joshua and the Israelites.

Details of the battle "by the waters of Merom" (Joshua 11:7), where the battle was joined, are not clear. There is a memory of the tactic of hamstringing the enemy's chariot horses, that is, hacking the tendons of the hind legs (Joshua 11:6), and of burning the chariots with fire. This kind of strategy requires first that the Israelite foot soldiers outrun the chariot horses and, second, that they immobilize the dangerous archers in the chariots. We are not told how this was accomplished, but presumably the sudden surprise attack (Joshua 11:7) panicked the charioteers, and the horses were disabled in the resulting confusion.

This victory is followed up by the extermination of the entire population from Sidon (in the extreme northwest) to Mizpeh (in the extreme northeast) (Joshua 11:8). Israel put to the sword all that breathed, until the cities were "utterly destroyed." Hazor was burned with fire (Joshua 11:11).

Some scholars believe there was but one military episode described in the Bible three times: first in connection with Joshua and the king of Hazor (Joshua 11:1-15), and then twice in Judges (a prose account in Judges 4:1-23 and a poetic account in Judges 5:1-31) in connection with Deborah and Barak against the same king of Hazor (at least as he is identified in Judges 4). Each account supplies details that seem to belong to the same war, and the war constructed from the details of the three traditions is in character with the other wars of the Israelites. If the three traditions are concerned with the same war of liberation, it is possible that successors to Joshua actually did the fighting.

Hazor

According to Yadin, who extensively excavated Hazor, a 200-acre major Late Bronze Age city there was destroyed no later than 1230 B.C. (Moshe Kochavi of Tel Aviv University would date this destruction as early as 1275 B.C.).[43] After an indefinite period, a small settlement of about 25 acres was established on the upper citadel area.[44] Yadin attributes the destruction and burning of the 200-acre city to Joshua, as described in Joshua 11:11-13. Yadin acknowledged the problem with the three traditions. His solution was that the prose description of the battle of Deborah (Judges 4) and her general Barak against "Jabin king of Hazor" is "a late editorial gloss . . . added to a basically authentic historic text." "If Hazor had already been destroyed in Joshua 11," he asks, "how could Deborah and Barak be fighting against its king in Judges 4?" "My own solution," he concludes, "is that the reference to 'Jabin king of Hazor' in Judges 4 is an editorial gloss by a later editor." He acknowledges, however that "we should not be dogmatic [about the details of the biblical account] . . . . We can pick and choose based upon the evidence in each case," he notes, but "it is not necessary either to accept each detail of the Biblical account, on the one hand, or to reject the basic historicity of the Conquest, on the other." His conclusion on this basis is that "archaeology broadly confirms that at the end of the Late Bronze Age (13th century B.C.), seminomadic Israelites destroyed a number of major Canaanite cities; then, gradually and slowly, they built their own sedentary settlements on the ruins, and occupied the remainder of the country."[45]

Was there a
military
conquest?

So we come back to the basic questions: Does the military strategy in the accounts of the conquest belong in the context of the settlement, as Malamat advocates, or does it belong to a later time? Next, does the archaeological record of the cities of the conquest narratives support the historicity of the accounts, even in broad outline, as Yadin maintains? Finally, was there a military conquest of Canaan by seminomadic Israelite invaders near the end of the 13th century B.C.?

If we take seriously Malamat's acknowledgement that the present biblical traditions of the Israelite conquest took shape long after the settlement, then it is quite likely that the "Israelite consciousness" of taking the land by force may also have developed long after the entry into Canaan. The biblical evidence itself suggests that the authenticating strategies on which Malamat relies came from a later period.

Much of the same evidence that weakens Malamat's arguments for a military conquest from the perspective of strategy also works against Yadin's claims based upon archaeological findings. Jericho and Ai are clearly embarrassments to his view, because he has to attribute the extensive narrative about the capture of Ai to later etiology and not to history. He dismisses Jericho with the generalized observation that "in many cases the Late Bronze Age people [his time for the conquest] did not actually build new fortifications but, rather, reused Middle Bronze fortifications . . . . It may well be that the Late Bronze Age settlement at Jericho reused the city wall from the Middle Bronze Age."[46] True, some Middle Bronze fortifications were reused, but there is no material evidence of it at Jericho, as there is at other sites where these fortifications were reused.

Even the attribution of an Israelite destruction of Hazor is not as unambiguous as Yadin maintains. First, the biblical accounts in Joshua 11 and Judges 4-5 are interrelated, and a certain amount of "picking and choosing" by the interpreter is necessary, as Yadin acknowledged. He chooses the account in Joshua 11 and attributes the mention of "Jabin king of Canaan, who reigned in Hazor" in Judges 4:2 to "a late editorial gloss."[47] Second, the 200-acre walled city of Hazor that was destroyed as early as 1275 B.C. and not later than about 1230 B.C. was probably the largest and most formidable city in Canaan at the time, far larger and stronger than other walled cities named in Judges 1:27-33 that were *not* taken by the Israelites. How "seminomadic" foot soldiers with their primitive arms could take a walled city like Hazor is attributed, somewhat unconvincingly, to the decadence of the city.[48]

Was there a "conquest" of Canaan, then, by invading Israelites who took the hill country and Galilee in a series of lightning military campaigns, as related in Joshua 1-12? As we have seen, the evidence is not convincing. Both the biblical accounts and the archaeological evidence leave enough contradictions and negative evidence that an advocate of a military conquest has to accept it with a blind leap of "faith," or make Yadin's confirmation "in broad outline" very broad indeed. I agree with Yadin that "it would be a mistake to argue either that the entire conquest account in Joshua and Judges is historically accurate in every detail or that it is historically worthless."[49] The question is at what point in the spectrum between "accurate in every detail" and "historically worthless" do we position ourselves. Before we answer this question, it may be well to look at the alternatives to a military conquest of Canaan that have been advocated over the last 60 years.

The biblical narratives of the conquest were given their present form long after the settlement actually took place. In their present form, we have what has been characterized as "history that preaches" to needs at the time of the Israelite monarchy. To achieve this purpose, the editors, or redactors, selected passages from the ancient sources available to them and told the story of Israel's beginnings from a theological perspective. The role of the Lord was emphasized, the need for absolute faith and obedience was preeminent and the rules for conducting "Holy War" (Deuteronomy 20:1-20) were imposed upon history. This reworking of the traditions created a barrier between the student of the Scriptures and the actual historical events of the settlement, because history has been obscured by layers of later traditions.

In a case of this kind, how do we get around the barrier of reinterpretations and get at the historical events themselves? Obviously, archaeology provides one way. We dig into the actual sites named in the biblical accounts and see what is there. But archaeology does more than this. More than a century of research in the countries of the Near East has helped restore the world of the Bible, its languages, history, literature, politics, personalities, inscriptions, letters, etc. At the time of the settlement in Canaan, Egypt was in the twilight of its greatness, the great Hittite kingdoms in Asia Minor were disintegrating, and newcomers to Canaan were on the move from all directions.

New perspectives on the Israelite settlement in Canaan

New perspectives for the study of the settlement of Canaan have emerged from the flood of new information that archaeological research has provided, all from vantage points outside the biblical traditions. Essentially, three views in addition to a military conquest have been put forward. First is the view that seminomadic Israelites peacefully infiltrated unoccupied areas of the hill country and gradually built settlements and became sedentary. Only later did they displace the Canaanites in the cities. Second, a peasant's revolt by villagers in the highlands against their Canaanite overlords has been proposed, analogous to the Habiru revolts in the same region a century earlier, as reflected in the Amarna letters. Third is the view that biblical Israel emerged out of the amalgam of a sparse local population augmented by newcomers from all directions, who settled some areas that were uncontested and joined together with local inhabitants in fighting for other territory. This latter view is more compatible with the accounts in Judges than with those in Joshua.

Peaceful infiltration

Let us consider each of these positions. In 1925, Albrecht Alt published (in German) "The Settlement of the Israelites in Palestine" which set forth his view of a seminomadic infiltration by Israelites of the central highlands.[50] Working primarily with Egyptian inscriptions that were contemporary or near-contemporary with the time of the settlement, Alt concluded that the central highlands were only sparsely settled at the time. At the end of the Amarna period, about 1350 B.C., Shechem was the only significant city-state in the hill country of Canaan between Jerusalem and the Jezreel Valley.[51] A century later, when the power of the 19th Dynasty pharaohs collapsed, the hill country still seemed to be relatively free of occupation.[52] This is the region where biblical traditions place the initial settlements of the Israelites.

Alt's view of the manner in which the Israelites acquired this thinly populated region is trenchant. Since little resistance would be encountered in the wide gaps in the city-state system, he concluded that settlement resulted from seminomadic Israelites following their flocks from east of the Jordan river into the hills west of the river. Eventually they began to build villages and become sedentary. Thus, the settlement occurred relatively peacefully, rather than by military conquest as indicated in Joshua 1-12. Alt's pupil, Martin Noth, found support for this view in the negative archaeological evidence at Jericho and Ai. More recently, Manfred Weippert, Noth's pupil, summarized Alt's view as follows:[53]

> "The tribal confederacy did not exist at the time when those who later became the Israelites entered Palestine . . . . One must suppose, rather, that it was a question of individual clans or confederacies of clans of nomads with small cattle (sheep and goats) who, during the winter rainy season and the spring, lived with their herds in the border territory between the desert and the cultivated land and who were forced, when the vegetation in that area ceased in the summer, to penetrate further into the cultivated land and to come to an understanding with the owners of the land about summer pasturage in the harvested fields and in the woods."

Weippert continues:[54]

> "The clans who entered the country in this way in the course of regular change of pasture then gradually settled in the relatively thinly populated wooded areas of the uplands, areas which were not directly exposed to the reach either of the Canaanite city-states or of Egyptian sovereignty, and began to practice agriculture once they had turned these wooded areas into arable land. This peaceful process of transition on the part of nomads to a sedentary life was, according to Alt, the real process of settlement and it was, in the nature of things,

a peaceful development, since the interest of any landowner in the area would not be harmed."

Military encounters, Alt believed, occurred in a second stage of Israelite settlement, which he characterized as "territorial expansion." This was late in the period of the Judges and the early monarchy, when Israel took the plains and valleys that had long been occupied by groups of Canaanites. It was a long process in which the Israelites won some fortified cities, and also lost some battles. Presumably, the memory of these wars would account for what Malamat characterizes as "a basic element of Israelite consciousness . . . that Canaan was 'inherited' by force."[55] The military confrontations came at the end of the 11th century B.C., when the tribes were beginning to coalesce into a monarchy, instead of at their first entry into Canaan at the end of the 13th century B.C.[56]

Alt's view, which finds more accommodation to the Book of Judges than to Joshua, has sparked controversy for more than half a century, first with Albright and his pupils, and more recently with Israeli scholars such as Yadin and Malamat. Some parts of his arguments, however, are still very persuasive. We have noted that the accounts of lightning military conquests in Joshua 1-12 find little support in archaeological research. The other side of this conclusion is that Alt does have support for his infiltration theory.

Moshe Kochavi recently reported that at this time "a wave" of newcomers moved into the "more or less empty hills of Ephraim" and planted almost a hundred settlements.[57] In the region between Hebron and Shechem, Lawrence Stager found some 90 new village settlements of people who apparently moved into the open areas of the hills from the west and northwest.[58] The major weakness in Alt's position is his characterization of the Israelites as nomads who, like modern Bedouin, followed their flocks seasonally into the highlands after harvest and exploited any weakness they found in control of the territory. Lacking specific evidence of this, he worked from analogy based on the sedentarization of Bedouin in this century and conjectured that the same process occurred in the Israelite settlement.

Increasing evidence, however, indicates that most of the newcomers to the highlands at the end of the 13th century B.C. were primarily farmers and secondarily herdsmen, as will be noted in detail below, and not what we would characterize as nomads. However, there were movements into the highlands to occupy sites peacefully, as Alt maintained, and this conclusion has kept Alt's position at the forefront of discussions of the Israelite settlement.

Another recent suggestion that has commanded serious attention is that Israel emerged not as a result of outsiders coming into the country but as the result of a peasants' revolt against Canaanite overlords. Advocated by George E. Mendenhall and, with minor modifications, more recently by Norman K. Gottwald,[59] this view rejects the characterization of the Israelites as nomads or seminomads who infiltrated the highlands in

Peasants' revolt

search of pasturage.[60]

According to this view, Israel emerged from the melting pot of Canaanite culture in a revolutionary social movement among the peoples already in Canaan. For Mendenhall, it was a peasant's revolt against Canaanite overlords in the cities, an internal uprising pitting the villages against the cities, "ignited by Hebrews who advocated commitment to, and covenant solidarity with, Yahweh, the liberating God of the Exodus."[61] This revolution began in Transjordan "where Yahweh-worshipping fugitives from Egypt joined with discontented elements of the population to overthrow the Amorite kingdoms of Sihon and Og, . . . and spread across the Jordan to the west bank, where the rural population, restive under the Canaanite city-state system, 'rejected the old political ideologies in favor of the covenant community of Yahweh.' "[62]

The model for this view is taken from the Habiru revolts in the same region a century earlier during the Amarna age. The Habiru were rebels against the city-states of Canaan then ruled by vassal princes appointed by Egypt. The Habiru sought to overthrow Egyptian rule in what was essentially a political struggle between oppresed villagers and Canaanite rulers; as reflected in the famous Amarna letters which document this struggle, there is no mention of a religious dimension to the struggle.

Gottwald, like Mendenhall, sees early Israel as an alliance of suppressed and disenfranchised elements of Canaanite society, "including peasants, farmers, pastoralists, outlaws, mercenaries, and adventurers . . . ."[63] Gottwald's model, however, is the historical cultural materialism of Karl Marx, which gives priority to materialism over religion.[64] Mendenhall believes that the social revolution sparked by the Hebrews was to some extent "created by the new Yahwistic religion"; Gottwald, on the other hand, believes that Yahwism was created to support the social ideals of early Israel, and "arose as a function of the revolution."[65] For this reason, Mendenhall vehemently denies that he is the "father" of Gottwald's theory.[66] In both views, however, the so-called conquest of Canaan is seen as a revolution effected inside the land by population elements already there. There was no unified military campaign conducted by forces from the outside, and there was no mass killing of the inhabitants of the land.

The social revolution hypotheses are attractive because they have, in some measure, parallels with movements in this century. However, both hypotheses lack supporting evidence from inscriptions contemporary with the events that would have occurred about 1200 B.C. In addition, the systematic surveys of biblical Ephraim and Manasseh cited by Kochavi show a significant occupational decline during the 14th-13th centuries B.C. in the inland regions, leaving the "region between Shechem and Bethel void of any major Canaanite town at the time."[67] There is also a radical decrease in population and occupied sites in the region between Shechem and Jezreel, leaving the hills "more or less empty," in Kochavi's words.[68] Thus, the views of Mendenhall and Gottwald lack a demonstrable population to carry out the events that are postulated. Their arguments from historical analogy and modern social movements do not find support in the material evidence from the time.

There seems little doubt that a considerable influx of newcomers to the hill country of Canaan occurred at the end of the 13th century B.C. In a recent survey of ancient agricultural terraces and village sites from Hebron to Shechem, Lawrence Stager of Harvard University found that the density of permanent settlements increased dramatically in the transition from Late Bronze to Iron Age I.[69] By about 1200 B.C., the number of villages in an area of some 2,600 square miles had increased from 23 in the Late Bronze Age to 114 in Iron Age I, and the estimated population increased from about 14,000 to more than 38,000.[70] This increase occurred too rapidly to be ascribed to natural growth, Stager notes. Clearly, a significant population of newcomers moved into the highlands.

New archaeological evidence

These villagers, however, were not nomads or seminomads, as Alt had conjectured. They were primarily farmers and secondarily herders of sheep and goats who brought with them fixed cultural patterns of village life. The convincing archaeological evidence indicates that two new subsistence technologies enabled the settlers to establish villages in marginal and even inhospitable areas of the semiarid hill country where villages had not been located before. First, the houses on hilltop sites in the Bethel-Ai region had their own bell-shaped cisterns hewn out of solid rock with metal chisels to provide for household water supplies. Tell en-Nasbeh, southwest of Bethel, has been characterized as "truly a place of cisterns," because a total of 53 were excavated.[71] And second, agricultural terraces were constructed on the contours of steep hillsides never before planted in crops for the cultivation of wheat, barley and vegetables. For instance, the Iron Age I village houses at Ai (et-Tell) were founded on terraces that provided a relatively level foundation on the steep east slope of the acropolis area, and one terrace system extending more than 325 feet was discovered in the cultivated area just below the village.[72]

Moshe Kochavi of Tel Aviv University recently reported on archaeological surveys principally in biblical Ephraim and Manasseh, including the northern part of the area surveyed by Stager and the hill country north of Shechem to the Esdraelon plain, as they relate to the settlement of this region. "The major change that occurred between the Late Bronze and Iron Age was not the sudden destruction of Canaanite urban civilization," he said. Toward the end of the Late Bronze Age, he noted, small unfortified settlements are almost unknown. "However, with the beginning of the Iron Age, they suddenly appear by the hundreds."[73]

Kochavi goes on to say that "the more or less empty hills of Ephraim were washed over by a wave of settlers moving from northeast to southwest, a wave that left in its wake almost a hundred settlements in this region alone."[73] The movement from east to west "is attested by the

appearance of later ceramic forms and more developed sites" as one
follows the direction of movement. Although Kochavi's graphic
statements seem to reflect fast-moving events in the establishment of new
villages, he actually sees a process stretching over a considerable period
of time, during much of the period of the Judges. This, for him, was
the first phase of the Israelite settlement.

The second phase was one of expansion "into the surrounding
lowlands," which "began later and gained momentum only with the
Monarchy."[75] "It is in this period," he concludes, "that we have to look
for the *Sitz-im-Leben* (life situation) of the biblical concept of the
Conquest and Settlement."[76]

In addition to the evidence that newcomers moved into the hill country
from the west, north and northeast, recent excavations at Tel Masos and
Beersheba in the northern Negev indicate movements also from the south.
There seem to be memories of this in Numbers 13:17-33, which reports
the sending of spies into the land of Canaan from the south, and in
Numbers 14:39-45, which tells of an abortive effort to take the hill country
from the south.

The late Yohanan Aharoni believed that settlements were established
in the Beersheba region at the end of the 13th century B.C., and that
they spread northward into the land of Canaan and southward across
the southern Negev over the next 200 years, or until the beginning of
the monarchy under Saul and David. This penetration and settlement
of the region from the south "occurred mainly in unoccupied or sparsely
settled areas," Aharoni noted, "a picture that corresponds to the
description in the Book of Judges, contrasting to the picture of unified
conquest reflected in the Book of Joshua."[77]

Archaeological evidence thus indicates a far more complex process of
settlement in the land of Canaan at the end of the Late Bronze Age than
one would assume from the biblical accounts. This was a time of political
upheaval in the eastern Mediterranean area caused by the demise of
Egyptian authority, the fragmentation of the Hittite empire in north Syria
and Asia Minor into small warring city-states, and the Dorian invasion
of the Greek mainland causing uprooted Sea Peoples from the Aegean
area to migrate eastward to the Syrian coast, southeastward to the
Palestinian coastal area, and across the sea to North Africa and Egypt.
The Sea Peoples in turn pushed the less militant "Canaanites" inland
toward the mountains of Lebanon and the central hill country of Canaan,
where they found "a refuge and redoubt" in inaccessible hilltop villages
such as Khirbet Raddana and Ai (et-Tell) north of Jerusalem. Hittites and
Hivites also settled in the region of Gibeon, possibly in Jerusalem (the
Jebusites) and north to the slopes of Mt. Hermon. People of Aramean
background moved southward into northern Transjordan and into the
hills of Canaan. And on we could go. When one adds to this mix
whatever number of Hebrew refugees from slavery in Egypt were involved
in the Exodus, we have a "melting pot composed of diverse elements
living under various 'ad hoc' political and religious circumstances"[78] out

of which biblical Israel emerged.

Exactly how and when Israel emerged as a people with a national consciousness is a matter of intense debate among scholars, and the outcome of this debate is by no means clear. Perhaps a truly national consciousness did not emerge until the reign of King Solomon. The disintegration of the kingdom after Solomon suggests that it may not have occurred even then. Baruch Halpern sees the first evidence of solidarity among the tribes that became Israel in the time of Deborah, toward the end of the 12th century B.C. "From the time of Deborah," he says, "ten Israelite tribes constitute some sort of Israel: within a century or so, the twelve-tribe empire of the United Monarchy will enter full bloom."[79] But before the time of Deborah, any reconstruction is largely speculative.

An intriguing Egyptian monument dating to about 1207 B.C. mentions Israel, spelling it in hieroglyphic signs. Known as the Merneptah Stele, after the pharaoh whose reign it commemorates, it provides us with the earliest extant reference to Israel. For that reason, it is also known as the Israel Stele. Merneptah's victory ode provides in part:[80] **The Merneptah Stele**

"The princes are prostrate, saying 'Peace!'
Not one is raising his head among the Nine Bows.
Now that Tehenu [Libya] has come to ruin, Hatti is pacified;
The Canaan has been plundered into every sort of woe:
Ashkelon
has been overcome;
Gezer has been captured;
Yano'am is made non-existent.
Israel is laid waste and his seed is not;
Hurru is become a widow because of Egypt."

Unpronounced hieroglyphic signs called determinatives are sometimes attached to words to indicate the category of the word to which it is attached. Thus, the determinative for a "city-state" is attached to the words for Ashkelon, Gezer and Yano'am. The determinative for a "foreign land" is attached to Canaan. By contrast, the determinative for a "foreign people" is attached to the hieroglyphic signs for Israel.

Tons of ink have been spilled interpreting the Merneptah Stele. Was Israel already established in Canaan in about 1207 B.C. so that Merneptah could—albeit with obvious exaggeration—claim that he had "laid [him] waste and his seed [was] not"? Many have argued this. If it is true, the Exodus and conquest must have occurred earlier.

Another, more recent view that has been garnering support is that the "Israel" referred to in the Merneptah Stele is not the Israel that was involved in the Exodus, but instead is the Israel whose roots were in Canaan long before the time of the Merneptah Stele. In a recent article, Lawrence Stager focused on the last two lines of the victory ode, the meaning of which, he claimed, can be understood in terms of its parallel poetic construction. Consider this stanza:[81]

"Israel is laid waste and his seed is not;

Merneptah Stele (above). Commissioned by Pharaoh Merneptah about 1207 B.C., this monument contains the earliest reference to Israel. A victory stele that commemorates a military campaign into Canaan, it states in the second line from the bottom (closeup, below) that "Israel is laid waste and his seed is not." This suggests that Israel was already in the land at this time, although the description of its demise is obviously an exaggeration.

Hurru is become a widow because of Egypt."

"Hurru and Israel form a distinct complementary pair in the ode," says Stager, "viz. husband (Israel) and wife/widow (Hurru)."[82] Since the term Hurru usually referred to the region of Syria-Palestine, or to a lesser area of the region, the parallel construction with Israel indicates an entity larger than the city-states of Ashkelon, Gezer and Yano'am, also named on the stele. Hurru is spelled with the determinative for "land." Israel, however, is spelled with the determinative for a " people" rather than a "land" or a "state." It apparently had a population capable of fielding a sizable fighting force against pharaoh's chariots. A depiction of the pharaoh's enemies in a battle scene at Karnak has been identified by Stager's colleague Frank Yurco at the University of Chicago's Oriental Institute as the people called "Israel" on the Merneptah stele.[83] Their dress is decidedly Canaanite in style and not that of nomads, such as the "Shasu" depicted elsewhere in the battle scene. Stager suggests that Israel's fighting strength may have been diminished by this defeat as well as by the incursions of the Sea Peoples (including the Philistines) into the region. But Stager does not suggest any more specific identification for Israel as referred to in the Merneptah Stele.

Israel emerged from a "melting pot"

A more specific identification of "Israel" is suggested by J. Maxwell Miller of Emory University. Miller argues that "Israel" in the Merneptah stele refers to a group of loosely allied Canaanite tribes in the central part of the country. Miller notes that the Book of Judges tends to focus on "the tribe of Ephraim and three neighboring tribal groups—the Benjaminites, the Manassites, and the Gileadites—all three of which appear to have been dominated by or aligned with Ephraim in some fashion.[84] Ephraim covered that part of the hill country between Shechem and Bethel. Benjamin, which means "sons of the south," was in the Bethel-Ai region, reaching south toward Jerusalem and focusing around Gibeah. Manasseh, north of Ephraim, between Shechem and the Jezreel Valley, spilled over into Transjordan. Gilead was opposite Ephraim in Transjordan.

Miller notes that this group of tribes, "loosely associated" in a satellite or client tribe relationship, was dominated by Ephraim. He continues: "Probably this loose alliance of tribes was the premonarchical 'Israel' to which the Merneptah inscription refers to."[85] Since the Merneptah inscription dates to before the time of Deborah (sometime in the 12th century B.C.), we can postulate an evolution in tribal alignments, beginning at least with the four tribes of the loose Ephraimite alignment, i.e., Ephraim, Manasseh, Gilead and Benjamin.[86] By the time of Deborah, there seems to have been an alliance of ten tribes; they are listed in the "Roll Call of the Tribes" in Judges 5:12-18.[87] Eventually, when the monarchy was established in Jerusalem, there were 12 tribes. These tribes were probably of diverse origins and ethnicity, as well as religion. Their emergence into a nation with a national religion was the result of a long process of struggle shaped internally by dynamic leaders we know as

JOE SEGER

Gezer calendar. Inscribed in soft limestone in the tenth century B.C., this tablet is the oldest known Hebrew inscription of significant length. Small enough to be held in one hand, it lists by month a farmer's duties—planting, reaping, vine-tending, and so on.

Judges, and externally by political pressures exerted primarily by the Philistines.

In short, Israel seems to have emerged from a "melting pot" of peoples in the land of Canaan at the beginning of Iron Age I, peoples whose origins can be traced only rather generally and in many different directions. Among these were the refugees from slavery in Egypt, who may have brought with them a new "Yahweh" religion that came to dominate the composite people Israel. This scenario, admittedly, is more complex than we would suppose from a casual reading of Joshua and Judges, but it finds support from a careful reading of the biblical text as well as from archaeological research.

Both the Book of Judges and the results of archaeological research indicate that the village was the basic form of social organization in the highlands of Israel during the period of the Judges, what archaeologists call Iron Age I (about 1200 to 1000 B.C.). As attested by archaeology these villages share features of house design, village layouts and an economy of dry farming supplemented by animal husbandry. Before about 1200 B.C., permanent settlements had been located near natural water sources, but with the settlement of the central hills of Canaan, villages subsisted on rainwater captured in rock-cut cisterns. Hillsides around village sites were terraced to slow and capture runoff water, thus allowing cultivation of wheat, barley, vegetables and olive trees at sites not served by natural water sources, such as streams.

The village was an economic entity within itself, independent of other villages and, for the most part, not subject to any market or trade system. It featured a subsistence system dependent more on the vagaries of nature than on political or economic influences. Anthropologists characterize this aspect of village life as "isolation,"[88] but to some extent this is a misnomer. Although we find very few imported artifacts in excavated villages, there are exceptions: bronze tools obtained in trade, or the ingots from which these tools were made, which were bartered or purchased. Thus isolation was not complete, although it was the village's predominant characteristic.

The village's self-sufficiency and pragmatic isolation have implications for the larger social structure of the people and its political organization. These characteristics lead to a natural tendency to resist political unification and social conformity because they threaten the integrity of the village unit.

The dominant socioeconomic unit within the village was the household. A household consisted of an extended family compound separated from other compounds by dividing walls or space. Stager has noted that these household compounds "probably reflect the socioeconomic unit known from biblical sources as the bet-'ab," the house of the father.[89] Gottwald has observed that "a bet-'ab customarily includes the family head and his wife (or wives), their sons and unmarried daughters, the sons' wives and children . . . as far as the biological and affinal links extended generationally."[90] The biological link was not the sole determinant, however, because slaves and strangers who shared the mutual dwelling were also considered part of the bet-'ab.

The beth-'avot were grouped together in what the biblical text refers to as the mishpahah or clan. The concept of mishpahah can extend, as Gottwald has noted, not only to a group of related families but also to a more neutral characterization of a "protective association of extended families."[91] In the case of small Iron Age I villages, the village itself could be the equivalent of the biblical mishpahah. Indeed, the concept of clan and village often coincided.[92]

Tribes were made up of a group of clans, and, as Miller has noted, they were essentially territorial in character. "Thus," he says, "the name 'Ephraim' probably originated with reference to the people living in the vicinity of Mt. Ephraim."[93] The same would be true of Gilead, Benjamin (son of the south), Naphtali, etc. The names of places, on the other hand, were also closely related to the names of constituent clans, so that the tribe was not purely territorial in nature, but also had a proto-ethnic context.

Political leadership among the tribes seems to have been clan- or village-oriented. The isolation of village life encouraged a highly individualistic kind of leadership, allowing the emergence of a diversity of leadership types. Local affairs were managed by elders of the clans, probably made up of the heads of different expanded families.

The tribal leader is exemplified by Jephthah in Judges 11:1; he is referred to as a "mighty warrior, but the son of a harlot." When the elders of Gilead were threatened by the Ammonites, they went to Jephthah in "the land of Tob," apparently a place of exile where his half-brothers had driven him because he was the son of a harlot. Jephthah initially responded: "Did you not hate me, and drive me out of my father's house? Why have you come to me now that you are in trouble?" (Judges 11:7). However, in the end he relented when the elders promised to make him head of the tribe if he would fight with the Ammonites.

Also certain leaders, such as Deborah, seem to have risen above the tribal level. Deborah is said to have sat under a palm tree between Ramah and Bethel in the hill country of Ephraim, "and the people of Israel came up to her for judgment" (Judges 4:5). Evidently she had acquired a reputation as a wise settler of disputes and arbitrator of justice that transcended clan and tribal limitations. When the Israelites were threatened by an alliance of Canaanites, Deborah issued a call to all the tribes to join forces; six of ten Israelite tribes responded, according to Judges 5.

The tribal allotments   Although Joshua 13-22 states that 12 tribes were given allotments of territory after the conquest, a close reading of Joshua and Judges indicates an evolution in the relationships of tribes and groups of tribes that spanned most of the period of the Judges. As noted above, Miller suggested that the "Israel" of the Merneptah inscription, dated about 1207 B.C., was probably composed of Ephraim and at least three "client" or "satellite" tribes: Manasseh, Gilead and Benjamin.[94] He notes further that the patriarchal narratives appear to support this view. The stories about Jacob, also named "Israel" (Genesis 32:27-28, 35:10), "have their setting primarily in the territory of these Ephraimite-dominated tribes." Joseph and Benjamin are depicted as favorite sons of Jacob/Israel, with Benjamin as the younger. Manasseh and Ephraim are identified as Joseph's sons, with Ephraim as the one destined to dominate (Genesis 48).[95] In the Book of Joshua, occasional references to "the house of Joseph . . . pertain to these three related tribes—Ephraim/Benjamin and Manasseh" (see Joshua 17:14-18).[96] And "after the death of Solomon, the territory of these same tribes became the core of the northern kingdom, which in turn is referred to interchangeably as 'Ephraim,' 'Israel' and 'Samaria' (after the capital city)."[97]

The Galilee-Jezreel tribes of Asher, Zebulon, Issachar and Naphtali are described in Judges 1:30-33 as living among the Canaanites who dominated them and who subjected Zebulon to "forced labor" (Judges 1:30). These tribes were involved in two battles against oppressors in which the Ephraimite tribes took the initiative. First, Gideon of Ophrah led an attack on Midianites and Amalekites from the east who had taken over part of the Valley of Jezreel. Asher, Zebulon and Naphtali responded to the call (Judges 6:35), and the raiders from east of the Jordan were defeated. Second, when the Canaanites led by Sisera of Harosheth-ha-goiim (Judges 4:2) oppressed the Galilee tribes, Deborah of Ephraim/ Benjamin summoned Barak of Naphtali to lead an army against the oppressors. Zebulon joined forces with the men from Naphtali, and apparently a contingent from Ephraim was involved. In any case, the Ephraim group seems to have taken the initiative, and the Canaanites were defeated. In the victory ode of Judges 5:12-18, ten tribes are mentioned, although not all of them took part in the battle. These accounts indicate that the Ephraim/Israel tribes assumed leadership roles over the Galilee tribes.[98]

The tribes of Dan, Judah, Reuben and Gad were located peripherally to the Ephraim/Israel tribes and do not figure significantly in leadership roles. The Danite clans, located along the Mediterranean coast, were pressed back into the edge of the hill country of Ephraim by the Amorites (Judges 1:34-35), and to find relief from oppression, migrated to Laish (later Dan) at the foot of Mt. Hermon in north Galilee (Judges 17-18).

The Judah clans occupied the hill country south of Benjamin and into the Negev; they were separated from Ephraim by the alliances of Hivite and Jebusite villages in the vicinity of Jerusalem. Judah did not play a significant role during the period of the Judges, and, in fact, did not become prominent until the time of David.

Gad and Reuben are associated with Transjordan in the patriarchal narratives (Genesis 29:31-32, 49:3-4), and are allotted territory east of the Jordan in Joshua 13:15-28. They are not even mentioned in the Book of Judges.

Thus, it seems that the Ephraim/Israel tribes were the focus of leadership during the period of the Judges and were the historic center of the Israel that emerged as a monarchy during the time of Saul. The focus of leadership changed during the emergence of David and the reign of Solomon, but reverted to local leaders when Solomon died and rival monarchies were set up at Shechem and Jerusalem.

The Book of Judges reflects considerable diversity in the premonar-chical religion of Israel, and this is confirmed by archaeology. The final editors of the book had a rather idealistic view of religious conditions—the Levites led the other tribes in the worship of Yahweh, which contrasted sharply with the idolatry of the Canaanites. Once we get behind the editorial framework of the compilers, however, we find a far more complex situation. For instance, when Gideon was called upon to deliver Israel from the Midianite oppression, an angel of Yahweh appeared before him at Ophrah and commanded him to "pull down the altar of Baal which your father has, and cut down the Asherah that is beside it; and build an altar to the Lord your God on top of the stronghold . . ." (Judges 6:25-26). Gideon proceeded to pull down the

Early Israelite religion

altar by night, because he feared his family and the men of the town; he built the altar to Yahweh, and offered a bull upon it. When the men of the town discovered what he had done, they went to the house of Gideon's father and demanded that he be brought out so they could execute him.

Apparently the altar to Baal served as a village shrine. Joash, Gideon's father, interceded and saved his son from the townspeople. However, after Gideon defeated the Midianites, he received from the Israelites the loot taken from the Midianites (Ishmaelites)—golden earings, crescents and pendants, as well as purple garments worn by the kings of Midian. Gideon proceeded to make from this material (the Hebrew word is "it," so we can't be sure if the antecedent is the gold or the robes) an ephod. An ephod can be a decorated priestly garment, as in Exodus 28:4, or it can be an image clothed in a cultic garment, as appears to be the case in the Gideon incident, because it "became a snare to Gideon and to his family" (Judges 8:27).

In another episode, Micah, the Ephraimite, steals 1100 pieces of silver from his mother, for which she curses him (Judges 17:2ff.). Repentant, Micah restores the silver; his mother then gives him 200 pieces of silver, which he turns over "to the silversmith, who made it into a graven image and a molten image; and it was in the house of Micah" (Judges 17:4). The account continues: "And the man Micah had a shrine, and he made an ephod and teraphim, and installed one of his sons, who became his priest" (Judges 17:5).

This description of a household shrine finds an echo in Iron Age I houses excavated at Khirbet Raddana by the writer, two of which had small platforms built up of stones beside the roof support pillars of the greatroom. In one house, two offering stands were recovered.[99] The account of Micah's household shrine suggests, as does this excavation, that the religion of Yahweh that we meet later in the Bible went through a process of development. We cannot trace this development to an imageless Yahweh with any certainty.

A collection of ancient Hebrew and Phoenician inscriptions from a later period was recovered in 1975 and 1976 at Kuntillet 'Ajrud in the desert southwest of Kadesh Barnea. Although they date to the eighth century B.C., they have implications for the period of the Judges as well. These inscriptions contain the names of El and Yahweh (spelled YHWH as in the Hebrew Bible), suggesting to the excavator that the site was a religious center, or shrine.[100] The inscriptions and some primitive drawings were found on large storage jars and on the plaster of the building. One Phoenician inscription apparently written on the plaster of a door jamb reads ". . . blessed be Baal in the day of . . . ."[101] It refers to Baal rather than Yahweh, but its appearance on a door jamb recalls the injunction in Deuteronomy 6:9 to write the biblical text on "the doorposts of your house and on your gates." One of the storage jars at Kuntillet 'Ajrud was inscribed with poorly preserved drawings and a blessing that reads:[102]

"Amaryau said to my lord . . . may you be blessed by Yahweh and by his Asherah. Yahweh bless you and keep you and be with you." The reference to Asherah in this inscription is highly controversial, as, indeed, is the meaning of Asherah in the Old Testament.[103] Asherah is found in Canaanite literature, where she is the female consort of Baal, and is always condemned in the Bible as a pagan deity. But here, in the eighth century B.C., the time of the classical prophets, we find Asherah, at least according to some interpreters, as a consort of Yahweh. What we seem to have here is a grassroots-level syncretism that called for periodic religious reform throughout Israel's history. Examples are King Hezekiah's reform of the eighth century B.C. and King Josiah's reform of the seventh century B.C. If this syncretism of Yahwism and Baalism persisted until the time of Kuntillet 'Ajrud, then it certainly existed in the period of the Judges.

We do not know the origins of Yahweh worship. Exodus 6:3 attributes the revelation of Yahwism to Moses, in the land of the Midianites south of Canaan. Moses married a Midianite woman whose father is called "the priest of Midian" (Exodus 18:1); he officiated at a cultic celebration of Yahweh's deliverance of Israel from Egypt (Exodus 18:10-12). J. Maxwell Miller points out that "certain poetical texts associate Yahweh in a special way with the south, and speak of Yahweh coming from that area to aid Israel in warfare" as in Judges 5:4-5 and Deuteronomy 33:2.[104] If Yahwism did have its origins among the desert peoples of the south, its acceptance among the tribal groups in Canaan apparently occurred over a long period of time, during which different factions emerged. These different factions were associated with different cult symbols. The ark of the covenant seems to have been a symbol of southern origin; other symbols, such as the brazen serpent, finally removed from the Temple during Hezekiah's reform (2 Kings 18:4), seem to have Canannite origins. The evolution and triumph of Yahwism in Israel came about through intense internal struggles among competing factions.

The period of the Judges, when "there was no king in Israel; [and] every man did what was right in his own eyes" (Judges 21:25), lasted about 200 years—from about 1200 to 1000 B.C. When, however, the periods of time given for each episode in the Book of Judges are added together, the total far exceeds 200 years. It even exceeds the 480 years the Bible says elapsed between the Exodus and the founding of Solomon's Temple (1 Kings 6:1). This is because the episodes are not to be joined as consecutive events; some undoubtedly occurred contemporaneously. Secondly, there is a recurrence of the numbers 20, 40 and 80 in the data given. These are highly symbolic numbers, and are not necessarily to be taken literally. Numbers in the biblical world often have more sophisticated vocations than counting.

The Judges— prelude to monarchy

The stories of the Book of Judges have been arranged in a theological pattern in which historical detail often yields to theology. The theological pattern is given in Judges 2:11-23:

(1) turning from Yahweh to Baal;

(2) incurring the wrath of Yahweh, who allows an enemy to oppress Israel;

(3) raising up Judges to deliver the people from oppression; and

(4) allowing a time of peace before the next apostasy.

Miller notes that "the basic assumption behind this theological pattern is that fidelity to Yahweh was the determinative factor in the vicissitudes of ancient Israelite history."[105] The writer's or editor's purpose is religious instruction, not history. As a result, the modern historian must interpret the text accordingly.

The transition from the period of the Judges to the beginning of the monarchy under Saul occurred during the priestly career of Samuel, the last of the Judges. His father was an Ephraimite from the town of Ramah, south of Bethel, who went on annual pilgrimages to the sanctuary at Shiloh. On one of these pilgrimages Hannah, Elkanah's barren wife, was promised a child: The birth of her son Samuel is described as a miraculous event. In gratitude to Yahweh, Hannah entrusted Samuel to Eli, the priest at Shiloh, to rear and educate. Samuel became an exemplary man of God, and was recognized widely as a prophet and a Judge. He worked an annual circuit that took him to Bethel, Gilgal, Mizpah and back to Ramah where he built an altar to Yahweh (1 Samuel 7:3-17).

Samuel's sons, however, were not of Samuel's caliber and the elders of Israel called on Samuel to appoint a king to rule over them. Samuel's position on this matter is unclear, because there are two or three traditions in 1 Samuel that give conflicting opinions. In 1 Samuel 8:6-22, Samuel is instructed by Yahweh to oppose the appointment of a king; in 1 Samuel 9:15-24, Samuel is instructed to anoint Saul secretly as king. Perhaps Samuel was of two minds on the question. In any event, Samuel played a decisive role in the creation of the monarchy.

Thus the era of the settlement and Judges ended. Israel was embarked on the road to nationhood.

F O U R

The United Monarchy

Saul, David and Solomon

ANDRÉ LEMAIRE

T HE UNITED KINGDOM WAS THE MOMENT OF ISRAEL'S GLORY ON
the international scene—a moment to be remembered and
recalled for millennia. What led to the creation of the Israelite
monarchy? In the words of William E. Evans, "The impetus for the origin
of [the] Israelite monarchy [was] the Philistine military threat."[1] It was
external pressure that brought an end to the loose tribal confederacy—
if that is what it was—by which Israel had been led and protected.
Charismatic tribal leaders who arose as the need arose were no longer
adequate to the times.

The United Kingdom of Israel lasted for about a century (c. 1030?-
931 B.C.). Three strong personalities occupied the throne: Saul, David
and Solomon. Then the United Kingdom split in two: Israel in the north
and Judah in the south.

Under Saul, the Israelite monarchy was a small, petty, local state. Under
David and then Solomon, Israel was transformed into a large, unified
kingdom with vassal states subject to it. It assumed an international role
to which other powers in the ancient Near East, mainly Phoenicia and
Egypt, were required to give due regard.

The principal difficulty in reconstructing the history of the period is
that we are dependent almost exclusively on the Bible. The assurance
that comes from a variety of sources is missing here, and the biblical
account is sometimes tendentious and includes traditions that are not
completely reliable as history. To understand this period of Israel's

history, we must consider questions of literary criticism, as well as differences in the various traditions preserved in the Bible. Finally, we must consider the light archaeology sheds.

On the other hand, we are fortunate in this period: The biblical record is copious because this period was later conceived as a kind of "golden age"; indeed, it was often idealized by tradition. The Bible probably devotes more space to this century than to any other in ancient Israel's history. We find accounts of this period in both of the Bible's parallel sets of historical books—from 1 Samuel 8 to 1 Kings 11 and from 1 Chronicles 3 to 2 Chronicles 9.

Saul (c. 1030?-1009 B.C.)

As presented in the Bible, Saul is a study in contrasts. Although he was Israel's first king, he was ultimately rejected (1 Samuel 15:10). His dark, fitful personality suffers by contrast with the two other legendary figures between whom he seems wedged—Samuel, the prophet-priest, and David, Saul's hero-successor.

The Philistine threat   The Philistines are known from the Bible and from extra-biblical sources.[2] Egyptian inscriptions mention them as one of the so-called Sea Peoples. They apparently came originally from the Aegean area or from southern Anatolia. Other Sea Peoples included the Tjekkar, the Sheklesh, the Danùna and the Weshesh. The Sea Peoples destroyed a number of cities of the Syro-Phoenician coast at the beginning of the 12th century B.C. and even tried to subdue Egypt. However, they were stopped in a large-scale battle, fought both on land and on sea, in the eighth year of the reign of Pharaoh Ramesses III (c. 1177 B.C.). Reliefs and hieroglyphic accounts of this battle appear on Ramesses III's temple at Medinet Habu in Thebes.[3] Probably with Egypt's agreement, the Sea Peoples settled in various parts of the Egyptian province of Canaan: The Philistines occupied the coastal plain between Gaza and Jaffa; the Tjekkar occupied the Sharon plain, around the city of Dor; the Cherethites (Cretans?), perhaps another Sea People, settled the so-called Negev of the Cherethites (1 Samuel 30:14).

In the coastal plain, the Philistines organized themselves into a pentapolis, a confederation of five cities: Gaza, Ashdod, Ashkelon, Gath and Ekron. Each city was ruled by a *sèren*, the only Philistine word that is known with certainty (Joshua 13:3; Judges 16:5,8,18,23,27; 1 Samuel 5:8,11); it may be connected with the Greek word *tyrannos*.[4]

The Philistines seem to have used the most advanced weapons and military equipment of their time, both in bronze and in increasingly available iron. Actually, until about 1200 B.C., bronze was the predominant metal in the ancient world; in the 12th-11th century B.C., iron technology developed in the Aegean, in Cyprus and in Canaan. In Cyprus and Canaan, this development apparently had an Aegean connection.[5]

Eventually, the Philistine military expansion near Aphek brought the Philistines close to the territory occupied by the Israelite confederation. The Israelites mustered in the hill country overlooking Aphek. A two-stage battle between the Israelites and the Philistines ensued. In the first phase of the battle "Israel was defeated by the Philistines, who slew about four thousand men on the field of battle" (1 Samuel 4:2). In desperation, the Israelites brought the Ark, which had been installed at Shiloh, to lead them in battle. In the second phase of the battle, the Israelites were again defeated, and the Ark was captured by the Philistines. After the battle of Ebenezer (1 Samuel 4), the Philistines occupied at least part of the Ephraimite hill country. Moving in on their victory at Ebenezer, the Philistines had installed garrisons (or governors) in the hill country of Ephraim and Benjamin, the most important of which was at Geba (1 Samuel 13:3-5).

Like the *Habiru* of the Late Bronze Age, hundreds of years before, and the Jews of the Maccabean revolt, hundreds of years later, some Israelites took to the hill country, hiding in natural caves in this part of the country (1 Samuel 14:11,22).

In these dire circumstances, the Israelite tribes determined that they must have a king. The story of the choice of Saul as king appears in three different traditions: In the first, Saul is looking for his father's lost she-asses; he meets Samuel who anoints him prince (*nasi*) over Israel (1 Samuel 9:3-10:16). In the second tradition, at Mizpah, Saul hides among the baggage while Samuel casts lots to choose the king (1 Samuel 10:17-27); in the third tradition, the story of the Ammonite war, probably the most reliable historically,[6] Saul at the head of Israelite columns rescues Jabesh-Gilead from an Ammonite attack; the people, with Samuel's agreement, proclaim their allegiance to Saul at Gilgal (1 Samuel 11-12). In each of these accounts,[7] Saul is installed and anointed as king by Samuel, now an old man. Samuel was regarded as the last of the Judges (1 Samuel 7:6,15, 8:1), the charismatic leaders who emerged at times of crisis. Another tradition, probably a later one, regarded Samuel as a prophet (1 Samuel 3:20). He also officiated at the tabernacle at Shiloh, where the Ark was kept, so he was also a priest. Obviously, Samuel's leadership was regarded as insufficient. The tribal elders apparently felt that the appointment of a king was a historical necessity: ". . . now appoint for us a king to govern us like all the nations" (1 Samuel 8:5). Saul, a Benjaminite, seems to have been chosen because he was tall and strong and well qualified to wage war against Israel's enemies.

The choice of Saul

Like earlier charismatic leaders, Saul's principal task was to conduct a war of liberation. Saul had led a successful expedition to rescue Jabesh-Gilead from the Ammonites (1 Samuel 11:1-11),[8] and this was no doubt an important consideration in his selection. Now he was called upon to lead the people against the Philistines, a people who were well organized, well equipped and motivated by an expansionist ideology that included plans to bring the whole country west of the Jordan under its control.

The first battle—at Michmash—was a victory for Israel. The details are given in 1 Samuel 13:5-14:46. The decision to appoint a king seemed a wise one. But this was by no means the last battle of the war:

Saul, the warrior

"There was hard fighting against the Philistines all the days of Saul; and when Saul saw any strong man, or any valiant man, he attached him to himself" (1 Samuel 14:52).

The Philistine war thus became a guerrilla war, characterized by ambushes and surprise attacks against enemy posts. Generally, it did not involve great numbers of fighters. Saul had only "about six hundred men with him" near Gibeah (1 Samuel 14:2). Unfortunately, the Bible gives only brief intimations regarding the details of the continuing wars with the Philistines. Saul probably succeeded in driving the Philistines out of the central part of Israel. But the Philistines did not give up. They apparently attacked from the south, threatening Judah in a confrontation in which a young Judahite named David distinguished himself (1 Samuel 17).

Saul seems to have been generally successful as long as he fought in the hills; however, his troops could not win a battle in the open plain. Witness what happened near Mt. Gilboa. The Philistines attacked from the north through the Jezreel Valley. The Israelites should never have come down into the plain to fight. Saul, his son Jonathan and most of their soldiers were killed by the Philistines at the battle of Mt. Gilboa (1 Samuel 28-31):

"The Philistines fought against Israel; and the men of Israel fled before the Philistines, and fell slain on Mt. Gilboa . . . . Thus Saul died, and his three sons, and his armor-bearer, and all his men, on the same day together. And when the men of Israel who were on the other side of the valley and those beyond the Jordan saw that the men of Israel had fled and that Saul and his sons were dead, they forsook their cities and fled; and the Philistines came and dwelt in them" (1 Samuel 31:1,6-7).

Other than the Philistine war, which seems to have been the principal feature of Saul's reign, the biblical text mentions wars against the Moabites, the Ammonites, the Edomites, the king of Zobah and the Amalekites (1 Samuel 14:47-48).

The main battle of the war with the Amalekites is described in 1 Samuel 15. The Amalekites were the Israelites' special enemies; among other things, the Amalekites had been the first to attack Israel in the wilderness after the Israelites left Egypt; the Amalekites, without provocation, had attacked Israel from the rear (Exodus 17:8-16). After Saul's victory over the Amalekites, Saul and his men were to kill all the Amalekites and their animals, according to the tradition of *hérèm* (compare Joshua 6:18 and 7), which allotted the fruits of victory to the Lord alone. However, Saul spared from *hérèm* the Amalekite king Agag

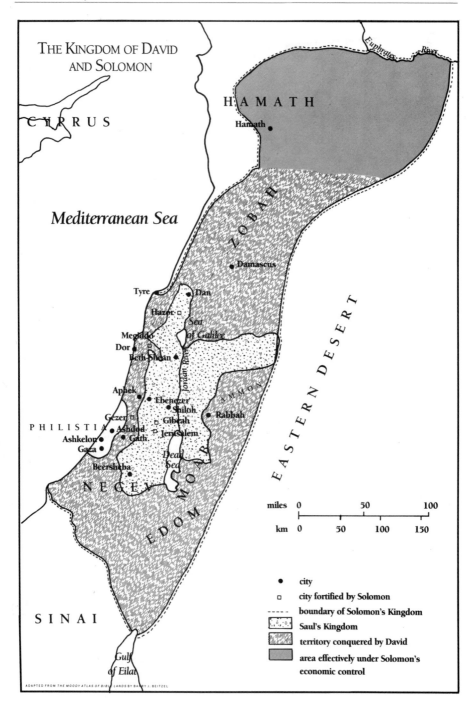

THE KINGDOM OF DAVID
AND SOLOMON

CYPRUS

HAMATH

Hamath

Mediterranean Sea

ZOBAH

Damascus

Tyre

Dan

Hazor

Sea
of Galilee

Megiddo

Dor

Beth-Shean

Jordan River

EASTERN DESERT

Aphek

Ebenezer

Shiloh

AMMON

Gezer

Gibeah

Rabbah

PHILISTIA

Ashdod

Jerusalem

Ashkelon

Gath

Gaza

Dead
Sea

Beersheba

NEGEV

EDOM

SINAI

Gulf
of Eilat

miles 0   50   100

km 0   50   100   150

● city

□ city fortified by Solomon

----- boundary of Solomon's Kingdom

Saul's Kingdom

territory conquered by David

area effectively under Solomon's
economic control

ADAPTED FROM THE MOODY ATLAS OF BIBLE LANDS BY BARRY J. BEITZEL

and the best of the Amalekites' domestic animals. For this sin, Samuel denounced Saul and declared that the Lord had irrevocably rejected him. Samuel "never saw Saul again" (1 Samuel 15:35).

Saul's stormy reign   The following chapters (1 Samuel 16-27) describe, sometimes according to varying traditions, the stormy relationship between Saul and the young David. David had distinguished himself in the Philistine wars and had been given Saul's second daughter, Michal, in marriage. Saul became increasingly jealous of David, accusing David of conspiring against him. On several occasions, Saul tried to kill David. David fled to Judah, but Saul pursued him. Finally, David took refuge in Philistine territory. The chapters describing these events were clearly written from David's point of view and already belong to David's history. We shall discuss them in more detail in connection with that history.

We do not know how long Saul ruled. According to the traditional Hebrew text (the Masoretic text), which unfortunately is badly preserved at this point, Saul became king when he was one year old (!) and his reign lasted only "two years"(1 Samuel 13:1).[9] Two years seems improbable and several commentators correct it to "twenty-two years," which remains conjectural.

Although the length of Saul's reign is conjectural, we have information about the general economic and political conditions of Israelite society at the time from two biblical passages:

"Now there was no smith to be found throughout all the land of Israel; for the Philistines said, 'Lest the Hebrews make themselves swords or spears'; but every one of the Israelites went down to the Philistines to sharpen his plowshare, his mattock, his ax, or his sickle; and the charge was a pim [= two-thirds of a shekel] for the plowshares and for the mattocks, and a third of a shekel for sharpening the axes and for setting the goads. So on the day of the battle there was neither sword nor spear found in the hand of any of the people with Saul and Jonathan; but Saul and Jonathan his son had them" (1 Samuel 13:19-22).

The passage reflects a nonspecialized society of peasants and shepherds in which even iron implements were rare.

The second passage describes Saul's family:

"Now the sons of Saul were Jonathan, Ishvi, and Malchishua; and the names of his two daughters were these; the name of the firstborn was Merab and the name of the younger Michal; and the name of Saul's wife was Ahinoam, the daughter of Ahimaaz. And the name of the commander of his army was Abner the son of Ner, Saul's uncle" (1 Samuel 14:49-50).

This passage demonstrates that Saul's kingship was essentially a family matter. The principal specialized responsibility, the army, was in the hands of Saul's cousin Abner.

It is very difficult to make a balanced historical assessment of Saul's reign.[10] In the biblical tradition he seems to be presented as the typical "bad" king,[11] in contrast to his adversary David, presented as the typical "good" king. This contrast is the central theme of the stories in 1 Samuel 16-27, the bulk of which seems to have been written by David's companion Abiathar (cf. 1 Samuel 22:20) or someone close to him.[12] These chapters may contain some reliable information,[13] but it is presented in a one-sided and tendentious way. The stories tend to demonstrate that David was right[14] in revolting against Saul and seeking refuge in Philistine territory. But they also reveal that people from Bethlehem in Judah joined Saul in his wars against the Philistines when the Philistines tried to invade the central hill country from the southwest (1 Samuel 17:1). Saul obviously exerted some political influence south of Jerusalem in the territory of Judah and prepared the way for the federation of Israel and Judah under David.

The historicity of Saul's other wars is more doubtful. The wars against the Moabites, the Edomites, the king of Zobah and even the Amalekites (1 Samuel 14:47-48, 15) may simply be a transposition from David to Saul because the Judahite historian had so little information about Saul. Such wars far from Saul's home base seem improbable, especially because the Philistine threat was so strong and Saul's army was so poorly organized.

Unfortunately, we are left with little solid information about Saul or his reign. All that can be said with confidence is that Saul seems to have been recognized as king in order to lead the Israelites in their wars against the Philistines.

Saul's "kingdom" was not very large. It included Ephraim, Benjamin and Gilead; it also exerted some influence in Judah and in the Jezreel Valley. Instead of a capital or a palace, Saul maintained his tent "in the outskirts of Gibeah under the pomegranate tree which is at Migron" (1 Samuel 14:2) or in Gibeah, where Saul sat "under the tamarisk tree on the height with his spear in his hand, and all his servants were standing about him" (1 Samuel 22:6).

Saul's "kingship," as might be expected, left hardly a trace, archaeologically speaking. Excavations at places like Izbet Sartah[15] basically reveal farms or small villages or open cult places on hilltops. By contrast, the latest excavations at Tell Qasile, Tell Ashdod, Tell Gerisa, Tell Miqneh (Ekron) and Tell Ashkelon reveal a flourishing Philistine urban civilization in the 11th century B.C.[16] The principal Israelite site of this period, Shiloh, seems to have been destroyed in the mid-11th century B.C.[17] by an intense conflagration. This destruction is often attributed to the Philistines as a follow-up operation after their victory over the Israelites at Ebenezer (1 Samuel 4). Shiloh is mentioned only once in the stories of Saul and David (1 Samuel 14:3).

Archaeology seems to confirm that until about 1000 B.C., the end of Iron Age I, Israelite society was essentially a society of farmers and stockbreeders without any truly centralized organization and administration.[18] A recent population estimate sets "a figure of about 50,000 settled Israelites west of the Jordan at the end of the eleventh century B.C."[19]

With Saul's tragic death his reign ended in total failure. After the rout on Mt. Gilboa, the Israelite revolt against Philistine domination seemed hopeless. The Israelite fight for independence against the Philistines, which was the *raison d'être* of Saul's kingship, was taken up again, however, under the leadership of Saul's adversary, David.

David (c. 1009/1001-969 B.C.)

With David's reign, Israel indisputably becomes a national entity, in contrast to a loose confederation of tribes. Its existence as a nation is easily confirmed by its king, its army, its administration, its territory and its relations with neighboring countries. Moreover, even the most critical historians, like Mario Liverani[20] and J. Alberto Soggin, [21] who hesitate to say anything about the early history of Israel, agree that from about 1000 B.C., "the History of Israel leaves the realm of pre-history, of cultic and popular traditions and enters the arena of history proper."[22] That does not mean, however, that everything is clear or without historical problems.

David, the model of a good king

The Bible tells the story of David's reign in detail (1 Samuel 16-1 Kings 2:11), reflecting its importance, as well as its length. David "reigned over Israel for forty years, seven in Hebron and thirty-three in Jerusalem" (c. 1009/1001-969 B.C.). His long reign was later regarded as Israel's "golden age"; David himself was regarded as the model of the good king.

David's later glorification may seem paradoxical in light of the fact that he was a Bethlehemite, from the tribe of Judah, and not from any of the original, northern Israelite tribes (Ephraim, Manasseh and Benjamin). Moreover, David was one of Saul's adversaries, banned because he was considered the personal enemy of the first Israelite king. Furthermore, at the time of Saul's death, David was serving as a mercenary in the army of the Philistines, Israel's bitter enemy.

According to 1 Samuel 16:1-13, David was the youngest son of Jesse. The prophet-priest Samuel "anointed him in the midst of his brothers; and the Spirit of the Lord came mightily upon David from that day forward."

Saul had taken David into his service as his "armor-bearer" (1 Samuel 16:14-23). David, having killed the Philistine champion Goliath in single combat (1 Samuel 17), was officially presented to Saul as a hero. At that time David's three older brothers were already in Saul's army. The biblical account of David's rise to power may well represent an amalgamation of different traditions concerning the early relationship between David and Saul.

In any event, with the support of his friend Jonathan (Saul's son), David was "made . . . a commander of a thousand [in the army]; and he went out and came in before the people. And David had success in all his undertakings; for the Lord was with him" (1 Samuel 18:13-14).

This happy situation did not last. David was soon accused of conspiring against Saul (1 Samuel 22:8). David decided it would be prudent to flee to the hill country:

> "David departed from there and escaped to the cave of Adullam; and when his brothers and all his father's house heard it, they went down there to him. And every one who was in distress, and every one who was in debt, and every one who was discontented gathered to him; and he became captain over them. And there were with him about four hundred men " (1 Samuel 22:1-2).

Among them were Abiathar, the son of Ahimelech the son of Ahitub the priest of Nob, descendant of Eli the chief priest at Shiloh (1 Samuel 22:20), and Gad the prophet. The fact that these religious personalities joined David suggests the importance of Yahwism among David's partisans.

After some time in various locations of Judah where Saul pursued him, David sought refuge in Philistine territory:

> "So David . . . and the six hundred men who were with him [escaped to the land of the Philistines] to Achish son of Maoch, king of Gath. And David dwelt with Achish in Gath, he and his men, every man with his household and David with his two wives" (1 Samuel 27:2-3).

After a while "Achish gave him [David] Ziklag"[23] (1 Samuel 27:6). David fought Judah's enemy the Amalekites (1 Samuel 27:8, 30:1ff), attempting to maintain good relations with the leaders of the territory of Judah (1 Samuel 30:2-31).

This good relationship with Judah proved fruitful. After Saul's death at the battle of Mt. Gilboa,

> "David went [to Hebron in the territory of Judah] and his two wives also, Ahinoam of Jezreel, and Abigail the widow of Nabal of Carmel. And David brought up his men who were with him, every one with his household; and they dwelt in the towns of Hebron. And the men of Judah came, and there they anointed David king over the house of Judah" (2 Samuel 2:2-4).

This does not seem to have provoked any Philistine reaction; at least at first, the Philistines apparently were pleased that one of their vassals controlled the territory of Judah.

> "Now Abner the son of Ner, commander of Saul's army, had taken Ishbosheth the son of Saul, and brought him over to Mahanaim;[24] and he made him king over Gilead and the Ashurites and Jezreel and Ephraim and Benjamin and all Israel. Ishbosheth, Saul's son, was forty years old when he began to reign over Israel; and he reigned two years" (2 Samuel 2:8-10).

A "long war" ensued between the house of Saul and the house of David (2 Samuel 3:1). But in the meantime a disagreement soon split Abner and Ish-Bosheth (Eshbaal). Both of them were killed, apparently as a result of personal vengeance (2 Samuel 3-4).[25] The way was open for David to become the king of all Israel.

> "All the elders of Israel came to the king at Hebron; and King David made a covenant with them at Hebron before the Lord, and they

anointed David king over Israel" (2 Samuel 5:3).

David's   The Philistines could no longer remain indifferent in face of the
military   unification of their long-time enemy. They attacked twice in the central
accomplishments   hill country, once near the Valley of Rephaim and probably once near
Gibeon. But David defeated them both times (2 Samuel 5:17-25).[26] They
then gave up their efforts at military expansion.

After driving off the Philistines, David was free to attack the Jebusites
of Jerusalem and take the city, which until then had remained in
Canaanite hands: "And David dwelt in the stronghold [of Jerusalem] and
called it the city of David" (2 Samuel 5:9).

Jerusalem soon became not only the political capital of Judah and
Israel, but also the religious center of all Israel. To accomplish this, David
brought the Ark to the City of David (2 Samuel 6). This was the Ark
that, according to tradition, had accompanied Israel in the Sinai, that
had rested in the tabernacle of Shiloh before being captured by the
Philistines, that had remained in storage at Kiriath Yearim after being
returned by the Philistines. When David brought the Ark to Jerusalem
the religion of Yahweh became a unifying factor, cementing the
relationship between Judah and Israel.

From the beginning of his career, David had shown himself to be a
fervent Yahwist. His religious devotion is confirmed by the presence in
his retinue of the priest Abiathar and the prophet Gad when he fled
from Saul. David's devotion to Yahweh probably made it easier for the
leaders of Israel to accept him as their king.

David also made politically important marriages to cement his relations
with internal as well as external political and national groupings. His
wives included Abigail of Carmel; Ahinoam of Jezreel; Maacah, daughter
of the Transjordanian king of Geshur (2 Samuel 3:2-5).[27]

Militarily, David had already developed a cadre of well-trained troops
when he fled from Saul. These devoted soldiers were ready to follow
him anywhere, and, in fact, had followed him from the wilderness of
Judah to Gath, Ziklag, Hebron and finally to Jerusalem. These troops
became his personal guard and the core of his regular army. The chief
of the army was his nephew Joab (2 Samuel 8:16).

After checking the Philistine advances on Israel's western border, David
was free to enlarge his kingdom on the eastern border. There he defeated
the Moabites, who then became a vassal state, paying tribute to David
(2 Samuel 8:2). As discussed below, David also fought with the
Ammonites, although the precise sequence of these wars is unclear. A
campaign to Edom, after a victory in a battle in the Valley of Salt, led
to David's appointing "garrisons (or governors) in Edom; throughout all
Edom he put garrisons, and all the Edomites became David's servants"
(2 Samuel 8:14).

In the biblical tradition, after the Philistines, the Israelites' most
important war was with the Ammonites. The Ammonite war began as
a result of a diplomatic incident. Nahash, the king of the Ammonites,

had been David's friend. When Nahash died, he was succeeded by his son Hanun. David sent Hanun condolences on his father's death. Hanun treated with contempt the entourage that carried David's message. Hanun cut away half of their beards and half of their garments, accusing them of being David's spies (2 Samuel 10:1-5). Hanun probably thought he could get away with this because of an alliance he had made with the Aramean kingdoms of northern Transjordan and southern Syria[28] (1 Samuel 10:6).

David's general, Joab, attacked close to the Ammonite capital. An Ammonite ally—Hadadezer the Rehobite, king of Zobah—summoned other Arameans from "beyond the Great Bend of the Euphrates" (2 Samuel 10:16) to join forces against David. David met and defeated this Aramean army at Helam (2 Samuel 10:17-18). He "took from him [Hadadezer] a thousand and seven hundred horsemen, and twenty thousand foot soldiers; and David hamstrung all the chariot horses, but left enough for a hundred chariots" (2 Samuel 8:4). Apparently, chariots were not used much in David's army; otherwise, he would not have crippled the chariot horses.

As a result of this enormous victory, David was able to conquer Rabbah, the Ammonite capital. David then "took the crown of their king (or of Milkom) from his head . . . and it was placed on David's head." The Ammonites became David's subjects (2 Samuel 12:30-31). In addition, the kingdom of Zobah, headed by Hadadezer, became David's vassal: "David put garrisons (or governors) in Aram of Damascus; the Syrians [Arameans] became servants to David and brought tribute" (2 Samuel 8:6). Finally, "All the kings who were servants of Hadadezer . . . they made peace with Israel and became subject to them" (2 Samuel 10:19). Among them was Toi, the king of the important kingdom of Hamath (2 Samuel 8:9-10).

David thus extended his direct or indirect political control from the Red Sea to the Great Bend of the Euphrates, David's kingdom, or empire, also became an economic power. He controlled the international trade routes and became rich from the spoil and tribute brought to Jerusalem. Hiram, the Phoenician king of Tyre, traded with him, especially after David made Jerusalem his capital (2 Samuel 5:11-12).

The expansion of David's kingdom also changed the status of Jerusalem. From a small Canaanite city-state with a territory of a few square miles, it became the capital of the united Israelite and Judahite kingdoms. These kingdoms, after David's victories, extended far and wide. The United Kingdom itself extended from Dan to Beersheba, but its many administrative territories and vassal states extended far beyond. *Jerusalem, the new capital*

The capital of such an empire needed new buildings (2 Samuel 5:9-10) and a new administrative organization. This David provided.

"So David reigned over all Israel; and David administered justice and equity to all his people. And Joab the son of Zeruiah was over the army; and Jehoshaphat the son of Ahilud was recorder; and Zadok the son of Ahitub and Ahimelech the son of Abiathar were priests; and Seraiah was secretary; and Benaiah the son of Jehoiada was over the Cherethite and the Pelethites; and David's sons were priests"[29] (2 Samuel 8:15-18; cf. also a slightly different list in 2 Samuel 20:23-26).

The spoils of war, the levies from the administered territories, the tributes of vassal kings—all flowed into David's royal treasury. In addition, produce of royal properties also served to fill the royal coffers (1 Chronicles 27:25-31).

Justice was administered at the local level by the elders of the cities, but an appeal could now be taken directly to the king (2 Samuel 14:15).

The guiding principle was centralization. But this process of centralization only began during David's reign. It was later applied more broadly by his son and successor Solomon.

David also planned a new temple at Jerusalem (2 Samuel 7) and organized a census, probably as a basis for administrative, taxation and conscription reorganization (cf. 2 Samuel 24:1-9). Both the temple project and the census met internal opposition. Only in Solomon's reign were they realized. Even the prophet Gad, one of David's oldest and most loyal companions, was against the census, although he supported the construction of an altar on the threshing floor of Araunah the Jebusite, the site David purchased for the temple (2 Samuel 24:18).

Internally, the problem of succession loomed large. It was doubtless exacerbated by the unstable union of the houses of Israel and Judah. This problem is treated at great length in the Bible. Indeed, this is the principal subject from 2 Samuel 6 to 1 Kings 2, often called the "History of the Succession."

Initially, David tried to gain the good will of the Saulides.[30] He even married Michal, Saul's daughter. David also welcomed to his table on a regular basis Merib-Baal (Mephibosheth), a cripple who was Saul's heir. True, this seeming act of kindness permitted David to control Merib-Baal's activity (2 Samuel 9). And in the end David more or less abandoned Michal, who "had no child to the day of her death" (2 Samuel 6:23). When David allowed the Gibeonites to take vengeance on seven of Saul's descendants, reconciliation between the two houses was no longer possible (2 Samuel 21:1-14).[31]

David's own house was also beset with rivalries and jealousies among his sons. His eldest son, Amnon, was killed by order of David's third son Absalom (2 Samuel 13). Absalom himself was killed by the general of David's army Joab after an almost successful *coup d'état* (2 Samuel 15-19). This revolt, led by Absalom, was connected with the rivalry between Israel and Judah and with Benjaminite opposition to David (compare the role played by Shimei and by Sheba son of Bichri, both Benjaminites [2 Samuel 19:16-23, 20:1-22]).

After Amnon and Absalom were killed, Adonijah became David's heir apparent. David's old retainers, including his general Joab and the priest Abiathar, were ready to support Adonijah (1 Kings 1:5-7). However, according to 1 Kings 1, the aged David promised Bathsheba that their son Solomon would become king. With the help of the prophet Nathan, the priest Zadok and the chief of the guards Benaiah, Solomon was recognized as king while David was still alive. David himself died peacefully some time afterward (1 Kings 2:10-12).

In the absence of any contemporary text outside the biblical tradition, a historical appreciation of David's reign is difficult. A literary analysis of the biblical tradition seems to indicate, however, that a good deal of it was written either in David's or Solomon's time, close enough to the events to be reliable witnesses, although there are doubtless later additions and glosses reflecting the influence of the so-called Deuteronomistic historians until the sixth century B.C.[32]   *Assessing the biblical text*

Of course, even early traditions can be tendentious, and it does seem that most of the account of David's reign was written to glorify and justify David and his son Solomon. This is particularly true of the stories concerning David's accession, which reflect the most attractive side of his personality and justify his claim to the kingship.[33] This is also true of the account of Solomon's accession, which explains how Solomon, although one of the younger sons of David, could be his legitimate heir. The aged David's promise to Bathsheba to make her son Solomon king sounds more like literary artifice than history. Or perhaps Bathsheba, with the help of the prophet Nathan[34] and the priest Zadok, succeeded in convincing an old and weakened David to support their conspiracy to elevate Solomon and thus to legitimate what was in effect a "*coup d'état.*"[35]

The account of David's external policies also bears the marks of tendentiousness; the biblical text emphasizes David's military victories more than his political control of the conquered territories. If David was victorious against the invading Philistines, he was nevertheless probably unable to control the Philistine territory itself, despite the ambiguity of 2 Samuel 8:1,12 (cf. 2 Samuel 5:25: David defeated the Philistines only as far as Gezer, on the eastern border of Philistine territory). Gezer itself did not become part of Israel until Solomon's reign, see below.

David's relations with Hiram king of Tyre must also be looked at critically. The relationship was essentially commercial; there was no vassal submission. Actually the Phoenicians were technologically superior to the Israelites. Moreover, even this commercial relationship probably dated to the end of David's reign, or even more probably, to the beginning of Solomon's reign.[36]

After the Ammonite war, if David indeed took for himself the Ammonite crown, he probably dismissed the ruling Ammonite king Hanun only to put in his place another son of Nahash as the head of the Ammonites—"Shobi the son of Nahash from Rabbah of the Ammonites," who supported David during Absalom's revolt (2 Samuel 17:27-29). In the foreign territories that David administered (Damascus, Edom, etc.), the governors were probably chosen from among local leaders. In the vassal kingdoms (like Moab), their own kings continued to rule, although they paid tribute to David. Sometimes it is difficult to tell the difference between a vassal state and an allied kingdom—for instance, Toi, king of Hamath, probably considered himself as much an ally as a vassal (see 2 Samuel 8:9-10).

Even if David's influence did extend from the Red Sea to the Great Bend of the Euphrates, one must distinguish various kinds of political control and influence.[37] David's control of the outlying areas was superficial and sometimes even theoretical.

The archaeology of David's reign is unfortunately sparse. Yohanan Aharoni[38] thought that Dan and Beersheba were rebuilt by David and that the Iron Age gates of these cities could be dated to the beginning of the tenth century B.C., but this is disputed and few archaeologists today support his conclusions. It is difficult to date so precisely either an artifact or architecture to the *beginning* of the tenth century. Most of the building activity in the tenth century probably occurred later, during King Solomon's reign. At the very least, both reigns must be studied together from an archaeological viewpoint.[39]

Despite all these reservations, however, David's reign represents a glorious achievement. A strong and brilliant personality[40] seized the opportunity occasioned by the weakness of Assyria and Egypt[41] to unify the houses of Israel and Judah, to create a new capital at Jerusalem and to make this unification the basis of his empire. Within this favorable international context, David created, for a time, one of the most important powers in the ancient Near East. He also laid the foundations of religious institutions that would support the worship of the Hebrew God Yahweh for millennia.

Solomon (c. 970/969-931 B.C.)

David was occupied chiefly with wars, achieving the expansion of his kingdom both by military and political means. Solomon was concerned mainly with consolidating this expansion and organizing the administration of the kingdom after strengthening his personal power during the first years of his reign.

Threats to Solomon's rule—internal and external

Solomon was confronted first with an internal and then an external threat. As long as Adonijah, David's oldest surviving son, lived, this apparent Davidic heir would be a danger; there was always the possibility that he would present himself as the legitimate successor to David. Solomon seized an early opportunity to rid himself of this threat: Adonijah was executed as soon as he was suspected of scheming against Solomon. David's general Joab, one of Adonijah's chief supporters was also executed; Abiathar the priest, another of Adonijah's supporters was exiled to his own estate in Anathoth (1 Kings 2:13-35). Solomon also put to death Shimei, a supporter of the house of Saul (1 Kings 2:36-46). "So the kingdom was established in the hand of Solomon" (1 Kings 2:46).

Outside of Israel, pharaoh, the king of Egypt, probably Siamun,[42] tried to take advantage of the change in rulers to intervene. He organized a military expedition that seized and destroyed Gezer (1 Kings 9:16), a destruction that now seems confirmed by archaeological excavations.[43] Apparently pharaoh did not go further, however; that is, he did not enter Solomon's territory. On the contrary, perhaps because he was aware of Solomon's power, he made an alliance with Solomon[44] and gave one of his daughters to Solomon as a wife (1 Kings 3:1, 7:8, 11:1), with the city of Gezer as a dowry. Such an unusual marriage [45] reflects Egypt's weakness at the time. Perhaps Solomon promised not to attack Egypt's Philistine territory, which was, at least theoretically, under Egyptian sovereignty.

Except for the addition of Gezer, Solomon's kingdom was probably the same as David's kingdom, at least during the first part of his reign. No significant change in external policy occurred except, perhaps, a greater development in commercial relations with Hiram, king of Tyre (1 Kings 5:1-18).

Like David, Solomon entered diplomatic marriages to ensure the fidelity of neighboring kingdoms. He probably married "Naamah the Ammonitess" whose son later became King Rehoboam (1 Kings 14:21).[46] Like his father, "Solomon ruled over all the kingdoms from the River [the Euphrates] to Philistia, as far as the Egyptian frontier; they were bringing gifts (or tribute) and were subject to him all his life" (1 Kings 4:21).

Solomon also reorganized the administration of his kingdom, a task to which he devoted very considerable effort and for which biblical tradition accords him the title "wise" (*hakam*)—that is to say, he was both a clever politician and a good administrator. Various areas of administrative reorganization can be distinguished.[47] First was the central government, in which a new royal cabinet was nominated:

"and these were his high officials: Azariah the son of Zadok was the priest; Elihoreph and Ahijah the sons of Shisha were secretaries; Jehoshaphat the son of Ahilud was recorder; Benaiah the son of Jehoiada was in command of the army; Zadok and Abiathar were priests;[48] Azariah the son of Nathan was over the officers; Zabud the son of Nathan was priest and king's friend; Ahishar was in charge of the palace; and Adoniram the son of Abda was in charge of the forced labor" (1 Kings 4:2-6).

In comparison with David's royal cabinet (2 Samuel 8:16), Solomon's appointments reflect a certain continuity, a son often taking his father's position. We can also detect an Egyptian influence[49] in the bureaucratic structure. There are new officials such as the governors, the man in charge of the administration of the palace and the man in charge of the forced labor levy. In general, the bureaucracy becomes more complex and more pervasive.

Two sons of the prophet Nathan were made members of this cabinet, probably because of the prominent part their father played in the designation of Solomon as king (1 Kings 1:11-38).

Israelite territory now included a number of annexed Canaanite city-states, such as Dor, Megiddo and Beth-Shean. As expanded, Israel was divided into 12 administrative districts or provinces.[50] Each province had at its head a prefect or governor appointed by the king. Administration was thus centralized. In 1 Kings 4:8-19 we find a list of the governors with their territories and principal cities. At least two governors married Solomon's daughters (1 Kings 4:11,15), another way of centralizing and controlling the administration of government.

Each administrative district was required to provide for the king and his palace for one month a year (1 Kings 4:7, 4:27-28). This was a heavier economic responsibility than it might at first seem. It included the expenses of the royal harem, of a number of functionaries and of equipping the army with horses and chariots (1 Kings 5:8 = 4:28 in English). As in David's reign, the royal treasury also received income from royal properties. Although the royal treasury did not receive as much booty in Solomon's reign as in David's reign, Solomon's treasury was supplied regularly with tribute from administered territories and from vassal lands (cf. 1 Kings 4:21).

Trade and construction during Solomon's reign

Solomon also developed an important new source of income from the international trade that became so important during his peaceful reign. The government operated this trade, and the royal treasury profited from it in various ways:[51] Trade with Phoenicia provided timber (cedar and pine) and technical aid (mainly for Solomon's official buildings). In exchange, Israel provided agricultural produce (wheat and olive oil) (1 Kings 5:8-11). In cooperation with the Tyrians, Solomon sent trading expeditions to Ophir[52] through the Red Sea. These expeditions brought back gold, precious stones and tropical products (*almug* wood, apes and baboons) (1 Kings 9:26-28, 10:11,22). Caravans through the Arabian desert brought back spices (1 Kings 10:1-10,13).

Although Solomon's reign was peaceful—David was almost continually at war—Solomon nevertheless took care to modernize his army.[53] He equipped it with large numbers of chariots imported from Egypt, for which he imported horses from the kingdom of Que (Cilicia) (1 Kings 10:26-29).[54] Solomon also built special garrisons in various administrative districts for his chariots and chariot horses (1 Kings 4:26-28, 9:19).

Solomon is also famous for his building activities. He fortified Jerusalem with a wall and built three fortified cities, Hazor, Megiddo and Gezer (1 Kings 9:15). These building activities can be related to military defense (see also 1 Kings 9:17-18).[55] He built new public buildings in his capital, Jerusalem, including the *millo*, the Temple and the royal palace (1 Kings 9:15). No one is certain what the *millo* was. The most likely suggestion is that it was some terracing, since the word seems to be related to the word for "fill."

Solomon's public works in Jerusalem were major accomplishments. It took him seven years to build the Temple (1 Kings 6:37-38) and 13 years to build his royal palace (1 Kings 7:1, 9:10).

Gezer gate. In 1 Kings 9:15 we learn that Solomon built the cities of "Hazor, Megiddo and Gezer." In this view from inside Gezer, we see six chambers of a tenth-century B.C. gate, no doubt built by King Solomon. Nearly identical gates were found at Hazor and Megiddo that also probably date to the tenth century B.C.

To plan and construct these official buildings Solomon needed the technical aid of the Phoenicians, who provided assistance not only with the basic architecture and structure, but also with the decoration of the buildings and the raw materials (wood, ivory, gold). These imports were expensive. Indeed, during the second part of his reign, "King Solomon gave to Hiram twenty cities in the land of Galilee" (1 Kings 9:11-13) to balance the trade deficit between the two kings.

To cast the many bronze objects decorating the Temple and the royal palace, Solomon used his metal works in the Jordan valley "between Succoth and Zarethan," but the origin of the metal is not specified. The casting seems to have been supervised by a Phoenician who specialized in bronze craftsmanship (1 Kings 7:13-47). Solomon's copper mines—if they existed—have not been found.[56]

The Bible's detailed description of Solomon's public buildings, especially of the Temple (1 Kings 5-6), reflects these monuments' importance to the people. Jerusalemites, as well as pilgrims, were no doubt proud to see such achievements. However, to build and maintain them Solomon needed a reservoir of cheap manpower. His solution was the corvée, forced labor required not only of non-Israelite peoples (1 Kings 9:20-21), but of Israelites as well. The statement in 1 Kings 9:22 that "of the people of Israel Solomon made no slaves" seems contradicted by 1 Kings 5:13-18, 11:28, 12:4. The corvée of Israelites and the

Ivory winged sphinx. Solomon's "great throne of ivory" described in 1 Kings 10:18 may have been decorated with ivory plaques. Although there is no evidence that ivory-working was an Israelite craft in Solomon's day, ornamenting thrones and beds with ivory was a well-known specialty of the Phoenicians, Solomon's trading partners.

On this ninth- or eighth-century B.C. plaque from Samaria is a sphinx, a mythological creature with a lion's body and a human head. This sphinx also has wings, a "Phoenician apron," a curled wig and the flattened royal double crown of Egypt. The relief technique used by the artist is called ajouré or openwork—in places the ivory is completely carved away.

conscription of Israelites (1 Kings 9:22) into Solomon's army probably provided the principal sources of popular dissatisfaction with Solomon's reign.[57]

As often happens during long reigns, internal dissatisfaction grew in the latter half of Solomon's rule; at the same time serious external threats surfaced. The biblical tradition gives us a few hints of the dissension inside Israel, as well as of disturbances in the vassal states (1 Kings 11).[58]

The text speaks of two foreign adversaries (*satan*) of Solomon: The first one is "Hadad the Edomite, he was of the royal house in Edom"[59] who sought refuge in Egypt and even married a sister of the Queen (Tahpenes) before trying to go back to his country (1 Kings 11:14-22). The second adversary of Solomon is "Rezon the son of Eliyada" who left his master Hadadezer king of Zobah and took to the hills as the chief of a small troop: "They went to Damascus, and dwelt there and made him king in Damascus" (1 Kings 11:23-24).

In Israel itself, internal dissatisfaction led to a revolt spearheaded by Jeroboam, an Ephraimite who had the support of the prophet Ahijah from Shiloh: "Solomon sought therefore to kill Jeroboam; but Jeroboam arose and fled into Egypt, to Shishak king of Egypt and was in Egypt until the death of Solomon (1 Kings 11:29-40).[60]

The dissatisfaction with Solomon's rule probably had many sources, but the biblical tradition insists principally on the people's objections, based on religious grounds, to Solomon's many foreign wives.

"For when Solomon was old his wives turned away his heart after other gods . . . He went after Ashtoreth, the goddess of the Sidonians, and after Milcom, the abomination of the Ammonites . . . Then Solomon built a high place for Chemosh the abomination of Moab, and for Molech[61] the abomination of the Ammonites, on the mountain east of Jerusalem"[62] (1 Kings 11:4-7).

The biblical tradition again mentions the wisdom of Solomon (1 Kings 11:41; see previously 1 Kings 4:29-34 and 10:1-13) and fixes the length of his reign at 40 years (1 Kings 11:42).

As with David, it is difficult to assess as history the biblical traditions concerning Solomon's reign. The principal parts of 1 Kings 1-11 contain an early literary tradition that does seem to be taken from a story of Solomon's reign probably written not long after Solomon's death. However, this early tradition is often mixed with later Deuteronomistic additions and emendations by later editors.[63] Two different literary traditions seem to have been combined in 1 Kings 9:26-10:15, which concerns the journey to Ophir and the visit of the queen of Sheba. Part of the early tradition preserved in the Book of Kings tries to justify and exalt Solomon. This is even more true of later traditions. For example, 2 Chronicles 8:3-4 refers to Solomon's expedition to northern Syria: "And Solomon went to Hamath-Zobah and took it. He built Tadmor [Palmyra] in the wilderness and all the store-cities which he built in Hamath." However, the Hebrew text of 1 Kings 9:15-18 does not mention Hamath-Zobah or Tadmor and these names are probably a conforming alteration of 1 Kings 9:15-18 by the author of Chronicles.[64] In the same way, the Hebrew text of 1 Kings 9:19 mentions "Lebanon," in addition to Jerusalem, as a place where Solomon conducted building activities; however, "Lebanon" is missing in some manuscripts of the Greek translation known as the Septuagint and probably has no historical basis.

If we put aside overstatements and later additions, and discount for the flattering style of most of the texts, the principal points of the biblical

Biblical text vs. history

tradition seem generally trustworthy. For a historically reliable picture, we should rely on passages that are close to the style of contemporaneous annals and administrative texts.

Our extra-biblical knowledge of the history of the region during this period provides information regarding several aspects of Solomon's reign, especially in connection with his relations with Egypt,[65] but also with Phoenicia and Sheba. And archaeology helps us to understand Solomon's reputation as a builder and of the social transformation during his reign.

Although Egypt is hardly mentioned as a political power in the biblical tradition concerning David, several pharaohs do play an important political role during Solomon's reign. At the beginning of Solomon's reign, a pharaoh attacked Gezer; this pharaoh, as earlier mentioned, was probably Siamun, one of the last pharaohs of the 21st Dynasty.[66] Although Egyptian texts thus far discovered do not confirm the matrimonial alliance between Solomon and pharaoh's daughter, several studies have tried to show that there was a strong Egyptian cultural influence at Solomon's court. As evidence, these studies cite the way the royal cabinet was designed[67] and Solomon's organization of the country into 12 administrative districts.[68] Some scholars contend, however, that as to the organization of the country into 12 administrative districts, the influence was in the opposite direction.[69] The fact that the same type of administrative organization appears at about the same time in Israel and in Egypt is probably not a mere coincidence, although the direction of influence is not entirely clear. It is even possible that the literary tradition of the 12 sons of Jacob and of the 12 tribes of Israel finds its origin in this organization into 12 administrative districts, as G. W. Ahlström has suggested.[70] If true, the notion of 12 tribes of Israel could be a retrojection back from this period to the patriarchal period.

Another pharaoh mentioned in the biblical account of Solomon's reign (in connection with Jeroboam's revolt [1 Kings 11:26-42]) is called "Shishak." This is Sheshonk, the founder of the 22nd Dynasty. Shishak was a strong personality who wanted to restore Egyptian power, especially in the ancient Egyptian province of Canaan. His accession to the throne probably marks a turning point in Solomon's reign (c. 945 B.C.). Instead of an ally and friend, in Shishak Solomon was confronted with a hostile pharaoh who encouraged all of Solomon's opponents. Finally, in the fifth year of the reign of Solomon's successor, his son Rehoboam, Shishak organized a military expedition against the kingdoms of Judah and Israel (1 Kings 14:25-28).[71] It is therefore not surprising to find Shishak supporting Jeroboam's revolt. This political and military threat—and the independence of Damascus—probably increased the financial strains on Solomon. He received less tribute and had to spend more money on defense.

A literary tradition sheds some light on the relationship between Israel and Phoenicia at this time. Preserved in Phoenician annals, the tradition has been transmitted to us second- or third-hand through Menander of Ephesus, Alexander Dius Polyhistor and Josephus.[72] Although we must read these works with some caution,[73] because they evolved indirectly via two or three Greek intermediaries, they do comprise a serious literary tradition; they reflect the use of actual Tyrian archives or annals telling about the principal military expeditions and building activities of the Phoenician kings. Therefore some kind of Solomonic annals probably existed, containing a contemporaneous parallel—and may well have been inspired by the Phoenician annals. Thus Josephus quotes Dius Polyhistor, probably from his history of Phoenicia:[74]

"On the death of Abibalus [Abibaal], his son Hirom came to the throne. He leveled up the eastern part of the city with embankments, enlarged the town, united it by a causeway to the temple of Olympian Zeus, which was isolated on an island, and adorned it with offerings of gold; he also went up to Libanus and had timber cut down for the construction of temples . . . ."

Similarly, Menander of Ephesus, as quoted by Josephus, tells us:[75]

"On the death of Abibalus, the kingdom passed to his son Hirom, who lived fifty-three years and reigned thirty-four. He laid the embankment of the Broad Place, dedicated the golden pillar in the temple of Zeus, went and cut down cedar wood on the mount called Libanus for timber for the roofs of temples, demolished the ancient temples, and built new shrines dedicated to Heracles and Astarte. That of Heracles he erected first, in the month Peritius."

Even if these texts present historical problems of their own and are different in detail, they are probably based originally on the same annals of Tyre and so shed some light on the cultural and commercial relations between Hiram and Solomon. Furthermore, other later traditions as well as some Phoenician inscriptions confirm the important part played by the Phoenicians, mainly by the Tyrians, in the maritime trade of the Red Sea during the first millennium B.C.[76]

The queen of Sheba

Although in the Bible the story of the Ophir expedition through the Red Sea is now intertwined with the expedition of the queen of Sheba (1 Kings 9:26-10:22), these two events should not be confused. The queen of Sheba did not come on Phoenico-Israelite ships plying the Red Sea but traveled instead on camels and brought with her principally spices. These two features are characteristic of the Arabian peninsula. Although the story of the queen of Sheba contains various literary and legendary themes and was clearly written to glorify Solomon, Assyrian texts of the eighth-seventh centuries B.C. do mention a kingdom of Sheba in northern Arabia and several queens of northern Arabian kingdoms.[77] In light of these texts, the queen of Sheba could well have come from the Transjordanian desert, rather than from extreme southern Arabia.

Epigraphical discoveries from the period of the United Kingdom are still very rare. An exception is the famous Gezer calendar, a small limestone tablet containing a list of the 12 months with the agricultural work performed in each month. Despite this paucity, the period of David and Solomon was probably an important period of literary creation, much of it composed to support ideological and political goals of the government. Although a matter of considerable scholarly dispute, Israelite historiography probably began at this time.[78] It may have begun with a history of David's accession written by Abiathar the priest or by someone close to him. This probably paralleled the development of Phoenician historiography (see above). David and, even more so, Solomon probably promoted the writing of a history that brought together the early Israelite traditions originally connected with different sanctuaries (Shechem, Hebron, Beersheba, Shiloh, etc.). The original unification of these early traditions may have been the work of the famous and much discussed "Yahwist,"[79] also called J. The Yahwist or J identifies the earliest strand of tradition in the Pentateuch, according to the so-called documentary hypothesis, which divides the Pentateuch into four different strands, the other three being E (for Elohist), P (Priestly code) and D (Deuteronomist). J probably established the tradition of the 12 sons of Jacob and was the first to present Abraham, Isaac and Jacob as members of the same family.

Solomon's complex state administration required officials who could read and write. The development of national historical and legal traditions, as well as a new royal ideology, also required literate scribes. We may therefore assume that there were schools in Jerusalem and in the capitals of the administrative districts[80] as well as in some of the ancient city-states. The tradition of Solomon "the wise . . . who declared 3,000 proverbs and 1,005 songs" is clearly an exaggeration (1 Kings 4:32); nevertheless, the Solomonic period, probably in part under Egyptian influence, no doubt saw the birth of an important stream of Hebrew literature connected with royal ideology.

Solomon and archaeology   Archaeology also sheds some light on the activities of Solomon as a builder and on his transformation of Israelite society. According to William G. Dever, the tenth-century B.C. architectural remains "are not only the earliest evidence we possess of monumental architecture in ancient Israel but [the buildings] are among the most impressive."[81]

The Solomonic Temple was probably completely destroyed in 587 B.C. After the Israelites returned from the Babylonian Exile, a second temple was built. This was rebuilt by Herod the Great, but the Romans burned this edifice in 70 A.D. According to Ernest-Marie Laperrousaz, however, part of the Solomonic retaining wall of the Temple Mount can still be seen on the eastern side of the Temple Mount as it exists today.[82] This particular part of the wall begins north of the so-called straight joint that can be found on the eastern wall of the Temple Mount, 105.5 feet north of its southeast corner.

The most recent excavations in the City of David (a spur south of the present Temple Mount), led by Yigal Shiloh, have uncovered a huge stepped-stone structure probably built to support an enlarged platform on top of the northern part of the City of David. The platform may have supported a public building—perhaps the royal palace;[83] or the stepped-stone structure may also be the famous *millo* mentioned in 1 Kings 9:15.

RAPHAEL MAGNES

Jerusalem stepped-stone structure. Founded on the stubs of 13th-century B.C. Canaanite walls, this massive, 50-foot-high structure, right, may have been a retaining wall for an earthen platform atop Jerusalem. It may originally have been built in pre-Davidic Jebusite times and then reused by David and Solomon.

As noted, in 1 Kings 9:15-17 we are told that Solomon rebuilt three Canaanite cities which became part of his kingdom—Hazor, Megiddo and Gezer. Major excavations have been conducted at each of these three sites and Yigael Yadin[84] has shown that these three cities were rebuilt about the middle of the tenth century B.C. (the time of Solomon) according to almost identical fortification plans: a casemate wall* around the city and a gateway with three chambers on each side (that is, with four pairs of piers) of nearly the same dimensions. The ashlar stones of these three gateways are dressed the same way. All these similarities can best be explained as being part of the plans of the same architect or the same school of architects during Solomon's reign.

More generally, many archaeological sites in ancient Israel seem to have been built or rebuilt about the middle of the tenth century; some

* A casemate wall consists of two parallel walls with internal walls or casemates in effect creating internal rooms for storage, etc.

of them were later destroyed by Pharaoh Shishak's military expedition in about 925 B.C. These sites include new cities as well as new fortresses. Indeed a network of early Iron Age fortresses in the Negev can probably be connected with Solomon's reign.[85]

Israelite areas were inhabited not only by farmers and stockbreeders in villages but, beginning in the tenth century, also by craftsmen, merchants and functionaries serving in the army or in government administration and living in royal fortified cities. This social change, from a tribal society to a unified nation under a central administration probably accounts for the appearance of many public buildings in the new cities— the governor's palace,[86] storehouses, administrative buildings. At about this time, we begin to find many small precious objects. "The change in material culture during the tenth century is discernable not only in luxury items but also especially in ceramics"[87] which is of a higher quality. The economic growth and development of new cities was probably connected with an important population boom, natural in a period of peace and prosperity. In the area inhabited by Israel, the population probably doubled in a century, from the beginning of Saul's reign to the end of Solomon's.[88]

The rights of secession

This transformation of Israelite society and the burden of the new state administrative structures[89] encountered resistance at many levels of Israelite society.[90] This was especially so among the "house of Israel" (the northern tribes). The "house of Israel" wanted to retain its own religious and political traditions. Social tensions were also produced by the interchange of population involved in Solomon's military conscription and the forced levy (the corvée). No doubt all this served to sharpen the antagonisms between Israel and Judah.[91] The men of Judah probably got the better positions in the civil and military administration of the country, and this was doubtless resented by the "house of Israel." Solomon's death and the political errors of his successor soon revealed the unstable base on which David and Solomon had set their achievements.

Plate 1. The Sinai peninsula, the "great and terrible wilderness" (Deuteronomy 8:15) traversed by the Israelites on their Exodus wanderings. This view to the north was taken by a NASA satellite miles out in space. (Chapter II)

Plate 2. Wall painting in a tomb at Beni-hassan, Egypt. Painted about 1890 B.C., this fresco shows brightly garbed western Semites arriving in Egypt to trade. (Chapter II)

Plate 3. Ai (et-Tell). White stone ruins mark the site of the excavations. Whether there was a settlement here at the time the Bible says the Israelites conquered it is a matter of intense scholarly debate. (Chapter III)

Plate 4. Philistine pottery. Archaeologists have discovered distinctive Philistine artifacts, contradicting the millennia-old reputation the Philistines bear as a warlike society devoid of aesthetic values. (Chapter IV)

Plate 5. Ammonite king. No one knows for sure where this illegally excavated life-size limestone head, bearing a crown, was unearthed, but it was probably near Amman, Jordan, in the territory of the ancient Ammonites. The Ammonites often clashed with the Israelites. (Chapters IV and V)

Plate 6. Israelite bull figurine. Standing roughly 5 inches high, this bronze figurine dates to about 1200 B.C., the time of the Judges. It may resemble the statues set up by Jeroboam (921-910 B.C.) at Bethel and Dan. (Chapter V)

Plate 7. Wall relief from Sennacherib's palace at Nineveh. A family from the conquered Judahite city of Lachish walks barefooted into exile. Other panels from the series show the Assyrians storming Lachish and carrying off booty. (Chapter V)

Plate 8. Herodium. In 23 B.C. Herod the Great built this volcano-like palace-fortress in the Judean wilderness. Starting with a natural hill, he created an artificial mountain over and around it. Within the casemate walls that surround the palace-fortress are seven stories of rooms. (Chapter VIII)

WERNER BRAUN

Plate 9. Masada. This mountain palace-fortress in the Judean wilderness, built by Herod the Great (37-4 B.C.), was occupied by Jewish fighters during the First Revolt against Rome. (Chapter VIII)

F I V E

The Divided Monarchy

The Kingdoms of Judah and Israel

SIEGFRIED H. HORN

A FTER SOLOMON DIED, HIS KINGDOM FELL APART—JUDAH IN THE south and Israel in the north. What may have appeared to be a strong and united empire broke in two. The causes are found in Solomon's own reign. The outward glory of his kingdom—the sumptuous court ceremonials, the strong new fortresses, the powerful army, the great trading enterprises with foreign nations—none of this could hide the fact that by the time Solomon died about 931 B.C., his empire was badly fissured. His countrymen were quietly groaning because of the high taxes and forced labor he had imposed. The subjugated nations, also disgruntled, were just waiting for a sign of weakness to break loose from Jerusalem. The Bible mentions three rebels who had been active before Solomon's death—Jeroboam, an Israelite from the tribe of Ephraim; Hadad, an Edomite prince; and Rezon, an Aramean (1 Kings 11:14-40). There may have been a number of other incipient revolts during Solomon's lifetime.

Biblical writers, who were more concerned with the religious life of their heroes than with the political life of Israel, attribute the decline of Solomon's power and the breakup of his empire principally to the fact that the king strayed from the straight path of religious duty. True, he had built the Temple of Yahweh and at its dedication had offered a prayer reflecting a deep spiritual experience (1 Kings 8:22-61); nevertheless he fell into unprecedented polygamy and idolatry (1 Kings

11:9-11) that led him to adopt foolish policies and so hastened the fall of his kingdom.

Before recounting this chapter in the history of the Divided Kingdom of ancient Israel, a word about the sources is in order. Our chief source is the Bible, especially the historical books of Kings and Chronicles. Some additional historical information comes from the prophetic books, such as Hosea, Amos, Isaiah and Jeremiah. Kings was compiled during the Exile and Chronicles after the Exile, hence hundreds of years after the early events described in them; however, their narratives were often based on written biographical, chronological and annalistic records, such as the "Book of the Acts of Solomon" for that king's reign (1 Kings 11:41) or the "Book of the Chronicles of the Kings of Israel" for Jeroboam I (1 Kings 14:19) and the "Book of the Chronicles of the Kings of Judah" for Rehoboam (1 Kings 14:29).

The factual information contained in the historical books of the Bible has generally proved to be trustworthy and accurate insofar as this can be determined from contemporary cuneiform records that have turned up in Assyrian and Babylonian archives. Wherever events recorded in the Bible for this period are mentioned in such secular documents, they either corroborate or supplement the biblical information. Archaeological discoveries, such as the Siloam inscription from Jerusalem and the excavations at Lachish and other sites provide supplemental and corroborative information on King Hezekiah's reign. This archaeological material is but one example. In the course of this chapter, we will mention a number of others.

As soon as Solomon closed his eyes forever, the troubles started. Rehoboam, Solomon's son and the crown prince, appears to have been accepted immediately and without opposition as king by the southern tribes of Judah and Benjamin. Strong political ferment among the northern tribes, however, showed Rehoboam that he would need the northern tribes' approval and confirmation before he could rule effectively over the entire country. Accordingly, representatives of all the tribes of Israel were summoned to Shechem for Rehoboam's coronation as king over the whole nation. Shechem lay not in Judah, but in the heart of the territory settled by the northern tribes. It may have been chosen as the site of the convocation as a concession to the northern tribes, although it already had historical precedent as an Israelite rallying place (see Joshua 24).

Grievances over Solomon's excessive tax burdens and forced labor policy broke into the open at the Shechem convocation. Jeroboam, an Ephraimite, assumed the role of spokesman for the dissidents.

Jeroboam had once served as foreman of a labor gang in one of King Solomon's building enterprises in Jerusalem. Apparently he was a subversive even then; Solomon learned of his activities and sought to kill him. Jeroboam fled to Egypt, where Pharaoh Shishak I received him with open arms (1 Kings 11:26-40).

Rehoboam's folly

On hearing of Solomon's death, Jeroboam returned from exile and assumed the leadership of the northern tribes who had come to Shechem to negotiate with Rehoboam about the conditions under which they would accept Rehoboam as king.

Rehoboam rejected the advice of his more experienced counselors and refused to accede to all reasonable demands; instead, he threatened to increase the burdens. Open revolt erupted among the northern and eastern (Transjordanian) Israelites. Fearing for his life, Rehoboam fled from Shechem to Jerusalem, while the rebellious tribes announced their secession from the house of David and proclaimed Jeroboam their king (1 Kings 12:1-20; 2 Chronicles 10:1-16). Thus was born the kingdom of Israel, composed of the ten northern tribes. Rehoboam was left only with Judah and Benjamin, which now became the kingdom of Judah.

The prophet Shemaiah counseled Rehoboam not to go to war against the northern tribes. Although initially Rehoboam heeded Shemaiah's advice, later he apparently fought several bloody wars with Jeroboam (1 Kings 12:24, 14:30; 2 Chronicles 12:15).

In the fifth year of Rehoboam's reign (c. 926 B.C.) the Egyptian Pharaoh Shishak I (Sheshonk in Greek sources) cut a devastating swath through Judah (1 Kings 14:25-28; 2 Chronicles 12:2-4), a historic attack that Shishak commemorated in a victory relief on a wall of the temple of Karnak.[1] Shishak's attack may account for the fact that Rehoboam fortified a number of cities that guarded the roads leading to Jerusalem (2 Chronicles 11:5-12).

Rehoboam, like his father Solomon, had a large harem. Rehoboam's mother, an Ammonite woman in Solomon's harem, probably influenced him to promote the worship of pagan gods, whose rites were considered an abomination by the conservative strata of Judahite society (1 Kings 14:22-24; 2 Chronicles 11:21, 12:5). He ruled for 17 years and died about 913 B.C.[2]

Jeroboam becomes king of Israel

After Rehoboam fled from the Shechem tribal convocation, where he had expected to be crowned king of all Israel, Jeroboam was made king by acclamation of the northern and eastern (Transjordanian) Israelite tribes (1 Kings 12:20.

Jeroboam used Shechem as his first capital (1 Kings 12:25),[3] but later transferred his capital to Tirzah (1 Kings 14:17). Tirzah was probably at the present mound of Tell el-Far'ah, about seven miles northwest of Nablus. Excavations have been carried out at this mound, which is larger than Megiddo. Definite clues as to its identification as Tirzah have not yet been found.[4]

Jeroboam of Israel was forced to fight continual wars against his disgruntled southern neighbor, first against Rehoboam and then against Rehoboam's successor Abijam (1 Kings 14:30, 15:7). Moreover, Israel as well as Judah was devastated during Shishak's military campaign of 926 B.C. Although the Bible mentions only Judah and Jerusalem as the victims of the Egyptian attack, the evidence clearly shows that Shishak invaded the northern kingdom as well. He inscribed the names of many northern cities on his Karnak victory relief.[5] A fragment of one of Shishak's victory stelae was even discovered at Megiddo, one of the northern kingdom's most important cities.[6] Why Shishak attacked the northern kingdom is not entirely clear. He had welcomed Jeroboam when Jeroboam had fled from Solomon. Perhaps Jeroboam had agreed to become Shishak's tribute-paying vassal and had then reneged. It is difficult to understand otherwise why Shishak so quickly turned against Jeroboam once he became king of the northern tribes.

Jeroboam's religious apostasy   For political reasons, Jeroboam introduced religious rites and practices in Israel that drastically departed from the worship of an invisible god Yahweh. At Bethel and Dan—at opposite ends of his kingdom—he built temples or open-air sanctuaries in competition with the Judahite temple in Jerusalem. At Bethel and Dan, Jeroboam set up images of young bulls to represent Yahweh in visible form (1 Kings 12:27-31) (although some interpret the bulls as pedestals on which the invisible Yahweh stood). For two centuries, the worship of these golden calves was known as the "sin of Jeroboam." Except for three of his successors, all the kings of Israel followed Jeroboam in this aberration.

An ostracon* found at Samaria throws an interesting light on this calf worship. The inscription on the ostracon includes the name of a man called Egelyau, which means either "Yahweh is a calf" or "The calf of Yahweh." The name suggests that Yahweh was worshipped in the form of a young bull, just as the Canaanites of Ugarit worshipped their god El as a bull. Recently, excavations in northern Samaria revealed a cult site with a bronze bull that had undoubtedly served as an object of worship.[7] Although this find dates to the period of the Judges, it serves as a good example of what Jeroboam's cult places and images may have looked like.[8]

Jeroboam established new festivals in the eighth month of the Hebrew ecclesiastical calendar; the principal festivals in Judah, in contrast, continued to be observed in the seventh month (1 Kings 12:32-33). From a study of Israelite chronology it would appear that Jeroboam also introduced a civil calendar that began in the spring, in contrast to the one in use in the southern kingdom, where the civil year began in the autumn. The kings of Judah used the traditional accession-year system to reckon their regnal years, so Jeroboam—to differentiate his own kingdom—introduced the Egyptian non-accession-year system.** In these ways, Jeroboam widened the religious and cultural chasm between Israel and Judah as much as possible.

---

* An ostracon (plural, ostraca) is an inscribed potsherd (the inscription being either written on with ink or scratched into the surface with a sharp instrument).

** See next page for this footnote.

COURTESY OF THE ISRAEL DEPARTMENT OF ANTIQUITIES AND MUSEUMS

Cult stand. This elaborate Canaanite pottery stand from Taanach (about five miles southeast of Megiddo) dates to the late tenth century B.C. Four registers contain tableaux modeled in high relief, and a platform with a shallow basin crowns the 21-inch-high stand. The bottom register depicts a nude female figure, perhaps the mother-goddess Asherah, holding the ears of flanking lions. Winged sphinxes seem to stand guard on each side of the opening in the second register.

Lions appear again on the flanks of the third register; between them, two goats stand in heraldic positions and nibble on a stylized tree (perhaps a "tree of life"), a motif associated with Asherah. The top register displays a calf facing left between a pair of voluted columns. A winged sun-disc seems to ride upon the calf's back. The calf may represent the Canaanite storm-god Baal, who is generally associated with a bull in Near Eastern iconography.

Jeroboam ruled over Israel for 22 years and died about 910 B.C.

Before continuing to trace the separate histories of the northern

** The "accession-year system" employed, for example, by the Assyrian, Babylonian and Persian kings, counted the remainder of the calendar year in which a king had come to the throne as his "Accession Year." The regnal year which began at the first New Year's Day in his reign was consequently labeled "Year One."

The "non-accession-year system," on the other hand, employed, for example, in Egypt, considered the remaining part of the calendar year in which a king came to the throne as his "Year One," regardless of its length. The regnal year that began with the first New Year's Day in his reign was consequently labeled Year Two." (See Edwin R. Thiele, *The Mysterious Numbers of the Hebrew Kings* [Grand Rapids, MI: Zondervan, rev. ed., 1983], pp. 53-55).

kingdom of Israel and the southern kingdom of Judah, a warning may be in order. The succession of kings and dynasties in this period is laboriously complex, and there is no way to present the interlocking, overlapping and simultaneous reigns and events in an easily comprehensible way. To make matters worse, the names of the various kings are confusingly similar. Sometimes the same name is even repeated. In other cases, a king may have more than one name.

One reason for the similarity in names is that ancient names were often hypocoristic—that is, they consist of a compressed sentence. One of the most common elements in these names is an abbreviated form of the ineffable name of the Israelite God, Yahweh (YHWH). One abbreviated form of this name consists of the Hebrew letters *YH* or *YHW*, which might be pronounced "Yah" or "Yahu," respectively. As incorporated into ancient names and transliterated into Latin letters, *Yah* and *Yahu* appear as *Jeh-* or *Jo-* or *Jeho-* at the beginning of names (*J* being the Germanic transliteration of the Hebrew *Y*) and as *-iah* at the end of names. Thus we have Jehu, Joash, Jehoahaz, Jotham, etc. We also have Athaliah, Amaziah, Uzziah, Zachariah, Hezekiah, Josiah, etc.

To present this complex succession of kings in some orderly fashion, I have made divisions by chunks of time, beginning at the end of the tenth century B.C. with the deaths of Rehoboam and Jeroboam (we may now refer to the latter as Jeroboam I). In this way, we proceed through 723/722 B.C., when the Assyrian conquest of Samaria brought an end to the northern kingdom of Israel. Then, with but one kingdom left, we proceed to 586 B.C. when the Babylonian destruction of Jerusalem brought an end to the southern kingdom of Judah.

The divided kingdom at a glance   From the standpoint of religion, the nadir in this period was the reign of King Ahab in Israel. The zeniths were the important religious reforms instituted first by King Hezekiah and then by King Josiah, both of Judah, in the late eighth and late seventh centuries B.C. Both kings sought to centralize worship of Yahweh in the Jerusalem Temple and to obliterate outlying shrines dedicated to Yahweh and other gods. Throughout this period, the prophets exhorted king and commoner alike to adhere to the way of Yahweh.

The most important military events were the conquest of Israel by the Assyrians in 723/722 B.C. and the conquest of Judah by the Babylonians in 586 B.C. Also of considerable significance was the Syro-Ephraimite war (c. 734-732 B.C.).

Politically, the southern kingdom of Judah was far more stable than the northern kingdom of Israel. Judah retained the Davidic dynasty with only a minor break of a few years throughout its history. (The exception was its only woman ruler, Athaliah.) The northern kingdom of Israel, on the other hand, changed royal families so often that when its 209 years of existence ended in 722 B.C., 20 different kings belonging to 10 different families or dynasties had reigned over the country. Born in rebellion, the kingdom of Israel struggled through its brief history with

city
★ capital city
▲ mountain peak

miles 0 10 20 30 40
km 0 10 20 30 40 50 60

PHOENICIA

★ Damascus

Tyre ★

Dan ●

DIVIDED KINGDOM
ISRAEL AND JUDAH

ARAM

Mt. Carmel ▲

Sea of
Galilee

Megiddo ●

Ramot-Gilead ●

Tirzah ★
Samaria ★
★ Shechem

Jordan River

*Mediterranean
Sea*

I S R A E L

● Rabbah

Bethel ●

A M M O N

Ashdod ●
● Ekron
★ Jerusalem

Ashkelon ●
Lachish ●

● Bethlehem

Gaza ●

● Hebron

Dead Sea

P H I L I S T I A

● Arad
● Beersheba

M O A B

J U D A H

★ Kir-Hareseth

Wadi Zered

● Bozrah

E D O M

E A S T E R N
D E S E R T

ADAPTED FROM *THE MOODY ATLAS OF BIBLE LANDS* BY BARRY J. BEITZEL an unending series of coups d'état and political upheavals. Although both in territory and population, it was much larger than Judah, Israel was never able to match Judah in political stability.

I. The First Half of the Ninth Century B.C. (913 to 841)

IN JUDAH:

In 913 B.C. Solomon's son Rehoboam was succeeded by his son Abijam (also called Abijah), who reigned only till 911 B.C. Nevertheless, this was enough time for Abijam to fight a war with Israel, which at the time was still ruled by Jeroboam I. According to the biblical text, Abijam had all the vices of his father Rehoboam (1 Kings 15:1-8; 2 Chronicles 13:1-14:1).

With the accession of Abijam's son Asa, once more a good king, like David, ruled Judah (911-869 B.C.). Asa banished all the male prostitutes from his realm and suppressed idol worship. He also removed his Ammonite grandmother (Solomon's widow) from influence at court because she had erected an image for Asherah (1 Kings 15:10-13).

The first years of Asa's reign, which he devoted to religious reforms, were peaceful. But later Asa was attacked by the Cushites under Zerah, probably Ethiopians from the eastern shore of the Red Sea (2 Chronicles 14:9-14).[9] Then about 895 B.C. King Baasha of Israel occupied part of northern Judah (2 Chronicles 16:1). Asa did not dare meet Baasha's army with his own inferior forces, so he induced Benhadad of Syria to attack Israel. For this lack of faith in Yahweh's help Asa was severely rebuked by the prophet Hanani (2 Chronicles 16:1-10). In his last years, because he suffered from poor health (2 Chronicles 16:12), Asa appointed his son Jehoshaphat co-ruler (as the chronological data indicate: 1 Kings 15:9-24; 2 Chronicles 14:1-16:14).

Asa's son Jehoshaphat (872-848 B.C.) continued the religious reforms of his father. Although Jehoshaphat failed to remove all pagan high places, he directed the Levites and priests to travel throughout the country and preach the law (1 Kings 22:43; 2 Chronicles 17:7-9). Jehoshaphat also ended the long feud between Judah and Israel by allying himself with the Israelite dynasty of Omri. Indeed, Jehoshaphat even gave his son Jehoram,* the crown prince of Judah, in marriage to Athaliah, the daughter of King Ahab of Israel (2 Kings 8:8, 26), a union that unfortunately opened the door to Baal worship in Judah, as we shall see. Jehoshaphat also assisted the northern kings in their military campaigns. With Ahab he fought against Ramoth-Gilead (1 Kings 22:4-33; 2 Chronicles 18:28), and with Joram* of Israel he fought against Moab (2 Kings 3:4-27). He also fought a strong confederacy of Edomites, Moabites and Ammonites (2 Chronicles 20:1-30). Some nations, such as the

---

* The names Jehoram and Joram are used interchangeably in the Bible. For the sake of convenience and clarity, however, Jehoram is used in this chapter to designate the son of Jehoshaphat, king of Judah, and Joram to designate the son of Ahab, king of Israel (see 2 Kings 8:16).

Israel's Kings

Saul	*c. 1020-1000 B.C.*
David	*c. 1000-961 B.C.*
Solomon	*c. 961-921 B.C.*

Kingdom of Judah *921-586 B.C.*		Kingdom of Israel *921-722/1 B.C.*	
Rehoboam	*921-913*	Jeroboam I	*921-910*
Abijam (Abijah)	*913-911*		
Asa	*911-869*		
		Nadab	*910-909*
		Baasha	*909-886*
		Elah	*886-885*
		Zimri	*885*
Jehoshaphat	*872-848*		
		Omri	*885-874*
		Ahab	*874-853*
		Ahaziah	*853-852*
Jehoram	*854-841*	Joram	*852-841*
Ahaziah	*841*		
Athaliah	*841-835*	Jehu	*841-814*
Jehoash	*835-796*	Jehoahaz	*814-798*
Amaziah	*796-790*	Joash	*798-782*
Uzziah		Jeroboam II	*793-753*
(Azariah)	*790-739*		
		Zachariah	*753-752*
		Shallum	*752*
Jotham	*750-731*	Menahem	*752-742*
		Pekahiah	*742-740*
Ahaz	*735-715*	Pekah	*740-732*
		Hoshea	*732-723/722*
Hezekiah	*729-686*		
Manasseh	*696-641*		
Amon	*641-639*		
Josiah	*639-608*		
Jehoahaz	*608*		
Jehoiakim	*608-598*		
Jehoiachin	*598-597*		
Zedekiah	*597-586*		

Destruction of Jerusalem *586 B.C.*

Philistines and Arabs, were so impressed with Jehoshaphat's accomplishments that they sought his friendship. Jehoshaphat also attempted to revive Solomon's Ophir expeditions, but this effort failed when Jehoshaphat's ships were wrecked at Ezion-Geber (2 Chronicles 20:35-37; 1 Kings 22:48).

At first, Jehoshaphat's son Jehoram (854-841 B.C.) was associated on the throne with his father. Of Jehoram, however, nothing good is said. Influenced by Athaliah, his wicked and idolatrous wife from Israel, Jehoram went so far as to encourage Baal worship in Judah (2 Kings 8:18). He fought unsuccessful wars with the Philistines and Arabs (2 Chronicles 21:16-17, 22:1), and lost Edom, which became independent again (2 Kings 8:20). In the end, he died of an incurable disease, as the prophet Elijah had predicted (2 Kings 8:16-24; 2 Chronicles 21:12-19).

Jehoram's son Ahaziah (841 B.C.) followed the corrupt ways of his father and his mother Athaliah. Ahaziah joined his uncle Joram of Israel in an unsuccessful war against the Syrians (2 Kings 8:26-29). On a visit to Joram of Israel, Ahaziah was wounded in a coup d'état. The coup brought an end to the reign of Joram of Israel—and to the Omride dynasty. Ahaziah fled to Megiddo but soon died there from his wounds (2 Kings 9:14-28; 2 Chronicles 22:1-9).

About this time, a religious center flourished at Kuntillet 'Ajrud, a site halfway between Beersheba and Elath (about 40 miles south of Kadesh-Barnea) in the Sinai desert. Here in 1975 and 1976 Ze'ev Meshel excavated buildings that apparently were used by travelers from Phoenicia and the kingdoms of Israel and Judah. The travelers deposited votive objects as offerings and prayed for help and blessings to the gods El, Baal, Yahweh and, according to one interpretation, Yahweh's consort Asherah. The pottery and script of the inscriptions, as well as the names mentioned in the inscriptions, indicate that this religious center operated in the late ninth or early eighth century B.C. This was the time when several Judahite kings enjoyed close relations with the kings of Israel and, through Israel, were influenced by Phoenician culture and religion. It was a time when pagan idolatrous rites and cults were rampant in both Hebrew kingdoms, as the Bible clearly states (1 Kings 18:19; 2 Kings 11:18), and as the inscriptions of Kuntillet 'Ajrud confirm.[10]

IN ISRAEL:

Nadab murdered—a new dynasty in Israel In Israel, Jeroboam I was succeeded in 910 B.C. by his son Nadab (910-909 B.C.). Nadab's reign was cut short, however, when he was murdered by Baasha. What official position Baasha had before he murdered Nadab is not known. The Bible records only his father's name, Ahijah, and that he came from the tribe of Issachar. Nadab's assassination ended the first dynasty of the northern kingdom of Israel (1 Kings 15:15-29). This fearful precedent was to be repeated again and again.

Kuntillet 'Ajrud. At this desert way-station halfway between Beersheba and Elath, ninth- to seventh-century B.C. travelers rested and prayed. Modern archaeologists have discovered abundant evidence here of idolatrous worship.

Nadab's murderer Baasha became king of Israel (909-886 B.C.), thus beginning a new dynasty. Baasha harassed Judah and even occupied parts of its territory. He lost this territory, however, when he was attacked by Benhadad of Damascus, who had received a bribe from Asa of Judah for that purpose (1 Kings 15:16-16:7). Baasha's dynasty ended like Nadab's before him. Baasha's son Elah (886-885 B.C.) was murdered by Zimri, one of Baasha's generals, in the capital Tirzah after a reign of less than two years (1 Kings 16:8-10).

Elah murdered—a new dynasty in Israel

Zimri then assumed the kingship of Israel but reigned only seven days (885 B.C.). He made use of his brief reign, however, by killing all of Baasha's relatives and friends. As soon as it became known that Zimri had assassinated Baasha's son Elah, the army, then engaged in a campaign against the Philistines, proclaimed Omri, another general, king. Omri marched on Tirzah and attacked. Although he knew that resistance was futile, Zimri refused to surrender. He set fire to the palace and perished in the flames (1 Kings 16:11-18).

The Omride dynasty　　Omri (885-874 B.C.) founded a new dynasty of four kings who successively occupied the throne over a period of 44 years (885-841 B.C.). At the outset, Omri had to fight another contender for the throne, Tibni, who seems to have had a considerable following. Only after four years of internal strife was Omri able to exterminate Tibni and his followers (1 Kings 16:21-23).[11]

Omri's 12-year reign was more important politically than the Bible indicates. He moved the capital from Tirzah to Samaria. By selecting this strategic site for his capital, Omri did for Israel what David had done more than a hundred years earlier in selecting Jerusalem. Samaria was built on a 400-foot-high hill situated in a cup-like plain; it could be easily defended. It appears never to have been taken by force of arms; in the end, it surrendered only for lack of water or food. Excavations at Samaria have verified the fact, intimated in the biblical records, that the site had been uninhabited before Omri's time. With the transfer of his capital from Tirzah to Samaria, Omri began an extensive defense-building operation, which his son Ahab completed.[12]

Whether Omri himself had military encounters with the Assyrians to the east is unknown, but the Assyrian records for the next 100 years refer to Israel as "the land of the house of Omri," even long after Omri's dynasty had vanished. Omri's personality, political success and business enterprises must have made him famous not only in the eyes of his contemporaries but to later generations as well.

Omri established cordial relations with his Phoenician neighbors and married his son Ahab to Jezebel, daughter of the king of Tyre. This alliance introduced the worship of Baal and Asherah into Israel to an extent previously unknown (1 Kings 16:25). He also granted economic concessions to Damascus and allowed Syrian traders to operate shops in Samaria's bazaars (1 Kings 20:34).

Omri was also successful in subduing Moab and making it an Israelite vassal, as the lengthy inscription on the famous Mesha Stele admits. In the Mesha Stele (or Moabite Stone, as it is also called), Mesha, king of Moab, states that "Omri, king of Israel, had oppressed Moab many days, for Kemosh was angry with his land."[13] How valuable the possession of Moab was for Israel can be seen from the tribute paid by Moab to Omri's son Ahab. It is said to have amounted—probably annually—to "a hundred thousand lambs, and the wool of a hundred thousand rams" (2 Kings 3:4).

Ahab　　In 874 B.C. Omri was succeeded on the throne of Israel by his son Ahab. A morally weak ruler, Ahab had neither the strength nor the resolve to resist his strong-willed Phoenician wife Jezebel, who was determined

Mesha Stele. Erected by Mesha, king of Moab in the ninth century B.C., the basalt stele stands about 40 inches high and about 24 inches wide. The inscription in Moabite, which is closely related to Hebrew, expresses Mesha's gratitude to his god for delivering the Moabites from Israelite rule.

to make her own religion supreme. By bringing from her homeland hundreds of cult personnel of Baal and Asherah, by introducing the rites of the Canaanite cult system and by persecuting and killing the worshippers of Yahweh, Jezebel caused a religious crisis of the first magnitude (1 Kings 18:4, 19). Because of this crisis and because of the fact that some of the most prominent religious leaders of that age, Elijah and Elisha, lived and worked in the northern kingdom, the Bible devotes much space to Ahab.

Elijah stands out in the fight for the survival of Yahwism. A three-and-a-half-year drought, predicted by the prophet as a judgment of Yahweh, brought Ahab's land close to economic ruin. The drought ended when Elijah was victorious over the priests of Baal on Mt. Carmel in a contest between the power of Yahweh and Baal (1 Kings 18:17-40).

Nevertheless, as long as Ahab ruled, the cult of Baal flourished.

Strangely enough, Ahab did not give Baal names to his own children—probably he did not dare. All their known names—Ahaziah, Joram and Athaliah—contain the abbreviated form of Yahweh. Ahab's subjects, however, had fewer scruples in this regard. Numerous personal names in subsequent periods were connected with Baal—Abibaal, Baala, Baalzamar, Baalzakar and others—as ostraca found during the excavations of Samaria show.[14]

Ahab was famous for his "ivory house" (1 Kings 22:39; Amos 3:15). Numerous beautifully carved ivory plaques found in the excavations of Samaria reveal that the interior of his palace and some of its furniture were probably paneled with ivory. The designs of these ivory plaques are similar to those found in ivory decorations discovered in the ruins of ancient palaces in Syria and Assyria.[15]

As a warrior, Ahab was moderately successful. Twice he defeated the Syrians. Loot from these two victorious wars enriched him tremendously, and his victories won him economic concessions in Damascus (1 Kings 20:21, 34). Hence, for a time, he became one of the most powerful rulers west of Assyria. When the Assyrian king Shalmaneser III advanced against Ahab's old enemy Syria, Ahab this time joined Syria and other allies to make common cause against the Assyrians. Ahab mustered the greatest number of chariots of any of the allies. Thus states Shalmaneser in a list of his opponents in the battle of Karkar in northern Syria.[16] The historic rock inscription on the upper Tigris states that of the 3,940 enemy chariots fighting against the Assyrians, 2,000 belonged to Ahab; the other ten allies had mustered altogether only 1,940 chariots. Of the 52,000 foot soldiers arrayed against the Assyrians, Ahab furnished 10,000.[17] When the battle of Karkar had checked Shalmaneser's advance, Ahab, conscious of his strength, immediately turned against Syria. His aim was to regain possession of the Transjordanian city of Ramoth-Gilead, but his army was beaten and he died in the battle (1 Kings 22).

Joram murdered—a new dynasty in Israel

Ahab was succeeded by his son Ahaziah (853-852 B.C.), the third ruler of the Omride dynasty in Israel. Nothing important happened in Ahaziah's short reign except perhaps the abortive expedition to Ophir made in cooperation with Jehoshaphat of Judah (2 Chronicles 20:35-37). Since he left no son, Ahaziah was succeeded on the throne by his brother Joram (852-841 B.C.), the last of the Omrides. During Joram's reign, Mesha king of Moab rebelled. A military expedition against Moab was undertaken in cooperation with the forces of Judah and Edom. Initially the expedition was disastrous for Moab. Nevertheless Israel proved unable to reestablish control over Moab, as the Bible record hints (2 Kings 3:4-27), and as the inscription of King Mesha on the Moabite Stone clearly claims.[18]

Joram also fought several wars against the Syrians. Through the intervention of the prophet Elisha, near disasters were twice averted (2 Kings 6 and 7). Like his father Ahab, Joram attempted to regain the

Transjordanian city of Ramoth-Gilead from the Syrians, but he too failed in the effort. Wounded by Hazael of Syria, Joram went to the city of Jezreel to recuperate. There he was murdered by one of his army commanders, Jehu. Jehu proceeded to wipe out all members of the royal house of Omri, including Jezebel, the Phoenician queen mother. Jehu then usurped the throne himself (2 Kings 8:28-29, 9:24-10:17).

Since the story of the accession of Jehu to the throne throws an interesting light on the awesome political power that some of the prophets of Israel wielded, a little more may be said about it. It was Elisha who had Jehu, a general of the army, anointed as king while Joram, the legitimate king, was still alive and on the throne. This act was apparently accepted without protest by Jehu's fellow officers, by the army and by the population in general (2 Kings 9:1-13). Elisha could contemptuously talk in public to the king without fear of being killed or even arrested; in 2 Kings 3:13-14, Elisha is said to have consented to talk to King Joram only because he was in the company of the king of Judah, whom the prophet respected. While Israel's kings considered prophets such as Elijah and Elisha their "enemies" (1 Kings 21:20), these kings seem to have had a superstitious fear that they dare not lay hands on the prophets. Elijah never fled from King Ahab, whose wrath he evidently did not fear, but Elijah was afraid of the foreign queen Jezebel and was well aware of her muderous designs on his life (1 Kings 19:1-3).

II. From the Middle of the Ninth to the Middle of the Eighth Century (841-750 B.C.)

IN JUDAH:

When we left the Judahite story, King Ahaziah of Judah had died from wounds received in the coup d'état that occurred while he was visiting his uncle Joram, king of Israel. The coup brought an end to the Omride dynasty in Israel.

When Ahaziah of Judah died, his mother Athaliah seized the throne and ruled for six years (841-835 B.C.). She was not, of course, a descendant of King David; her six-year rule marked the only interruption in the direct line of Davidic rulership in the kingdom of Judah. A daughter of the cruel and unscrupulous Queen Jezebel of Israel, Athaliah exterminated "all the seed royal" in Judah so that her own rule might be assured. However, her henchmen missed the infant prince Jehoash,* who was rescued by the high priest Jehoiada and his wife (2 Kings 11:1-3).

A woman on the throne of Judah

The high priest Jehoiada raised and educated Jehoash in his own home. When Jehoash was seven years old, Jehoiada had Jehoash crowned king (835-796 B.C.). Crying "Treason, treason," Athaliah was murdered

---

* The names Jehoash and Joash are used interchangeably in the Bible. For the sake of convenience and clarity, however, Jehoash is used in this chapter to designate the son of Ahaziah, king of Judah, and Joash to designate the son of Jehoahaz, king of Israel.

by Jehoiada's men (2 Kings 11:4-21).

As long as the young king allowed his mentor, the high priest Jehoiada, to guide his affairs, he acted prudently and piously, removing Baal worship and promoting extensive Temple repairs (2 Kings 12:1-16; 2 Chronicles 24:1-14). After Jehoiada's death, however, Jehoash became indifferent, and even had his benefactor's son Zechariah stoned to death for reproving him because of his evil deeds (2 Chronicles 24:15-22).

When Hazael of Damascus marched against Jehoash he bought the Syrians off with some of the Temple treasures. This act of cowardliness and Jehoash's murder of Zechariah, together with the people's domestic and religious grievances, apparently created deep-seated resentment and opposition to Jehoash. As a result, he was assassinated by his own servants. He was buried in the city of David, but, because of his unpopularity, not in the royal sepulchers (2 Kings 12:17-21; 2 Chronicles 24:25).

Jehoash's son Amaziah (796-767 B.C.) first disposed of his father's murderers and then consolidated his own position as ruler. Next he planned the reconquest of Edom, which had formerly belonged to Judah, but had successfully rebelled. Amaziah hired 100,000 mercenaries from Israel, but later discharged them at the direction of "a man of God." With his own Judahite forces he was victorious over the Edomites and conquered their capital, Sela.[19] Meanwhile, the discharged and disgruntled mercenaries plundered the cities of northern Judah on their way back to their own homeland.

Israel and Judah at war   Returning from his victorious campaign against the Edomites, Amaziah became so overbearing that he challenged Joash of Israel to fight. This unwise move proved disastrous, for Judah was soundly defeated and humiliated. It then became for all practical purposes a vassal of Israel. Having turned away from Yahweh and having adopted "the gods of the men of Seir" as "his gods," Amaziah lost the confidence of his people. They rose up against him in open revolt, and he was forced to flee for his life. He got as far as Lachish, where he was assassinated (2 Kings 14:1-20; 2 Chronicles 25:1-28).

Amaziah was succeeded on the throne by his son, Azariah, whose second and better-known name—probably a throne name—was Uzziah. Uzziah reigned from 790 to 739 B.C. His reign is described as upright, successful and prosperous. He promoted the economic development of the country (2 Chronicles 26:10) and raised a large and well-equipped army (2 Chronicles 26:11-15). With this army he waged successful campaigns against the Philistines and Arabs (2 Chronicles 26:7), recovered Elath (Ezion-Geber) at the Gulf of Elath (2 Kings 14:22) and probably also Edomite territory lying between Judah and the gulf. The Ammonites decided to buy Uzziah off with gifts (2 Chronicles 26:8). During Uzziah's reign a severe earthquake apparently occurred, for it was remembered for centuries and was referred to by later writers (Amos 1:1; Zechariah 14:5).

BRITISH MUSEUM

Black Obelisk. In one of the 20 reliefs on this black stone monolith, King Shalmaneser III of Assyria (859-824 B.C.) depicted King Jehu of Israel kneeling before him while Jehu's attendants offered tribute. The annals of Shalmaneser III date this event to 841 B.C.

During Uzziah's reign, both Egypt and Assyria were politically weak, which helped Uzziah as well as Jeroboam II of Israel to make their nations prosperous and powerful. In 750 B.C. the realms of the two kingdoms approximated the area that David and Solomon had ruled over. This period of prosperity was to be the last. In 745 B.C. a strong Assyrian king, Tiglath-pileser III, ascended the throne. His rule marked the rebirth of the Assyrian empire and the beginning of a rapid decline in the power of both Israel and Judah.

IN ISRAEL:

Jehu was the Israelite general who murdered King Joram, thus bringing an end to the Omride dynasty. Even before the murder, Jehu had been anointed king at Ramoth-Gilead by a messenger of Elisha.

Thus began the dynasty of Jehu. Jehu ruled from 841 to 814 B.C. He eradicated Baal worship as thoroughly as he could. For his righteous zeal in this respect he was commended by the prophet Elisha, and a promise was made that his descendants would sit on Israel's throne to the fourth generation (2 Kings 10:30). Accordingly, his dynasty reigned over the country for about 90 years, nearly half the time of Israel's existence. However, Jehu did not break with Jeroboam's calf worship, and his reform was, as a result, considered incomplete (2 Kings 10:31).

Jehu voluntarily became a vassal of the Assyrian monarch Shalmaneser

Jehu

III. Jehu began paying tribute to Assyria as soon as he ascended the throne. This vassal relationship is depicted on the four sides of Shalmaneser's Black Obelisk, now in the British Museum, which Austen Henry Layard discovered in 1846 at Nimrud. The Israelite king Jehu—the earliest for which a contemporary representation exists—is shown kneeling before Shalmaneser, while Jehu's attendants carry as tribute "silver, gold, a golden *saplu*-bowl,* a golden vase with pointed bottom, golden tumblers, golden buckets, tin, a staff for Shalmaneser and a wooden *puruhtu*.**"[20] This event is dated 841 B.C. in the Assyrian records[21]—which was the first year of Jehu's reign. Jehu evidently considered it prudent to reverse Israel's policy toward Assyria, which had been one of hostility, in order to secure Assyrian help against Israel's chief enemy, Hazael of Syria.

When Jehu died in 814 B.C., his son Jehoahaz ascended the throne of Israel (814-798 B.C.). The 17 years of Jehoahaz's reign were marked by continual wars against the Syrians, who oppressed Israel, first under Hazael and later under Hazael's son Benhadad III (2 Kings 13:1-3). Israel lost much of its territory and its army in these wars; it was left with only 10 chariots, 50 horsemen and 10,000 foot soldiers (2 Kings 13:7). A comparison of Jehoahaz's ten chariots with Ahab's 2,000 chariots 50 years earlier reveals the great loss of power the kingdom of Israel suffered. We do not know who finally rescued Israel from the Syrians; in 2 Kings 13:5 a "savior" is referred to, but not identified. It may have been Jehoahaz's son Joash (see 2 Kings 13:25), or Adad-nirari III, king of Assyria; or perhaps some other person altogether.

Jehoahaz died in 798 B.C.; he was succeeded by his son Joash (798-782 B.C.). Joash is listed by Adad-nirari III as having paid tribute to Assyria.[22] This seems to have freed Joash to wage war against the Syrians. Fortunately, he had more success with this ancient foe than his father Jehoahaz had had. Joash defeated the Syrians three times and recovered all the territory lost by his father (2 Kings 13:25). Challenged by Amaziah of Judah, Joash was unwillingly forced to fight his southern neighbor—the first war in 100 years between the two brother nations. Joash bested Judah's army at the battle of Beth-Shemesh, captured the Judahite king and victoriously entered Jerusalem. He broke down part of the city's defenses and took vessels from the Temple, royal treasures, and some hostages back to Samaria (2 Kings 14:8-14).

The chronological data require a co-regency between Joash and his son, Jeroboam (referred to as Jeroboam II) for about 12 years. Political prudence on the part of Joash may have led to this measure. Knowing the danger a state experiences when a sudden vacancy on the throne occurs, he probably appointed his son as co-ruler and successor when he began his wars of liberation against Syria. In this way, continuity of the dynasty was assured even if the king lost his life during a military

* An Assyrian word whose meaning is still unknown.

** An Assyrian word whose meaning is still unknown.

campaign.

Jeroboam II's recorded reign began in 793 B.C. and lasted 41 years (793-753 B.C.), including the 12 years of co-regency with his father. Unfortunately, little is known of his apparently successful reign. The Bible devotes only seven verses to his life (2 Kings 14:23-29), but they indicate that he regained so much lost territory that, with the exception of the territory held by the kingdom of Judah, his kingdom was almost as large as the empire of David and Solomon. He restored Israelite rule over the coastal and inland regions of Syria to the north, conquered Damascus and Hamath, and occupied Transjordan south to the Dead Sea, which probably means that he made Ammon and Moab vassals to Israel. These tremendous gains were possible only because Assyria was suffering a period of political weakness and was unable to interfere.

During Jeroboam II's reign two prophets—Amos and Hosea—arose in the northern kingdom. Their messages have survived as individual books in the Bible. Amos, the first of the two, actually came from Tekoa in Judah, a small town west of Bethlehem on the fringe of the wilderness. Amos was of low origin—being a shepherd and gatherer of sycamore fruit—who felt called by Yahweh to go to the north and raise his voice against the evils in that kingdom. Jeroboam II's political success seems to have brought the country a wave of prosperity, which as is often the case, was accompanied by moral decay, lawlessness and crime. The rich oppressed the poor, while officialdom dispensed justice to the highest bidder (Amos 2:6-7, 3:10, 15, 4:1, 5:7-13, 6:4-6, 8:4-6). Sparing neither king nor priest, nobility nor common people, Amos castigated them all in simple but sharp messages of reproof and denunciation, evidently delivered in Bethel, one of the sanctuary cities of the northern kingdom (Amos 7:10-13). In the midst of its prosperity and evident political security, Israel did not realize that only a few decades later its doom would come, as predicted by the prophet; Amos warned that only complete repentance by king and people, and a turning again to Yahweh, whom they had forsaken, could avert the approaching catastrophe.

Shortly after Amos, Hosea, a citizen of the northern kingdom (he refers to Jeroboam II as "our king") began denouncing the evils of his nation. Occasionally he even included Israel's southern neighbor Judah in his messages of rebuke. The vices he identified (Hosea 4:1-2, 8, 6:10, 9:1, 9) are similar to those mentioned by Amos—lawlessness and corruption—although Hosea also emphasized the worship of foreign gods, especially Baal. Apparently after King Jehu had extinguished it, Baal worship returned to the country with renewed force (Hosea 2:8, 13, 17). Neither Hosea's ministry nor Amos's warnings seem to have made a lasting impression on the nation; the people did not change their lifestyle.

From all appearances, Jeroboam II was a strong ruler, although he lacked the prudence and foresight of his father Joash. Unlike Joash, Jeroboam made no provision to guarantee continuity of rule, and his kingdom broke up almost immediately after his death. His son Zachariah

Amos and Hosea

reigned for only six months (753-752 B.C.), and then fell victim to a murderous plot (2 Kings 15:8-12). Thus ended Jehu's dynasty. The kingdom quickly returned to the political impotence that had characterized it during most of its short history.

III. The Latter Part of the Eighth Century, Including the Fall of the Kingdom of Israel (750-715 B.C. in Judah and 752-723/722 B.C. in Israel)

IN JUDAH:

We left the history of Judah in King Uzziah's reign. Although Uzziah ruled from 790 to 739 B.C. we interrupted our account of his reign about 750 B.C., for two reasons: First, that date marks the beginning of the encounter of both Judah and Israel with the rising power of the new Assyrian empire (which in three decades would put an end to the northern kingdom of Israel). Second, about 750 B.C. the Judahite king Uzziah made his son Jotham co-regent.

By 750 Uzziah had had a long and successful reign. About this time, however, he contracted leprosy—according to the Bible, as a punishment for his having illegally entered the Temple of Yahweh to offer incense (2 Chronicles 26:16-20). His son Jotham was then appointed co-regent (2 Kings 15:5), a wise move to guarantee the continuity of the dynasty. This policy of appointing the crown prince as co-regent was followed in Judah thereafter for more than a century, from Uzziah to Manasseh.

The biblical account of Uzziah's leprosy indicates that a quarantine was imposed on the victim. Even a king was required to be isolated during his life and was given a separate burial when he died. In 1931 a square stone slab, 14 inches (35 cm) on a side, mentioning Uzziah, was found in the collection of the Russian Archaeological Museum on the Mount of Olives at Jerusalem; it is now in the Israel Museum in Jerusalem. It contains the following inscription in Aramaic: "Hither were brought the bones of Uzziah, king of Judah—do not disturb!"[23] The form of the script indicates that it was inscribed about the first century A.D. or perhaps a bit earlier; that was probably when Uzziah's bones, for some unknown reason, were collected and moved to a new resting place.

Uzziah's son Jotham reigned in Judah for nearly 20 years (750-731 B.C.), including 12 years when he ruled for his leprous father Uzziah. Like his father, Jotham was a comparatively upright ruler. Three contemporary Hebrew prophets, Isaiah, Hosea and Micah, possibly exerted influence upon him. Jotham was king during an abortive invasion of Judah led by Rezin II of Syria and Pekah of Israel (2 Kings 15:37). The invasion may have been what prompted Jotham to appoint his son Ahaz as co-regent.

A Hebrew seal, found by Nelson Glueck during the excavations at Tell el-Kheleifeh, at the Gulf of Elath, in 1940, carries the inscription "Belonging to *Ytm*." The identification of the owner of this seal with King Jotham, first made by Glueck, was endorsed by William F. Albright as "almost certain." However, more recent paleographic evidence seems to indicate that the seal must be dated to the seventh century B.C. and thus has nothing to do with King Jotham of Judah.[24]

As indicated, Jotham appointed his son Ahaz co-regent in the 16th year of his 20-year reign. Ahaz, who ruled from 735 to 715 B.C., was unaffected by the message of the prophets; he imitated the cult and worship practices of the northern kingdom:

> "He walked in the way of the kings of Israel, caused his son to pass through the fire . . . and sacrificed and burned incense on high places, on hills, and under every green tree" (2 Kings 16:3-4).

When Judah was attacked by Rezin II of Syria and Pekah of Israel—an encounter referred to as the Syro-Ephraimite war—the prophet Isaiah offered divine help to King Ahaz (Isaiah 7:3-13). Ahaz rejected the prophet's offer and turned instead to Tiglath-pileser III of Assyria, whose aid Ahaz bought with treasures from the Temple of Yahweh and from his own palace (2 Kings 16:7-8). The tribute of Ahaz is mentioned also in an Assyrian inscription of Tiglath-pileser III.[25] When Tiglath-pileser conquered Damascus (Syria), Ahaz was part of the royal Assyrian entourage.

In Damascus Ahaz absorbed the Assyrian mode of worship and immediately proceeded to introduce it into his own kingdom—probably at the prodding of the Assyrian king. From Damascus Ahaz sent instructions to Jerusalem to have an altar made, like the Assyrian one he had seen in Damascus. This new altar replaced the one Solomon had set up for burnt offerings, and was kept in use for some time (2 Kings 16:10-16).

Ahaz appointed his son Hezekiah as co-regent about 729 B.C., when he saw that the kingdom of Judah would probably be threatened by Asssyria (see 2 Kings 18:1, 9-10). The kingdom of Israel was in fact extinguished during Ahaz's reign (in 723/722 B.C.).

IN ISRAEL:

We left Israel with the murder of Zachariah in 752 B.C., a murder that brought an end to the 90-year dynasty of Jehu. Israel had but three decades of life remaining.

Zachariah murdered—a new dynasty in Israel

Zachariah's murderer, Shallum, became the new king of Israel, ushering in a 30-year period of anarchy and political decline. Shallum reigned only one month (752 B.C.); he was assassinated by Menahem (2 Kings 15:8-15).

Menahem (752-742 B.C.) was a cruel ruler who put down all opposition by extremely severe measures (2 Kings 15:16). By this time, it seems clear, the vast Syrian territories that Jeroboam II once controlled had been lost, although the fact is not mentioned in the Bible. Recognizing his inability to resist Assyrian power, Menahem voluntarily paid enormous sums in tribute so that Tiglath-pileser III would leave him in peace. Tiglath-pileser was placated; at that time he was busy restoring Assyrian rule to large sections of Syrian territory. Menahem's tribute, levied from the population by a special tax, is mentioned both in the Bible (2 Kings 15:19-20) and in Assyrian records.[26] Menahem died, apparently of natural causes, in 742 B.C.

Pekahiah, Menahem's son, was able to hold the throne for only two years (742-740 B.C.), when he, like so many other Israelite kings, was assassinated. His murderer, Pekah, assumed the throne and reigned for about eight years (740-732 B.C.).[27]

Pekah changed the pro-Assyrian policy of his predecessors and concluded an anti-Assyrian alliance with Rezin II of Damascus and other Syrian rulers. Thus, the Syrians had no reason to attack Israel. But they did go to war against Judah—a war already referred to, the Syro-Ephraimite war. This war was intended to force Judah's participation (with Israel) in the anti-Assyrian league. Although the confederates did great damage to Judah and annexed some of its territory, they failed to force Judah to join the anti-Assyrian alliance. Instead, the Judahite king Ahaz, as has already been noted, asked and received the assistance of Tiglath-pileser III of Assyria, who moved into Pekah's kingdom, occupied part of Israel (the greater part of Galilee and Gilead) and deported the Israelite inhabitants of these regions to northern Syria and northern and eastern Mesopotamia (2 Kings 16:5-9, 15:27-29). This unexpected Assyrian invasion of Israel broke the unnatural alliance between Israel and Syria, the more so since Tiglath-pileser III also marched against the Syrians, conquered Damascus and captured King Rezin II (732 B.C.). Syria and the conquered parts of Israel were made Assyrian provinces and henceforth were administered by Assyrian governors.[28]

Pekah
murdered—a
new dynasty
in Israel

Pekah's unhappy reign in Israel ended with another assassination. Hoshea, the assassin, ascended Israel's throne as its 20th and last king (732-723/722 B.C.) (2 Kings 15:30). Tiglath-pileser III claimed to have put Hoshea on the throne, and indicated that Pekah was overthrown by his subjects as a result of his disastrous policies.[29] Hoshea paid heavy tribute to Assyria, first to Tiglath-pileser III and then to his son and successor Shalmaneser V, in exchange for the right of being tolerated as a vassal to the king of Assyria (2 Kings 17:3).[30] The amount of annual tribute must have been unbearable for the little state, which now consisted of but an insignificant part of its former kingdom.

The Assyrian
conquest—
the end of the
northern
kingdom of
Israel

Israel in desperation decided to revolt. Hoshea formed a hopeless alliance against Assyria with a weak king of the 24th Dynasty of Egypt whose residence was at Säis and whose authority covered only part of the Nile country (2 Kings 17:4)[31] Shalmaneser V then marched against Israel. He laid siege to Israel's strongly fortified capital at Samaria, but captured it only after three years of fighting (2 Kings 18:10). The fall of Samaria probably occurred in the last year of Shalmaneser's reign (723-722 B.C.), possibly shortly before his death. Sargon II, Shalmaneser's successor, claimed in inscriptions, produced several years after the events had occurred, that he was the one who had captured Samaria during the first year of his reign.[32] He probably had no right to this claim, at least not as king. He may have been Shalmaneser's army commander at that time and in that capacity may have conquered the city and after his predecessor's death deported, according to his own claim, 27,290 Israelite captives.[33]

The fall of Samaria marked the end of the northern kingdom of Israel, after a tragic history of little more than two centuries. Conceived and born in the spirit of rebellion, Israel had no chance of survival. Twenty kings, each ruling an average of ten and a half years, had sat upon the throne; seven of them had murderered their predecessors. The first king, Jeroboam, had introduced a corrupt cult system and set up idolatrous representations of Yahweh. All succeeding rulers had followed him in this "sin," some adding to it the worship of Baal and Asherah. Had it not been for the tireless ministry of such reformers as Elijah, Elisha and other prophets, the kingdom of Israel might not have endured as long as it did (2 Kings 17:7-18).

IV. From the Last Part of the Eighth Century to the First Part of the Sixth Century, Including Hezekiah's Reforms, Josiah's Reforms and the Fall of Judah (729-586 B.C.)

With Israel's fall, the double strand ends. We have only to follow the story in the southern kingdom of Judah now. It lasted for another 135 years.

When we left the story of Judah, Ahaz had appointed his son Hezekiah co-regent, in 729 B.C., probably because he felt threatened by the same Assyrian pressure that just a few years later destroyed the northern kingdom of Israel.

Hezekiah

For Hezekiah's reign considerable information is available both in the Bible and in extra-biblical sources. The events described in 2 Kings 18-20 are paralleled in Isaiah 36-39 and 2 Chronicles 29-32. Other information is given in Jeremiah 26:17-19 concerning the prophet Micah in Hezekiah's time. The inscriptions of Sargon II and Sennacherib of Assyria provide extra-biblical source material for the Assyrian campaigns and Hezekiah's involvement.

Hezekiah was a co-regent with his father Ahaz for 14 years before Ahaz died. During those years the young co-ruler of Judah saw not only the death struggle of his country's brother nation Israel, but also the deportation of its population to foreign countries (2 Kings 18:1, 9-10). During these early years, Hezekiah may well have been strongly influenced by a religious leader, possibly the prophet Isaiah.

Whatever the roots of his deep-seated religious convictions, Hezekiah is described in the Bible as a good ruler who initiated a series of important religious reforms when, as sole ruler, he had the authority to do so. These reforms included abolishing illegitimate sanctuaries and

Beersheba horned altar. Dating to the eighth century B.C. this is the first example discovered of an Israelite horned altar for animal sacrifice. The animal may have been tied to the horns. Although the altar had been disassembled and its blocks then built into a wall, archaeologists had no trouble distinguishing the altar blocks from those of the rest of the wall. The altar blocks had been carefully cut—to different heights for the different courses—from calcareous sandstone, which differs in color and hardness from the common limestone of the wall.

destroying cult objects throughout the country (2 Kings 18:3-4), thus centralizing worship in the Jerusalem Temple. One of the objects of his religious zeal was evidently the temple or open-air sanctuary at Beersheba to which the prophet Amos had made reference in his earlier denunciation of cult places in Israel and Judah (Amos 5:15, 8:14). Yohanan Aharoni discovered the large stone altar from this temple during his 1973 excavations of the eighth-century B.C. storehouse complex of Beersheba. In the storehouse walls he found, in reuse, some well-smoothed blocks of calcareous sandstone among the limestone blocks commonly used in the Beersheba buildings. When put together these reused smooth sandstone blocks formed a large, horned altar over five feet high. Three of its four horns had been preserved and protruded from the corners.[34] The cult structure in which this altar had stood has not been located; apparently the altar was dismantled (and perhaps the building in which it stood destroyed) as part of Hezekiah's religious reforms.

For his religious reforms Hezekiah was highly commended in the Book of Kings (2 Kings 18:3-7). In chronicling Hezekiah's life, the author of Kings drew heavily on the written records of Isaiah (possibly Hezekiah's mentor), as is evident from the fact that some passages in Isaiah are

Hezekiah's tunnel. Anticipating an attack by Sennacherib of Assyria, the Judahite king Hezekiah built a 1,749-foot-long tunnel to bring the water of the Gihon Spring within the city walls of Jerusalem. This building project is referred to in 2 Kings 20:20 and 2 Chronicles 32:4.

appropriated word-for-word in the Book of Kings. Hezekiah also turned out to be a forceful and progressive ruler in other ways. He established control over areas of Philistia, strengthened the national defense system, especially of Jerusalem, and promoted trade and agriculture (2 Kings 18:8; 2 Chronicles 32:28-29).

Hezekiah was also responsible for a remarkable technical accomplishment, the boring of a 1,749-foot-long tunnel in Jerusalem—from the Gihon Spring in the Kidron Valley to a lower pool inside the city (2 Chronicles 32:4, 30; 2 Kings 20:20). In this way he assured Jerusalem of a protected water supply in time of siege. Even now, after more than 2,500 years, the waters of Gihon still flow through this tunnel into the Pool of Siloam.

In 1880 boys wading through the tunnel accidentally discovered a Hebrew inscription, now in the Archaeological Museum at Istanbul, which had been cut into the rock after the completion of Hezekiah's tunnel. It reads as follows:[35]

"[The completion of] the piercing through. And this is the story of the piercing through. While [the stone-cutters were swinging their] axes, each toward his fellow and while there were yet three cubits to be pierced through, [there was heard] the voice of a man calling to his fellow, for there was a crevice [?] on the right . . . . And on the day of the piercing through, the stone-cutters struck through each to meet his fellow, axe against axe. Then ran the water from the Spring

Siloam inscription. Discovered in 1880, the inscription celebrates the completion of Hezekiah's tunnel. The inscription was carved into the wall of the tunnel about 20 feet from its end at the Siloam Pool.

to the Pool for twelve hundred cubits, and a hundred cubits was the height of the rock above the head of the stone-cutters."

Sennacherib's invasion of Judah

Hezekiah is best known, however, for his faith in Yahweh at the time of one of Sennacherib's invasions of Judah. Hezekiah had inherited the Assyrian vassalship from his father and for several years seems to have continued paying to Assyria the required annual tribute. In one of Sargon's inscriptions, Judah's tribute is listed with tribute sent by Philistia, Edom and Moab.[36] During the reign of Sargon II, Judah apparently had no serious problems with the Assyrians, unlike the Philistines against whom Sargon II directed three military campaigns.[37] Sargon subjugated Gaza in 720 B.C. Then came a second and a third Philistine campaign (in 716 and in 712 B.C.). The Assyrian attacks on the Philistine cities of Ekron and Gibbethon are depicted on reliefs discovered in Sargon's palace at Khorsabad;[38] his conquest of Philistine Ashdod is known from Sargon's Annals and the so-called Display Inscription, as well as from three fragments of a victory monument set up by the Assyrian king in Ashdod itself.[39] The short note in Isaiah 20:1, the only passage in which Sargon is mentioned in the Bible, refers to his campaign against Ashdod. Hezekiah probably also lost some territory to Sargon at this time; Sargon calls himself in one inscription from Nimrud "the subduer of the country of Judah."[40]

In the later years of his reign Sargon became heavily engaged in Mesopotamia and refrained from conducting military campaigns in the west. Sargon died in 705 B.C. and was succeeded by his son Sennacherib. After his father's death Sennacherib faced a number of rebellions in various parts of the Assyrian empire. Hezekiah too made plans to shake off the Assyrian yoke. He strengthened his defenses and allied himself with the Ethiopian kings of the 25th Egyptian Dynasty. The prophet Isaiah vehemently opposed this policy (Isaiah 18:1-5, 30:1-5, 31:1-3), but was unable to change Hezekiah's mind. The prophet even went public with his warnings when he saw that his messages were being ignored. He walked "naked and barefoot" in the streets of Jerusalem and solemnly, but unsuccessfully, proclaimed his prophecies against Egypt and her allies, predicting that only slavery and misfortune would result if the anti-Assyrian policies continued (Isaiah 20). Hezekiah remained unmoved. Determined to break with Assyria whatever the cost, he formally severed his connection with the empire. As a result, he had to meet Assyrian forces head on.

Before the Assyrians carried out any punitive action, however, Hezekiah became ill. His sudden sickness, described in 2 Kings 20, must have occurred in the same year as the Assyrian invasion.[41] The prophet Isaiah promised that Hezekiah would be healed and assured him that Sennacherib would not take Jerusalem. Hezekiah soon recovered.

Shortly after Hezekiah's recovery, Babylonian messengers from Marduk-apal-iddina, the biblical Merodach-baladan, arrived in Jerusalem. Merodach-baladan was a self-proclaimed king of Babylon who had been a thorn in the Assyrian side for some time, although at the time of this event he was living in exile. When Merodach-baladan learned of Hezekiah's rebellion against his Assyrian overlord and of his miraculous healing from a serious disease, Merodach-baladan decided to contact Hezekiah. Perhaps Hezekiah would help Merodach-baladan to regain the throne of Babylon by causing trouble for the Assyrians in the western part of the empire, thus keeping the Assyrian army away from Babylonia. Hezekiah, for his part, was eager to ally himself with anyone who was ready to resist the Assyrian war machine; he received Merodach-baladan's messengers with delight. Isaiah, however, was just as opposed to an alliance with Babylonia's king in exile (2 Kings 20:12-18) as he was to an alliance with Egypt.

Shortly after these events, but still in the same regnal year (2 Kings 18:13)—in 701 B.C.—Sennacherib himself appeared on the scene. His army went through the land like a steamroller, leaving in its path destruction and terror. Too late, Hezekiah reversed his policy and quickly sent a heavy tribute to Sennacherib at Lachish, less than 30 miles southwest of Jerusalem. This tribute is recorded in the Bible (2 Kings 18:14-15) as well as in the Assyrian king's annals;[42] the accounts differ only in the amount of silver Hezekiah paid. The Bible lists the tribute as 30 talents of gold and 300 talents of silver; according to Sennacherib's records, it was 30 talents of gold and 800 talents of silver. Even this was not enough for Sennacherib, however. He demanded unconditional surrender, which was unacceptable to Hezekiah. When disaster seemed imminent, something must have happened elsewhere in Sennacherib's vast domain, because he decided to withdraw without attacking Judah's well-fortified capital. The Assyrian records clearly state that Jerusalem was not taken during this campaign. They say that Sennacherib had made

Hezekiah "a prisoner in Jerusalem . . . like a bird in a cage," but they do not claim that Sennacherib captured either Hezekiah or his capital.

About 12 years later, when Taharka of Egypt (689-664 B.C.) had come to the throne (see 2 Kings 19:8), Sennacherib returned to Palestine to force a showdown with the defiant Hezekiah. (It should be noted that many scholars attribute the events described in this paragraph to Sennacherib's 701 B.C. campaign, rather than to a second campaign 12 years later.[43]) Sennacherib, during his siege of Lachish, first dispatched a letter calling upon Hezekiah to surrender. The king of Judah, encouraged by Isaiah, refused this demand and eventually saw his faith in Isaiah's sure promise of divine intervention rewarded.

In the meantime the Assyrian army conquered the strong fortress of Lachish. Sennacherib left us richly illustrated details of the siege and conquest of this city: a series of sculptured stone reliefs decorating the walls of one hall in his palace at Nineveh. Now in the British Museum, these reliefs sequentially depict, just as the pictures of a comic strip, the various stages of the attack and conquest of the city. We see on them the arrival of the army and the assault on the city—both by battering rams and by foot soldiers armed with bows and arrows or slings. The rams were moved toward the foot of the fortress wall over an artifical ramp constructed by the Asssyrians. After scenes of fierce fighting, we see the final surrender of the city; then the leaders of Lachish appear before the Assyrian king and plead for mercy. Evidently, this was denied; another panel shows these leaders flayed and impaled, while the Judahites from Lachish are deported. David Ussishkin, the excavator of Lachish, recently discovered the city's own counter-siege ramp, along with arrows and other objects that provide eloquent testimony to this unhappy chapter in Lachish's history.[44]

From Lachish the Assyrian army marched on Jerusalem, Judah's capital, and began a siege. But before the gates of Jerusalem, the army met with a dreadful disaster (2 Kings 18:17-19:36; 2 Chronicles 32:9-21; Isaiah 36:2-37:37). According to the Bible, an unusually large number of Assyrian soldiers died in a single night, thanks to a miracle.[45] The Assyrian records are silent on this campaign, as it was their custom never to record any misfortunes or adversities. Perhaps a serious and devastating disease, such as cholera or the plague, so decimated the Assyrian army that they lifted the siege and allowed the remnants of their forces to return home. Herodotus, the Greek traveler and historian, who visited Egypt in the fifth century B.C., heard stories there about a disaster that Sennacherib's army had suffered; the disaster had originated from some unusual causes and had forced the army to return to its homeland; it then attempted to invade Egypt.[46]

Hezekiah probably spent the last 15 years of his life rebuilding his devastated country. Some ten years before his death he made his son Manasseh co-regent.

Manasseh   Manasseh reigned for 55 years (696-641 B.C.), including ten years as co-regent with Hezekiah. According to his biblical biographers, Manasseh's reign was filled with wickedness. He rebuilt the altars of Baal, served Asherah, practiced witchcraft, sacrificed infants and "worshipped all the host of heaven" (2 Chronicles 33:1-10). A Jewish Midrash* to 2 Kings 21:16 emphasizes his shedding of "innocent blood." This Midrash claims that Manasseh hated Isaiah and killed him by having him sawed in two.[47] If true, Isaiah at that time must have been a very old man since he had served and advised—sometimes with little success—four kings of Judah over more than half a century.

The Assyrian kings Esarhaddon and Ashurbanipal both mention that Manasseh paid them tribute,[48] an indication that Manasseh became a vassal of Assyria after his father's death. However, at some time during his reign Manasseh must have rebelled, since one of these two Assyrian kings came and "bound him with fetters, and carried him to Babylon" (2 Chronicles 33:11). It seems somewhat strange that he was taken to Babylon instead of to Nineveh, the Assyrian capital. It is possible that the Assyrian ruler Esarhaddon, whose mother was a Babylonian and who rebuilt and embellished Babylon after his father Sennacherib had destroyed it, considered it practically his second capital. Manasseh's offense cannot have been very serious, for he was pardoned and restored to his former position (2 Chronicles 33:12-13). In the meantime, however, Assyrian officials had administered Judah and probably thoroughly looted it.

Manasseh, upon his return from Babylon to Judah, found an extremely impoverished country; an Assyrian document states that the country of Ammon paid a tribute of two minas of gold, Moab paid one mina of gold, while poor Judah paid only ten minas of silver.[49] Manasseh's troubles finally brought him to the point of conversion; the Bible credits him for becoming an ardent worshipper of Yahweh after returning from Assyrian captivity (2 Chronicles 33:12-20).

After Manasseh's death, his son Amon came to the throne (641-639 B.C.). Amon was just as wicked as his father had been before his conversion. Amon was so unpopular that his servants killed him after a brief reign of two years (2 Kings 21:18-26; 2 Chronicles 33:21-25).

Amon's son Josiah ascended the throne at the age of eight years. He reigned for 31 years (639-608 B.C.). Josiah apparently was raised by a pious tutor who had continued to live in the religious tradition of Hezekiah, for young Josiah proved to be a deeply religious man. At the age of 15 or 16, he began to abolish the high places, sacred pagan pillars and Baal altars (2 Chronicles 34:3).[50] In his 18th regnal year (622-621 B.C.), during repair work on the Jerusalem Temple, a "book of the law"— almost certainly the book known to us as "Deuteronomy"—was found. Josiah, then about 25 years old, became familiar with its precepts and

Josiah

---

* Midrash is a Jewish traditional exposition or supplementary embellishment of a biblical passage.

DAN COLE

Arad temple. The Israelite temple at Arad in the Negev desert remained in use through four phases of building and remodeling—from the tenth till the late seventh century B.C.

Limestone incense altars flank steps that lead into a four-foot by four-foot niche with two stone pillars against the rear wall. When the temple was abolished by a religious reform, probably King Josiah's, the altars were reverently laid on their sides and covered with earth. This is the only Israelite temple discovered in an archaeological excavation.

inaugurated a thorough purge of paganism and idolatry not only throughout the kingdom of Judah, but also in adjacent areas of the former kingdom of Israel (2 Kings 22-23; 2 Chronicles 34:6-7). This indicates that Josiah had established some kind of political control over territories that had, since 722 B.C., been Assyrian possessions.

Some archaeological evidence of Josiah's religious reforms has come to light at Arad in the Negev and possibly also in Jerusalem. In the northwestern corner of the Israelite citadel at Arad, Yohanan Aharoni

ZEV RADOVAN, COURTESY ISRAEL DEPARTMENT OF ANTIQUITIES AND MUSEUMS

Fertility figurine. Excavated recently in the Jewish Quarter of Jerusalem's Old City, this clay figurine may be a household fertility amulet representing the Canaanite goddess Asherah. It probably dates to the time of King Josiah, whose drastic religious reform of 621 B.C. outlawed such images.

found a temple dedicated to Yahweh that remained in use with slight alterations until the seventh century, when it was destroyed, most probably by Josiah. Luckily, a casemate wall built over it preserved its foundation walls and cult paraphernalia, including two incense altars and a cult stele; the altars and the stele are now in the Israel Museum in Jerusalem.[51]

In Jerusalem, excavations at the eastern slope of Ophel revealed a small sanctuary and an adjoining cave. About 1,300 objects—mainly pottery, but also hundreds of broken animal and human figurines—were discovered there. The human figurines, hollow, so-called pillar figurines, undoubtedly represent a fertility goddess. Each one was deliberately broken before it was deposited in the cave. Some archaeologists suggest that this large deposit of destroyed cult objects (together with an abandoned temple) must be associated with Josiah's drastic religious reforms. However, Kathleen Kenyon, the excavator, dated the associated pottery closer to the time of Hezekiah than to Josiah's. Hence, it is possible that these finds from Jerusalem are witnesses to Hezekiah's religious reforms.[52]

The early sixth-century B.C. Lachish Letters attest that Josiah's efforts at eradicating the worship of pagan gods had some lasting effect. These missives, written by military men, always begin with an introductory

Lachish letter. Written about 586 B.C., just before the Babylonians completed their conquest of Judah, this inscribed *ostracon* (plural, *ostraca*) was probably composed by a soldier to his superior officer. The sender's name is Hosha'yahu, and the officer's name Ya'ush—both contain forms of the name Yahweh (Yahu and Ya). Hosha'yahu's letter begins, "Your servant Hosha'yahu has sent to inform my lord Ya'ush: May Yahweh let my lord hear good tidings!"

This *ostracon* and more than 20 others excavated in a guardroom of Lachish's city wall constitute one the most important collections of Hebrew letters from the time of the First Temple.

formula that mentions Yahweh, such as "May Yahweh let my lord hear good tidings," or "May Yahweh let my lord see peace." Furthermore, of the 22 personal names mentioned in the Lachish Letters, 14 are compounded with Yahweh. Examples are Gemaryahu or Ya'azanyahu.[53] Not one is compounded with Baal or the name of any other foreign god, like the names we find in the eighth-century B.C. Samaria ostraca.* The Samaria ostraca, discovered in the capital of the northern kingdom of Israel, contain several Baal names, such as Abibaal and Baalzakar. The contrast between the Samaria ostraca and the Lachish Letters suggests that Yahweh occupied a monopolistic position in the religious life of the people during the last decades of the kingdom of Judah.

On the other hand, statements made by the prophet Ezekiel indicate that the worship of pagan gods was still practiced secretly by some citizens of Judah, even prominent ones. According to Ezekiel, such worship was carried on even in the Temple of Yahweh, up to the very end of Jerusalem's existence (Ezekiel 8:5-16). Apparently, completely abolishing long-ingrained religious beliefs, customs and practices was extremely difficult.

During Josiah's reign the Assyrian empire disintegrated. Their kings Esarhaddon and Ashurbanipal overextended themselves when they invaded Egypt and made it part of their realm. So far from the center of the Assyrian empire, Egypt was hard to control, and the Assyrians had to keep a heel on the many other restless nations that repeatedly tried to shake off her yoke. The biggest blow to Assyrian power came when Nabopolassar, the Chaldean viceroy of Babylon, declared Babylonia independent and concluded an alliance with Media, which for some time had been causing Assyria trouble in the east. In quick succession after Ashurbanipal's death about 630 B.C. one part of the empire after another fell away. By 615 B.C. the Assyrians were defending themselves in their homeland; Asshur, one of their former capital cities, was attacked by the Babylonians. In the following year Asshur fell to a Median onslaught. Finally, in 612 B.C., the glorious Assyrian capital at Nineveh was destroyed by the combined Median and Babylonian armies, forcing the remnants of the Assyrian kingdom to set up temporary headquarters in the northern Mesopotamian city of Haran.

During these years the Assyrian empire naturally crumbled; Assyria could no longer effectively control its western possessions. It was in the period before Babylonia took over these possessions that Josiah extended his influence, perhaps even political control, over considerable parts of the territory that had formerly belonged to the kingdom of Israel (and had been administered more recently as Assyrian provinces). A zealous religious person, Josiah applied his power and influence to secure religious reforms throughout the land; he might have succeeded were it not for his untimely death in 608 B.C.

The rise of Babylon

---

* An ostracon (plural, ostraca) is an inscribed potsherd.

While the collapse of the Assyrian empire benefited Josiah, it also allowed a rebirth of Egyptian power. When Assyrian strength in Egypt disintegrated, the kings of the 26th Dynasty took control over their own land; wherever possible, they also filled the vacuum created by Assyrian impotence in Syria and in the lands surrounding Israel and Judah. The Egyptians may have looked with apprehension on the emerging power of Bablyonia, fearing that the kings of Babylon, after extinguishing the Assyrian empire, might want to assume control over former Assyrian territories in the west. For this reason, the Egyptian kings, first Psamtik I (663-609 B.C.) and then Neco II (609-594 B.C.), apparently decided to try to prevent Assyria's complete collapse. For the Egyptians, a weakened but still viable Assyria would provide an effective buffer between Syria, which the Egyptians wanted to control, and Babylonia.

Josiah may have felt that the Egyptian pharaohs had other plans besides merely keeping Assyria alive: aspirations of rebuilding the former Egyptian empire in Asia. In any event, the Egyptian Pharaoh Neco II wanted to march through Judah to assist the Assyrians. Josiah may have actually made an agreement with Nabopolassar of Babylon to resist Neco in order to aid his Babylonian ally. Or perhaps Josiah took his stand merely on the basis of his conviction that if the Egyptians and Assyrians defeated the Babylonians, Judah would be forced to submit either to Egypt or to Assyria. One or the other reason must have prompted Josiah's unfortunate decision to resist Neco II by force to prevent him from marching north through Judah to assist the Assyrians.

Josiah chose the Carmel passes near Megiddo to try to stop Neco's army. That battle marked the failure of Josiah's pro-Babylonian policy, for he was badly wounded and died soon afterward (2 Kings 23:29; 2 Chronicles 35:20-24). His army was decisively beaten. Neco hurried on to the north without, for the present, following up his victory over Josiah. He was more concerned with a victory over Babylonia, since that would give him a free hand in Syria, in Judah, and in the other nations in the area.

Although Judah was spared the tragic fate that befell the northern kingdom of Israel at the hands of the Assyrians, Judah had been bled white by Assyria's heavy demands for tribute. In Hezekiah's time a glorious and miraculous deliverance had saved Jerusalem, but even then a terrible price had been paid for previous political blunders, and Judah had been devastated from one end to the other by the armies of the Assyrian king Sennacherib. The rise of Babylonia provided little respite. By the time of Josiah's death in 608 B.C., the country was not only threatened by Babylonia, but had suffered at the hands of a resurgent Egypt. The biblical writers, who viewed the political history of their nation in the light of faithfulness or disobedience to Yahweh, forcefully declared that the many misfortunes that came to Judah were the result of apostasy. Since half the kings who reigned during this period were considered to have been unfaithful to Yahweh, it is not surprising that the nation did not fare well.

As soon as the news of Josiah's death reached the nation, his 23-year-old son Jehoahaz was crowned in Jerusalem by popular demand, though Jehoahaz was not the oldest of the dead king's sons. He seems to have followed his father's policies, including a pro-Babylonian policy, which to Pharoah Neco II meant that he was anti-Egyptian.

After consolidating his position in northern Mesopotamia and Syria, Neco decided to punish Judah for having interfered with him during Josiah's reign. Accordingly, Neco summoned Jehoahaz to Riblah, his temporary headquarters in northern Syria. Jehoahaz obeyed—a clear indication that Judah suffered heavy losses in the battle of Megiddo during Josiah's reign, and that the country was powerless to resist Neco, who by then must have considered himself the unquestioned lord of Judah and the adjacent area. After Jehoahaz had reigned only three months, Neco took the young king and sent him as prisoner to Egypt. In his stead Neco allowed Eliakim, better known as Jehoiakim, an older brother of Jehoahaz, to become king. Jehoiakim's pro-Egyptian sympathies were apparently well known. The Egyptians also exacted a tribute of 100 talents of silver and one talent of gold; the new king Jehoiakim raised this from the people by an extra tax (2 Kings 23:30-35; 2 Chronicles 36:1-4).

Jehoiakim, who became king at the age of 25, ruled for 11 years (608-598 B.C.). His reign was marked by gross idolatry and wickedness; he was the exact opposite of his pious father Josiah. Jehoiakim distinguished himself by various godless acts, of which the most heinous was the murder of a prophet, Uriah son of Shemaiah. Of all the rulers of Judah and Israel, Jehoiakim was the only king who was charged by the Bible writers with such a shocking misdeed (Jeremiah 26:20-23).

Jehoiakim probably also planned to kill Jeremiah and his secretary Baruch for having rebuked the king's sins in public. However these two men went into hiding at the advice of friends and escaped the king's wrath (Jeremiah 36:19,26). Recently a series of seal impressions have come to light; one belonged to Baruch and another to Jerahmeel, the king's son.[54] Jerahmeel, a royal prince, was dispatched by King Jehoiakim to arrest Baruch and Jeremiah (Jeremiah 36:26). To find two bullae* with seal impressions of these two men together is certainly a curious coincidence. The impressions were without doubt made by seals belonging to the two biblical individuals mentioned, as the inscriptions clearly reveal: Baruch is called "son of Neriah, the scribe," exactly as in the Bible (Jeremiah 36:4,32), while Jerahmeel is called in Jeremiah 36:26 as well as on the bulla "Jerahmeel, the king's son."

Until his third regnal year, 605 B.C., Jehoiakim was probably an Egyptian vassal. In that year, according to a Babylonian (or Chaldean) chronicle discovered in 1956,[55] Nebuchadnezzar, the crown prince of

---

* A bulla (plural, bullae) is a round lump of clay into which a seal has been impressed. Bullae were generally attached to rolled-up ancient papyrus or parchment documents by means of strings. Both the scrolls and strings have in most cases long ago disintegrated in the humid climate of Israel, but the clay bullae have survived.

Bulla from a seal of Baruch, probably the scribe, or secretary, of the prophet Jeremiah. A *bulla* is the small lump of clay in which a seal was impressed to seal a document. About two-thirds of an inch long, this *bulla* bears an impression written in a script called old Hebrew, which was used in Israel and Judah before the Babylonian exile.

In three lines it reads "(Belonging) to Berekhyahu/ son of Neriyahu/ the scribe." Apparently, Baruch's full name was Berekhyahu, which means "blessed of Yahweh."

Babylon, was dispatched to fight against the Egyptians in northern Mesopotamia. In two battles, first at Carchemish and then at an unknown place near Hamath in Syria, Nebuchadnezzar decisively defeated the Egyptians, and consequently came into *de facto* possession of Syria, Judah, Israel and the adjacent areas. While following the defeated Egyptians toward their homeland, Nebuchadnezzar apparently appeared in Jerusalem and forced Jehoiakim to become a vassal of Babylon. Nebuchadnezzar carried away some of the Temple treasures as booty and certain princes as hostages—among them Daniel and his friends (Daniel 1:1-6).

Nebuchadnezzar
becomes king
of Babylon

News of his father's death sent crown prince Nebuchadnezzar back to Babylon by the shortest possible route to claim the throne. With his generals he left the prisoners already taken during the campaign, and gave orders to retreat to Mesopotamia, his homeland, with the prisoners.[56] A king's death always creates the opportunity for a usurper to attempt to seize the throne or for dissident elements to revolt. After his father died, Nebuchadnezzar did not want his army fighting in faraway Egypt when it might be urgently needed in Babylonia. Hence his order to the army to follow him.

Nebuchadnezzar found no opposition at home, however. He could thus return to the task of bringing under full control the western territories that, as the result of the battles in northern Syria, had fallen into his lap. We soon find him undertaking three campaigns in "Hatti-land," as the Babylonians called Syria and the area around Judah and Israel.

Resistance must have been light, because the only military action mentioned is the capture and destruction of Ashkelon. Nebuchadnezzar's campaigns served to organize the territory and to assure collection of the annual tributes.

It appears that during this period Jehoiakim of Judah remained a loyal vassal of Nebuchadnezzar (2 Kings 24:1). However, since the annual tribute to Babylon was so burdensome, Jehoiakim felt a strong urge to switch his allegiance back to Egypt, which was regaining strength. This directed Nebuchadnezzar's attention toward Egypt, the chief cause of his troubles with his vassals. A battle fought between Nebuchadnezzar's Babylonian army and the Egyptian army in Kislev (November-December), 601 B.C., seems to have ended in a draw, although the Babylonian army suffered especially heavy losses, as we can gather from the fact that the Babylonians withdrew—evidently without having obtained a victory. The records tell us that Nebuchadnezzar remained at home during the following year, probably to rebuild his army, weakened by this encounter with the Egyptians.[57]

The first Babylonian entry into Jerusalem

In the meantime Nebuchadnezzar seems to have allowed several of his western vassal nations, aided by some of his own troops, which had probably been left behind as garrisons, to raid and harass Judah (2 Kings 24:2). In December 598 B.C. some of these Babylonian troops were evidently able to penetrate Jerusalem and capture the king. Once more Temple treasures were sent to Babylon (2 Chronicles 36:7), and 3,023 Judahites were deported (Jeremiah 52:28). King Jehoiakim was placed in fetters in preparation for his own deportation to Babylon (2 Chronicles 36:6) in order to punish him for his flirtation with Egypt. But this deportation plan was never carried out. Apparently, before he could be deported Jehoiakim died, either at the hands of the enemy soldiers or from natural causes. His body was cast outside the city gates and lay there exposed to heat and cold for several days before it received a disgraceful burial—like that "of an ass" (Jeremiah 22:18-19; see also 2 Kings 24:6; 2 Chronicles 36:6; Jeremiah 36:30; Josephus, *Antiquities of the Jews*, X.97).[58]

Jehoiakim was succeeded by his 18-year-old son, Jehoiachin, who reigned only three months (598-597 B.C.). Nebuchadnezzar proceeded to Jerusalem to take the new king prisoner. When Nebuchadnezzar arrived at Jerusalem, Jehoiachin surrendered himself, his mother and his whole staff on Adar 2 (March 15/16), 597 B.C., a date established by the Babylonian chronicle.[59] Nebuchadnezzar took Jehoiachin to Babylon as hostage and made his uncle, Zedekiah, king in his stead, although, as we shall see, Jehoiachin continued to be recognized as king by his people at least during the first several years of his exile in Babylon. Nebuchadnezzar also transported to Babylonia all the remaining vessels of the Temple treasure, 7,000 soldiers and all the skilled craftsmen he could find (2 Kings 24:10-17; 2 Chronicles 36:9-10). The latter would be useful in Nebuchadnezzar's extensive building enterprises.

Jehoiachin, still considered by his people as the king of Judah, was more or less a hostage in Babylon. This conclusion is based on the fact that the Bible records agitation in Judah and among the Judahite captives in Babylon because of the unfulfilled expectations that Jehoiachin would be returned to the throne and the sacred vessels would be brought back to the Temple (Jeremiah 28:3-4 and chapter 29). Since the Jews in Babylon could not date events according to the regnal years of Jehoiachin without offending the Babylonians, they apparently reckoned such events—as Ezekiel did—by the years of his captivity (Ezekiel 1:2, 40:1).

These conclusions regarding Jehoiachin find some confirmation in archaeological discoveries. Several cuneiform tablets found in the palace ruins of Babylon contain lists of foodstuff provided by the royal storehouse for certain persons who were fed by the king. Among them Jehoiachin is repeatedly mentioned as "king of Judah," together with five of his sons and their tutor Kenaiah. On one of them, dated in the year 592 B.C.—five years after his surrender—Jehoiachin is still called king.[60] The use of this title and the fact that he received 20 times as much food rations as any other person mentioned in these records (probably needed to feed his entourage), and that there is no reference to his imprisonment seems to indicate that he was held by Nebuchadnezzar in anticipation of the day when he would be restored to his throne, if and when conditions in Judah might make such a course of action advisable.

At a later time, either in connection with the unrest among the exiled Jews in Babylon, described in Jeremiah 29, or at the time of Zedekiah's rebellion (to be described below), Nebuchadnezzar imprisoned Jehoiachin. His imprisonment continued for 37 years, when Nebuchadnezzar's son, Amel-Marduk, the biblical Evil-Merodach, released and exonerated Jehoiachin (2 Kings 25:27-30; Jeremiah 52:31-34). This event, however, falls in the period of the Exile, after the destruction, and will be dealt with in the next chapter.

When Nebuchadnezzar put Zedekiah, Jehoiachin's uncle, on the throne of Judah, the Babylonian king changed his name from Mattaniah, "Gift of Yahweh" to Zedekiah, "Righteousness of Yahweh." He probably did this so that the new name would serve as a continual reminder of his solemn oath of loyalty to Nebuchadnezzar, by his own God Yahweh who was considered to have acted as a just witness (2 Kings 24:17; 2 Chronicles 36:13; Ezekiel 17:15-19). Zedekiah, however, was a weak character, and although he was sometimes inclined to do right, he allowed himself to be swayed from the path of loyalty and fidelity by popular demands, as the history of his reign clearly shows.

For a number of years—according to Josephus, for eight years[61]— Zedekaiah remained loyal to Babylonia. Once he sent an embassy to Nebuchadnezzar to assure the Babylonian monarch of his fidelity (Jeremiah 29:3-7). In Zedekiah's fourth year (594/593 B.C.), he himself made a journey to Babylon (Jeremiah 51:59), perhaps having been summoned to renew his oath of loyalty. Later, however, under the constant pressure of his subjects, particularly the nobility, who urged him to seek the aid of Egypt against Babylon, Zedekiah made an alliance with the Egyptians (see Jeremiah 37:6-10, 38:14-28). In doing so, he disregarded the strong warnings of the prophet Jeremiah. This Egyptian alliance was probably made after Pharaoh Psamtik II had personally appeared in Judah in 591 B.C. and had given Zedekiah all kinds of assurances and promises of help.[62]

Nebuchadnezzar had prudently refrained from attacking Egypt, in order to avoid the trap that the Assyrians had earlier fallen into. Nevertheless, he was unwilling to lose any of his western possessions to Egypt; he therefore marched against Judah as soon as Zedekiah's Egyptian alliance became apparent. Nebuchadnezzar systematically devastated the land, practically repeating what Sennacherib had done a century earlier.

From this unhappy period come the famous Lachish Letters discovered in 1935 and 1938 in the gate of the ruins of Lachish. These letters, written in ink on broken bits of pottery, were sent by an officer in charge of an outpost between Azekah and Lachish to the commandant of the latter fortress. Their language is practically identical with that found in the Book of Jeremiah, and some of the expressions are very similar. One of these letters, No. 16 in the official publication,[63] refers to a prophet whose name ends in [-ya]hu. Identifying this "prophet" either with Jeremiah (*Yeremiyahu*) or Uriah (*'Uriyahu*) would be hazardous, though both hypotheses have been suggested. In fact, many prophets were operating in Judah at this time (see Jeremiah 29:1, 8, 19; 32:32), and some of their names probably ended in *-yahu*—for example, the false prophet Hananiah (*Hananyahu*) mentioned in Jeremiah 28:1-17.

Another of these letters, No. 4, must have been written in the very last days of the existence of the kingdom of Judah. It states that the sender of the letter, the officer already mentioned, was still watching the signals of Lachish, sent out probably by means of smoke during the daytime or fire at night, but that he and his men no longer could see the signals of Azekah. This letter must have been dispatched to Lachish shortly after the events recorded in Jeremiah 34:7, which states that of all the cities of Judah, only three—Jerusalem, Lachish and Azekah—remained unconquered by the Babylonians.[64] The discovery of the letter inside Lachish proves that the letter reached that city before it fell to the Babylonian army, while Azekah—lying only 11 miles due north of Lachish—had evidently already been captured, for its signals could no longer be seen.

The Lachish Letters

The siege of Jerusalem began in earnest on January 15, 588 B.C., and lasted until July 19, 586 B.C. (2 Kings 25:1-2; Jeremiah 39:1-2),[65] when the Babylonian army finally broke through the walls of the city. A severe famine had devastated the city (Jeremiah 38:9). Jerusalem had been able to hold out for over two and a half years—vivid testimony to the strength

The Babylonian destruction of Jerusalem

of its walls and the thoroughness and effectiveness of its defensive measures. During recent excavations in the Jewish Quarter of the Old City of Jerusalem, archaeologists discovered one of the defensive towers of the pre-Exilic period and a 213-foot-long stretch of the lower part of the city wall, which had an average thickness of over 22 feet. At the foot of the tower a group of five arrowheads came to light—silent witnesses to the last fierce fight before the city fell.[66]

The 30-month-long siege of the city was interrupted once briefly with an unsuccessful attempt by Judah's ally, Egypt, to defeat the Babylonians (Jeremiah 37:5).

When the Babylonian army finally broke into the city, King Zedekiah attempted to escape. In the confused fighting that followed the breakthrough, he managed to leave the city and reach the plain of Jericho, but was overtaken there by his enemies. Carried to Nebuchadnezzar's headquarters at Riblah in northern Syria, Zedekiah witnessed his sons being killed; then his own eyes were put out and he was sent to Babylon in chains. His chief ministers were executed, and all others were carried into captivity (2 Kings 25:4-7, 19-21; Jeremiah 52:5-11).

Jerusalem was systematically looted and then destroyed. The horrible evidence of this destruction has been found wherever excavators have reached this level. The city walls were torn down and the Temple was burned. The fire that destroyed the city raged for three days—August 15-18, 586 B.C., as the two dates of 2 Kings 25:8 and Jeremiah 52:12-13 seem to indicate.

Many Judahites were transported as captives to Babylonia, although some, including the poor, remained behind. Nebuchadnezzar appointed a governor for them, a Judahite by the name of Gedaliah, who chose Mizpah as his administrative center (2 Kings 25:22; 2 Chronicles 36:20). The ruined site of Tell en-Nasbeh, situated about 7.5 miles north of Jerusalem, is generally identified with biblical Mizpah. It was excavated by William F. Badè during five campaigns between 1926 and 1935.[67]

Gedaliah seems to have governed for only a short time, although the lack of a year in 2 Kings 25:25 leaves uncertain how long after the fall of Jerusalem he held his post—until he was assassinated.

Jeremiah, who was a prisoner in Jerusalem when the city fell, was released by Nebuchadnezzar's army commander and joined Gedaliah at Mizpah. Also, several Judahite field commanders who had escaped from the debacle found their way to Mizpah. Among them was Jaazaniah, "a captain of the forces" (2 Kings 25:23; Jeremiah 40:8) whose seal was probably found during the excavations of Tell en-Nasbeh. This seal of banded agate depicts a cock in the lower register, and above it a Hebrew inscription, "belonging to Jaazaniah, officer of the king."[68]

Another of the old Judahite officers, Ishmael, a relative of King Zedekiah and a fanatical royalist who was in the pay of Baalis, king of Ammon, killed Gedaliah, along with his staff and the few Babylonian soldiers whom Nebuchadnezzar had left as a garrison in Mizpah. During the recent excavations at Tell el-'Umeiri in Jordan, a seal impression of

Milkom-'ur, minister of Ba'al-yasha' was discovered. The biblical Baalis is a shortened and somewhat distorted form of the original Ba'al-yasha'. This discovery is the first extra-biblical attestation of the existence of this Ammonite king.[69]

Having thus eliminated Gedaliah and the last remnants of the administration of Judah, Ishmael took captive the remaining citizens of Mizpah, including Jeremiah and his secretary Baruch, and tried to join the Ammonites in Transjordan. This plan was thwarted by Johanan, another former general of Zedekiah, who intercepted Ishmael at Gibeon and liberated his captives. Ishmael escaped with eight men to the Ammonites (2 Kings 25:22-25; Jeremiah 40:6-41:15).

The escapees from Ishmael, fearful that Nebuchadnezzar would hold them responsible for Ishmael's murder of Gedaliah, decided to go to Egypt. Although Jeremiah assured them of their safety, they refused to heed him and forced him and his secretary, Baruch, to go with them to Egypt. There Jeremiah joined other, earlier refugees from Judah—part of the Egyptian diaspora. Thus ends the pre-Exilic history of Judah.

S I X

Exile and Return

From the Babylonian Destruction to the Reconstruction of the Jewish State

JAMES D. PURVIS

I. The Exile to Babylonia

"The rest of the people who were left in the city and the deserters who had deserted to the king of Babylon, together with the rest of the multitude, were carried into exile by Nebuzaradan the captain of the guard. But the captain of the guard left some of the poorest of the land to be vinedressers and plowmen."

2 Kings 25:11-12

THE CALAMITIES THAT BEFELL JUDAH IN 587 B.C., WHEN NEBUCHAD-nezzar, king of Babylon, crushed Zedekiah's rebellion and destroyed Jerusalem, are stated concisely but poignantly in the narrative prose accounts in 2 Kings 25:7-21 and Jeremiah 39:1-10 and 52:1-16: the execution of the king's sons before his eyes; then his own blinding and imprisonment; the burning of the Temple; the execution of Temple officials, military commanders and noblemen; and, finally, the exile of the survivors.

After this, Nebuchadnezzar appointed Gedaliah governor. Gedaliah established his administrative center at Mizpah. Although the extent of Gedaliah's authority is not indicated, there was apparently some hope for peace and economic recovery under his leadership.[1] This hope was thwarted, however, by Gedaliah's assassination and the flight of his supporters and others to Egypt. Thus, in addition to the destruction of Jerusalem and the exile of its leaders to Babylonia, the nation was further weakened by a dispersion to Egypt (2 Kings 25:22-26; Jeremiah 40:1-44:30).

How many   In reprisal for Gedaliah's assassination, the Babylonians deported still
exiles?   more Jews to Babylon. According to Jeremiah, 745 people were deported
in 582 B.C. (Jeremiah tells us that previously 832 people were deported
in 587 B.C. and 3,023 in 597 B.C., when King Jehoiachin was defeated
[Jeremiah 52:28-30]).

There are several surprises in Jeremiah's figures. First, the number of
deportees to Babylonia at the time of Gedaliah's assassination was not
much smaller than the number of those taken into exile at the
destruction of Jerusalem (only 87 fewer); second, the number deported
in the exile of 587 B.C. is itself not very large (832); and third, neither
of these deportations was as large as the exile of 598 B.C.—of the total
number of deportees (4,600), virtually two-thirds (3,023) went into exile
with the capitivity of King Jehoiachin in 598 B.C.

No figures are given in 2 Kings for the number of deportees in 587
B.C. (when Jerusalem was destroyed), and no reference is made to a
deportation following Gedaliah's assassination. Numbers are given,
however, for the first deportation under Jehoiachin. According to 2 Kings
24:14, 10,000 people were exiled at that time (of whom 7,000 were
soldiers and 1,000 craftsmen and smiths). This number greatly exceeds
the figure given in Jeremiah.

The lack of specific figures in 2 Kings for the exile of 587 B.C. is
not surprising; what the writer wished to stress was the destruction of
the city and its Temple and the fate of the survivors. But one thing is
clear: for the writer of 2 Kings, as for the editor of Jeremiah, the Exile
began in 597 B.C., when Nebuchadnezzar removed and imprisoned King
Jehoiachin and appointed Zedekiah as a puppet-king to reign in his
stead.

Neither is it surprising then that the concluding words of 2 Kings
concern King Jehoiachin. There we learn that in the 37th year of his
exile (i.e., 561 B.C.) the king was released from prison and granted a
position of status by the Babylonian king Evil-merodach (Amel-Marduk
in Babylonian records) (2 Kings 25:27-30; see also Jeremiah 52:31-34).
Why was this important to the biblical writers? Because their hope for
the restoration of the Davidic dynasty (the divine election of which played
such an important role in their theology of history) lay with Jehoiachin,
not with Zedekiah. Zedekiah had been appointed king by the
Babylonians only after Jehoiachin had been taken hostage; Zedekiah's
reign was viewed by many as only temporary.[2] In Babylonia, Jehoiachin
was regarded as the exiled Judahite king, both before and after the
deportation of 587 B.C. It was certainly not accidental that the leader
of the first wave of Jewish exiles to return to Jerusalem was Jehoiachin's
son, Sheshbazzar, and that the builder of the Second Temple was his
grandson, Zerubbabel.*

In short, according to the editors of 2 Kings and Jeremiah, the Judean

Exile to Babylonia began in 597 B.C. when King Jehoiachin was taken
hostage by Nebuchadnezzar (2 Kings 24:12-17; Jeremiah 52:28-30). This
was the first and largest of three separate deportations; a second
deportation occurred at the time of the destruction of Jerusalem in 587
B.C. (2 Kings 25:8-12; Jeremiah 52:12-16) and, according to Jeremiah,
a third occurred after the assassination of Gedaliah in 582 B.C. (Jeremiah
52:30).

The Book of Chronicles presents quite a different picture: Here there
is only one deportation—at the time of the destruction of the Temple
in 587 B.C., and indeed very little is said about it (2 Chronicles 36:20-
21). Although the Chronicler records the deportation of Jehoiachin
himself in 597 B.C. (2 Chronicles 36:10), he does not associate the
beginning of the national exile with that event. Rather, the Chronicler
states that it was "the precious vessels of the house of the Lord" that
were removed to Babylon with the exile of Jehoiachin; the removal of
the Temple vessels is what is important, not the removal of the people.

What is found in 2 Chronicles is a simplified retelling of the story
in which the historian has stressed what he considered important. The
Temple—its plan, construction, furnishings, administration and service—
is of paramount importance throughout the Chronicler's history. In Ezra
1-6 (a continuation of the narrative of 2 Chronicles 36), the Chronicler
regards the return of the Temple vessels at the end of the Exile as an
important link in establishing continuity between the cultic establishment
of the First and Second Temples (Ezra 1:7-11, 5:14-15, 6:5).[3] For the
Chronicler, when the Jews returned from Exile, they returned not with
a king to reestablish the older political order, but with the Temple vessels
to continue the cultic order that had allegedly existed in ancient times.

Equally important for the Chronicler is his claim that the Exile resulted
in the land's becoming desolate and lying fallow (in effect keeping its
own sabbath) (2 Chronicles 36:21). This condition of the land seems to
have been derived from a tradition (Leviticus 26:1-39) preserved in the
Holiness Code; the code states the punishment for idolatry as banishment
to a foreign land, with the result that the land lies fallow:

"And I will scatter you among the nations, and I will unsheath the
sword after you; and your land shall be a desolation, and your cities
shall be a waste. Then the land shall enjoy its sabbaths as long as
it lies desolate, while you are in your enemies' land; then the land
shall rest, and enjoy its sabbaths" (Leviticus 26:33-34).

The Chronicler also made use of Jeremiah's prophecy of an exile of 70
years (Jeremiah 25:11, 29:10), not simply to indicate that this would be
the duration of the Exile, but to stress that the land would have a ten-
fold (seven years times ten) sabbath rest:

"to fulfill the word of the Lord by the mouth of Jeremiah, until the
land had enjoyed its sabbaths. All the days that it lay desolate it kept

---

* Understanding Shenazzar of 1 Chronicles 3:18 to be Sheshbazzar. See B.T. Dahlberg,
"Sheshbazzar," IDB, Vol. 4 (Nashville, TN: Abingdon, 1962), pp. 325-326.

sabbath, to fulfill seventy years" (2 Chronicles 36:21).

If the number 70 was important, one had to begin counting at some point. The Chronicler chose to begin with the time of the destruction of Jerusalem in 587 B.C.,[4] not the captivity of Jehoiachin in 597 B.C.

The Chronicler's account of the Exile appears to have been shaped by his editorial concerns. It is thus less useful for historical reconstruction than the traditions in 2 Kings and Jeremiah, especially when Chronicles is in disagreement with these two sources. What does seem fairly certain, however, is that the Babylonian Exile began before the destruction of Jerusalem in 587 B.C. When the deportees in 587 B.C., and at any subsequent time, reached Babylonia they joined a Jewish community that was already established, with its own social structures, beside "the waters of Babylon."

Indeed, even earlier, in the late eighth century B.C., exiles from Israelite Samaria had been settled by the Assyrians in western Syria, Mesopotamia and Media (see 2 Kings 15:29, 17:6; 1 Chronicles 5:26). The annals of Sargon II indicate a deportation/settlement (and also military conscription) of about 27,000 Israelites.[5] The preaching of Ezekiel shows that not all of these communities had been assimilated by pagan cultures; much of this biblical book is concerned with the reunification of the Judean and Israelite branches of the nation after the destruction of Jerusalem in 587 B.C. Indeed, some passages in Ezekiel read as if they are actually directed at specific Israelite—that is, northern—communities in exile. The Jews of the military colony at Elephantine in Egypt (see below) may also have been of northern, Israelite origin.[6]

Thus, while we may date the Babylonian Exile from 597 B.C., this event was but part of a process of Israelite/Judahite settlements in Mesopotamia and Babylonia that had begun earlier and that would continue. Not all of Israel was deported, and not all of the descendants of the exiles returned; the Jewish people had become both a people in their ancestral homeland and in the Diaspora.

II. "By the Waters of Babylon": The Jewish Exiles in Babylonia

The familiar words of Psalm 137, "by the waters of Babylon, there we sat down and wept, when we remembered Zion," constitute an oft-cited cliché to express the mood of the Babylonian exiles. This is not surprising; the psalm is a poem of great beauty, in which plaintive lyricism is mixed both with frustration ("How shall we sing the Lord's song in a foreign land?") and with nostalgia and loyalty ("If I forget you, O Jerusalem, let my right hand wither!"). What it expresses was certainly part of the experience of Exile for many of the deportees. But it falls short of expressing all we know of Jewish life in Babylonia and thus ought not to be taken as characteristic of the Exile experience as a whole. A more representative text—certainly of the social and economic dimensions of life by the waters of Babylon—is found in a letter written by Jeremiah to the deportees after 597 B.C.:

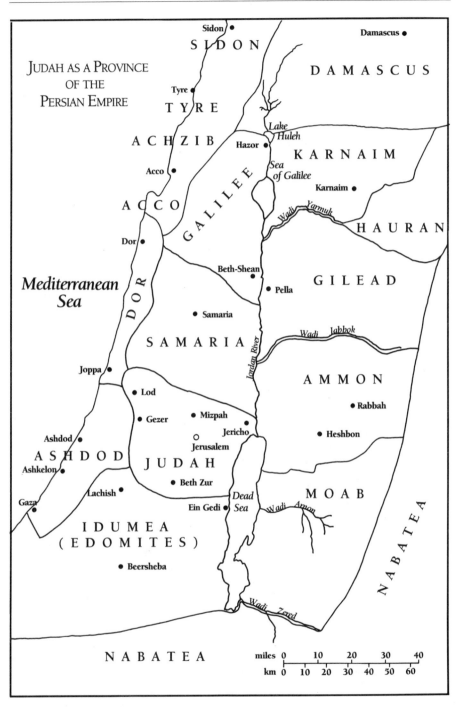

JUDAH AS A PROVINCE
OF THE
PERSIAN EMPIRE

Sidon

Damascus

S I D O N

D A M A S C U S

Tyre

TYRE

ACHZIB

Hazor

Lake
Huleh

KARNAIM

Acco

Sea
of Galilee

Karnaim

ACCO

GALILEE

HAURAN

Dor

Beth-Shean

Pella

GILEAD

Mediterranean
Sea

DOR

Samaria

Wadi Jabbok

SAMARIA

Jordan River

AMMON

Joppa

Lod

Rabbah

Gezer

Mizpah

Jericho

Heshbon

Ashdod

Jerusalem

ASHDOD

JUDAH

Ashkelon

Beth Zur

Gaza

Lachish

Ein Gedi

Dead
Sea

MOAB

Wadi Arnon

NABATEA

IDUMEA
(EDOMITES)

Beersheba

Wadi Zered

NABATEA

miles 0   10   20   30   40

km 0   10   20   30   40   50   60

"Build houses and live in them; plant gardens and eat their produce. Take wives and have sons and daughters; take wives for your sons, and give your daughters in marriage, that they may bear sons and daughters; multiply there, and do not decrease. But seek the welfare of the city where I have sent you into exile, and pray to the Lord on its behalf, for in its welfare you will find your welfare" (Jeremiah 29:5-7).

This seems to be as things worked out, though hardly in deference to the prophet's appeal.

Although our knowledge of Jewish life in Babylonia is fragmentary, we are nonetheless able to put together a general picture of the situation from allusions in contemporary biblical texts, from later biblical texts and from extra-biblical sources.

Life in   With the exception of some members of the royal Judahite family and
Babylonia   aristocracy, the people did not live in "captivity"; they were settled on land where they were free, as Jeremiah says, to "build houses and live in them and plant gardens and eat their produce." Their status probably did not permit them to be landowners; more likely, they were land-tenants on royal estates.[7] We know that some Jews were settled beside "the river Chebar" (Ezekiel 1:1-3, 3:15,23), an irrigation canal of the Euphrates (Akkadian, *nâru kabari*) that flowed through Nippur. One Jewish settlement beside the Chebar was known as Tel-abib (Ezekiel 3:15); if this settlement was even then a tell, or mound containing a buried ancient city, it might be evidence that the Babylonians settled the Jewish deportees at or near the sites of ruined, abandoned cities, perhaps as part of a program to develop unutilized land resources. Further support for this suggestion comes from the fact that Jewish exiles were apparently also settled at Tel-melah and Tel-harsha (Ezra 2:59). Other places of Jewish settlement mentioned specifically by name are Cherub, Addan/Addon, Immer (Ezra 2:59 and Nehemiah 7:61), and Casiphia (Ezra 8:17). The locations of these cities are not known. Some Jews were probably also conscripted into military and other imperial services, as was the custom both of the Assyrians and of the Babylonians in their dealings with deportees.

Evidence of Jews in the *nâru kabari* (Chebar) region also comes from a number of cuneiform documents discovered in excavations at Nippur. The so-called Murashu texts contain the records of a large Babylonian family banking firm. Copies of contracts made by Jews and other documents concerning Jews testify to the existence of Jewish communities in 28 settlements in the Nippur area. Although dating from the Persian period (fifth century B.C.), these records indicate that Jews had prospered in agriculture, in trade and in banking during the century after their settlement there. There appears to be no discrimination against Jews, despite the fact that they were descendants of foreigners. Jews made the same kind of contracts and at the same interest rates as others. Several had positions of prestige, one in the Murashu firm itself, another in government service. One Jew held a military fief, for which he was obliged to render military services or to furnish a substitute.[8]

Indications that some of the Jews of the Exile managed to accumulate wealth also appear in Ezra 1:5-6 and 2:68-69, which speak of contributions in gold, silver and precious goods for the rebuilding of the Temple in Jerusalem. Ezra 2:65 mentions male and female slaves who returned with their Jewish masters. Not only were Jews permitted to own slaves, some were financially able to do so.

The recognized leader of the Jewish community during the Babylonian Exile was the Davidic monarch Jehoiachin. Although his leadership was only titular, it was nonetheless significant. From the very beginning of Jehoiachin's captivity in 597 B.C., there was apparently hope for his restoration to power, even though the prophet Jeremiah counseled against a naive optimism in this regard (Jeremiah 28-29). Ezekiel indicated his own loyalty to the hostage king by dating events from the year 597 B.C. and expressed the hope that Jehoiachin's family would again shepherd the people in their native land (Ezekiel 34:20-31, 37:24-28). In addition to the biblical texts, two sets of epigraphic data may testify to the status of Jehoiachin in exile: first, a number of seal impressions found over a wide range in Judah bear the inscription "Belonging to Eliakim, steward of Yaukin"; second, a cuneiform document from the official archives in Babylon lists rations of foods to be supplied from the royal storehouses to King Yaukin of Judah, his five sons and other Judahite officials. William F. Albright, the discoverer of the first of the Yaukin seals, at Tel Beit Mirsim, suggested that Eliakim was the Judahite administrator of the crown properties of Jehoiachin following his deportation and that Yaukin represented a form of Jehoiachin. (Recently, however, scholars have questioned this identification.*) Albright believed that Zedekiah, the puppet-king appointed by the Babylonians, decided not to confiscate Jehoiachin's wealth; because he was unsure of Jehoiachin's restoration[9] Zedekiah was himself insecure in his own position. As for the significance of the ration for Jehoiachin in the Babylonian cuneiform archives, we may cite Albright:[10]

*Jehoiachin
still king*

"Now we know that Jehoiachin was not only the legitimate king of the Jewish exiles in Babylonia from their own point of view; he was also regarded by the Babylonians as legitimate king of Judah, whom they held in reserve for possible restoration to power if circumstances should seem to favor it."

Jehoiachin was released from prison in 561 B.C. by Nebuchadnezzar's successor, Amel-Marduk, and thereafter received provisions by royal allowance (2 Kings 25:27-30 and the Babylonian cuneiform archives). Thus, the exiled king and his family enjoyed some measure of freedom in Babylonia. This did not, however, result in Jehoiachin's restoration to

---

* See Peter Machinist's review of *A History of Ancient Israel and Judah* by J. Maxwell Miller and John H. Hayes in "Books in Brief," *BAR*, Nov./Dec. 1986, p. 4.

Elephantine papyrus. In the fifth and fourth centuries B.C., during the period of the Exile and for some time thereafter, a Jewish community thrived on the island of Elephantine, in the upper Nile River. A collection of letters, deeds and other documents of this community included this well-preserved papyrus, folded several times, bound with a string and sealed with a *bulla*. The word "deed" is written in ink on the papyrus.

power in his native land. We do not know what prompted Jehoiachin's release, and we can only guess at how this action may have related to internal Babylonian politics.[11] All we know is that Jehoiachin spent the remainder of his life in Babylonia as the recognized head of the exiled Jewish community.

Jewish communal leadership in Babylonia appears to have been in the hands of officials known as "elders"—the elders of the Exile, of Judah and of Israel (Jeremiah 29:1; Ezekiel 8:1, 14:1, 20:1). Texts concerning the return to Jerusalem also mention "the heads of families" (e.g., Ezra 2:68, 8:1). The family was apparently the basic unit of social organization in Babylonia. Whether families kept the strict genealogical records indicated in Ezra 2 and Nehemiah 7 is moot; one group of priests was chided (and subsequently disenfranchised) for not having done so (Ezra 2:59-63; Nehemiah 7:61-65). The genealogical tables in Ezra 2:8 and Nehemiah 7:11-12 show a keen interest in the families of the cultic orders, i.e., priests, levites, *nethinim* (temple servants), and a group known as the "sons of Solomon's servants." A passage in Ezra 8:15-20 indicates that there were concentrations of these families in particular places; Ezra secured a number of levites and *nethinim* from "the place Casiphia."

A Temple in Babylon?   This raises the question of cultic or religious activities among the exiles in Babylonia. From the Elephantine papyri, we know that a Jewish temple existed in Egypt at Elephantine (Yeb) during the fifth century B.C.[12] From Josephus we know that in the Hellenistic period another Jewish temple was built in Egypt at Leontopolis.[13] From Josephus we also learn of a Samaritan temple on Mt. Gerizim.[14] Also during the Hellenistic period, a Jewish temple was probably constructed at the Tobiad center in Transjordan.[15] The Deuteronomic restriction on multiple shrines and the command to make pilgrimage to and perform cultic rites at only one place (Deuteronomy 12) was interpreted to apply only to worship in the land of Canaan, not outside. It thus leaves open the question of worship in the Diaspora.

Was there a Jewish temple in Babylonia? Most scholars who have addressed this question have said no, citing the absence of any specific reference to such a sanctuary and the difficulty Jews might have had in securing permission for its construction. But the silence of our literary sources means little, because they are so scant, and permission for the building of a modest shrine might have presented few difficulties. The possible existence of a Jewish temple in Babylonia has been suggested by Peter R. Ackroyd, who notes two biblical texts that may imply this.[16] One is the Ezra passage already cited, concerning the concentration of levites and *nethinim* at Casiphia. Ezra 8:17 refers to Casiphia (twice) as "the place [Hebrew, *maqôm*] Casiphia." In biblical Hebrew, *maqôm* sometimes refers simply to a place; but it is frequently used in the technical sense of "holy place" or "shrine." The other text is Ezekiel 11:16, which reads in the Revised Standard Version,

"Though I removed them far off among the nations, and though I scattered them among the countries, yet I have been a sanctuary [Hebrew, *miqdash*] to them for a while [or in a small measure] in the countries where they have gone."

This could mean, as the RSV translation suggests, that God himself has been a *miqdash* for the people in exile, that the divine presence has sufficed for, or has been better than, a sanctuary. Or it could indicate that, for a while, the people had a small-scale sanctuary in Babylonia.

It is sometimes suggested that the synagogue (as a substitute for the temple) came into being at this time. But there is no specific evidence for this, and the question has been debated with no clear resolution.[17] Part of the difficulty has been lack of agreement on exactly what is meant by synagogue: the institution known from later times with clearly defined functions in respect to the reading of the law and prayers?—Or simply a meeting place for community activities?[18] Whichever, the origins of the synagogue are obscure. Nor is it clear that its original purpose, functionally speaking, was to provide a place of worship for those who did not have a temple or who found it inconvenient to get to the temple. There were, for example, synagogues in Jerusalem during the Roman period before the destruction of the Second Temple; such synagogues clearly were not needed as substitutes for the nearby Temple and its rituals.

The question of how and where Jews may have worshipped in Babylonia needs to be addressed in the context of the communal character of Jewish prayer. Prayer may be offered in solitude, as was the case with Daniel in Babylon; Daniel prayed three times daily in his chamber, facing a window opened towards Jerusalem (Daniel 6:10-11). But the experience of prayer in Israel was rooted in community worship. It is through the shared experience of worship that one becomes accustomed to a specific number of daily prayers (the reference in Daniel is the earliest to the thrice-daily practice that later became standard in Judaism) and it is through group conditioning that prayers come to have a standard form: in the case of Daniel's prayer, thanksgiving, petition and supplication (Daniel 6:11). A shared experience similarly influences religious rites of fasting. It inculcates the custom of observance, determines the dates on which one fasts and sets the standards of what is appropriate for fasting (from what one abstains, conditions of sorrow and mortification, penitential prayers, personal adornment, etc.). We learn from Zechariah 7:1-6 that it had become the custom during the 70 years of Exile to fast in the fifth and seventh months, i.e., in the month in which the Temple had been burned (the seventh day of the fifth month, according to 2 Kings 25:8, although in Jeremiah 52:12 it is the tenth day of the fifth month) and the month in which Gedaliah had been assassinated (the seventh month [2 Kings 25:25; Jeremiah 41:1]). A longer catalogue of fast days appears in Zechariah 8:18-19, and includes fasts in the fourth and tenth months, i.e., in those months in which the wall of Jerusalem had first been breached by the Chaldeans/Babylonians (the ninth day of the fourth month [2 Kings 25:2; Jeremiah 52:6]) and, in the previous year, in the month in which the siege of Jerusalem had begun (the tenth day of the tenth month [2 Kings 25:1; Jeremiah 52:4]).

If Jews in Babylonia observed these fasts, they had to have some place to convene. Esther 4:16 indicates that fasting was a communal phenomenon among Jews in the Exile: "Go, gather all the Jews to be found in Susa, and hold a fast on my behalf, and neither eat nor drink for three days, night or day. I and my maids will also fast as you do." But neither a temple with sacred precincts nor a public house of prayer would have been necessary for such gatherings; any open place with adequate space could have sufficed. "The place (*maqôm*) Casiphia," with its concentration of levites and temple servants, skilled in liturgy, could have been such a place of gathering; if so, it was certainly not the only place. In this connection, Psalm 137 speaks of weeping (rites of mourning) beside the waters (i.e., water canals) of Babylon. Ezekiel 1:1-3:15 mentions the banks of the river Chebar (the canal *nâru kabari*) as the place of the prophet's "visions of God" (appropriately so, if it was a place of community worship). Later texts dealing with the Jewish Diaspora of the Greco-Roman world testify to the existence of public places of prayer by the seaside or beside rivers.[19] One such witness comes from the New Testament, in the story of Paul in Philippi:

"We remained in this city some days; and on the sabbath day we went outside the gate to the riverside, where we supposed there was a place of prayer . . ." (Acts 16:12-13).

Thus, while there may have been places of public assembly where religious rituals were performed, it is unclear whether there were buildings associated with these places, and if so whether they may be considered synagogues or temples.

Assimilation   We may assume that not all Jews were faithful to the religion of their fathers and that some may have assimilated into Babylonian culture. But of this we have no direct information. We do know that Ezekiel was

Seal impression. Made by a sixth-century B.C. seal only three-quarters of an inch long, this impression reads "Belonging to Yehoyishma, daughter of Sawas-sar-usur." Yehoyishma—"Yahweh will hear"—is a type of name that originated in Babylonia during the Exile. Sawas-sar-usur is a well-known neo-Babylonian name that means "Shamash protect the king!" (Shamash is the name of the Babylonian sun-god.)

The owner of this seal was a Jewish woman with a Yahwistic name; her father had a neo-Babylonian pagan name. How do we explain this phenomenon? Suppose one of the first exiles in Babylonia gave his son the name Sawas-sar-usur. By the time this man had a daughter, there was a great revival of religious and national feeling among the Jews. Perhaps in reaction to his own pagan name and as an expression of hope for divine help to return to Jerusalem, Sawas-sar-usur gave his daughter a purely Yahwistic name meaning "Yahweh will hear."

concerned with Jews adopting Babylonian cults (see Ezekiel 8:14). But his concern was directed primarily at the situation in the Jewish homeland rather than in the Exile. Deutero-Isaiah's oracles against idol worship (Isaiah 44:9-17, 46:1-13) are given in a context of contempt for paganism rather than rebuke of the Jewish people for practices they may have adopted. But the attraction of idols was, and remained, a problem for spiritual leaders in the Jewish Diaspora, as may be seen from later writings, including the Letter of Jeremiah and the Wisdom of Solomon 13-15 (from the Apocrypha). In addition, we know that some Jews adopted Babylonian names. Others, while using Hebrew/Aramaic names, replaced the more traditional Israelite/Jewish element *-yahu* (a form of Yahweh) with the more general divine element *-'el*.[20] This indicates a degree of assimilation, but not an abandonment of traditional Jewish religion.

Members of the house of Jehoiachin had Babylonian names probably out of deference to their royal patrons. Nahman Avigad has published a seal of a Jew who had a traditional Jewish name, but her father bore a Babylonian name, reflecting perhaps the renewal of national aspirations among Babylonian Jews of the second generation in Exile—to which the oracles of Deutero-Isaiah also bear witness.[21]

In short, the Jewish deportees were settled in Babylonia as land-tenants of royal estates in undeveloped areas. As such, they joined other ethnic minorities in the Mesopotamian/Babylonian region, including some previously settled Israelite communities. With the exception of some members of the royal family, the Judahites were not imprisoned or held as captives. They were free to engage in agriculture and commerce and to accumulate wealth, although on a modest scale. They were not coerced to abandon their traditional cultural ways or social organization. The imprisoned (and later freed) King Jehoiachin was their titular head, although de facto leadership was in the hands of elders and/or heads of families. Their corporate life included religious observances of prayer and public fasting. We have no evidence that they erected public buildings for such communal activities, although it is possible that they did. Some Jews were assimilated into Babylonian culture. Others were not; when the opportunity arose, a number of Jewish families returned to their homeland to reconstruct a national life there. Many, however, remained in Babylonia, where the Jewish Diaspora continued as an important cultural phenomenon for over two millennia.

III. "And these from the land of Syene"—The Jewish Diaspora in Egypt.

The fate of the Jewish exiles in Babylonia would probably be of little concern to us were it not for the fact that the restoration of the Jewish state in the late sixth-early fifth century was the work of Jewish leaders who came from Babylonia. It was they who led the initial return to Jerusalem, the subsequent rebuilding of the Temple under Sheshbazzar and Zerubbabel, and finally the cultic/national reforms and rebuilding of the city under Ezra and Nehemiah. In the books of Ezra and Nehemiah, the local Judean population (who had not been exiled) is regarded with contempt; the only citizens who seem to matter (and the only Temple personnel allowed to function) are those with proper genealogical records brought from Babylonia. Nonetheless, there were Jews who never left the land, and there were Jewish Diaspora communities in places other than Babylonia—most notably in Egypt.

The books of Ezra and Nehemiah mention no return of Egyptian Jews to Judea during this period. This may have been because there were none, or none worth mentioning, or none the Babylonian Jews wished to acknowledge. Nevertheless, we are reminded of the words of Jeremiah "concerning all the Jews that dwelt in the land of Egypt, at Migdol, at

Tahpanhes, at Memphis, and in the land of Pathros . . ." (Jeremiah 44:1-14):

"I will punish those who dwell in the land of Egypt, as I have punished Jerusalem, with the sword, with famine, and with pestilence, so that none of the remnant of Judah who have come to live in the land of Egypt shall escape or survive or return to the land of Judah, to which they desire to return to dwell there; for they shall not return, except some fugitives" (Jeremiah 44:13-14).

On the other hand, Deutero-Isaiah, a prophet active among the exiles in Babylonia, included the Jews of Egypt among those he envisioned participating in the return to Zion: "Lo, these shall come from afar, and lo, these from the north and from the west, and these from the land of Syene" (Isaiah 49:12).

"The land of Syene" was the southern frontier of Egypt at the first cataract of the Nile (modern Aswan), as in the formulaic expression "the land of Egypt . . . from Migdol to Syene, as far as the border of Ethiopia [or Nubia]" (Ezekiel 29:10). As Syene was located at the southern border, Migdol was located at the northeastern frontier. There were military encampments at both of these sites with settlements of foreign mercenaries and their families.

The existence of a Jewish community at Syene is known from the Elephantine papyri (the major fortress at Syene was on the island in the Nile later called Elephantine; Jewish troops stationed there referred to it as Yeb).

The existence of Jews in the Migdol area, on the northeastern border of Egypt, may also be alluded to in the Elephantine documents. Jeremiah, as we have seen, speaks of Jews at Migdol and at nearby Tahpanhes (later called Daphni, modern Tel Dafneh) and also at Noph (Memphis) and Pathros (Nubia). It was to the area of Migdol and Tahpanhes that Johanan ben Kareah led his group of refugees after the disruption of political and social order following Gedaliah's assassination (Jeremiah 43:8-13).

Archaeological evidence for the Egyptian diaspora

Excavations east of the Suez Canal under the direction of Eliezer Oren of the Ben-Gurion University of the Negev reveal that in the early sixth century B.C. this area of Jewish settlement was a fertile, densely populated region with a navigable water system, as well as irrigation and drainage canals. Migdol was not only a military center, but a commercial and industrial area. Imported pottery types testify to the existence of a large foreign element in the population, which is not surprising because the Egyptians had, since the reign of Psammetichus I (664-610 B.C.), come to rely on foreign mercenaries to garrison their border stations and to fill the ranks of their regular army. Nor is it surprising that Jeremiah's catalogue of areas of Jewish residence follows a line of defense systems established by the Egyptians, from the northeast border (Migdol) to Nubia (Pathros). It was in these centers that Jewish soldiers and their families lived and it was to these centers their compatriots would have come in settling in Egypt.[22]

A good deal of information concerning life in the Jewish settlement at the border station of Syene/Yeb during the fifth century B.C. comes from the Elephantine papyri. The papyri—archival documents in Aramaic including copies of correspondence, memoranda, contracts and other legal materials—first came to light in the late 19th century and were published by numerous scholars over a 60-year period (1906-1966). They have recently been the subject of intensive investigation (with corrections of some mistakes made by earlier scholars) by Bezalel Porten of the Hebrew University.[23] The documents date from 495 to 399 B.C., and are thus roughly contemporaneous with the reconstruction of the Jewish state under Ezra and Nehemiah, but the Jewish community at Elephantine had existed for at least a century before the earliest Elephantine documents.

The most intriguing aspect of Jewish communal life at Elephantine was a temple to the Hebrew God Yahu (YHW, a variant form of YHWH). According to the papyri, their temple had been destroyed by the Egyptians at the instigation of the priests of the local cult of Khnum in the 14th year of Darius II (410 B.C.). Exactly when it was built is unknown, but it was sometime prior to the Persian period (before 525 B.C.). Jedaniah, the Jewish communal leader at Elephantine, wrote to Bagohi the Persian governor of Judah, requesting assistance in rebuilding the Elephantine temple. Jedaniah also wrote to Delaiah and Shelemiah, the sons and successors of Sanballat, governor of Samaria, with the same request. Other correspondence with Jerusalem requested information on the correct procedure for observing the Feast of Unleavened Bread (Passover) and matters of cultic purity. Although Jedaniah represented his Elephantine temple as a regular Jewish sanctuary, just like the Jerusalem Temple, scholars have tended to regard the Yahu cult at Elephantine as a syncretistic mixture of Yahwism and native Canaanite (especially northern Canaanite) cults of Bethel, Anat-Bethel, Eshem, Eshem-Bethel, Herem-Bethel and Anath-YHW. This is because the names of these deities appear in judicial oaths and salutations used by Jews in the Elephantine documents. Accordingly, a northern, Israelite origin of these colonists has been suggested. Porten, on the other hand, contends that "the evidence for a syncretistic communal cult of the Jewish deity dissipates upon close inspection" (although "individual Jewish contact with paganism remains"). According to Porten, the temple was established by priests from Jerusalem who had gone into self-imposed exile in Egypt during the reign of King Manasseh (c. 650 B.C.) to establish a purer Yahwistic temple there.[24]

Whether or not the cult of Yahu at Elephantine was syncretistic or the Jews of Elephantine were syncretistic, one thing is nevertheless clear: pagan religion was more influential in the life of the Jews of upper Egypt than it was in the life of Jews in Babylonia. The tradition preserved in Jeremiah 44:15-30 records the worship of a goddess called "the Queen of Heaven" (compare Jeremiah 7:18) by the Jews of Johanan ben Kareah's community in the Pathros/Migdol area of Egypt. Similar tendencies probably prevailed among the Jews in upper Egypt. This may be why Jeremiah judges the Jews of Egypt so harshly. This may also be why we read nothing of any role the Jews of Egypt played in the reconstruction of the Jewish nation during the Persian period.

IV. Return and Restoration Under the Persians

"For we are bondmen; yet our God has not forsaken us in our bondage, but has extended to us his steadfast love before the kings of Persia, to grant us some reviving to set up the house of our God, to repair its ruins, and to give us protection in Judea and Jerusalem" (Ezra 9:9).

When Cyrus the Great, the Achemenid ruler of Persia, conquered Babylon in 539 B.C., the Persians succeeded the Chaldeans (or Babylonians) as the major imperial power of the Near East. In contrast to their Assyrian and Babylonian predecessors, the Achemenid Persians represented themselves to their subject-states as a benevolent power concerned not just with the garnering of taxes but with the maintenance of peace and order throughout the empire. The territories formerly administered by the Assyrians and Babylonians were reorganized into a system of satrapies and provinces; local governments were strengthened; roads and systems of communication were developed; and—most important for the Jews—displaced and exiled peoples were encouraged to return to their ancestral homelands to reestablish local religious and political institutions in order to play supportive roles in this new concept of empire.

This is the political background of the decree of Cyrus preserved in 2 Chronicles 36:23 and Ezra 1:2-4:

Cyrus's decree permitting the exiles' return

"Thus says Cyrus king of Persia, 'The Lord, the God of Heaven, has given me all the kingdoms of the earth, and has charged me to build Him a house at Jerusalem, which is in Judah. Whoever is among you of all his people—may His God be with him, and let him go up to Jerusalem which is in Judah and rebuild the House of the Lord God of Israel—He is the God who is in Jerusalem; and let each survivor, in whatever place he sojourns, be assisted by the men of his place with silver and gold, with goods, and with beasts beside(s) freewill offering(s) for the house of God that is in Jerusalem' " (Ezra 1:2-4).

Although the text of this decree is preserved only in the Bible, it is not dissimilar in spirit and style to the edict of Cyrus known as the Cyrus Cylinder. In this document Cyrus credits his accomplishments to the Babylonian deity Marduk, for the benefit of his Babylonian subjects, as he is here said to have acknowledged the assistance of Yahweh; his policy of rebuilding ruined sanctuaries and resettling dispersed population is also reflected in the Cyrus Cylinder:[25]

"From . . . to the cities of Ashur and Susa, Agade, Eshnunna, the cities of Zamban, Meturna, Der, as far as the region of Gutium, the holy cities beyond the Tigris whose sanctuaries had been in ruins over a

BRITISH MUSEUM

Cyrus Cylinder. The inscription written in cuneiform on this ten-inch-long clay barrel tells how the great god Marduk chose Cyrus (559-529 B.C.) to supplant the impious tyrant who preceded him as king of Persia, and of how Cyrus next conquered the equally odious king of Babylon, Nabonidas. It then proclaims, "I am Cyrus, king of the world, great king," and gives an account of his benevolent acts. Among Cyrus's acts was his decree that permitted the exiled Jews to return to Jerusalem in 538 B.C.

long period, the gods whose abode is in the midst of them, I returned to their places and housed in lasting abodes. I gathered together all their inhabitants and restored to their dwellings."

The exiled Jewish community of Babylonia greeted Cyrus as a liberator and saw his work as fulfilling a divine purpose in national redemption: "Thus says the Lord, your Redeemer, who formed you from the womb; 'I am the Lord, who made all things, who stretched out the heavens alone . . . .' who says of Cyrus, 'He is my shepherd, and he shall fulfill all my purpose'; saying of Jerusalem, 'She shall be built,' and of the Temple, 'Your foundation shall be laid.' " (Isaiah 44:24, 28)

But the task of national reconstruction was not without difficulties. The returning exiles found that their hope conflicted with new territorial hegemonies that had come into being during their absence—most particularly in regard to Samaria, which apparently had exercised control over the Judean territory.[26]

Rebuilding
the Temple

According to biblical sources, there were successive waves of repatriations of Jews under Persian rule. The first was led by Sheshbazzar, the son of King Jehoiachin who had been taken into captivity in 597 B.C. (Sheshbazzar is called Shenazzar in 1 Chronicles 3:18). This first return occurred not long after 539 B.C., when Cyrus conquered Babylon and subsequently issued a decree that provided for the rebuilding of the Jewish Temple (Ezra 1:1-11). Sheshbazzar was entrusted with the Temple vessels (Ezra 1:7, 5:14-15) and is reported to have laid the foundation for the rebuilt Temple (Ezra 5:16). The actual work of rebuilding, however, remained uncompleted. No figures are given for those who returned under Sheshbazzar. It was a modest and unpretentious beginning.

A major wave of returning exiles was then led by Zerubbabel, the son of Shealtiel and grandson of Jehoiachin, and by the priest Joshua/Jeshua, apparently during the early years of the administration of Darius (522-486 B.C.; Ezra 2:2, 3:2, 8; 4:2-3; 5:1-2; Nehemiah 7:7, 12:1, 47; Haggai 1:1, 2:2,; Zechariah 3:1-4:14).[27] Ezra 2:1-67 and Nehemiah 7:6-73 give a census of the returnees—who numbered 42,360 people, plus 7,337 servants and 200 singers.

Zerubbabel and Joshua established an altar on the Temple Mount in Jerusalem and again began the work of Temple construction, this time in the second year of Darius's reign (520 B.C.). The Temple was completed in the sixth year of Darius (516 B.C.), with the encouragement of the prophets Haggai and Zechariah and the support of the Persian court, despite strong local resistance (Ezra 6:1-15). For his work in rebuilding the Temple, the prophet Zechariah hailed Zerubbabel as "the branch," a messianic title.

This repatriation and restoration should be understood against the background of Darius's career. When Darius came to power in 522 B.C., he suppressed rebellions throughout his realm, including revolts in Babylon led by Nebuchadnezzar III (522 B.C.) and Nebuchadnezzar IV (521 B.C.). Darius also reorganized the satrapies and provinces and the command of the armies. He introduced imperial coinage, a road and postal system, and royal building projects. The return of the Jewish exiles and the appointment of Zerubbabel as governor over Judah was part of Darius's reform of the empire's political structure.[28] But if Zerubbabel's supporters saw in these circumstances the opportunity for the restoration of monarchy under Davidic rule, their hope was ill-founded. The messianic sentiments concerning Zerubbabel expressed by the prophet Zechariah ("and [he] shall bear royal honor, and shall sit and rule upon his throne" [Zechariah 6:13]) would hardly have been acceptable to the Persians.

It is commonly thought that Darius removed Zerubbabel from office because of these messianic claims. But of this there is no evidence. The argument is based primarily on the low state of Jewish affairs at the next wave of immigration and on the silence of our sources concerning Zerubbabel after the Temple construction began. It is not clear whether he was still in office in 516 B.C. when the work was completed. But Zerubbabel was not the only person in the post-Exilic history of Ezra/ Nehemiah who vanished from the scene without explanation. True, Zerubbabel was no ordinary figure; he was the last active claimant to the Davidic throne of whom we have knowledge from the Hebrew Scriptures. Naturally, we speculate on what may have happened to him. But the evidence for any clear conclusion is absent.

Equally intriguing, and subject to speculation, is the figure of Joshua/

Jeshua, the high priest who led the return with Zerubbabel. He receives as much attention as Zerubbabel (perhaps even more) in Zechariah 3-6. He and Zerubbabel are linked together as "the two anointed who stand by the Lord of the whole earth" (Zechariah 4:14). Joshua's authority in temporal affairs may have equaled or even exceeded Zerubbabel's. Yet, like Zerubbabel, he disappears without a trace.

The Samaritans   Unfortunately, Judah's Samaritan neighbors sought to influence the Persians to limit the development of the renascent Jewish community. Initially "the adversaries of Judah and Benjamin" (i.e., the rulers of Samaria) offered to assist Zerubbabel in the rebuilding of the Temple of Yahweh, claiming they too were worshippers of the Hebrew God and had been since they were settled in the land by the Assyrians. Zerubbabel rebuffed the Samaritans' proffered assistance, however, and this led to their harassing the returning Judeans by means of correspondence with Persian officials.

The Yahwistic inhabitants of what was formerly Israel, whose help Zerubbabel rejected, were the descendants of Syrian/Mesopotamians. After the Assyrians destroyed the northern kingdom in 722 B.C., they sent colonists to settle the district. These Syrian/Mesopotamian colonists subsequently adopted the religion of the land (2 Kings 17:24-41). The biblical writers explain the hostility of the Samaritans, as these people came to be known, as resulting from the petty jealousy of a people whose mixed ethnic background and syncretistic Yahwism precluded participation in a renewed Jewish cult. It is not difficult to see the political agenda, however, in strained relations between the peoples of these two regions. We are told that the "people of the land discouraged the people of Judah" throughout the reign of Cyrus (i.e., from 538 to 530 B.C.) to the time of Darius, and subsequently during the reign of Ahasuerus (Xerxes, 486-465 B.C.), and in the days of Artaxerxes I (465/4-424/3 B.C.; Ezra 4:4-23).

Reference to Artaxerxes brings us down to the time of Ezra and Nehemiah. Ezra came to Jerusalem in the seventh year of the reign of Artaxerxes (458 B.C.; see Ezra 7:7). Nehemiah came to Jerusalem in the 20th year of Artaxerxes' reign (445/4 B.C.; Nehemiah 2:1), and was governor until Artaxerxes' 32nd year (433 B.C.; Nehemiah 5:14). Nehemiah also served a second term as governor sometime before Artaxerxes' death (424/3 B.C.). We have followed the chronological sequence of Ezra and Nehemiah suggested by the present arrangement of the biblical materials. It should be noted, however, that from the late 19th century until fairly recently the prevailing opinion had been that Nehemiah preceded Ezra (understanding the Artaxerxes of Ezra 7:7 as Artaxerxes II [404-358 B.C.]) and that the two were not at any point contemporaries. An alternative opinion was that Ezra came to Jerusalem during the reign of Artaxerxes I, but that he was preceded by Nehemiah, of whom he was later a contemporary (the date "the seventh year of Artaxerxes" of Ezra 7:7 being understood as a scribal corruption, probably of "thirty-seven"). More recently these views have been challenged and historical reconstructions proposed in which the traditional order of Ezra and Nehemiah has been restored. These historical reconstructions have resulted, in part, from recent archaeological data, including comparative information on the ruling house of Samaria (the Samaritan papyri of Wadi Dâliyeh).[29] The whole matter remains problematic, however.[30]

According to the biblical record, the most dramatic and long-lasting **Ezra** cultural and political changes in the post-Exilic Jewish state occurred during the tenure of Ezra and Nehemiah. From the biblical perspective, Ezra's accomplishments were primarily in the religious sphere, although these should be understood within the larger context of Persian policy of fostering local religio-legal traditions for the purpose of social stability within the provinces. Ezra arrived in Jerusalem not as a governor but as a "scribe skilled in the law of Moses," with a copy of the law (Ezra 7:6, 10) and with a commission from Artaxerxes to establish magistrates and judges in order to enact and teach that law (Ezra 7:11-14, 25-26). Ezra was also given funds and precious goods to revitalize religious rites in Jerusalem (Ezra 7:15-20, 8:21-34). This may have required some rebuilding activity. According to Ezra 6:14, the rebuilding of the Temple was accomplished by the royal decrees of Cyrus, Darius *and Artaxerxes,* so Ezra may well have participated in it. Eventually, under Ezra's leadership, and after Nehemiah's arrival (Nehemiah 8:9, 10:1), the law was accepted as the constitutional basis of Jewish life. This was done by formal public ceremony and contractual agreement (Ezra 9:1-10; Nehemiah 8:1-10:39). The prohibition of intermarriage with non-Jews was an especially important dimension of the acceptance of Jewish law.

It is widely assumed that the "law of Moses" that Ezra brought to Jerusalem was the Pentateuch (the first five books of the Hebrew Bible); if not the Pentateuch in its entirety, then perhaps Ezra brought one of the law codes incorporated in the Pentateuch. One suggestion is that he brought the so-called P-source of the Pentateuch (one of the strands of the Pentateuch according to the documentary hypothesis, which divides the Pentateuch into four different principal strands). Ezra has thus been credited with a major role in the history of the development of the canon of Jewish Scripture and/or in the editorial process that produced the Pentateuch in the form in which it is now known. What is curious about this assumption, however, is that of the quotations from Ezra's law code in the books of Ezra and Nehemiah, none agrees with any specific passage of the Pentateuch (see, for example, Ezra 9:10-12; Nehemiah 8:14-15). Ezra's reform measures agree in general with dicta contained in various parts of the Pentateuch, although Ezra's prohibition against intermarriage is far more specific than any command in the Pentateuch. Ezra's law code may have been simply a précis or compendium of Jewish law in a form suitable for deposit in the Persian court archives. We know that Ezra came as a scribe of the law of Moses, commissioned by Artaxerxes to be the promulgator and enforcer of that law. We do not know the particular form of that law, however, or how that law related to the Pentateuch as it has come down to us in its canonical form.

Ezra is frequently referred to as "the father of Judaism," that is, the father of Judaism as a religious system based upon Torah, or law. He was certainly an important person in the history of Judaism and played a significant role in the revitalization of Jewish life based upon Torah. Without diminishing Ezra's importance, however, we must remember that he was not the originator of Judaism as a legal system. This legal system can be traced to the religious reforms of King Josiah in 621 B.C. (2 Kings 22-23; 2 Chronicles 34-35). It was Josiah who promulgated a code of law, most likely an edition of Deuteronomy. Ultimately, however, Judaism as a religion of Torah may be traced to the work of Moses, and to the role of the levitical priests in the teaching of Torah in early Israelite culture.

Against exaggerated claims for Ezra, we may note that when the Jewish sage Ben Sira extolled the great heroes of Judaism, from Enoch to Simon the Just (in his eulogy "Let us now praise famous men," Sirach 44-50), he did not even mention Ezra. For Ben Sira, the heroes of the Persian period were Zerubbabel, Joshua/Jeshua and Nehemiah.

According to Ben Sira, it was Nehemiah who "raised for us the walls that had fallen, and set up the gates and bars and rebuilt our ruined houses" (Sirach 49:13). Before reviewing Nehemiah's accomplishments, however, let us survey what is known about this period from archaeological sources.

Until fairly recently the Persian period had been characterized as the dark age of Israelite history. This is no longer true, not only because of the availability of newer materials but especially because of the work of Ephraim Stern of the Hebrew University. Stern's study, which reviews all the available data, could well serve as a model for future publications on the relation of archaeological materials to a biblical period.[31]

Stern makes a number of pertinent observations: During the Persian period, the land of Israel was divided into two culturally distinct regions. The separation was as definite as that between two countries. One region consisted of the hill country of Judah and Transjordan (and to a lesser extent Samaria); the other included Galilee and the Mediterranean coastal plain. Judah's local culture was a continuation of its earlier culture (as noted by William F. Albright, who called the Persian period Iron Age III), although its culture also reflected Assyrian, Babylonian and Egyptian influence. The Galilee and the Mediterranean coast were influenced, on the other hand, by Greek and Phoenician cultures. Strangely, the material culture of the Persian period reflects almost no influence of the ruling Persians—the exceptions being a few pottery types and some Persian-style jewelry manufactured by Phoenicians. The major influence of the Persians on Israelite culture seems to relate to government, military organization, economic life and taxation. The most direct influence can be seen in coins and seals. Changes in seals impressed on jar handles used in connection with the collection of taxes indicate administrative reforms, with increasing local control, at the end of the fifth century.[32] Imperial Achemenid motifs in seals and seal impressions gradually are replaced by designs in local Aramaic script. A similar change is noted in coins; there we find the gradual appearance of the province name in Aramaic. Sometimes we even find coins with the governor's name in Aramaic.

Nehemiah's principal accomplishments are described in the Book of *Nehemiah* Nehemiah. He rebuilt the gates and walls of Jerusalem, despite the concerted preventive efforts of Sanballat, governor of Samaria; Tobiah, governor of Ammon; and Geshem, the leader of the Arab Qedarite confederacy (Nehemiah 1-4, 6, 12:27-43). Nehemiah also enforced legislation on mortgages, loans and interest for the betterment of the economic life of the Judean citizens (Nehemiah 5). He repopulated Jerusalem by means of a public lottery in which one-tenth of the Jewish population was moved into the city (Nehemiah 11). He established Jewish control over the cultural and economic life of the city (Nehemiah 13:15-22). He established cultic reforms to assure that the levites and Temple singers would not disperse to the countryside (Nehemiah 13:10-14). Finally, he enforced Ezra's legislation concerning intermarriage, especially as it affected the priestly orders (Nehemiah 13:1-9, 23-29). These reforms were carried out over a period of time, including a second administration as governor sometime after 433 B.C. (the 32nd year of Artaxerxes; Nehemiah 13:6) and before 423 (the year of Artaxerxes' death). Of his varied accomplishments, the greatest attention is given to rebuilding the walls of Jerusalem—and for good reason; this was a major move in the establishment of national security and a political statement that Nehemiah's adversaries understood very well.

These reforms indicate that during Nehemiah's administrations as governor, he exercised far more authority and control over local affairs than did his predecessors. This is consistent with what we now know about administrative changes towards more autonomy in the western Persian provinces in the late fifth century. The hostility of Nehemiah's neighboring governors also reflects this situation. Each maneuvered for greater control over his own area and entered into alliances (in this case against Judah) aimed at establishing his own hegemony. The position of Sanballat as leader of the conspiracy against Nehemiah reflects the history of Samaritan hegemony over Judah after the collapse of Judah in 587 B.C. and the assassination of the puppet governor Gedaliah.[33]

The extent of Judean hegemony in the time of Nehemiah—that is, the *Reduced size* borders of the province of Yehud—is reflected in several toponymical *of population* references in Ezra and Nehemiah, as well as in the distribution of Yehud *on the exiles'* seal impressions and coins found in the area. Ezra (2:21-35) and *return* Nehemiah (7:25-38, 3:2-22, 12:28-29) list names of places in the territory of Benjamin, the Jordan valley from Jericho to Ein Gedi, the Judean hills from Jerusalem to Beth Zur, and the districts of Lod and Adulam in the

Yehud (the name for Judea during the Persian period) has been stamped on numerous pottery handles and on coins. "Yehud" stamps and coins have been discovered in archaeological excavations from Tel en-Nasbeh (biblical Mizpah) in the north to Beth Zur in the south, and from Jericho in the east to Gezer in the west. Such seal impressions and coins help modern scholars to establish the boundaries of the ancient province.

The pottery handles probably belong to wine jars. The *Yehud* impression was literally an official stamp of approval.

The small silver coin, found in the Jericho region dates to the fourth century B.C. On the obverse a falcon with spread wings shares space with the *Yehud* stamp; a lily appears on the reverse.

Shephelah. These names, as Stern has noted, correspond approximately to the range of finds of Yehud seals, seal impressions and coins (from Tel en-Nasbeh in the north to Beth Zur in the south and from Jericho and Ein Gedi in the east to Gezer in the west). Evidence of the borders also comes from archaeological surveys conducted by L. Y. Rahmani of Israel's Department of Antiquities and Moshe Kochavi of Tel Aviv University; these archaeologists have discovered lines of forts erected by the Jews during the Persian period as defenses against the province of Ashdod on the west and territories held by the Edomites in the south. The lines of demarcation of the province of Judah on the southwest and south as reflected in these forts correspond to the borders indicated in the biblical lists and to the distribution of Yehud impressions.

The list found in Nehemiah 11:23-35, on the other hand, gives much wider boundaries for Judah. This seems to be not a description of the actual borders of Judea, but rather a statement of the territory that Judea considered its own, an idealization based on older biblical boundaries. The actual borders were much smaller.[34]

The size of the province of Yehud and the size of its capital city Jerusalem were limited not simply by the amount of power Nehemiah and his successors could arrogate but also by the available Jewish population. Excavations in Jerusalem have shown that the city shrank in the Persian period, occupying only the eastern hill, as it had done much earlier in its history as an Israelite city.[35] All other indications of population size suggest a much smaller Jewish population in the country than during pre-Exilic times. Perhaps the biblical tradition that the land was denuded of its people in the early sixth century B.C. is not simply an overstatement by the editors of 2 Kings and Jeremiah or a fiction imposed by the Chronicler to promote the idea of sabbatical rest for the land. The rebuilding of the Jewish population took several hundred years; it was not until the second century B.C. that there was a sizable Jewish population in Jerusalem and Judea.

With the work of Nehemiah, biblical historiography ends. Our knowledge of Jewish life during the remainder of the Persian period (until the conquest of the area by Alexander the Great in 332 B.C.) is sketchy at best. From the Elephantine papyri we learn that the governor of Yehud in the year 408 B.C. was Bagohi and that in the same year Samaria was governed by Delaiah and Shelemaiah, sons of Sanballat, Nehemiah's adversary. The Jews of Yeb (Elephantine) wrote to these Samaritan and Judean leaders seeking assistance in rebuilding their temple. Josephus records an incident from the time of Artaxerxes II (404-358 B.C.) in which the Persians "defiled the sanctuary and imposed tribute on the Jews" (and also that "the people were made slaves") for a period of seven years. This, he says, resulted from the interference of Artaxerxes' general Bagoses who tried to appoint Jesus (that is, Joshua/Jeshua) son of Eliashib as high priest and became enraged when Jesus was murdered by his brother, the high priest Joannes (Johanan) (*Antiquities*, XI.297-301). Some scholars believe the Bagoses of this story is Bagohi, the governor of Judah known from the Elephantine papyri.[36]

The last Persian period incident recorded by Josephus occurred on the eve of Alexander's conquest of the area. According to Josephus, the Samaritans led by Sanballat built a temple on Mt. Gerizim. The reference is to Sanballat III,[37] grandson of the earlier Sanballat who had opposed Nehemiah's rebuilding of Judea. The building of a Samaritan temple on Mt. Gerizim about 332 B.C. is evident not only from Josephus and the sources he utilized (*Antiquities*, XI.304-347), but also from the archaeological evidence. Foundations of a temple at Tel er-Ras on Mt. Gerizim have recently been excavated.[38] Josephus claimed that this temple was built as a result of a schism in which expelled priests from the Jerusalem Temple and other malcontents from Jewish society took refuge with the Samaritans. This may or may not have been the case. It is more likely that this temple was an expression of the Samaritans' own national identity as a Hebrew people who claimed descent from the old Joseph tribes of the north (Ephraim and Manasseh) and who desired to worship God at the ancient and (from their understanding) true sanctuary at Shechem.

Because Josephus's account bears certain similarities to a brief note in Nehemiah 13:28 concerning Nehemiah's expelling of a son-in-law of Sanballat I from Jerusalem, some scholars have been inclined to date the building of the Samaritan sanctuary (and the alleged schism) to that earlier time (about 425 B.C.). An alternative dating is the time of Ezra (about 450 B.C.), although the biblical traditions on Ezra make no reference at all to the Samaritans, even in cases of intermarriage. In fact, the biblical record knows nothing of a Samaritan schism during the time of Ezra or Nehemiah. The history of the Samaritans as an autonomous religious community residing at Shechem belongs to a later time, not earlier than 332 B.C.[39]

In sum, the restoration of the Jewish nation in the land of Israel following Cyrus's edict of return was accomplished through successive waves of immigration, of both leaders and their followers, from the Babylonian Exile. We are not told of any role played by those who had remained in the land or by returnees from the Diaspora in Egypt. Although the biblical record covers a period of about 115 years (from 538 to 423 B.C.), or longer if Ezra was active during the reign of Artaxerxes II, the reporting of the period is episodic, focusing on specific roles played by five leaders: the return of the Temple vessels under Sheshbazzar, the rebuilding of the Temple under Zerubbabel and Joshua/ Jeshua, cultic renewal and the establishment of Mosaic law as the constitutional basis of society with the prohibition of mixed marriages by Ezra, and the rebuilding of the gates and walls of Jerusalem and the development of its economic and religious life by Nehemiah. Of these five leaders, Nehemiah is credited with the greatest specific political and social accomplishments. Resistance to the development of a Jewish state came primarily from Samaria because of cultural differences aggravated by political considerations. The biblical account may be understood against a dual background: the political history of the Persian empire and the archaeology of the land to which they returned. It is from the latter that we gain a clearer picture of the political realignments and the development of Judah as an autonomous province in the late fifth century B.C., under the leadership of Nehemiah.

S E V E N

The Age of Hellenism

Alexander the Great and the Rise and Fall of the Hasmonean Kingdom

LEE I. A. LEVINE

A LEXANDER THE GREAT (356-323 B.C.) CHANGED THE FACE OF Judea along with the rest of the then-known world. In 336 B.C. he became king of Macedon and of the Greek city-states conquered by his father, Philip II. Within a decade he defeated the Persians and fell heir to their empire.

Early in that decade, in 332 B.C., he conquered Judea, a conquest that was to have profound and far-reaching effects on Jewish history. Conquest itself was nothing new to the Jews; Judea had been subjugated on numerous occasions. This time the conqueror came from the west, rather than the east (as had Assyria, Babylonia and Persia). But this was not particularly significant. Two other factors made Alexander's conquest indeed historic. The first was cultural; the second, geographic.

The Greeks were interested not only in military victories, political expansion and economic gain; they were also committed to disseminating their way of life, their institutions, norms and ideas, to the world of the barbarians (as they called non-Greeks). In addition to political hegemony and imposition of taxes, Greek conquest exposed the eastern Mediterranean lands and beyond to an entirely different way of life—Hellenism.[1]

Perhaps the most effective means by which Hellenism was propagated in new regions was by the founding of a Greek city, or by reconstituting an already existing city, as a *polis*. Either step carried with it political,

Imposing Hellenism

religious, social and cultural ramifications. The newly founded city operated politically under a Greek constitution,* Greek deities were introduced into the city's pantheon, and Greek educational and entertainment institutions were established. Within a century of Alexander's conquest of Judea, Greek cities were founded along the Mediterranean coast, as well as inland at Beth-Shean and Samaria, and even to the east in Transjordan. These cities served as centers of Greek life and influence and reinforced one another through joint commercial, cultural and athletic enterprises.[2]

Judea's key location
The geographic consequences of Alexander's conquest also affected the course of Israel's history. In previous conquests Israel had invariably remained at the periphery of world empires, far from seats of power and authority. Its marginal geographic location assured the Jews a measure of stability and insulation. But with the death of Alexander in 323 B.C. and the breakup of his empire, Judea was thrown into the vortex of political and military activity. Geographically sandwiched between the two foci of power—the Seleucid kingdom based in Syria and the Ptolemaic kingdom of Egypt, the capital of which was in Alexandria—Judea served as a battlefield on which the Seleucids and the Ptolemies faced one another for the next century. No fewer than five major wars were fought between Egypt and Syria during the third century B.C., each lasting for at least several years. Garrison troops were posted all over Judea (including Jerusalem), and large armies were stationed throughout the country.

Either factor—exposure to Hellenistic culture or geographic centrality—would have been unsettling under any circumstances. But for the Jews of Judea these factors were wrenching, because in the centuries immediately preceding the conquest, these Jews had lived in a kind of splendid isolation. When Persia ruled the world, Cyrus maintained a policy of actively supporting ethnic and religious groups, encouraging them to rebuild their institutions and develop indigenous traditions. Naturally, this policy had been welcomed with open arms by Jewish leaders. The Persians had demanded only political loyalty and the payment of taxes. The district of Judea, or Yehud, consisted of a small area around Jerusalem that was far removed from the main cities and international highways of the country. Its location guaranteed it relative isolation from the surrounding world—geographically, socially and religiously.[3]

Thus, it is not surprising that, following Alexander's conquest, Judea's inundation by government officials, merchants, soldiers and others was traumatic for many Jews. Jerusalem was no longer able to remain insulated from the outside world—and many of its inhabitants did not want to be. The opportunities and attractiveness afforded by the wider

---

* A *boulé*, or legislative council, met regularly; *archei* (heads) were chosen from this body for the management of day-to-day affairs. A *demos* made up of ordinary citizens met infrequently.

culture were not to be denied. The silver coins minted by the Jerusalem authorities between about 300 and 250 B.C. provide striking expression of a positive Jewish response to Hellenistic influence. These coins bear representations of the Egyptian ruler Ptolemy I, his wife Berenike and an eagle—the latter the symbol of Ptolemaic hegemony. The presence of these motifs on Jewish coins is a clear attestation of a desire, at least by some, for successful integration into the new world order.[4]

It is difficult to assess how Jewish society as a whole, however, responded to this new reality. Did the Jews' isolated geographical circumstances (they lived mostly in the more remote hill country of Judea), combined with ethnic and religious differences, create a partial buffer between them and the outside world? Or was Jewish society profoundly affected by the changes, albeit at a somewhat slower pace than their pagan counterparts in the cities on the Mediterranean? Unfortunately, our sources are inadequate to answer these questions. The bits and pieces preserved offer but an inkling of the many and varied Jewish responses to the challenges of the new age. In general, we can say that the divisions in Jewish society deepened as a result of Hellenistic domination, political allegiances polarized into factions favoring the north (Seleucids) and south (Ptolemies), economic and social divergences became more exacerbated and traditional religious beliefs and practices were challenged.[5]

Assessing the Jewish reaction to Hellenism

However, the degree of Hellenization among Jews during the Hellenistic period (from Alexander's conquest to the establishment of the Hasmonean monarchy in 141 B.C.) remains unclear. Leading scholars have staked out quite different maximalist and minimalist positions. Some view the impact of Hellenism as profound (Bickerman, Hengel),[6] others as more negligible and superficial (Tcherikover, Sandmel, Millar).[7] In actuality, both positions contain some truth, and the reality was undoubtedly more complex than either extreme would suggest. Much depends to whom we are referring (an urban aristocrat or village farmer), the specific time period involved (the fourth or second century B.C.) and the particular areas of society under scrutiny (material culture, religious beliefs or social institutions). Much of the Jewish literature written or edited during the early Hellenistic period reflects a grappling with ideas from the outside world. The biblical Book of Ecclesiastes (Kohelet) remains the most explicit and detailed statement that we possess of the disturbing impact of this new environment on a Jew's religious and intellectual commitment.[8] Faith and certainty had been lost, and in their stead were doubt, hesitancy and skepticism. At the turn of the second century, Ben Sira composed a response to this type of thinking, called in Latin *Ecclesiasticus* (the little Ecclesiastes),* perhaps providing us with some indication of the gravity of the skepticism and loss of faith reflected

---

* Ecclesiasticus was included in the Greek translation of the Bible known as the Septuagint and remains a part of the Catholic Bible. For Jews and Protestants it is part of the Apocrypha.

in Ecclesiastes. In a similar vein, the Book of Jubilees presents an almost polemical emphasis on such basic commandments as circumcision (15:23-34) and the Sabbath (2:16-33), perhaps reflecting a certain laxity in observance resulting from exposure to the outside world. Finally, the rather graphic love song that came to be called the Song of Songs was probably edited about this time and reflects themes well attested in Hellenistic poetry.[9]

How much these intellectual and religious currents affected Jewish society at large is hard to gauge; the limited evidence offers conflicting signals. On the one hand, after the Seleucid ruler Antiochus III conquered Jerusalem (about 200 B.C.), he promulgated an edict granting privileges to the Jews of the city; this appears to confirm the traditional status and leadership of the city. Elders, high priest, priests and other Temple personnel were recognized as the leaders of the community and were accorded due privileges. The concerns expressed in Antiochus's edict focus on the Temple, the cult, religious precepts and the welfare of the city. It is probable that such issues stood at the forefront of Jerusalem affairs for decades, if not centuries.[10]

On the other hand, this almost idyllic picture becomes clouded when viewed from the perspective of other sources. The Jewish historian Josephus, for example, records a chronicle of the Tobiad family, whose members played an important role in Jerusalem politics at about this time. They represented Jewish interests to the Ptolemaic court in Alexandria and undoubtedly played a major role in internal Judean affairs as well. The Tobiads underwent a significant degree of acculturation during this period, adopting Greek names, mannerisms and life-styles.[11]

A second example of a more complex situation is preserved in 2 Maccabees 4. The Seleucid kings were often in desperate need of money to pay their annual tribute to Rome. In 175 B.C., Jason, a Jerusalemite of priestly lineage, offered the newly enthroned Seleucid monarch Antiochus IV a sum of money to secure for himself appointment as high priest in the Jerusalem Temple. Jason then added an additional amount for the right to convert Jerusalem into a Greek *polis*. This meant that Jerusalem's inhabitants would be registered as citizens of a *polis*, that the city would be restructured politically, that social institutions would be reorganized in the spirit of a Greek city, and that a *gymnasion* and *ephebeion* would be established.* [12]

There can be no question that this was an extremely bold step. Yet it is not clear to what degree Hellenization had penetrated Jewish society at that time. Phrased differently, did Jason have the backing, either active or passive, of a large segment of the population, or was this program of Hellenization only a superficial mimicry of Greek mannerisms by a small elite of Jerusalem society? Was this a sudden and dramatic step with little forethought or planning, or was it the culmination of a long

* Institutions for the training of Greek citizens. The *gymnasion* was roughly equivalent to today's high school with an emphasis on physical as well as academic subjects; the *ephebeion* was a more advanced school specializing in military training.

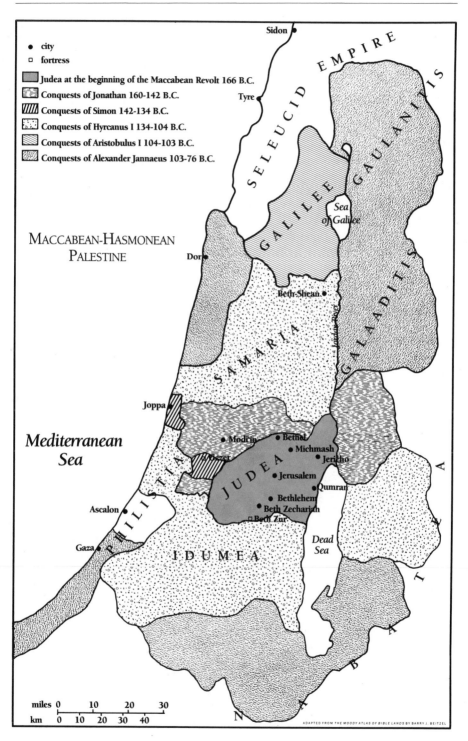

- **●** city
- **□** fortress
- ▓ Judea at the beginning of the Maccabean Revolt 166 B.C.
- ▤ Conquests of Jonathan 160-142 B.C.
- ▨ Conquests of Simon 142-134 B.C.
- ⣿ Conquests of Hyrcanus I 134-104 B.C.
- ▧ Conquests of Aristobulus I 104-103 B.C.
- ▨ Conquests of Alexander Jannaeus 103-76 B.C.

MACCABEAN-HASMONEAN
PALESTINE

SELEUCID EMPIRE

Sidon

Tyre

GALILEE

GAULANITIS

Sea
of Galilee

Dor

Beth-Shean

SAMARIA

GALAADITIS

Mediterranean
Sea

Joppa

Modtin
Bethel
Michmash
Gazer
Jericho
JUDEA
Jerusalem
Qumran
Bethlehem
Beth Zecharian
Beth Zur

Ascalon

PHILISTIA

NABATEA

Dead
Sea

Gaza

IDUMEA

miles 0   10   20   30
km 0   10   20   30   40

N

ADAPTED FROM THE MOODY ATLAS OF BIBLE LANDS BY BARRY J. BEITZEL

process? These fundamental questions cannot be answered with any certainty.

Nevertheless it is abundantly clear that by 175 B.C. many leading Jerusalemites, especially priests, were committed to a high degree of acculturation. Although we do not know the immediate reaction to Jason's initiative, during the years that followed, Jewish society was rocked by a series of events that shook it to its very foundations.

The heavy hand of Antiochus IV and the rise of the Maccabees

Soon after Jason became high priest by purchase and Jerusalem became a *polis*, the Seleucid overlord Antiochus IV (Epiphanes) visited Jerusalem (probably about 173 B.C.) and was greeted by the populace with a torchlight procession and overwhelming acclamation. At about the same time, the city sent a delegation to participate in the athletic games at Tyre, on the coast of Phoenicia. It is telling that the Jewish members of this delegation felt uncomfortable about offering the customary gift to the local deity at the opening of the games; instead, they gave their money to the host city's fleet.

In 172 B.C., another Jerusalem priest, Menelaus, sought to follow Jason's precedent by bribing the Seleucid king to appoint him high priest in place of Jason. In order to meet his financial commitment, however, Menelaus was forced to steal from the Temple treasury, an act that enraged the populace. The ensuing eruption of violence was quelled, but only with great difficulty. Tension between the followers of Jason and Menelaus continued.

Violence flared up again in 169-168 B.C., this time provoked by the Seleucid king Antiochus IV. First he pillaged the Temple, causing some destruction. Then he returned and, with unbridled fury, stamped out the unrest caused by Jason's challenge to Menelaus's authority. Massacre followed pillage and fire destroyed parts of the city. Not far from the Temple Mount, Antiochus built a fortress, named the Akra, which he garrisoned with Syrian troops.[13] Jerusalem churned with discontent, as it was clear that the presence of pagan troops meant the introduction of foreign cults into the Holy City.

About a year later, in the month of Kislev (December), 167 B.C., Antiochus issued a decree that banned circumcision, religious study, observance (including the Sabbath and festivals), and forced the Jews to commit what they considered the most unpardonable of sins—idolatry and eating forbidden foods. Antiochus proceeded to desecrate the Jews' most holy site by introducing idolatrous worship into the sacred Temple precinct itself.

Why did Antiochus do this? The primary sources (1 and 2 Maccabees) differ, as do modern historians. It is clear, however, that Antiochus's decrees were entirely unprecedented. Religious persecution had been hitherto unheard of in the pagan world. A conqueror might impose his deities on a local population, but he would never prohibit the practice of local traditions.*

Whatever may be said of Antiochus IV, his personality and quirks, he was educated in the best of Hellenistic traditions. Religious persecution was not part of his cultural and political heritage. Aware of the *sui generis* nature of this policy, historians have sought alternative explanations: The extreme Hellenizers under Menelaus were the real instigators of this upheaval (Bickerman, Hengel);[14] Antiochus was following a policy of religious persecution learned while in Rome (Goldstein);[15] Antiochus's religious persecution was part of an attempt to suppress a revolt that had already broken out in Jerusalem and that had a clear-cut religious character (Tcherikover).[16]

Whatever the reasons, these persecutions triggered responses of enormous consequence for subsequent Jewish history. The immediate reaction was one of disarray. Some Jews saw no way to respond other than to acquiesce passively. A number of Jews fled to the nearby Judean wilderness and perhaps beyond, outside the borders of Judea. Others despaired of worldly measures and took refuge in mystical-messianic dreams of divine intervention and salvation (see, for example, Daniel 7-12).

In the year following the imposition of these decrees, armed conflict broke out only in the remote town of Modi'in in northwest Judea. It was this response, however, that eventually led to a radical reshaping of Jewish society.

The Modi'in uprising was organized and led by a priest named Mattathias and his five sons, Judah Maccabee,** Simeon, Johanan, Eleazar and Jonathan. Eventually these sons would re-establish for the first time in 450 years a sovereign state, and a new dynasty of Jewish kings, the Hasmoneans.†

The 25-year struggle for an independent Jewish state

The Hasmonean rise to power, however, was a long and arduous process that succeeded only after a 25-year struggle. This quarter-century may be divided into four distinct periods:

1. *166-164 B.C.* These were years of continual guerrilla warfare. Led by the Maccabees, the Jews under the command of Judah Maccabee attacked the Seleucid armies as they attempted to reach Jerusalem and reinforce their garrison there. Seleucid forces approached the city from almost every direction—north, northwest, west and south—but each time they were defeated and their weapons appropriated to arm the growing Hasmonean irregulars. The heroic and almost always successful Hasmonean military efforts have been vividly recorded in both 1 and 2 Maccabees.[17] Only in an encounter at Beth Zur (south of Jerusalem),

---

* The one known example to the contrary, from the 14th century B.C., actually proves this point. Akhenaten's persecution of the traditional Egyptian clergy is more reflective of monotheistic zeal than of pagan intolerance.

** An additional name given to Judah and later applied to entire family as well. No satisfactory explanation as to the meaning of this name has thus far been suggested.

† The name Hasmonean refers to an ancestor of Mattathias and later became a family title of the Maccabees (*Antiquities* 12.265; *War* 1.36).

in the spring of 164 B.C., was the battle inconclusive, and a temporary armistice was declared as a result of the combined intervention of Jewish Hellenists and Roman envoys.[18] Six months later, however, Judah Maccabee and his troops surprised the Syrian garrison in Jerusalem, captured the city, purified the Temple and reinstituted the Jewish sacrificial rites. This occurred in the month of Kislev, 164 B.C., exactly three years after the persecution of the Jews had commenced. This recapture of Jerusalem, cleansing of the Temple and reinstitution of sacrificial rites is celebrated by Jews to this day in the holiday of Hanukkah.[19]

2. *164-160 B.C.* These years were marked by a number of dramatic changes in the fortunes of the hitherto victorious Maccabees. Having purified the Temple, the Hasmoneans proceeded to avenge Jews who had been attacked by gentile neighbors. Troops were dispatched to Transjordan, to the Galilee and to the Mediterranean coastal region. Many Jews were brought back to Jerusalem for resettlement. The success of these campaigns won the Hasmoneans unprecedented popularity.

But in 162 B.C. the Hasmoneans' fortunes plummeted. Antiochus V sent his Seleucid army to crush the rebels, and at a battle near Beth Zechariah, south of Jerusalem, the Seleucids were victorious.[20] They were denied the full fruits of their victory, however, when word came of a major crisis in Antioch that required the immediate presence of the commander, Lysias, and his troops. A hasty but, from the Jewish viewpoint, favorable peace treaty was arranged, in which the decrees banning the practice of Judaism were officially revoked. The Jews, for their part, accepted as high priest one Alcimus, a moderate Jewish Hellenist.

Most of the population appears to have been satisfied with this compromise, including the Hasidim, a pietist group that had joined the rebellion at its inception.[21] Only the Hasmoneans rejected this arrangement, and they were thus effectively isolated and forced to withdraw from Jerusalem.

In 161 B.C., Maccabean political and military fortunes changed once again, this time for the better. Judah Maccabee mustered a sizable army at Adasa, north of Jerusalem, and defeated the Greek general Nicanor in a major battle. His victory, though impressive, was short-lived. A year later a new Syrian army appeared in Judea, this time under the leadership of Bacchides. In a pitched battle in which the Jews were badly outnumbered, Judah Maccabee was killed. Any Hasmonean hope of soon gaining political power was dashed.[22]

3. *160-152 B.C.* These were years of declining Hasmonean fortune. Few Hasmonean partisans remained in Jerusalem. At first they fled to the region of Tekoa in the Judean wilderness, southeast of Bethlehem. Driven from there, they resettled at Michmash, near Bethel in northeastern Judea, where they lived in semi-isolation, removed from the arena of power and bereft of any titles or privileges.

4. *152-141 B.C.* This was the period of Hasmonean ascendancy that

Hasmonean Rulers of Judea, 142-37 B.C.

Simon	142-134
John Hyrcanus	134-104
Aristobulus I	104-103
Alexander Jannaeus	103-76
Salome Alexandra	76-67
Aristobulus II	67-63
John Hyrcanus II	63-40
Mattathias Antigonus	40-37

culminated in the establishment of an independent sovereign Jewish state. The change came about fortuitously.

In 152 B.C. Alexander Balas and Demetrius, both pretenders to the Seleucid throne, sought to win the support of Jonathan, Judah Maccabee's brother and a leader of the Hasmoneans, by outbidding one another in offers of privileges and honors. Finally, Jonathan threw his weight behind Demetrius and for this Jonathan was richly rewarded. He was made high priest, received permission to maintain troops and was given extensive tax benefits. Thus, despite their quasi-exile during the previous eight years, the Hasmoneans remained the only Jewish element in the country capable of mustering a sizable force—and this was ultimately the decisive factor. With the benefits Jonathan received from Demetrius, he was soon in firm control of Jewish society and was recognized as the undisputed representative of the Seleucids in Judea.

It is ironic that, less than a quarter of a century earlier, the Hellenizers Jason and Menelaus had acquired the high priesthood by bribing a gentile king; now the Hasmoneans followed suit; instead of bribes, the Hasmoneans paid with services to be rendered. As Seleucid officials, Jonathan and his brother Simon served the kingdom loyally, at one time even dispatching 3,000 troops to Antioch at the Seleucid king's request in order to quell an uprising there. During this decade the Hasmoneans were awarded more territories in the north and northwest of Judea.

Jonathan soon fell victim, however, to the same intrigues and political

machinations between royal pretenders that he had previously exploited
to his own advantage. He was treacherously killed in 143 B.C. by forces
opposed to his patron king.

Simon, the last of the Maccabean brothers, then assumed the high
priesthood and political leadership. He immediately drove out the
remnants of the Syrian garrison and the Jewish Hellenizers from the
Jerusalem Akra. Then, in an impressive public ceremony in 141 B.C.,
he declared his independence from Seleucid rule.

Accounting for the Maccabees' success in establishing an independent Jewish state

Looking back over these 25 years, we must ask ourselves why the
Hasmoneans succeeded as they did. Much of their success was
undoubtedly due to the charisma of the Maccabean family itself. Their
achievements in battle, the purification of the Temple and the fact that
many family members had given their lives in defending the Holy
Temple and the Holy City accorded them a strong claim to leadership.
They were able to consolidate large sectors of the Jewish population
behind them. Elders, rural and urban leaders, priests, levites and others
all participated in Simon's coronation ceremony, so vividly described in
1 Maccabees 14. In addition, Hasmonean tenacity in pursuing their
political goal, despite all obstacles, put them in a position to take
advantage of any opportunites that might—and indeed did—present
themselves.

Finally, the Hasmoneans were blessed with good fortune on the
international front. The mid-second century B.C. saw the decline of the
two major Hellenistic powers, the Ptolemies and the Seleucids. The
political vacuum in the region was quickly filled by petty ethnic
kingdoms (e.g., Itureans, Nabateans) and independent city-states (e.g.,
Tyre, Sidon, Ascalon). Precisely at this time the Hasmoneans too strove
for political independence; they took full advantage of these circumstances to reach their end. Only once before in the history of Israel had a
similar situation crystallized internationally, in the tenth century B.C.,
when David and Solomon carved out their far-flung and powerful
kingdom.

Combining political and religious power

With the emergence of the Hasmonean state, the political circumstances of the Jewish people altered radically. The power and trappings of
a self-governing political entity were now introduced into Jewish society.
Control of the various societal institutions carried with it enormous
authority and influence. From the outset, the Hasmoneans defined
themselves as the supreme leaders of the people, both in politics and
religion. Having already been appointed to the high priesthood (Jonathan,
as noted above, had been appointed high priest with Demetrius's help
in 152 B.C.), they assumed two more titles in 141 B.C.—*ethnarch* (head
of the people) and *strategos* (commander of the army). A generation later
(in 104 B.C.) the title "king" replaced that of *ethnarch*, and from that
time a dynasty of Jewish kings ruled Judea.

Combining the political authority of a sovereign state with the highest religious title in the land was indeed an innovation in Jewish history. Earlier, in the First Temple period, the high priesthood stood beside the monarchy; priest and king functioned as two distinctly independent sources of authority. Similarly, in the period following Hasmonean rule, Herod clearly separated these two realms, reserving the political one exclusively for himself and relegating the religious one, with its decidedly secondary status, to others. The combining of these two realms by the Hasmoneans was explosive, in both a positive and a negative sense, as it provided an ideological component that motivated and justified the most daring of political and military policies.[23]

One of the most remarkable achievements of the Hasmoneans was their radical redrawing of the map of Judea. What had once been a small, isolated subprovince in the Persian period and in the early Hellenistic period (after Alexander's conquest) became, by the end of the Hasmonean era, a major political entity embracing all of what is today modern Israel (minus the southern Negev and the northern coastal area), parts of southern Lebanon and western Jordan.

Expanding Hasmonean rule

Simon, who ruled the new state from 142 to 134 B.C., made a major military push northwestward, toward the sea. He conquered Gezer, expelled its gentile inhabitants, purified the town, and resettled it with observant Jews (1 Maccabees 13:43-48). From Gezer he proceeded to Joppa which, once taken, served as the major seaport emporium for the Hasmonean state.

Simon's son and successor, John Hyrcanus, ruled for 30 years (134-104 B.C.) and, like his father, expanded the country's borders dramatically. Enlarging his hold along the coast and even establishing a presence east of the Jordan River, he devoted his major effort against the various ethnic groups living in the hill country—the Idumeans in southern Judea and the northern Negev and the Samaritans to the north.[24] Hyrcanus probably conquered the Galilee as well, although the composition of its population at the time is unknown.

Hyrcanus was succeeded by his son Aristobulus I, the first Hasmonean to adopt the title "king." Although he ruled for only one year (104-103 B.C.), he successfully annexed Iturean territory in southern Lebanon.[25]

Aristobulus was succeeded by his brother Alexander Jannaeus (103-76 B.C.), the last and perhaps greatest military leader of the Hasmonean dynasty. Jannaeus annexed new territories in almost every direction. In the northwest, he gained control of Straton's Tower (later Caesarea) and Dor; in the southwest, he took the coastal district, including Gaza, one of the major Hellenistic cities of the time; in the northeast, he overran much of the Golan and Gilead (today's northwestern Jordan); and to the southeast, he conquered large areas of Moab.[26]

The control of neighboring peoples, cities, important trade routes and major ports was an obvious motivation that directed the course and extent of these Hasmonean conquests. The religious-nationalist dimension, however, was no less significant a factor in Hasmonean policy. The Hasmoneans regarded themselves as the successors of the great leaders of the past—the Judges and the kings of First Temple times. This is clearly, if subtly, reflected in 1 Maccabees, written toward the end of the second century B.C. under Hasmonean patronage. Both the language and the terms it uses are reminiscent of the books of Judges and Kings, consciously drawing an analogy between the Hasmoneans, on the one hand, and the development and institutionalization of Jewish political leadership in biblical times, on the other.[27] Simon's coronation ceremony, described in 1 Maccabees 14, provides the culmination of the book as a whole; it is a carefully written account, frequently alluding to the glorious days of King Solomon.

Another touch in the same vein: Hasmonean coins use the ancient Hebrew script resurrected from the First Temple period, rather than the square Aramaic script in use at the time. This was doubtless a conscious attempt by the Hasmoneans to identify their rule with the earlier Davidic monarchy.

Hasmonean religious ideology

In the religious sphere, the Hasmoneans were committed to ridding their territories of all idolatrous practices. Religious purification of the land became a basic policy. Sometimes this meant driving out the pagan inhabitants altogether and then purifying the site; at other times, conversion of the populace was required. Entire populations, both urban and rural, were thus brought into the Jewish fold. The two outstanding examples of this policy were the conversion of the Idumeans by John Hyrcanus and the conversion of the Itureans by Aristobulus I. How smoothly this policy was effected is difficult to determine. No mention of resistance is made in our sources, although undoubtedly some, either active or passive, must have occurred. It is hard to imagine, for example, that the choice between conversion or death offered to the inhabitants of the Hellenistic city of Pella in the Transjordan did not meet with outright hostility and serious resistance.[28]

The ideological component that accompanied Hasmonean successes was a two-edged sword. On the one hand, it undoubtedly provided a significant additional impetus and motivation for the Hasmoneans' conquests—and provided a transcendent cause firmly rooted in a biblical faith that overshadowed ordinary political concerns. On the other hand, such an anti-pagan attitude was bound to stir up animosity. Hasmonean zealousness might easily be interpreted, perhaps correctly, as an onslaught against gentile values and the pagan way of life. Some of the earliest evidence of pagan anti-Semitism—such as the negative description of Jews and Judaism by the advisors of Antiochus VII (as preserved by the Greek historian Diodorus) and the hostility of Posidonius of Syria (as noted by other early writers)—was in large part a reaction to Hasmonean anti-pagan drives. By the first century B.C., various anti-Jewish accusations were circulating widely: the Jews were misanthropes, Jewish religious precepts were engendering social animosity and moral perversion, Jewish worship in the Jerusalem Temple was primitive and barbaric, etc. Some of this anti-Jewish hostility seems to have been triggered by political and religious opposition to the Hasmoneans.[29] The fact that many pagans and Jews viewed the Hasmonean conquests as part of a struggle for ultimate control of the country, a struggle in which each side claimed possession of the land, no doubt further exacerbated pagan reactions.[30]

The Hasmonean combination of political power and religious ideology was equally problematic on the domestic front. Instead of being the art of the possible, politics was fraught with the tensions and passions born of ideological inflexibility. Indeed, the Hasmonean model of combining political and religious leadership was adopted by other elements in their society, particularly by religious groups. In contrast to the later Second Temple period, when the religious character of the various Jewish sects was predominant, during the Hasmonean era the political involvement of these groups was paramount. For example, we find leaders of both major sects, the Pharisees and the Sadducees, holding seats in the ruler's inner cabinet. Toward the end of the second century B.C., the Sadducees worked hand in glove with John Hyrcanus, who favored the priestly aristocratic classes: The joint political machinations of the Sadducees and the followers of John Hyrcanus finally forced the Pharisees out of government.[31] The Pharisees, however, quickly became a militant opposition; in fact, much of the unrest that occurred during the reign of Alexander Jannaeus was supported, encouraged and led by the Pharisees.[32] Open Pharisaic hostility and, at times, insulting behavior toward Jannaeus* finally led to severe countermeasures—including exile, persecution and even a mass crucifixion. The opposition, for its part, went to the extreme of inviting the Syrian king Demetrius VI to attack Jerusalem. When the battle was finally joined, the Seleucid side was bolstered by Jewish dissidents and the Hasmonean side was reinforced by pagan mercenaries!

Later, Jannaeus's wife and successor, Salome Alexandra (76-67 B.C.) reinstated the Pharisees and gave them complete control of the country's internal affairs. They lost little time in avenging themselves against the Sadducees and wealthy aristocrats who earlier had persecuted them.[33]

The most extreme reaction to this situation was taken by members of another Jewish sect—the Essenes, or Dead Sea sect. In protest against the political and religious leadership of the Hasmoneans, the Essenes left Jerusalem and settled in a remote region of the Judean wilderness, there to await the removal of the Hasmonean leadership as part of the messianic drama which, in their opinion, would imminently unfold.

Thus, political involvement of religious sects in Hasmonean society was endemic. All groups—Sadducees, Pharisees and Essenes—were organized as political parties no less than as religious sects. This injected

---

* According to Josephus (*Antiquities of the Jews*, 13.372) on the pilgrim festival of Sukkot, *etrogim* were thrown at the high priest. (An *etrog* is a small yellow fruit that looks like a lemon and is used in connection with Sukkot observance.)

into the political arena a certitude and ideological rigidity that only increased tensions.

A unique synthesis of Hellenism and Judaism   In a quite different area, the Hasmoneans established a pattern of behavior that deeply affected the cultural and social ambience of Jewish society; they introduced into Hasmonean Judea a particular synthesis between Jewish and Hellenistic elements. Elias Bickerman has aptly described the Hasmonean attitude as a form of moderate Hellenism;[34] the Hasmoneans were keen to adapt Hellenistic forms to Judaism—rather than Judaism to the dictates of Hellenism as the extreme Hellenizers among the Jews had advocated. Perhaps there is no better indication of the Hasmonean desire to integrate the two worlds than the coins they minted. On these tiny bronze issues, intended as small change and utilized for propagandistic purposes, we find symbols and inscriptions that convey a clear-cut message: The Jewish and Greek worlds are not irreconcilable. The language was either Greek or Hebrew; only a few issues are in Aramaic, the Semitic language in everyday use at the time. The Greek inscription uses the secular Hellenistic title of the Jewish ruler (king) and his Greek name (Alexander [Jannaeus]); the Hebrew coins use his Jewish title (high priest) and his Hebrew name (Jonathan). Moreover, the Hebrew script is not the later Aramaic "square" form, but an older style in vogue during First Temple times, but not used previously in Second Temple times.[35]

The symbols on these coins are also an important indication of the Hasmonean attitude to the surrounding culture. None of the symbols is uniquely Jewish. The palm branch, anchor, cornucopia, wheel/star, etc., are found on Ptolemaic, Seleucid or so-called city coins minted by and and in various cities of the region (such as Gezer, Tyre and Ascalon). The only exceptions to this rule are two issues minted by the grandson of Alexander Jannaeus and last of the Hasmonean rulers, Mattathias Antigonus (40-37 B.C.); on these two issues we find the menorah (candelabra from the temple) and table of shewbread from the Temple. For the most part, however, these Hasmonean coins display symbols of pagan origin, albeit carefully selected. Only the most neutral symbols were copied, those that bore no blatantly pagan overtones. Thus, a policy of compromise was adopted; Hellenistic symbolism yes, but nothing offensive to Jewish concepts and practices then in vogue.

A similar contrast and synthesis is found at the magnificent Hasmonean winter palace recently excavated near Jericho.[36] Some of the finest amenities of the Hellenistic world were found there—a large swimming pool, baths, a grand pavilion, frescoed walls with geometric designs, carefully hewn Doric columns and friezes. Yet between the pool and palace were a number of ritual baths (*mikva'ot*). These were used by the Hasmoneans who, in their role as priests, were required to be ritually pure before partaking of the free-will offerings (*terumah*) given by the people. *Mikva'ot* were unknown in earlier periods; no archaeological remains of such installations have been uncovered at sites

Bronze *prutah* of John Hyrcanus I (134-104 B.C.). The double cornucopia, a pagan symbol, but one that was not offensive to Jews, shows that the Hasmoneans blended Hellenistic culture with the Jewish world.

The other side of the coin, by contrast, demonstrates Jewish nationalism. The language of the inscription, including the name and title of the ruler, is Hebrew, not Greek: "Jehohanan the High Priest and the council of the Jews." Moreover, the script is not the "square" Aramaic script current at the time, but an old Hebrew script used in First Temple times.

of pre-Hasmonean date, nor are they ever mentioned in biblical sources. Thus, the Hasmoneans not only adopted Hellenistic architectural styles and associated social-recreational amenities, they also created a uniquely Jewish institution like the ritual bath.

Jewish society at large reflected this basic willingness to absorb Hellenistic influences, albeit with a significant amount of selectivity and adaptation in the process, which usually meant the rejection of overtly pagan forms.

Let us consider several examples. The funerary remains from the Jerusalem area reflect an enormous degree of outside influence, invariably imitating known Hellenistic models. The well-known tomb of Jason, a wealthy Jerusalem aristocrat from the first century B.C., had a pyramidal form; the tomb of the sons of Hezir (*Bnei Hezir*) in the Kidron Valley east of the Old City followed another Egyptian tradition with its columned facade and adjacent funerary monument. The deceased were regularly buried in *kokhim* (*loculi*), small cavities about the length and width of a human body, cut into the walls of caves. This form of burial was derived from Hellenistic models that originated in fourth-century Alexandria. No less Hellenistic in origin were the tomb facades and the series of outer courtyards (as at Jason's tomb). Columns, capitals, friezes and architraves of various Greek orders are always found at these tombs. Inscriptions were recorded in Greek, Hebrew and Aramaic. What is uniquely Jewish about these tombs, however, is their artistic expression; here we find a major break with the pagan world. Figural representation is common on pagan tombs in Palestine (for example, at Marissa we find figures in a musical procession) and throughout the Hellenistic world. Figural representations are practically nonexistent on Jewish tombs, however.[37]

This absence of figural representation reflects a significant religious and cultural development in the Hasmonean era. Throughout the previous 1,000 years of Jewish history, figural representations had been common. The cherubs over the Holy Ark, the lions of Solomon's throne, the oxen supporting the huge basin in the Temple courtyard, the bronze serpent for healing used from the days of Moses until King Hezekiah's time, and the calves at the sanctuaries of Dan and Bethel all attest to the use of figural art in the biblical period. The innumerable figurines excavated at Israelite sites, not to speak of coins with human and animal depictions minted in Jerusalem in the late Persian and early Hellenistic periods, provide additional evidence of Israelite use of figural art. Commencing with the Hasmoneans, however, and continuing for about 300 years—until the time of Bar-Kokhba (died c. 135 A.D.)—the Jews manifested an almost total aversion to figural art. Josephus and rabbinic literature, as well as archaeological remains from the late Second Temple period, all confirm a widespread adherence to this strict prohibition. Why this happened is not entirely clear. Perhaps it was a traumatic reaction to the decrees of Antiochus IV, who, to the horror of the Jews, introduced idols into the sacred Temple precincts; after all, the Second Commandment's proscription of images was, at its core, directed against idolatry. Or perhaps it was due to the dominance under the Hasmoneans of a more conservative (Sadducean?) interpretation of the Torah generally, and of the Second Commandment of the Decalogue in particular. Instead of banning only figural art for idolatrous purposes (the more lenient position taken both in the biblical period and, later, in the talmudic period), the Hasmoneans prohibited *all* figural depictions. In this Jewish reaction against regnant Hellenistic practice, the Jews clearly distinguished themselves from their surrounding culture.

Another illustration of the synthesis of Jewish and Hellenistic cultures is preserved in a small apocryphal work, the Greek Additions to the biblical Book of Esther. In these Additions, an attempt is made to give the Book of Esther a more pious, Jewishly oriented character. The biblical account as it stands raises some thorny issues. Why is God never mentioned? Why are no expressions of traditional Jewish piety, such as prayer, included? Why does a respectable Jewish girl like Esther marry a gentile king? Or sleep with him? Or eat from his table? The Additions deal with these issues by supplementing the biblical text with a particularistic, religious tone advocating a pro-Jewish and anti-pagan outlook. What is especially fascinating—indeed, ironic—is that the Additions were written in fine Greek literary style, and in Jerusalem; moreover, they were written by a Jewish priest named Lysimmachus and were brought to Alexandria by a levite named Ptolemy. Thus, some highly educated and acculturated Jews (notice their names!) had made a clear bifurcation between their Hellenistic education and their strong Jewish loyalties.

People's names often indicate cultural proclivities. Thus, in addition to the Greek names of the Hasmonean rulers (Hyrcanus, Aristobulus, Antigonus, Alexander), many members of the leading political and diplomatic families of the Hasmonean kingdom also bore Greek names.[38]

Hellenistic influence was not restricted only to material culture (art and architecture) or to Greek names and language. It penetrated deeper, affecting even religious institutions and religious beliefs of Hasmonean society. We have already discussed funerary practices.[39] Rabbinic sources shed interesting light on developments regarding marriage laws. Tradition has ascribed to Simeon ben Shetaḥ, a leading Pharisaic figure who flourished during the first half of the first century B.C., a major alteration in the *Ketubah*, the wedding document containing the obligation of the groom towards the bride.[40] Previously, the groom was required to set aside a sum of money or property, usually depositing it with the bride's family, with whom he made the contract. This arrangement had its roots in earlier Mesopotamian practice. According to at least one rabbinic tradition, this arrangement made divorce too easy; the husband had little to lose, for whatever he owed the bride in case of divorce had already been set aside. In the fourth or third century B.C. another arrangement, emanating from Egypt, was introduced into non-Jewish marriage contracts. The contract was negotiated directly between husband and wife, stipulating that in case of divorce the groom was to pay the settlement from his own property; nothing was set aside at the time of marriage. This was intended to make divorce more difficult. Sometime in the early first century B.C. Simeon Ben Shetaḥ introduced precisely this Egyptian practice into the Jewish marriage ceremony, obviously inspired by Hellenistic models.[41]

The impact of Hellenism on Pharisaic tradition is not limited to the *Ketubah*. In most cases, however, it is more difficult to trace. For example, the Pharisaic academy (*beth midrash*) had much in common with the Greek philosophical school. The parallels are not so much in the material learned (although in the area of ethics, the overlap may have been substantial),[42] but rather in the very nature and organization of this institution. The *beth midrash* was a school of higher learning open to all, with rules governing its operation similar to those of the Greek philosophical schools. The relationship between master and pupil in the *beth midrash* and the prinicples of exegesis applied there also resembled those of its Greek counterpart.[43] Since no similar institution existed in Palestine before Hellenistic times, and as influences from the Greek academy permeated Pharisaic-rabbinic tradition later on as well,[44] it seems quite probable that the creation of this Jewish institution was inspired by the Greek model.

Several other Pharisaic concepts, such as afterlife in the form of bodily resurrection and the concept of a dual law (written and oral), may also have originated outside of Jewish tradition. Neither has any clear precedents in biblical literature, and both can be found, in one form or other, in non-Jewish (Greek and Babylonian) traditions.

No discussion of foreign influences on forms of Judaism during the Hasmonean period can ignore the evidence from the Dead Sea caves at Qumran. Time and again it has been demonstrated that the ideology of the Qumran sect was replete with ideas quite different from biblical formulations and remarkably similar to concepts of the surrounding, especially eastern, Hellenistic world.[45] Ideas and concepts relating to dualism, predestination, astrology, angelology, demonology, a solar calendar and the particular notion of wisdom and the spirit—all can be traced to Hellenistic, especially eastern Hellenistic, models. Other institutions at Qumran—communal living, the concept of "community" (yahad), initiation rites, penal code, celibacy and asceticism—although new to Judaism, have striking parallels elsewhere.[46]

Explaining such an array of outside influences on the ideology of a Jewish sect like the Essenes at Qumran is a formidable challenge. When one considers the fact that, of all groups, the Essene community at Qumran was the most self-consciously isolated one, having physically divorced itself from the rest of society, the fact of such massive foreign influence becomes even more perplexing. Several explanations have been offered, yet none seems entirely satisfactory. They all suppose that such influences were early and that the Qumran community at the time for which we have evidence was probably unaware of the origins of these traditions. One explanation, for example, assumes that the sect originated in the eastern Diaspora (Babylonia) and that by the time it reached Judea, it had already absorbed and internalized these concepts.[47] Another suggests that these foreign ideas were current in Judean society of the Hellenistic period and that the forerunners of Qumran adopted them quite early as an integral part of the legitimate religious and cultural baggage of their environment.[48] Whatever the explanation, the fact remains that such extensive influence on a major Jewish sect of the period is indeed astounding.

In surveying Hasmonean society as a whole, we must conclude that no area of society and no sector of the population remained wholly unaffected by Hellenistic culture. The question is only a matter of degree—how much, in what areas, with what intensity, and affecting which parts of the population.

The Hasmonean state has often been portrayed as a reaction against Hellenism, a reassertion of Jewish nationalist and religious will in the face of the demands, temptations and outright coercion of the larger world. This view, however, is only partly true, and as such is a distortion when taken alone. In a more profound sense, the Hasmonean state must be viewed, at least in part, as a product of Hellenism, as an affirmation of the surrounding culture no less than its rejection, an expression of national sovereignty nourished and shaped by its international context. Thus, the Hasmonean state embodied a new Jewish disposition that incorporated a resurgent Jewish identity with a high degree of Hellenism. Most Jews were prepared to adopt into their life-style many forms of Hellenism, albeit in varying degrees and with certain necessary adjustments and changes.

Jerusalem, the Temple and the priests under Hasmonean rule

The creation of the Hasmonean kingdom had a revolutionary effect on Jerusalem, its capital city. Since the beginning of the Second Temple period in the sixth century B.C., Jerusalem had occupied a small area that included only the ancient City of David and the area of the Temple Mount. Altogether, the city included about 30 acres; its population numbered only about 5,000 or 6,000. This situation had prevailed for nearly 400 years (c. 540-140 B.C.). Then, suddenly, in the short period of Hasmonean rule, Jerusalem expanded more than five-fold, stretching to over 160 acres and numbering approximately 30,000 inhabitants. It now encompassed the entire western hill (Mt. Zion) as far as today's Citadel of David (adjacent to the Jaffa Gate). Remains of the Hasmonean city-wall have been discovered in the Jewish Quarter of the Old City, in the Citadel itself and on the slopes of Mt. Zion. In many places this wall followed the same course as the Israelite wall from First Temple times; in fact, Hasmonean builders were not only aware of this earlier enceinte, they even integrated parts of it into their later fortifications.[49]

Precisely dating this wall is not easy. Although the literary sources are replete with references to construction of the city's fortifications under various Hasmonean rulers, none ever explicitly mentions any large-scale expansion of the city limits. Moreover, archaeological evidence for dating these walls is scanty and inconclusive. Since there were several stages to the Hasmonean wall (as seen most clearly in the Citadel area), it would appear that the wall was first built in the second century B.C., probably under Jonathan or Simon, and then repaired and reinforced periodically.[50]

Jerusalem's population during this period was overwhelmingly, if not exclusively, Jewish. The priests were the leading class within Judean society; they not only controlled the most important institution within the city (the Temple), but they were also an integral part of the local aristocracy. With the rise of the Hasmonean state, priests played a leading role not only in its religious, but also in its political, diplomatic and military affairs. For example, the names of emissaries sent to Rome, Sparta and elsewhere indicate that they were almost always of priestly stock.[51]

Evidence of priestly prominence has also been found in the already mentioned tomb of Jason (almost certainly a priest) and that of the Bnei Hezir family (also of priestly origins, 1 Chronicles 24:15); and in the above-mentioned Additions to Esther, which were written by a Jerusalem priest named Lysimmachus.

The priestly caste was undoubtedly a varied group. Some were Hellenistic enthusiasts as, for example, Jason, Menelaus and others who reportedly flocked to the *gymnasion* instead of performing their Temple duties. On the other hand, Josephus recounts the heroic and brave efforts of the Jerusalem priests during the Roman siege of Pompey in 63 B.C. Despite near starvation, they faithfully continued to perform their cultic obligations. Some were even massacred by the Romans while fulfilling their priestly duties.[52]

Throughout the ages the geographical focal point of Jerusalem had been the Temple and the Temple Mount.[53] Nevertheless, in the First Temple period, power and prestige were divided among three different types of leaders—the king, the high priest and the prophets. Each had his sphere of influence and each operated in a totally different setting—

the king from his palace and through his bureaucracy, the high priest in the Temple and the prophet in the marketplace. In the early Second Temple period, by the time of Ezra and Nehemiah, this power structure had altered dramatically. Kingship and prophecy had disappeared and were replaced by the wealthy aristocrat (like Nehemiah) and the scholar-scribe (like Ezra). From then until the destruction of the Temple almost six centuries later (in 70 A.D.), the priesthood reigned supreme; the high priest became the religious and political leader of the people, both internally and vis-à-vis other ruling authorities.

In the early Hellenistic period, at the time of Ptolemy I (353-285 B.C.), the high priest Hezekiah is mentioned as a leader of the people.[54] In the third century B.C., Sparta communicated for diplomatic purposes with the high priest Onias I.[55] The high priest Onias II served as representative of the people before the Ptolemaic court in Alexandria.[56] Another high priest, Simon the Just, in the late third century, was praised by Ben Sira as a leader of his people.[57] The high priest Jason radically altered the political and cultural institutions of Jerusalem in 175 B.C.[58] Thus, the stage was set for the Hasmoneans to bring this process to a culmination by combining the high priesthood with the most extensive temporal power enjoyed by a Jewish ruler since 586 B.C.—political sovereignty and commander of the army.[59]

The importance and prestige of the Temple increased under Hasmonean rule in proportion to the enhanced political status of the Hasmonean state. The sanctity of the Temple as the quintessence of Judaism is reflected in a particularly interesting way in 2 Maccabees, a book produced under Hasmonean auspices for political and religious purposes. It is a summary of a larger, five-volume work, now lost, written in the mid-second century (c. 150 B.C.) by Jason the Cyrene. It summarizes the events that took place in Jerusalem and Judea between 175 and 160 B.C. (to the death of Judah Maccabee). The book was written, however, in the early years of John Hyrcanus's reign (about 120 B.C.) to impress the Jews of Alexandria with early Hasmonean military and religious achievements—their triumph over the Seleucids, their purification of the Temple and the celebration of Hanukkah. Aside from the obvious historical value of 2 Maccabees, it is an important statement of Hasmonean propaganda. The sanctity of the Temple is its central theme. The book begins and ends with the preservation of the Temple's purity; it focuses on the purification of the Temple in 164 B.C. The political message of 2 Maccabees is clear. It was the Hasmoneans who fought and shed their blood for the sake of preserving the sanctity of the Temple, and this fact should accord them legitimacy and authority in the eyes of the people.

A number of practices emphasizing the centrality of the Temple had already developed by the first century B.C. These practices, which appear to have originated in the Hasmonean period, became widespread and normative in the late Second Temple period. The large-scale pilgrimages to Jerusalem by Jews in the Diaspora, as well as in Judea, and the half-shekel annual contribution were nurtured and encouraged by Hasmonean leaders.[60] These practices not only enhanced the religious status of the Hasmoneans as high priests, they also emphasized that Jerusalem—with its Temple—was the spiritual center of world Jewry.

Finally, the most prominent institutions of the period were located in the Temple precincts or on the Temple Mount. It served as the ritual center for the nation's many and varied celebrations over the course of the year, but it was also the meeting place of the highest courts of the land, and probably of the *ḥever ha-yehudim* (the governing body of the high council of the Jews), an important representative body mentioned on Hasmonean coins. One of the important markets of the city serving Temple needs operated there, and leaders of the different sects taught their disciples in these precincts.

No other institution in Jewish society rivaled the Temple in its sanctity and importance. Despite the absence of explicit references to the presence of a synagogue in Judea proper, there can be little doubt that this institution had already evolved substantially by the time of the Hasmoneans. But, although the synagogue appears to have had a distinctly communal nature with a number of religious functions (such as the reading of scriptures, their translation into Aramaic, sermons and perhaps communal prayers), in no way did it challenge the supremacy of the Temple. This remained true throughout the Second Temple period; only after the destruction of the Temple in 70 A.D. did the synagogue develop its own unique religious profile.[61]

In the Hasmonean period, the religion of the ordinary Jew focused to a large extent on the Temple, its rituals and requirements. Aside from the offerings to priests and levites, a Jew was obligated to bring first fruits (*bikkurim*), as well as the first produce of his flocks, to Jerusalem. Moreover, four times every seven years he was to spend a tithe of his earnings within the bounds of Jerusalem. These obligations were in addition to the half-shekel contribution and the requirement (often unobserved by those living at a distance) to be present in the Holy City on each of the three pilgrimage festivals (Passover [*Pesach*], Tabernacles [*Sukkot*], and Weeks [*Shavuot*]). As the occasion arose, individual Jews would betake themselves to the Temple to offer sacrifices for personal reasons—a sin or guilt offering, a free-will offering, an offering in fulfillment of a vow or following childbirth.

Aside from the Temple itself, the various sects comprised the only other major religious framework in this period. The term "sect" or "sectarian" requires some comment, however. In Christian terminology, a sect is a group that has severed itself from a mother church because of dissent from policies, personalities or ideologies regnant in a given society. The Essenes were the only Jewish group of this period that seems to fit this definition. The Pharisees, Sadducees, Hasidim and others, however, were associations that operated within the framework of Hasmonean society and its institutions, accepting the basic premises and

Pharisees, Sadducees, Essenes and others

parameters of the society while competing for religious and political preeminence.[62]

The growth of such groups was a direct result of the religious revolution introduced by Ezra. With the demise of prophecy and the establishment of the written Torah as the basis of Jewish life, Judaism attained a high degree of democratization. The word of God was no longer confined to a charismatic personality; now anyone could offer an interpretation of the Torah, and if he commanded a following, his group constituted *de facto* a sect within Jewish society.[63] Whether this or that particular group sustained itself in the course of time and developed a unique and appealing ideology and *halakhah* (religious law) was a matter of historical destiny. No authoritative body made such a decision. Our sources are completely silent about what kinds of sects, if any, developed in the centuries immediately following Ezra. However, with the rise of the Hasmoneans the picture changes dramatically.

The three sects mentioned specifically by Josephus—the Pharisees, Sadducees and Essenes—appear to have originated and crystallized in the mid-second century B.C. All extant sources, literary and archaeological, attest to this dating. The earliest remains of the Dead Sea sect at Qumran are from the years 140-130 B.C. According to rabbinic sources, the earliest Pharisaic sages known by name flourished in the 160s and 150s B.C., and these sources claim that the Sadducees emerged sometime in the mid-second century B.C.[64] Similarly, Josephus's first reference to these sects is in connection with events at the time of Jonathan the Hasmonean,[65] in about 150 B.C. While some scholars have tried to find earlier traces of these groups—in the fourth and third centuries B.C.— their conclusions are largely speculative and unconvincing. Not only do all available sources point to the second century as the time of their origin, but historical circumstances likewise tend to support such a date. The political upheavals of this period—the transformation of Jerusalem into a *polis*, the Maccabean revolt and, finally, the establishment of an independent state—undoubtedly affected the religious life of the society in a profound way. The sects we have mentioned were in large measure a reaction and response to these developments.

The Sadducees

The Sadducees offer a clear example of this phenomenon. With the usurpation of the high priesthood by Jason, Menelaus and, ultimately, the Hasmoneans, the sons of Zadok divided into three separate groups. In about 150 B.C., one branch of this family, the adherents of Onias IV, erected a temple in Leontopolis in Egypt under Ptolemaic auspices to rival the Jerusalem Temple then under Hasmonean control.[66] Another branch of the family withdrew to the Judean wilderness and was central in the formation of the Essene sect, as we shall see in more detail below. A third segment remained in Jerusalem, forming an alliance with the Hasmonean ruling power and becoming an integral part of that society for the next two centuries. These were the Sadducees* and they were largely, if not exclusively, a priestly aristocratic party commanding significant wealth and political prominence. Rabbinic literature[67] and Josephus[68] make this point patently clear. They served not only as diplomats but as military leaders as well.[69]

One might have expected that the priestly sons of Zadok would regard themselves as the sole legitimate bearers of the priestly tradition and that they would therefore array themselves as implacable enemies of the Hasmoneans. This indeed happened with the first two branches of the family described above, those in Egypt and those who retreated to Qumran. With the third branch, however, pragmatism proved decisive; by working very closely with the Hasmonean rulers, the Sadducees even succeeded in ousting their rivals, the Pharisees, from positions of power towards the end of the reign of John Hyrcanus (c. 110 B.C.). Sadducean political ascendancy maintained itself right through the era of Alexander Jannaeus (103-76 B.C.), and only in the reign of Janneus's wife, Salome (76-67 B.C.) did the Pharisees again rise to power and remove their opponents from all positions of authority.

Undoubtedly, the basis for Sadducean power lay in their claim to priestly status. As such, they were recognized as the official religious authorities of the people, as servants of the God of Israel in his holy sanctuary and as guardians of the Torah tradition. Josephus claims, however, that socially the Sadducees found their most loyal adherents among the wealthy and not the populace.[70]

We are at a distinct disadvantage in our effort to understand the Sadducees, however, because they themselves have left us no written documents. Whatever information we have originated in circles distinctly hostile to them. Rabbinic and New Testament material preserves many traditions about the Sadducees, the Dead Sea material preserves some and Josephus mentions them only on rare occasions. Each of these sources, however, is openly critical of Sadducean ideology and conduct.[71] What the Sadducees would have said about themselves would undoubtedly have been significantly different. Contrary to popular belief, no consistent pattern can be discerned in our sources regarding their positions in disputes with the Pharisees regarding religious law.[72] At times, the Sadducees were the more lenient of the two; at other times, the more rigorous. Sometimes they adopted a strict constructionist approach toward the biblical text, sometimes not. In several disputes, they clearly took positions reflective of their wealthy, aristocratic background; in others, this is not at all clear.

Josephus notes several doctrines associated with the Sadducees: they denied the notion of immortality of the soul, rejected any concept of future reward and punishment and espoused a doctrine of unlimited free-will.[73] Perhaps their most significant tenet emphasized a clear-cut distinction between the Torah of Moses, which they regarded as divine,

---

* A number of explanations have been offered for the etymology of the word Sadducee; it probably derived from Zadok, the high priest in the time of David, whose heirs served in that role throughout the Second Temple period.

and all other laws and regulations, which they considered man-made and thus religiously inferior. These non-biblical laws and regulations were of an *ad hoc* nature and carried no imperative for later generations. Thus, aside from the Torah, all laws and regulations merely had the status of decrees, valid for specific times and places.[74]

The Pharisees   The Pharisees, perhaps the best known of the sects and the one destined ultimately to shape Jewish life to our own day, also crystallized in this period and, as noted, played a central role in Hasmonean political and religious life.

The name "Pharisee" appears to derive from the Hebrew *parash*, meaning "separate" or "stand apart." We do not know what the first Pharisees objected to or from what they stood apart. Many suggestions have been offered; they opposed the dominant priestly class, the emerging Hasmonean dynasty and its political-military policies, those who were lax in the observance of purity and tithing laws, those overly enamored of Hellenistic influences—or a combination of the above.

Our primary sources also reflect this same vagueness regarding the basic thrust of early Pharisaism. Josephus, for example, describes the Pharisees, along with the Sadducees and Essenes, as essentially a philosophical sect. According to him, Pharisaic beliefs and opinions were, in the final analysis, not only distinctive, but decisive. It was their views of reward and punishment after death, their synthesis of free-will and determinism and their position with respect to the sanctity of the Oral Law that ultimately prevailed. On the other hand, rabbinic sources emphasize not the philosophical views of the sect, but a plethora of *halakhic* (religious, legal) matters, particularly differences between Pharisees and Sadducees. These differences ranged from holiday observances and cultic practices to civil and criminal law, as well as purity and family affairs. Josephus emphasizes the Pharisees' involvement in Hasmonean politics; rabbinic literature, on the other hand, largely ignores this dimension, with the notable exception of Rabbi Simeon ben Shetah, who lived toward the end of the Hasmonean era.

Modern theories dealing with Pharisaic origins also contrast strikingly.[75] Louis Finkelstein, for example, views the Pharisees as basically an urban proletariat whose outlook was dictated by social and economic circumstances. Isaac (Fritz) Baer, on the other hand, claims that Pharisaic roots are to be found in rural, pietistic circles which, perhaps ironically, offer striking analogies with the surrounding Greek world.[76]

When all is said and done, we know precious little about the Pharisees of the Hasmonean era. Josephus treats the sects only peripherally in his various historical accounts, for he did not regard them as the primary force in the political events of the nation, with which he was basically preoccupied. Rabbinic literature, too, has preserved very little data relating to the Pharisaic sages who lived at the time; we know a great deal more about the later Pharisees under Roman rule (63 B.C.-70 A.D.) than we do of their predecessors. The overwhelming majority of sayings attributed to the Pharisees in rabbinic literature come from the later sages, Hillel and Shammai and their academies (Beth Hillel and Beth Shammai). We have no idea how many of the anonymous references to the Pharisees actually apply to the Hasmonean period. With but rare exceptions, it is impossible to date such material confidently. It is no less difficult to understand why so few traditions of these early sages were preserved by the later rabbis. The relatively large time gap between the Hasmonean period and the first redaction of rabbinic sources in about 200 A.D. may in part account for this phenomenon. Perhaps the later rabbis also harbored certain reservations about the political involvements and religious priorities of their distant forebearers and thus chose not to include much of their material in the rabbinic corpus. Whatever the reason, this lack of any significant quantity of reliable information about the early Pharisees is a serious obstacle to understanding them.[77]

Because the data at hand are simply too limited, too late, often contradictory, and almost always tendentious—each in its own way—to allow us to reach any firm conclusions about the most fundamental characteristics of the Pharisees, their prehistory and origins, we will restrict ourselves to those aspects of early Pharisaism that are relatively well attested and free of controversy.

It is clear that these early sages constituted a rather diverse group. On the one hand, they looked to the high priest Simon the Just of Zadokite stock as a forebear; on the other hand, an otherwise unknown Jewish savant, the Greek-named Antigonus of Socho, was also numbered among them. Some Pharisees were city dwellers, others came from rural settings. They came from such diverse places as Jerusalem, Zereda in Judea and Arbel, probably in the Galilee. One Pharisee was later recognized as a magician and miracle-worker (Joshua ben Perahia), another was reported to have been a relative of the royal family and part of the court entourage (Simeon ben Shetah). The opinions and proclivities were equally as diverse, some being of an ethical nature, others cultic or narrowly ritualistic. Almost no one voiced his opinions on social or political issues, with the striking exception already mentioned, Simeon ben Shetah. Nevertheless, the Pharisees under the Hasmoneans were highly politicized.

The Pharisees appear to have enjoyed a significant degree of popularity among the people.[78] Both Josephus and rabbinic literature make this point, although each may be guilty of exaggeration. Their prestige as religious figures apparently won them their political prominence. Little else seems to have been working in their favor. The Sadducees, by contrast, were prominent in diplomatic, military and aristocratic circles, not to speak of their central role in Temple affairs. It is difficult to pinpoint any particular Pharisaic power base, either in the political, social or economic realm. Apart from Simeon ben Shetah, there was no Pharisaic personality who played a major role in the affairs of state. Prominence and acceptance as religious figures were probably the

Pharisees' chief political asset.

A basic Pharisaic doctrine differentiated the sect from others. For the Pharisees, the Oral Law was the authentic amplification of the Written Law of Moses. As such, the two stood side by side, and one was incomplete without the other. The Oral Law provided the correct interpretation and application of the Written Law, although the Written Law remained the ultimate authority, the primary text and the basic parameter within which the Oral Law evolved and developed. The crowning recognition of the Oral Law as legitimate and authentic was the Pharisaic claim that it, too, was given at Sinai; God gave not only the Five Books of Moses to the Jews, but the Oral tradition as well. Armed with this notion, the Pharisees presented themselves to the people as the sole legitimate bearers of Mosaic tradition. This view of the Oral Law ultimately prevailed.

The Essenes   Oddly enough, though he mentions them last, Josephus, describes the Essenes in far greater detail than either the Sadducees or Pharisees.[79] Although the Essene role in Judean affairs certainly was not even remotely comparable to either the Sadducees' or Pharisees', it is possible that Josephus presents them in such detail because he thought his readers would be fascinated by a group exhibiting curious and exotic behavior.

Josephus was probably right regarding the audience of his generation. The archaeological finds from Qumran have certainly increased our amazement at the Essenes. The descriptions of Josephus and Philo, in addition to the many hundreds of scrolls and fragments discovered in the Dead Sea Scroll caves, unfold before our eyes details of a sect unique in the annals of Judaism in late antiquity.[80]

At first scholars debated the identity of the Qumran or Dead Sea sectarians. Although the parallels between them and the Essenes (as described in our literary sources) are extensive and striking, some significant differences are also evident. For example, the scrolls speak of a war-oriented group; the literary sources, of pacifists; the scrolls and archaeological finds offer evidence for the presence of women in the sect; the literary sources speak of a group of celibates. As a result of these discrepancies, almost every other organized group among the Jews—the Pharisees, Zealots, Sadducees, Boethusians and early Christians—has been mentioned as a candidate for the identification of the Dead Sea sect. Nevertheless, there is a consensus today that the Dead Sea sect was indeed the Essenes. Whatever differences there are between the literary descriptions of Josephus and Philo, on the one hand, and the Dead Sea Scrolls, on the other, are to be accounted for in one of the following ways: the different characteristics refer to various subgroups within the Essene sect; the varying characteristics reflect different periods in the sect's history; the differences reflect tendentious presentations on the part of Josephus and Philo, each for his own apologetic purposes.

The Essenes flourished during the last centuries of the Second Temple period, and, like the Sadducees and Pharisees, they originated during the mid-second century B.C. In about 140 to 130 B.C., they moved to Qumran in protest against Hasmonean rule. (Their settlement was destroyed by the Romans in 68 A.D.) Although Qumran served as the group's headquarters, branches existed in other places as well, including perhaps Jerusalem itself.

The sect was a tight organization with rigorous rules for acceptance and clearly defined penalties and punishments. It was governed by a council of 12 that was headed by an "overseer" (*mevaqer*). Priestly influence was considerable, and the original founder, referred to as the Teacher of Righteousness, was himself a priest, as were the majority of its leaders in each generation.

The sect was organized as a commune. There was no private property, and everything was produced communally and shared equally. Community life focused on meals, scriptural readings, instruction, and religious and spiritual observances highlighted by prayer. Although marriage was permitted in certain subgroups, members of the Qumran community were almost all celibate. The group therefore sustained itself from generation to generation by attracting a continuous stream of newcomers from Jewish society at large.

Another unique feature of Qumran was its calendar. In contrast to the rest of Jewish society which was governed by a lunar calendar (with periodic corrections), the Essene one was based on solar calculations. The year was divided into 12 months of 30 days each. Each three months constituted a season. Seasons were separated from one another by a single day that was not counted in either season. The Essene calendar was thus comprised of a 364-day year. Holidays fell on the same day of the week each year. Beyond the solar nature of the calendar, the sun was regarded as sacred by the sectarians. Prayer was directed to the east, and members were enjoined never to expose private parts of their bodies to the sun. It has been suggested that the sect's calendar may have been the basic reason for its withdrawal from Jewish society. Believing that the lunar calculations were false and the holidays were thus not being celebrated at their "appointed times," as commanded by Scripture, the Essenes chose to distance themselves from other Jews in order to practice the biblical prescriptions in what they assumed to be the "right" way.[81]

There were other, no less distinctive, aspects of Essene Judaism. For one, the sect firmly believed in a messianic doctrine according to which the world was imminently coming to an end and they themselves would participate in this final drama. To emphasize their high degree of messianic expectation, the sect divided itself into battalions, and even wrote a detailed scenario (the War Scroll) of the final series of battles that would bring human history to its culmination. Perhaps the most distinctive type of literary genre found at Qumran was the *pesher*, a kind of scriptural interpretation that assumed that all messianic references in the Bible, particularly from the Prophets, were being fulfilled in their own day.

Other components of Qumran ideology included dualism and

predestination. The sect viewed the world as being governed by two conflicting forces, good and evil, each at times gaining the upper hand. Only in the end would the forces of good prevail. Even the heavens were divided into opposing camps of angels functioning in the service of these two forces. Just as the final denouement of the world had been carefully programmed in advance, so the life and fortunes of each individual were predestined. For the Essene, there was no room for individual free-will.

The recovery of the Essene library at Qumran has had an enormous impact on our understanding of ancient Judaism. Because many of their ideas and customs seem to be unique within Judaism, they raise intriguing questions as to what indeed was the nature of Jewish religion at the time. What influence did this group have on Jewish society as a whole? Were Essene practices and beliefs *sui generis*, or did they have an effect on other segments of Jewish society as well? Given the striking parallels between the Dead Sea doctrines and communal organization, on the one hand, and those of early Christianity, on the other, these questions take on even greater import. No firm answers have been forthcoming to date, but there can be little doubt that future publication of Dead Sea Scrolls and further study of those already known will continue to have enormous bearing on our understanding of Jewish life in the Hasmonean period.

The end of Jewish sovereignty

As we shall see in the next chapter, Jewish sovereignty was lost to the Romans when Pompey conquered Judea in 63 B.C. Was this avoidable? Could the Hasmonean kingdom have overcome or averted this sudden and dramatic reversal of fortunes? Josephus answers in the affirmative, claiming that all was lost because of the internecine conflict between Hyrcanus II and Aristobulus II (67-63 B.C.). These warring brothers brought ruin to their kingdom through their failure to present a unified front against Rome. Josephus was certainly correct in his appraisal that Hasmonean weakness contributed heavily to the demise of their kingdom. There is no doubt that, had the brothers coordinated their efforts and jointly negotiated with Pompey, they could have avoided such serious losses. However, Josephus is certainly wrong in suggesting that even a unified stand would ultimately have made a difference. Rome was destined to conquer the East irrespective of internal Hasmonean politics. The Hasmoneans could only have hoped to mitigate the conditions of conquest. By demonstrating a unified stand and a willingness to cooperate, their kingdom might have survived much longer and remained more intact than it in fact did. Their failure in this regard was a major political mistake, one that cost them their independence and hegemony over Jewish society.[82]

E I G H T

Roman Domination

The Jewish Revolt and the
Destruction of the Second Temple

SHAYE J. D. COHEN

T HE ROMANS ENTERED JUDEAN POLITICS, IRONICALLY, BY INVITA-
tion of one Jewish faction that was in a power struggle with
another. In 76 B.C.* Alexander Jannaeus, the last great king of
the Hasmonean line, died. He was succeeded by his widow Salome
Alexandra, who herself died in 67 B.C. The royal couple's two sons,
Hyrcanus and Aristobulus then fought each other for succession to the
throne. Both Hyrcanus (usually called by scholars Hyrcanus II) and
Aristobulus (usually called by scholars Aristobulus II) appeared before
the Roman legate in Syria, each asking to be recognized as the ruler of
Judea. Other Jews appeared as well, asking the Romans to reject the
claims of both—by this time many Jews were thoroughly disillusioned
with Hasmonean rule.

The Romans at first supported Aristobulus II, but when they realized
he was a potential troublemaker, a suspicion amply confirmed by
subsequent events, they transfered their support to Hyrcanus II.
Aristobulus considered fighting the Romans, but realizing the
overwhelming might of Rome and the hopelessness of his situation, he
surrendered in 63 B.C. to the Roman general Pompey. The supporters
of Hyrcanus opened the city of Jerusalem to the Romans.

* Shaye Cohen and several other authors of this volume customarily use the abbreviations
"B.C.E." and "C.E." as do many historians. These stand for "Before the Common Era"
and "Common Era." They have permitted the change to the more familiar B.C. and A.D.
in the interest of conformity with the remainder of the volume.

Pompey takes   But that was not the end of the battle for Jerusalem. Although the city
Jerusalem   was in Roman hands, many of Aristobulus's supporters garrisoned
themselves in the Temple and refused to surrender. After a three-month
siege and some fearsome fighting, however, the Temple fell to Pompey's
legions (63 B.C.).

To punish the Jews for refusing to yield peacefully to Roman dominion,
Pompey greatly reduced the territory under Jewish jurisdiction. The
empire the Hasmoneans had created through war and struggle was
dismembered at a single stroke. The high priest of Jerusalem now ruled
only those areas populated by a heavy concentration of Jews, primarily
Judea (the district around Jerusalem) and Galilee. Although these Jewish
areas were not legally incorporated into the Roman empire, they were
now *de facto* under Roman rule.[1]

Pompey's conquest of Jerusalem closed one chapter in Roman-Jewish
relations and opened another. A hundred years earlier Judah the
Maccabee had sought and obtained an alliance with the Romans, who
were then just becoming the dominant power in the eastern Mediterranean. At that time, the Romans eagerly supported anyone who would
help them weaken the power of the Seleucid kings of Syria. Judah's
successors followed the same strategy of seeking Roman support in their
struggles for independence from the Seleucids.

Gradually, Rome's power grew; her policy in the region, however, never
wavered: Any power that might pose a threat to Roman interests was to
be weakened. When the Jews were a useful ally against the Seleucids,
they were embraced. When the Hasmonean state expanded, the Romans
had no desire to see it become, in turn, a new threat to Roman interests.
By the middle of the first century B.C., when the Romans at long last
decided that the time had come to incorporate the eastern Mediterranean
into their empire, the Jews were no longer allies but just another ethnic
group that was to be brought into the inchoate imperial system.[2]

Although the struggle for succession between Hyrcanus II and
Aristobolus II and their appeals for Roman support provided the occasion
for the Roman takeover of the Hasmonean state, we may be sure that
in one way or another the Romans would have found a satisfactory excuse
to exercise hegemony over the Jewish state.

The 30 years after Pompey's conquest of Jerusalem (63 to 31 B.C.)
were extremely turbulent not only for the Jews of Judea but for the entire
Roman world, especially in the East. This was the period of the decline
of the Roman republic, of the struggle between Julius Caesar and Pompey,
of Pompey's death and Caesar's ascension to sole power, of Caesar's
assassination (on March 15, 44 B.C.), and of the struggle between the
senate and Caesar's supporters and later between Octavian (Augustus)
and Mark Antony. The dust did not settle until the sea battle of Actium
in Egypt (31 B.C.), where Octavian defeated Mark Antony and became
the sole ruler of the Roman empire. During the 20s B.C. Octavian

consolidated his power and assumed the name "Augustus." He established a pattern of imperial administration that would endure for centuries.

As the Romans were changing their mode of government, so were the Jews. Under the Persian and the Hellenistic monarchies, the Jews had been led by high priests who wielded political as well as religious power. However, during the initial period of Roman rule after Pompey's conquest of Jerusalem, the high priesthood lost virtually all its temporal powers and a new royal dynasty emerged that was not of priestly stock. Its opponents claimed that it was not even wholly Jewish! The Romans, for their part, were delighted to install a dynasty that owed its very existence to Roman favor and therefore could be counted on to provide loyal support.

The rise of the Herodian dynasty

This new dynasty, usually called the Herodian after its most famous member, was founded by Herod's father, Antipater the Idumean. The Idumeans, who lived in the area south of Judea, had been incorporated into the Hasmonean empire and converted to Judaism by John Hyrcanus (Hyrcanus I). Antipater gradually insinuated himself into the circle of Hyrcanus II. When Julius Caesar came to Syria in 47 B.C., he conferred various benefits on the Jews. Hyrcanus II was appointed *ethnarch* (literally, ruler of the nation), and Antipater the Idumean was appointed *procurator* (literally, caretaker).

A rival soon assassinated Antipater, and his mantle then fell to his son Herod. In 40 B.C. the Parthians invaded Syria, captured Hyrcanus II and installed the son of Aristobulus II as king and high priest of the Jews. Herod, now the Roman procurator, fled to Rome and persuaded the senate that only he could restore Roman rule in Judea. With Roman support Herod returned to Judea and, after some severe fighting, reconquered Jerusalem in 37 B.C.

Herod remained the undisputed leader of the Jews for over 30 years (37-4 B.C.).

Herod the Great

Herod is an enigmatic figure.[3] A tyrant, a madman, a murderer, a builder of great cities and fortresses, a wily politician, a successful king, a Jew, a half-Jew, a gentile—Herod was all these and more. He is perhaps best known to posterity as the murderer of several of his wives, children and other relations. The murders were prompted by Herod's suspicions (often justified) of all those who had an equal or better claim to the throne than he. In the first years of his reign, Herod executed the surviving members of the Hasmonean aristocracy. Since he was married to Mariamme the daughter of the Hasmonean king Hyrcanus II, this meant that Herod murdered his wife's relations—her brother, her aunt and her father. Finally, he murdered Mariamme too. At the end of his reign, he executed the two sons Mariamme had borne him.

Herod also executed various other wives, sons and close relations. The Christian tradition of Herod's "massacre of the innocents" (Matthew 2) is based on his unpleasant habit of killing anyone associated with the old aristocracy, including many teachers and religious leaders.

Herod created a new aristocracy that owed its status and prestige to him alone. He raised to the high priesthood men from families that had never previously supplied high priests, including families from the Diaspora (the Jewish communities outside the land of Israel).

Herod was also a great builder. Many of the most popular tourist sites in Israel today were Herod's projects—Masada, Herodium, Caesarea and many of the most conspicuous remains of ancient Jerusalem, including "the tower of David," the "western wall" and much of the Temple Mount. As a result of Herod's works, Jerusalem became "one of the most famous cities of the east"[4] and its Temple, which he rebuilt, was widely admired. In the new city of Caesarea, Herod created a magnificent harbor, utilizing the latest technology in hydraulic cement and underwater construction. Herod also founded several other cities, notably Sebaste (on the site of ancient Samaria). He bestowed gifts and benefactions on cities and enterprises outside his own kingdom. Athens, Sparta, Rhodes and the Olympic games all enjoyed Herod's largess.

Herod's building program had several purposes.[5] A network of fortresses (Masada, Herodium, Alexandrium, Hyrcania, Macherus) was designed to provide refuge to Herod and his family in the event of insurrection. Herod rebuilt Jerusalem and the Temple so that his kingdom would have a capital city worthy of his dignity and grandeur and he would win the support of the Jews both in the land of Israel and in the Diaspora. Herod built Sebaste and other pagan cities (even Caesarea was a joint Jewish-pagan city) because he saw himself as the king not only of the Jews but also of the country's substantial pagan population. And last, but not least, the benefactions to the cities of the eastern Mediterranean were prompted by Herod's megalomania. Throughout his life Herod was hungry for power and prestige. He wanted desperately to be recognized as an important personage. He obtained that recognition through his lavish gifts. Even the city of Athens honored him with a public inscription.

Herod tried to win support and recognition from both the Jews and the pagans, both within his kingdom and outside of it. The support of these groups, however, would have meant nothing if Herod had not been supported by Rome. In 37 B.C, as we have seen, the Romans made Herod the leader of Judea. In the struggle that developed soon thereafter between Antony and Octavian, Herod supported Mark Antony. This was perhaps because Antony was headquartered in the East. But, as noted above, at the battle of Actium in 31 B.C., Octavian defeated Antony, and the entire eastern Mediterranean, including Egypt, came to the hands of Octavian.

Herod had supported the losing side. He was obviously in deep trouble. But, ever the survivor, Herod managed to convince Octavian that everyone's best interests would be served if he were to remain king of Judea. He had been loyal to Antony, Herod argued, and now would be loyal to Octavian. Octavian accepted Herod's argument and never had cause to regret his decision. Herod was true to his word, and during the course of his long reign was rewarded several times by the emperor (now Augustus) with grants of additional territory.

Like all other vassal kings subservient to the Romans, Herod was authorized to govern his subjects as he pleased as long as he maintained peace and stability, did not engage in any unauthorized activities outside his kingdom, and actively supported Roman administrative and military activities in the area. Herod knew his place and followed these rules. At home he was the tyrant, but in his dealings with the Romans he was ever the dutiful subject. Before engaging in any major enterprise (killing his sons, for example), he consulted the Roman governor of Syria, or even the emperor himself.

Herod's popularity during his own lifetime is hard to estimate. Our major evidence, indeed virtually our only evidence, is provided by Josephus, whose two histories, *The Jewish War* and the *Jewish Antiquities*, were written in the last quarter of the first century A.D., a full hundred years after Herod's reign. Moreover, the two books give somewhat varying appraisals. In the earlier work, *The Jewish War*, completed in the early 80s A.D., Josephus paints a portrait of Herod that is basically favorable: a brilliant and successful king who was plagued by personal disaster and calamity. Nevertheless, even here Josephus reports Herod's madness and the fact that he was widely hated. It is in *The Jewish War* that Josephus tells the (true?) story that Herod, fearing that his funeral would be an occasion for rejoicing among the Jews, planned to assure general mourning by ordering that the distinguished men of the country be gathered and killed upon the news of his death. Nevertheless, as a rule, *The Jewish War* treats the king kindly and regards him as unfortunate rather than mad, and as powerful rather than unpopular. Here is its final verdict:[6]

> "In his life as a whole he was blessed, if ever man was, by fortune; a commoner, he mounted to a throne, retained it for all those years and bequeathed it to his own children; in his family life, on the contrary, no man was more unfortunate."

Although the *Jewish Antiquities*, completed in 93/4 A.D., repeats this verdict in almost identical words,[7] its perspective is somewhat different. The *Jewish Antiquities* includes much more material unfavorable to Herod. *The Jewish War* either deemphasizes this unfavorable material or omits it altogether.

According to the *Jewish Antiquities*, Herod maintained his rule through terror and brutality. His secret police were everywhere, and reported to the king any murmurings of discontent. Many citizens were taken to Hyrcania, one of Herod's fortresses, never to be seen again. Herod is even supposed to have prohibited his subjects from assembling in public. These security measures were required because of the general dislike for Herod among the Jews.

The *Jewish Antiquities* recounts broadly two major complaints the Jews had against Herod, aside from his violence and brutality. First was his violation of traditional Jewish laws. He built a theater and an amphitheater in Jerusalem (neither has yet been discovered by archaeologists) where he staged gladitorial games and other forms of entertainment that were foreign to Judaism and inimical to many Jews. He built pagan cities and temples, and seemed to favor the pagan and Samaritan elements in the population over the Jews. Many of his judicial and administrative enactments were not in accordance with Jewish law. Certain elements in the population were offended at his introduction of Roman trophies into the Temple and his erection of a golden eagle over its entrance.

The second reason for the general dislike of Herod was his oppressive taxation. Someone had to pay for Herod's munificent benefactions to the cities of the East, generous gifts to the Romans and extravagant building projects at home. The Jewish citizens of Herod's kingdom had to foot the bill, and they objected.

But if the *Jewish Antiquities* condemns Herod in these respects, it also reflects a certain ambivalence. It includes pro-Herodian material as well. Even if in his private life Herod did not follow the traditional Jewish observances (for example, Jewish law does not approve of the murder of one's wife and children), in his public life he often took care not to cause offense. He built no pagan temples or cities in the Jewish areas of the country, and ordered that only priests were to work on the construction of the sacred precincts of the Temple in Jerusalem. Coins he intended for use in Jewish areas of the country were struck without images. Foreign princes who wished to marry a woman of the Herodian house had to be circumcised first. Moreover, it is in the *Jewish Antiquities* that we find reports of several reductions in taxes. Here too Josephus notes that Herod was conspicuously generous in the distribution of food to the people during a famine.

Because of the bad press Herod has received, both in Josephus and in the New Testament, he is occasionally vilified by contemporary scholars as a "malevolent maniac" or worse, but he is too complex a figure to be dismissed so easily. As we have seen, even in the *Jewish Antiquities*, which is the major source of anti-Herodian material, we find a more nuanced picture. Herod aimed to be both king of the Jews and king of Judea; he benefitted the Jews both of the land of Israel and of the Diaspora. But he never lost sight of the fact that his kingdom consisted of other groups as well.

Perhaps Herod's policy was dictated by the fact that he himself was the offspring of one of these groups, the Idumeans, who had been converted to Judaism only three generations earlier. Herod's court historian, Nicolaus of Damascus, claimed that Herod was a scion of one of the noblest families of Judea, which had returned from Babylonia in the time of the Persians, but Herod's detractors called him a "half-Jew," or even a gentile, because of his Idumean extraction.[8] His marginal status in the native Jewish community perhaps explains his eagerness to solicit the support of the Samaritans and the gentiles of the country. Herod was also an astute politician who never forgot that the key to his success lay in the hands of the Romans. Above all else, he was resilient and resourceful. Protected by his paranoia, he succeeded in reigning 33 years in a period of tremendous upheaval and instability.

Herod's death released the accumulated passions and frustrations of the people who had been kept in check by his brutality. As Herod lay on his deathbed, two pious men and their followers removed the golden eagle that Herod had erected over the entrance to the Temple and hacked the bird to pieces. Immediately after Herod's death, riots and rebellions broke out in Jerusalem, Judea, Galilee and the Transjordan (Perea). The leaders of the riots had diverse goals. Some were simply venting their anger at a hated and feared regime; others were eager to profit from a period of chaos and disorder; still others dreamed of ridding themselves of Roman rule and proclaiming themselves king.

From the death of Herod to the First Jewish Revolt

These riots illustrate the underside of Herodian rule. Herod's high taxes and extravagant spending caused, or at least accelerated, the impoverishment of broad sections of the population. A clear sign of social distress was the resurgence of brigands—landless men who marauded the countryside in groups and were either hailed by the peasants as heroes (like Robin Hood) or hunted as villains. Brigandage had surfaced earlier, decades after Pompey's conquest in 63 B.C. Although Pompey himself had respected the Temple and the property of the Jews, the governors he left behind (Gabinius and Crassus) did not. They engaged in robbery and pillage; Crassus even plundered the Temple. Perhaps as a result of these depredations Galilee was almost overrun by brigands. In 47/6 B.C. Herod routed and suppressed the brigands. Several years later, they resurfaced and Herod again suppressed them. Brigandage reemerged in the years after Herod's death, especially, as we shall see below, in the period from 44 A.D., to the outbreak of the Jewish rebellion against Rome in 66 A.D. The impoverishment of the country and its consequent social distress were an unfortunate legacy of Herod the Great.[9]

The history of the Jews from the death of Herod in 4 B.C. to the outbreak in 66 A.D. of the great war known as the First Jewish Revolt lacks a single theme or focal point. Josephus presents the history of the first century A.D. in the form of discrete episodes, with the decline in Roman-Jewish relations the sole connecting link.

During the first half of the first century A.D., the Romans used vassal kings to govern those areas of the eastern empire that, like Judea, were neither urbanized nor greatly "Hellenized" but were home to vigorous national cultures. Administration through a vassal king, a native aristocrat who could understand the peculiar ways of the population, was thought preferable to direct Roman rule. Thus, throughout eastern Asia Minor,

Roman-Jewish relations

northern Syria, and Palestine, native dynasts governed their territories in accordance with the wishes of the Romans. In accordance with this policy, after Herod's death, his kingdom was divided among three of his sons. Antipas got Galilee and Perea; Philip, the Golan heights and points east. Archelaus became ruler of the largest and most important part of Herod's kingdom—Judea. In 6 A.D., however, the Romans deposed Archelaus for misrule and Judea, along with Idumea, Samaria and much of the Mediterranean coast, was annexed to the province of Syria. Henceforth Judea was administered by functionaries in the Roman civil service, known as *prefects*, or (after 44 A.D.) *procurators*. The rest of the country remained in the hands of Antipas and Philip for another 30 years, but then became the domain of Herod's grandson Agrippa I. In 41 A.D. Agrippa I received from the emperor Claudius the kingship over Judea as well, thereby reigning over a kingdom almost as large as Herod's own. Agrippa I died, however, three years later, in 44 A.D. After his death, all of the Jewish portions of the country were governed by Roman procurators. For a few years, from the middle of the century until the end of the First Jewish Revolt in 70 A.D., a small piece of Galilee was given to Agrippa's son, known as Agrippa II, but an overall change in Roman policy and administration is unmistakable. At the beginning of the first century, the land of Israel was governed by vassal rulers—men like Herod and his sons; by the middle of the century it was governed by Roman procurators (with the exception of Agrippa II). This same shift can be found elsewhere in the Roman east.[10]

Judea, on the other hand, was governed by Roman prefects from 6 A.D. Of the six or seven Roman prefects who governed Judea following Archelaus's deposition, most are bare names to us. Even Josephus has little to say about them. The exception is the Roman prefect Pontius Pilate (c. 26 to 36 A.D.). Pilate receives a negative assessment in the Gospels, in Philo, as well as in Josephus. According to the Gospels, Pilate massacred a group of Galileans (Luke 13:1) and brutally suppressed a rebellion (Mark 15:7), quite aside from crucifying Jesus. According to Philo, Pilate introduced into Herod's former palace in Jerusalem some golden shields inscribed with the name of the emperor Tiberius. The Jews objected strenuously, because they felt that any object associated with emperor worship, not to mention emperor worship itself, was idolatrous and an offense to the Jewish religion. Previous Roman governors had respected Jewish sensitivities in this matter, but Pilate did not. After being petitioned by the Jews, the emperor ordered Pilate to remove the shields from Jerusalem and to deposit them in the temple of Augustus in Caesarea, a mixed Jewish-pagan city. Josephus narrates a similar incident (or perhaps a different version of the same incident) involving the importation of military standards (which of course contained images) into Jerusalem. The people protested loudly, saying they would rather die than see the ancestral law violated. Pilate relented and ordered the images to be removed. Ultimately, Pilate was removed from office when the Jews complained enough to his superiors.[11]

When a procurator like Pilate was brutal or corrupt, the Jews could appeal to the governor of Syria or even to the emperor himself to remove the malefactor. But when the emperor was responsible for actions that were deleterious to the Jewish community, the Jews had nowhere to turn. This was the dilemma that confronted the Jews of both Alexandria and the land of Israel during the reign of the emperor Caligula (37-41 A.D.).

The Romans realized that Judaism was unlike the numerous other native religions of the empire; the Jews refused to worship any god but their own, refused to acknowledge the emperor's right to divine honors, refused to tolerate images in public places and buildings, and refused to perform any sort of work every seventh day. Aware of these peculiarities, the Romans permitted Jewish citizens to refrain from participation in pagan ceremonies; allowed priests of the Jerusalem Temple to offer sacrifices on behalf of, rather than to, the emperor; minted coins in Judea without images (even if many of the coins that circulated in the country were minted elsewhere and bore images); exempted the Jews from military service and ensured that they would not be called to court on the Sabbath or lose any official benefits as a result of their Sabbath observances. In many of the cities of the East, the Romans authorized the Jews to create *politeumata*, autonomous ethnic communities, that afforded the Jews the opportunity for self-government of their communal affairs.[12]

The mad emperor Caligula and his legate in Egypt withdrew, or attempted to withdraw, these rights and privileges. Riots erupted first in Alexandria—the "Greeks" (that is, the Greek-speaking population of the city, most of whom were not "Greek" at all) against the Jews. Exactly who or what started the riots is not clear. The root cause of the conflict, however, was the ambiguous status of the city's Jews. On the one hand, the Alexandrians resented the Jewish *politeuma* and regarded it as a diminution of the prestige and autonomy of their own city. On the other hand, the Jews thought that membership in their own *politeuma* should confer on them the same rights and privileges the citizens of the city had. The result of these conflicting claims was bloodshed and destruction. Aided by the Roman governor of Egypt, the Greeks attacked the Jews, pillaged Jewish property, desecrated or destroyed Jewish synagogues and herded the Jews into a "ghetto." The Jews were hardly passive during these events, and resisted both militarily and diplomatically. The most distinguished Jew of the city, the philosopher Philo, led a delegation to the emperor to argue the Jewish cause.

The Alexandria riots

While in Rome Philo learned of another, even more serious, assault on Judaism by the state. Angered by the Jews' refusal to accord him divine honors, Caligula ordered the governor of Syria to erect a colossal statue of the emperor in the Temple of Jerusalem. Whether something more than coincidence ties together the anti-Jewish riots in Alexandria with Caligula's assault on the Temple is not clear, especially because of some uncertainty in the relative chronology of the two sets of events.[13] In any case, the rights of the Jews of Alexandria and the sanctity of the Temple in Jerusalem were threatened simultaneously. The Roman governor of Syria, Publius Petronius, realizing that the execution of Caligula's order to erect his statue in the Temple could not be accomplished without riots and a tremendous loss of life, procrastinated. In a letter to Caligula, Petronius explained that the matter should be delayed because otherwise it would interfere with the harvest; in a second letter, he asked the emperor to rescind his order outright. In the meantime, Agrippa II, who was a friend of Caligula's, convinced the emperor to rescind his demand. Caligula did so, but was angered when he received Petronius's second letter, which indicated that Petronius had no intention of following the imperial order. In reply, Caligula ordered Petronius to commit suicide. Petronius received this ultimatum, however, only after he learned that Caligula had been assassinated. This brought to an end the potential troubles in the land of Israel. The troubles in Alexandria were settled by Claudius, Caligula's successor, who ordered both the Jews and the Greeks to return to the status quo: The Jews were to maintain their *politeuma*, but were not to ask for more rights than was their due.

Perhaps one of the most significant aspects of these events was the refusal of the Jews even to consider rebellion against the empire. In Alexandria, the Jews took up arms only in self-defense and only with reluctance—at least this is what Philo tells us. The Jews directed their fighting against their enemies, not against the emperor or the Roman empire. In the land of Israel itself, when Caligula's edict to erect a statue of himself in the Temple became known, the Jews assembled before Petronius *en masse* and declared that he would have to kill every one of them before they would allow the Temple to be desecrated. But the Jews did not threaten rebellion. Instead, in anticipation of Mahatma Gandhi in India in the 20th century, they offered passive resistance. Because Petronius was an ethical man with a conscience, he was convinced by these mass demonstrations not to carry out his assignment. Even a governor with less moral fiber might be persuaded by these tactics: Pontius Pilate removed the golden shields from Jerusalem after the Jews protested and declared that they would rather be killed than allow the images to remain in the Temple. At no point in either story do "brigands" or revolutionaries make an appearance.

Agrippa I   Despite the success of this policy of passive resistance, the years after Caligula's reign saw the growth of violent resistance to Roman rule. Caligula's madness seems to have driven home the point that the beneficence of Roman rule was not secure, and that the only way to ensure the safety and sanctity of the Temple was to expel the Romans from the country and to remove those Jews who actively supported them.

This process might have been prevented had Agrippa I been blessed with as long a reign as his grandfather Herod the Great. Instead, Agrippa I ruled for only three years (41-44 A.D.). Despite his short reign, he was a popular king; both Josephus and rabbinic literature have only nice things to say about him. In some respects he resembled his grandfather. He was a wily and able politician. He sponsored pagan games at Caesarea and bestowed magnificent gifts on Beirut, a pagan city. But, unlike Herod, he was not criticized for these donations, for in other respects he was Herod's superior. He lacked Herod's brutality. While Herod refrained from flouting traditional Jewish laws in the Jewish areas of his domain, Agrippa was conspicuous for observing them. In the political sphere, he tried to attain a modest degree of independence from Rome. He even began the construction of a new wall on the northern side of Jerusalem; had it been completed, Josephus says, the city would have been impregnable during the Jewish revolt that erupted in 66 A.D.

Had Agrippa reigned a long time, perhaps the disaffected elements in Judea would have been reconciled again to foreign dominion. On Agrippa's death in 44 A.D., however, Judea once again became the domain of the Roman procurators. There was no longer a Jewish authority who, despite ultimate subservience to Rome, could satisfy Jewish nationalist aspirations.

Moreover, the procurators after 44 A.D. were incompetent and insensitive at best, corrupt and wicked at worst. A country that, even in the face of Caligula's assault on its religious sensitivities, had maintained the peace was brought to rebellion after a little more than 20 years of rule by the Roman procurators who followed Agrippa I. Josephus narrates a long string of minor incidents, disturbances, riots, assassinations and lootings, which, in retrospect, were forerunners to the great revolt. The participants in these incidents probably never realized that they were preparing the way for war. Nevertheless, various elements in the population were expressing their frustrations with the status quo, and the procurators were using the power of their office for fun and profit.

In the fall of 66 A.D., after Gessius Florus (who would be the last of the procurators) had stolen money from the Temple treasury (for overdue taxes, he claimed), a particularly violent riot led to the massacre of the Roman garrison in Jerusalem. The governor of Syria intervened, but even he failed to restore the peace. He was forced to withdraw from Jerusalem, suffering a major defeat. The Jews of Judea had rebelled against the Roman empire.

Before recounting the story of this rebellion and its disastrous consequences, let us pause to look at the religious atmosphere generally and the social texture of Palestine in the first century A.D.

Judaism at the time was a remarkably variegated phenomenon.* Above all, Judaism was a *belief* in the God of Moses, who created the world, ***Variegated Judaism***

* The word "Jew" derives from the Greek *Ioudaios* and the Latin *Judaeus*, which originally meant "an inhabitant or a native of the district of Judea; a member of the tribe of Judah." The English equivalent is "Judean." However, by the Hellenistic period the term began to have another meaning as well, one that approximates the English term "Jew." The Jews' manner of life (their religion) was called *Ioudaismos*, "Judaism."

who chose the Jews to be his special people and who rewarded and punished his people in accordance with their loyalty to him. Judaism was also the *practice* of the laws and rituals that Moses had commanded in God's name, most conspicuously the rituals of circumcision, Sabbath and prohibited foods. The Jews vigorously debated among themselves the precise meaning and content of their beliefs and practices, but on the general outlines all, or almost all, were in agreement.

Judaism during this period, was different from, or at least was not identical with, the religion of pre-Exilic Israel.[14] Judaism in this period was a "book religion"; at its center was the recitation and study of a collection of sacred writings, the most important of which was the Torah (Instruction) of Moses. By this time, many Jews added two other categories of sacred literature to the Torah: the Prophets and the Writings. These three groups of writings together comprise *the Bible,* called the Old Testament by Christians and the Tanakh* by Jews. Pre-Exilic Israel, by contrast, did not have such a sacred book; to be sure, it preserved in written form many sacred traditions, but it was not a "book religion." Pre-Exilic Israelites communicated and communed with God through the sacrificial cult in the Jerusalem Temple and through the revelations of the prophets. By Hellenistic times, however, and certainly by the first century of our era, the institutional access to God through the Temple and the charismatic access to God through the prophets were being supplemented, and to some degree supplanted, by new forms of piety, especially regular prayer and study of scripture.

The institutional home of this new piety was the *synagogue* (assembly or gathering) or *proseuche* (prayer-house), which is first attested in Egypt in the third century B.C. By the first century of our era, there were synagogues not only in every Diaspora settlement but also throughout the land of Israel. The archaeological remains of synagogues from this period have been discovered at Masada, Herodium, Gamla and various Diaspora sites.[15]

Pre-Exilic Israelite religion focused on the group, the community and the clan; first-century Judaism, by contrast, focused on the individual Jew. First-century Judaism enjoined the individual Jew to sanctify his (or her) life through the daily performance of numerous rituals. Sanctity was not to be restricted to the Temple; God's presence was everywhere, and the Jew was to be continually mindful of this fact. Every moment was an opportunity for the observance of the Commandments, the sanctification of life and subservience to God. Not only was the people of Israel collectively responsible to God, but each individual Jew was as well. The cult of the Temple therefore was supplemented by a religious regimen that focused on the individual rather than the group.

Prophecy too no longer was what it had been. Many Jews believed that prophecy had ceased, or at least had so transformed itself that it no longer

---

* Tanakh is an acronym for *Torah,* the five books of Moses; *Neviim,* the Prophets; and *Ktuvim,* the writings.

WERNER BRAUN

Synagogue at Herodium. During the First Jewish Revolt against Rome the reception/dining room of Herodium (45 feet long and 30 feet wide) was transformed into a synagogue by the addition of benches around the walls and four columns to support a new roof. In 23 B.C. Herod the Great had created Herodium in the Judean wilderness by building up a mountain on top of a natural hill. Within the mountain he fashioned a seven-story palace-fortress that included living rooms, the reception/dining room, cisterns, and a bathhouse.

had the prestige and the authority it had commanded when the classical prophets like Isaiah and Jeremiah of the eighth and sixth centuries B.C. spoke. Those Jews who continued to see heavenly visions and hear heavenly voices no longer saw and heard them in the manner of their predecessors. The new literary genre, called by modern scholars *apocalypse* (revelation), assigned a much greater role to complex symbolic visions and angelic intermediaries than did biblical prophecy. Apocalyptic thinking was dominated by a sense that the world was in the throes of a final crisis that would be resolved by the immediate arrival of the end of time. Not only were the *style* and the *atmosphere* of apocalypse different from those of biblical prophecy, but much of its *content* was different as well. In pre-Exilic Israel, the Israelites believed that God rewarded the righteous and punished the wicked in this world, and did so by rewarding or punishing either the actor himself or his children. By the first century A.D., this doctrine had been rejected, and replaced by the idea that every individual received his or her just desserts from God either in this world or in the world to come. Elaborate theories were developed about the rewards and punishments that awaited people after death or at the end of time, or both. Then there would be a resurrection of the dead and a final judgment, and the nation of Israel, the plaything of gentile kingdoms in this world, would finally receive its due; God would send a redeemer, either a human being or an angel, who would restore Israel's sovereignty. The nations of the world would then recognize the Lord and accept the hegemony of the Jews. These new ideas were widely accepted in society, even though apocalyptic literature was so esoteric that it could be appreciated only by the few.

The new ideas, rituals and institutions that gradually emerged were adopted in their most extreme forms by various pietistic groups, but also had an impressive impact on broad reaches of the population. The evidence for "popular religion,"[16] either in the land of Israel or the Diaspora, is very meager, but the literary evidence of Josephus, Philo and the New Testament shows that popular piety included the study of Scripture and the participation in synagogue services on the Sabbath; the observance of the Sabbath, the dietary prohibitions and various other rituals; adherence to a strict moral code; separation from pagans and anything connected with pagan religious ceremonies; and going on pilgrimage to the Temple in Jerusalem for the festivals. Many Jews of Jerusalem, rich and poor alike, believed in the ultimate resurrection of the dead. This is demonstrated by their practice of reburial. A year or so after burying the corpse in a temporary grave, they would dig up the bones, carefully arrange them in a special box known as an *ossuary,* and deposit the ossuary in a cave or some other safe location. Thus the dead would be ready for the resurrection; all the bones were united safely in one place, awaiting reassembly.[17] In the Diaspora the most conspicuously observed rituals, to judge from the testimony of pagan writers, were circumcision, the Sabbath and the dietary prohibitions (notably the avoidance of pork).

"Popular religion," at least in the land of Israel, also contained a strong element of the "magical" and the "miraculous." Magic brought divine activity into direct and immediate contact with humans. Teachers and holy men of all sorts roamed the countryside, preaching repentance and performing "miraculous" cures. Jesus spent much of his time exorcising demons and performing faith healings, but he was hardly unique in this respect.

Holy men, who often modeled themselves to some extent on the prophet Elisha, answered the immediate needs of the populace, which was more concerned about good health and abundant harvests than about salvation and redemption.[18]

Pharisees, Sadducees and Essenes   More conspicuous in our literary record is the religion of "virtuosi" or "pietists." The Hasmonean period witnessed the birth of the Pharisees, Sadducees and the Essenes of Qumran (see the previous chapter). In the first century A.D. several new groups emerged: the Sicarii, various other revolutionary groups and, of course, Christianity. The nature and social setting of each of these groups has been much debated, and many uncertainties remain.[19] What term most accurately describes these groups—elite, order, movement, sect, church, class, guild, association? Josephus treats the Pharisees, Sadducees and Essenes as ancestral "schools" or "schools of thought," that is, legitimate expressions of the Jewish philosophy. He regards the Sicarii and the other revolutionary groups as "intrusive" or illegitimate. Thus, in order to disqualify the Sicarii, Josephus appeals to "authenticity," but otherwise he does not resort to this quality.

Even if Josephus regards the Pharisees, Sadducees and Essenes as equally authentic, however, he strongly implies that the masses of the Jews did not:[20]

[Regarding the Pharisees:] They are . . . extremely influential among the townsfolk; and all prayers and sacred rites of divine worship are performed according to their exposition. This is the great tribute that the inhabitants of the cities . . . have paid to the excellence of the Pharisees. [Regarding the Sadducees:] There are but few men to whom this doctrine has been made known, but these are men of the highest standing. They accomplish practically nothing, however. For whenever they assume some office, though they submit unwillingly and perforce, yet submit they do to the formulas of the Pharisees, since otherwise the masses would not tolerate them. [Regarding the Essenes:] They send votive offerings to the temple, but perform their sacrifices employing a different ritual of purification. For this reason they are barred (or they distance themselves) from those precincts of the temple that are frequented by all the people and perform their rites by themselves . . . . The men who practice this way of life number more than four thousand.

Thus, according to Josephus, the Pharisees had the support of the masses, especially the urban masses, while the Sadducees had the support of only the well-to-do. As a result, the Sadducees had to accept the dictates of the Pharisees and conduct all public rituals in accordance with Pharisaic rules. The Essenes, in contrast, distanced themselves from general society and from the Temple and were supported only by their own members, who numbered somewhat more than 4,000.

The Dead Sea Scrolls from Qumran, many of which are of Essene origin, confirm and supplement Josephus's portrait. The Essenes were a secretive brotherhood that lived apart from general Jewish society. They were a consecrated, sacral group, led by priests and affecting priestly ways. They believed that the end time was imminent, at which point there would be a great battle between "the sons of light" and "the sons of darkness," and a new temple would apparently be built and administered in accordance with the rules and practices of their sect. The Essenes had a distinctive calendar, purity rules, festivals, theology and exegesis of Scripture. In sum they were a *sect*: a small, organized group that separates

YIGAEL YADIN

**Temple Scroll. One of the famed Dead Sea Scrolls, this scroll is named for
its long passages that describe in great detail plans for a temple—perhaps
a visionary one—to be built in Jerusalem. Israeli archaeologist Yigael
Yadin, who published the scroll, believed that it was written by the Essenes
and was considered by them to be part of their Holy Scriptures, equal in
authority to the Pentateuch.**

itself from a larger religious community and asserts that it alone embodies
the religious ideals of the larger group.[21] Not all the Essenes separated
themselves completely from Jewish society by fleeing to Qumran in the
Judean wilderness; both Josephus and the Qumran scrolls indicate that
some Essenes lived among their fellow Jews. Some even married in order
to have children.

The Sadducees were apparently not a "community" or "group"at all
but a social class. They were the aristocracy—the priestly families from
which the high priests were selected, and the lay families with whom
the priests intermarried. Aside from denying the resurrection of the dead
(they appparently believed that God metes out reward and punishment
in this world—not a surprising position for the well-to-do), very little
is known of the Sadducees' philosophy or way of life.

The characteristics and identity of the Pharisees have long exercised
scholars. Were the Pharisees the leaders of Jewish society? Were all public
rituals conducted in accordance with Pharisaic rulings? Was—or is—
"Pharisaic Judaism" virtually synonymous with "Judaism"? Were the
Pharisees the "norm" from which all other expressions of Judaism
deviated? The Gospel of Matthew (especially chapter 23) seems to

indicate they were the leaders of Jewish society and that public rituals were conducted in accordance with Pharisaic rulings. Josephus and rabbinic sources agree. Rabbinic sources, indeed, go further; according to them, the Pharisees provided the "norm" according to which other Jewish "deviations" were measured; in short, Pharisaic Judaism was, for the rabbis, synonymous with "Judaism."

Although Matthew, Josephus and rabbinic sources provide convergent testimony about the Pharisees, they were written after the destruction of the Temple and may reflect to some extent the conditions of that time— when the rabbis, the heirs of the Pharisees, were on the ascendant. Although in Matthew's field of vision the Pharisees loomed large, this may prove only that his Christian community in the 80s A.D. saw the Pharisees as their chief Jewish competitors; Matthew does not necessarily prove that Jesus and the disciples regarded the Pharisees as Matthew depicts them. Similarly, the testimony of Josephus proves only that in the 90s A.D., Josephus regarded the Pharisees as the most powerful Jewish group; Josephus's testimony does not necessarily prove that the Pharisees were powerful several generations earlier. (Of course, if it could be proven that Matthew and Josephus in their descriptions of the Pharisees were using sources that derived from the Second Temple period, this conclusion would not follow.)[22]

Rabbinic literature, a third source, provides evidence consistent with Matthew and Josephus. However, the rabbis had a vested interest in presenting their ancestors as the group that controlled Jewish society, a position they themselves strived to attain in the centuries following the destruction of the Temple. Accordingly, we must view our sources on first-century Pharisaism with considerable skepticism.

What seems to have made the Pharisees distinctive was both their scrupulous observance of the laws of the written Torah and their loyalty to "ancestral traditions" that were not incorporated in the Torah of Moses. To judge from the New Testament stories about the disputes between Jesus (or his disciples) and the Pharisees, these traditions included numerous details in the observance of the Sabbath, purity and oaths. Rabbinic literature too ascribes to the proto-rabbinic figures of the first century, most of whom we presume to have been Pharisees, intense interest in the laws of purity. The Pharisees sought to sanctify their life to such a degree that they regarded the food on their table as akin to food on the altar; it was to be consumed only in a state of purity. Since the laws of purity created social barriers between those who observed them and those who did not, the Pharisees must have separated themselves to some extent from the people (for example, they would not eat with publicans and sinners). The Pharisees were thus a pietistic or elitist group that, like the Essenes, separated itself from the people, but that, unlike the Essenes, was supported by the masses. It seems reasonable to conclude that the Pharisees were not a "sect," but a religious elite that was very influential even if it did not have official political power (note that the Pharisees are absent from all the versions of the trial and execution of Jesus).

Christians   Of the groups that emerged in the first century A.D., the Christians are the most famous. Jesus, their leader, was a holy man and a teacher who, like many other such people, attracted admirers and disciples. Like many of his contemporaries, he apparently believed that the end time was imminent and that he was sent by God to prepare the way for its arrival. He therefore prophesied that the Temple would be removed because a new and more perfect temple would be erected by God as part of the new, perfect and permanent order of the end time. The high priests, however, regarded Jesus as a troublemaker and handed him over to the Romans for execution. In a paradoxical way his death marked not the end but the beginning of Christianity (a development outside the purview of this book).

The earliest Christian community, as described by the book of Acts, had many sectarian features; that is, it was a Jewish sect. It was, like the Essenes, "a small organized group that has separated itself from a larger religious body." The apostles controlled this group; property was held in common, disbursements were made to the faithful from the common till and disobedience to one's superiors was not tolerated (Acts 5:1-11). The group dined and prayed together. New members were "converted" through baptism and repentance (Acts 2:38-42). Like the Essenes, the Christians attempted to create a utopian community. A sense of alienation from the rest of society is apparent in the numerous calls for repentance and in the eschatological fervor of the group. Although Christianity began as a Jewish sect, or at least as a pietistic group with many sectarian features, it ceased to be a Jewish sect when it ceased to observe Jewish practices. It abolished circumcision and became a religious movement overwhelmingly gentile in composition and character. This process was accompanied by the elevation of Jesus to a position far higher and more significant than that of an angel or any other intermediary figure in Judaism. The separation of Christianity from Judaism, however, was not an event but a process.[23] The separation was accomplished when Christianity's practices no longer conformed to those of the Jews, when its theology was no longer that of the Jews and when its members were gentile. Then it was a separate religion.

Social ferment   The first century A.D. was an age not only, as we have seen, of religious ferment, but also of social ferment. Indeed, the great revolt of 66-70 A.D. was in large part, especially in its early phases, a civil struggle among Jews—between the rich and the poor, between the upper classes and the lower, between the city dwellers and the country folk. As we have noted, brigandage, that unmistakable symptom of social distress, increased significantly in the countryside after Agrippa I's death in 44 A.D. Jerusalem too was racked by social turmoil. In the early 60s A.D., work on the Temple Mount, begun by Herod the Great many years earlier, was finally completed. Faced with the prospect of having 18,000 laborers added to the ranks of the unemployed, the priests suggested to Agrippa II that the porticoes be torn down so that they could be rebuilt! Agrippa II wisely remarked that it was easier to destroy than to build such edifices and suggested that the laborers devote their energies to repaving of the streets. His suggestion was accepted. The laborers were paid for a full day of work even if they actually worked for only an hour. In short, the city of Jerusalem became, in effect, a welfare state, dependent on "make-work" projects for the maintenance of social peace.[24] The wealthy, in contrast, lived their lives and buried their dead in opulence and splendor. Aristocrats in Jerusalem and throughout the country maintained bands of armed retainers to threaten their opponents and to work for their own interests. Within the priesthood there was strife and violence between the upper and the lower clergy. Peasants in Galilee in 66-67 A.D. wanted nothing more than to attack and loot Sepphoris, Tiberias and Gabara, the three largest settlements of the district. After the great revolt commenced in 66 A.D., many peasants of both Galilee and Judea fled to Jerusalem where they turned on both the city aristocracy and the priestly elite. These tensions within Jewish society often surfaced violently during the great revolt. For many of the participants in the war, the primary enemies were not Roman but Jewish.[25]

In one sense the great revolt against Rome derived from the internal religious and social tensions just described. In this internal struggle, the Romans supported the status quo and kept the aristocrats in power. As a result, hatred of the upper classes and the aristocracy translated into hatred of the Romans. This hatred was supported by a variety of religious ideologies. The holy land had to be purified of foreign contagion. It was an affront to Judaism that the Temple and its rituals were under the aegis of the Romans. "Zeal for the Torah" demanded that the Jews rise up and destroy the sinners in their midst, namely, all those who supported the Romans and allowed them to maintain their rule.

The revolutionaries may also have believed that they were living at the threshhold of the end time. Josephus narrates that "what more than all else incited them to the war was an ambiguous oracle, . . . found in their sacred scriptures, to the effect that at that time one from their country would become ruler of the world."[26] In the years immediately preceding the revolt, many "eschatological prophets" were active, predicting the imminent approach of the end time or attempting, by means of a symbolic action (for example, splitting the Jordan River), to hasten or implement its arrival. But, although Josephus states that the equivocal prophecy quoted above was the primary inducement for the Jews to go to war, in the body of his narrative he seldom even alludes to the eschatological expectations of the revolutionaries. Perhaps some of the revolutionary leaders regarded themselves as messiahs, or were so regarded by their followers, but Josephus nowhere makes this point explicit. Accordingly, while few scholars would deny that eschatological expectations played a role in the motivation of the revolutionaries, the relative importance of this factor remains the subject of debate.[27]

The social tensions and eschatological expectations that impelled Judea to war with Rome were not uniquely Jewish. In fact the war of 66-70 A.D. follows a pattern evident in other native rebellions against the Roman empire. Tensions between rich and poor, and between city and country, were endemic to ancient society, and often contributed to native rebellions. Like the uprising in Judea, other native rebellions were often led by aristocrats, although peasants, day laborers, and landless poor formed the bulk of the revolutionary army. As so often happens in revolutions ancient and modern, in its initial phases the struggle is led by aristocratic (or bourgeois) elements which, as the struggle continues, are ousted, usually with great violence, by more extremist (or proletarian) groups. Like the Jews, other rebels in antiquity too dreamed of subjugating the universal Roman empire. The revolt of the Gauls in 69 A.D. was prompted in part by a Druid prediction that Rome would be destroyed and that the rule of the empire would devolve on the tribes of Transalpine Gaul. The Jewish revolt was, therefore, hardly unique in the annals of Rome.[28] What makes it special is its intensity, its duration and, most important of all, the fact that an ancient historian saw fit to write its history in great detail. Because of Josephus's *The Jewish War*, we are better informed about this war than any other native revolt against Rome.

The reliability of Josephus   Before recounting the events of this cataclysmic war, we must assess briefly the reliability of Josephus, since his work is our chief source.

Josephus was a participant in the war, a Jewish leader who, in the end, surrendered to the Romans. In 67 A.D. Josephus was the commander of the Jewish revolutionary forces in Galilee. When the Romans arrived, Josephus and his forces fled to the fortress of Jotapata. After a siege of 47 days the fortress was taken, and Josephus and some of his men took refuge in a nearby cave. When the Romans discovered them, Josephus's companions argued that they should commit mutual suicide rather than be taken prisoner. But Josephus, remembering the "nightly dreams in which God had foretold to him the impending fate of the Jews and the destinies of the Roman sovereigns," realized that God was on the side of the Romans and that surrender to the Romans was the only legitimate course of action. Since his comrades insisted on suicide, Josephus reluctantly agreed to draw lots with the rest, but as luck would have it (?), he drew one of the last. After the others had killed themselves, Josephus was left with only one companion and had no trouble convincing him that surrender was a wiser course than death. Upon emerging from the cave Josephus was taken to Vespasian; he predicted that the general would become emperor of Rome, the master of land, sea and the entire human race—a prediction that subsequently proved accurate. Josephus's account of his surrender to the Romans is clearly a mixture of history, fantasy, apology and propaganda.[29]

After the Roman destruction of Jerusalem, Josephus was taken to Rome in the entourage of the Roman general Titus, Vespasian's son. With his newly acquired Roman patrons looking over his shoulder, Josephus wrote his account of the rebellion, *The Jewish War,* completing it in the early 80s. The major purpose of Josephus's *The Jewish War* was to restrict Jewish guilt in the eyes of Rome. The Jewish people as a whole was innocent of rebellion against the Roman empire; that is the book's major theme. The Jewish religion too was not to be blamed for the revolutionary ardor of the combatants. On the contrary, most of the blame for the war belonged to various hotheads, fanatics and criminals within the Jewish community who in no way represented either Judaism or the Jews and who fomented rebellion for their own selfish and ignoble purposes. Josephus labels the revolutionaries "brigands," "impostors," "insurgents," "deceivers," "assassins" (Josephus uses the Latin term *sicarii*), "tyrants" and "wicked ones." This abusive terminology emphasizes that the leaders of the war were not the "real" representatives of Judaism and the Jews. Consistent with this perspective, Josephus tends to lump the revolutionaries together, masking the distinctions between the various groups. He also argues that the real leaders of the Jews—the high priests, the aristocrats and King Agrippa II—unanimously opposed the war. The Pharisees, Sadducees and Essenes (the three "legitimate" expressions of the national philosophy of the Jews) took no part in the war. According to Josephus, just before the outbreak of hostilities the "most notable of the Pharisees" joined the high priests and other aristocrats in appealing to the revolutionaries not to begin a war they could not possibly win.[30]

By restricting war guilt to the revolutionary parties alone, a patently false thesis, as we shall see, Josephus was trying to facilitate a rapprochement between the Jews and the Romans after the war. The Romans should not hold all the Jews responsible for the misdeeds of a few, all of whom were killed or captured during the war. True, Josephus argues that the revolutionaries should not receive *all* the blame for the catastrophe—the last two Roman procurators were so wicked that they virtually prepared Jerusalem for its destruction and deliberately provoked the war in order to cover up their crimes. But this does not detract from the guilt of the revolutionaries.

Josephus's apologetic for the Romans is also evident from his account of the war itself. Vespasian and Titus, the Roman generals, are perfect gentlemen who gave the Jews every opportunity to come to their senses and surrender. They even commiserated with the poor innocents who must suffer the tyranny of the revolutionaries and the horrors of war. According to Josephus, Titus did his best to save the Temple (see below) and wept when he beheld the destruction of the city and the house of God. Josephus is clearly saying that Titus and the Romans bear no responsibility for the destruction of the Temple, and that this unfortunate consequence of the war should not bar the resumption of normal relations between the Romans and their Jewish subjects.

In his second major work, the *Jewish Antiquities,* completed in 93/4 A.D., Josephus writes anew about the prehistory of the war. Here he is much less concerned about war guilt and much more ready to admit that responsibility for the war should not be ascribed to the revolutionaries alone. In *The Jewish War* Josephus wanted to cover up any connection between the revolutionaries and the "official" representatives of Judaism; in the *Jewish Antiquities* he no longer felt constrained to do so. For example, in the *Jewish Antiquities*, one procurator even colludes with the assassins in order to remove an opponent; another empties the prisons of all those who had been arrested for seditious activity. The emperor Nero, by favoring the pagan element of the city of Caesarea in its dispute with the Jewish citizenry, also bears some responsibility for the ensuing catastrophe.[31]

Here the corruption and incompetence of the Roman procurators is far more evident.

Most modern scholars see the war as the result of a complex array of factors, both internal and external. The perspective of modern scholarship resembles that of the *Jewish Antiquities* much more than that of *The Jewish War*. Moreover, unlike Josephus, many modern scholars admire the revolutionaries or at least do not condemn them. For Josephus, even in the *Jewish Antiquities,* they are villains and scoundrels, the dregs of society. For modern Israelis and for many others they are heroes who were trying to reclaim what was rightly theirs.

The rabbis of the Talmud shared the perspective of Josephus in *The Jewish War*: the revolutionaries were crazed fanatics who did not listen to the sage counsel of the rabbis and persisted in their folly. They brought disaster upon the entire house of Israel. In the Talmudic account the hero of the war is Rabban Yohanan ben Zakkai, a man who fled from Jerusalem, went over to the Roman side and acknowledged the suzerainty of Vespasian, the Roman general and soon-to-be emperor. Isaiah's prophecy "Lebanon shall fall to a mighty one" (Isaiah 10:34) was interpreted by Yohanan ben Zakkai to mean that the Temple (constructed from the cedars of Lebanon) would fall into the hands of Vespasian (a mighty one). The rabbinic hero thus hailed the Roman general as victor and emperor well before his actual victory and his elevation to the purple. From the perspective of the revolutionaries, this was treason; but from the perspective of the rabbis, viewed with acute hindsight, this was wisdom, a course of action that to their regret had not been followed.

Whether the historical Rabban Yohanan did anything even remotely approximating the deeds ascribed to him in the rabbinic account is, of course, unknown and unknowable. The story probably tells us much more about the political outlook of the rabbis of the third and fourth centuries than about the actions of Rabban Yohanan in the first.[32]

The course of the First Jewish Revolt
With this background, let us turn to the course of the war itself. In the fall of 66 A.D., no one knew that a war between the Jews and the Romans was imminent. Some revolutionaries, perhaps, were dreaming of a final conflict, but even they had no way of knowing precisely when the conflict would erupt or what form it would take.

The spark was provided by the procurator Florus when he seized 17 talents from the Temple treasury to compensate, he said, for uncollected back taxes. This act was not significantly worse than the depredations and misdeeds of previous procurators, and the riot it provoked was not significantly worse than the riots that had erupted during the tenures of previous procurators.

This riot, however, was the first act of a war, because it came at the end of a period of almost 20 years of unrelieved tension and lawlessness. When Florus brutally suppressed the riot, the people responded with even greater intensity, with the result that Florus had to flee the city.

At this point various revolutionary factions stepped forward. It is difficult to determine the interrelationship of all these groups. Some scholars argue that all of the anti-Roman forces formed in the aggregate a single "war party," which for purposes of convenience can be called *Zealots* after its most distinctive constituent group. Others argue that no single "war party" ever existed and that each of the groups and figures has its or his own history. The diverse groups shared a common willingness to fight the Romans, but differed from each other in many other respects, which explains why they spent so much time fighting each other. The latter interpretation is much more plausible than the former.[33]

At the outbreak of the war, an aristocratic priestly revolutionary party, led initially by Eleazar, son of the high priest Ananias, seems to have controlled the revolution. Eleazar suspended the sacrifice, which until then had been offered every day in the Temple, for the welfare of the emperor and the Roman empire.[34] This act was tantamount to a declaration of war. As if to emphasize the point, Eleazar and his supporters turned on the Roman garrisons Florus left in the city, after Florus had retreated, and besieged them.

Whether the aristocratic priestly revolutionaries were truly committed to the revolution, or were merely playing for time in the hope of forestalling the emergence of more radical and more dangerous elements is debated among scholars. Josephus seems to give contradictory answers: Although they probably began as revolutionaries who deeply resented the Roman diminution of their prestige and prerogatives, when they were faced with the opposition of other revolutionary groups whose primary targets were the Jewish aristocracy, it is likely the priestly revolutionaries began to hope for a peace agreement with the Romans.[35]

In any event, these priestly revolutionaries were soon eclipsed by another group, the Sicarii, led by one Menahem. In the fall of 66 A.D., the Sicarii entered Jerusalem. In addition to attacking the Roman forces that remained in the city, however, the Sicarii also attacked the Jewish aristocracy. They looted the homes of the well-to-do and massacred many of the nobility; the most prominent of their victims was Ananias the high priest, the father of Eleazar, who had led the priestly revolutionaries. The priestly group, headquartered in the Temple, fought back and killed the Sicarii leader, Menahem. Menahem's followers then fled to Masada, one of Herod's great fortresses, in the Judean wilderness. There they remained for the rest of the war, doing nothing to help the struggle. Other bands of fighters, however, were already, or would soon become, active in Jerusalem.

Revolutionary ardor also spread outside Jerusalem. In Caesarea and in many other cities of Palestine and Syria, Jews and pagans attacked one another. The hostility towards pagans and paganism that motivated the revolutionaries in Jerusalem seems also to have motivated Jews throughout the country. The pagans, for their part, gave vent to the same animosities that had exploded in the anti-Jewish riots in Alexandria 30 years earlier.

The Roman governor of Syria went to Judea to restore order, but after entering Jerusalem he decided that he was not strong enough to take the Temple from the revolutionaries. In the course of his withdrawal, his troops were beset by the Jews and had to abandon much of their equipment.

After the defeat of the Roman general of Syria, the revolutionaries, led by the priestly revolutionary party, assigned generals to each district in the country. Most of the commissioned generals were priests. Their task was to prepare the country for war, in anticipation of either negotiations or hostilities with the Romans. The general about whose activities we are best informed is naturally Josephus. He was sent to Galilee, where he spent the next six months feuding with local leaders, trying to impose his rule on a fractious population that had little desire to fight the Romans. He fortified several key locations, raised and trained an army, brought local brigands under his employ, and intimidated the cities of the district (notably Sepphoris, which supported the Romans, and Tiberias, which was divided).

Josephus had had no military or administrative experience, and was not temperamentally suited to cooperative leadership; it is no surprise that he ultimately failed in his mission. With the appearance of the Roman army, led by the Roman general Vespasian, in the summer of 67 A.D., Josephus's army all but disappeared, and the Romans had little difficulty in subduing the district. Only one location gave them trouble, the fortress of Jotapata, a hilltop town fortified by Josephus, which became the refuge for the remnants of Josephus's army, such as it was. It held out for almost seven weeks before falling to the Roman assault. Josephus himself was captured and delivered his prophecy to Vespasian, as noted above. Galilee was now pacified.

The revolutionaries in the Golan congregated at Gamla, but after some fierce fighting, that fortress too was taken. The entire northern part of the country was once again brought under Roman rule.

After taking a winter break Vespasian resumed operations in the spring of 68 A.D. and by early summer had pacified the entire countryside; Jerusalem alone (and some isolated fortresses, notably Masada) remained in the hands of the rebels.

A respite in the war is wasted	Everything seemed prepared for an immediate attack on Jerusalem, but during the summer of 68 Vespasian learned of the emperor Nero's

assassination. The death of a reigning emperor meant that Vespasian's commission as general expired; accordingly, he discontinued his military activities. The cessation was extended because in the summer of 69, Vespasian had himself proclaimed emperor. He left Judea to establish his own imperial power in Rome. By the end of the year 69 he was successful. In the spring of 70, Vespasian once again turned his attention to the situation in Judea.

The two-year hiatus should have been a great boon to the revolutionaries in Jerusalem, allowing them time to organize their forces, fortify the city, lay away provisions, etc. But the opposite was the case. As the refugees entered Jerusalem from the countryside, internecine strife intensified. The party of Zealots now emerged, consisting for the most part of Judean peasants. They turned against the aristocratic priests who until that point had been in charge of the war, and appointed a new high priest by lot. The Zealots enlisted support from the Jews of Idumea, country peasants like themselves who could be counted on to hate the city aristocracy.[36] At first the Idumeans supported the Zealots in their attacks on the aristocracy, but after a while even they, says Josephus, were disgusted by the excesses of the Zealots and withdrew.

Thus 68 A.D. was spent in fighting between the aristocratic (or "moderate") revolutionary groups and the more radical proletarian ones. The latter triumphed. In 69 A.D. the radical revolutionaries themselves fell to attacking one another. John of Gischala, supported by his contingent of Galileans, turned on his former allies the Zealots and ulitmately succeeded in ousting their leader and bringing them under his control. But a new revolutionary faction then emerged, led by Simon ben Giora, a native of Gerasa (a city of the Transjordan). He had a radical social program like the Zealots and drew much of his support from freed slaves. The intense fighting among these various groups had disastrous consequences. Large stocks of grain and other provisions were destroyed. When the Roman siege began in earnest in 70 A.D., a famine soon ensued.

The Roman siege of Jerusalem

Vespasian had by then securely established himself as emperor and wanted a resounding success to legitimate his new dynasty. In his propaganda, Vespasian had pictured himself as the savior of the empire, the man who, after a year and a half of political chaos, had restored order and stability. There was no better way to prove this point than to bring to a successful conclusion the protracted war in Judea. In order to emphasize the dynastic implications of the victory, Vespasian appointed his son Titus to command the Roman army in its assault on the holy city of the Jews. In the spring of 70 A.D. the Romans, under Titus, besieged the city and cut off all supplies and all means of escape.

The fighting for the city and the Temple was intense. The major rallying point of the revolutionaries, and consequently the major target of the Romans, was the Temple. The Temple was a veritable fortress, but it still was a temple. The priests maintained all the customary rituals, even with death and destruction all around them. Three weeks before the final catastrophe the *Tamid*, the "continual sacrifice" which was offered every morning and evening, ceased because of a shortage of lambs. Josephus has many gruesome tales illustrating the severity of the famine, but the Jews were still willing to sacrifice two lambs every day to God. Their only hope for success was through divine intervention, and only a properly maintained cult would convince God to aid the faithful.

Divine help, however, was not forthcoming. The Romans advanced methodically toward their goal. The Jews were weakened by famine and internecine strife and, although Titus made some serious tactical errors in prosecuting the siege, the Roman victory was only a matter of time. Each of the city's three protective walls was breached in turn, and the Romans finally found themselves, by mid-summer 70 A.D., just outside the sacred precincts.

At this point, according to Josephus, Titus called a meeting of his general staff and asked for advice. What should he do with the Jewish Temple? Some of his adjutants argued that it should be destroyed, because as long as it was left standing it would serve as a focal point for anti-Roman agitation. According to the "rule of war" in antiquity, temples were not to be molested, but this Temple had become a fortress and therefore was a fair military target. No opprobrium would be attached to its destruction. Titus, however, argued that the Temple should be preserved as a monument to Roman magnanimity. Indeed, according to Josephus, during the siege Titus offered the revolutionaries numerous opportunities to surrender or, at least, to vacate the Temple and carry on the fighting elsewhere. Even at the end Titus was eager to preserve the Temple. But Titus's plan was thwarted. On the next day, a soldier, acting against orders, tossed a fire brand into the sanctuary, and the flames shot up, immediately out of control. Josephus insists that Titus did his best to douse the flames, but Josephus's apology for Titus is as unsuccessful as Titus's attempt to halt the conflagration.[37] It is very unlikely that this fantastic account of Roman magnanimity and self-restraint contains any historical truth. Scholars debate whether this portrait of moderate generals was concocted for a Jewish or a Roman audience, but most agree that at the least it is as exaggerated as Josephus's other claim that the Jews were compelled by the revolutionaries to fight a war they did not want.

On the tenth of the month of Ab (in rabbinic chronology on the ninth), late August of 70 A.D., the Temple was destroyed. Titus and his troops spent the next month subduing the rest of the city and collecting loot as the reward for their labors.

Upon his return to Rome in 71 A.D., Titus celebrated a joint triumph with his father, the emperor Vespasian. In the procession were the enemy leaders Simon Bar Giora and John of Gischala, and various objects from the Temple (notably the menorah, table and trumpets). Simon was beheaded, John was probably enslaved, and the sacred objects were

Arch of Titus relief. Erected in Rome in 80 A.D., the arch celebrates the Roman victory over the Jews and the conquest of Jerusalem. This relief on the inside of the arch shows the victory procession of 71 A.D., after the Romans returned. Sacred objects from the Temple—the golden menorah, the gold table and a pair of trumpets—are carried aloft.

deposited in the Temple of Peace in Rome.[38] Two triumphal arches were erected in the following years to celebrate the victory; one was destroyed in the 14th or 15th century; the other still stands, the Arch of Titus, with its famous depiction of the sacred objects from the Temple carried in the procession. The other arch, which is now destroyed, bore the following inscription:[39]

The senate and people of Rome (dedicate this arch) to the emperor Titus . . . because with the guidance and plans of his father, and under his auspices, he subdued the Jewish people and destroyed the city of Jerusalem, which all generals, kings and peoples before him had either attacked without success or left entirely unassailed.

To punish the Jews for the war the Romans imposed the *fiscus Judaicus,* the "Jewish tax." The half-shekel, which Jews throughout the empire had formerly contributed to the Temple in Jerusalem, was now collected for the temple of Jupiter Capitolinus in Rome. The imposition of this tax, which was collected throughout the empire at least until the middle of the second century A.D., shows that the Romans regarded all the Jews of the empire as partly responsible for the war. Dio Cassius, a Roman historian of the third century A.D., records that the Judean revolutionaries were aided by their co-religionists throughout the Roman empire.[40] Josephus implicitly denies this, but it is perhaps confirmed by the Jewish tax on Diaspora, as well as Judean, Jews.

The Romans did not, however, institute any other harsh measures against the Jews. They confiscated much Jewish land in Judea, distributing it to their soldiers and to Jewish collaborators (like Josephus),

Lots cast by the defenders of Masada? Atop Masada, a few hundred Jewish fighters—a small free remnant of the land of Israel—held off Rome's mighty army for three years. Finally, historian Josephus tells us, when defeat was just hours away, these fighters resolved to lie down and die with their families rather than become Roman slaves. By lot they picked men who would slay the rest of the community. These 11 sherds, each inscribed with a different name, may have been those lots, says Yigael Yadin, excavator of Masada. The sherd second from the right in the second row bears the name "ben Yair," the commander of this extraordinary band of men, women and children. However, Shaye Cohen questions Yadin's interpretation. Based on Josephus's account, the first drawing would have required hundreds of lots and the second only ten lots.

but this was a normal procedure after a war. They did not engage in religious persecution or strip the Jews of their rights. On the contrary, Josephus reports that the non-Jewish citizens of Antioch petitioned Titus to allow them to expel their Jewish population, but Titus adamantly refused; the Jews were still entitled to the protection of the state.

Masada   Titus's triumph in Rome in 71 A.D. marked the official end of the war. A few "mopping up" operations remained. Three strongholds, all originally fortified by Herod the Great, were still in rebel hands, but only one of them caused any real trouble for the Romans. This was Masada (which fell in either 73 or 74 A.D.). The archaeological excavations confirm Josephus's description of the magnificence of the site and the difficulty of the siege. The Romans built a ramp against one side of the plateau and pushed a tower up against the wall of the fortress. We may assume that this activity was accompanied by a constant hail of arrows and stones thrown by the rebels, although Josephus does not mention this. (He does not mention even a single Roman casualty!)

When the Masada rebels saw that the end was near, they had to decide whether to continue their struggle or not. At this point Josephus narrates a very dramatic tale. The leader of the Sicarii, Eleazar ben Yair, assembled the "manliest" of his comrades and convinced them that an honorable self-inflicted death was preferable to the disgrace of capture and enslavement. Acting upon his instructions each man killed his own wife and family. Then ten men were chosen by lot to kill the rest. Finally, one was chosen to kill the remaining nine and then himself. All told, 960 men, women and children perished. When the Romans entered the fortress the next day, they expected a battle, but all they found was silence.

The historicity of this famous account is uncertain. The basic elements of the story are of course accurate and confirmed by the archaeological findings—evidence of the rebel presence at Masada, the Roman siege works, the Roman camps, and the Roman ramp remain in a remarkable state of preservation. Even the stones hurled by the Romans from their siege tower were found. Some of the Jews slew their families, burnt their possessions, and set the public buildings on fire. Some of them killed themselves. That some tried to escape, however, is suggested by 25 skeletons found in a cave; these people were probably found by the Romans and killed.

Josephus probably invented or exaggerated the use of lots in the suicide process. True, Israeli archaeologist Yigael Yadin found 11 "lots," but the first drawing required several hundred lots and the second only ten. Moreover, many of the details in Josephus's account are irreconcilable with the archaeological evidence. For example, Josephus says that all the possessions were gathered together in one large pile and set on fire, but archaeology shows there were many piles and many fires. Josephus says that Eleazar ordered his men to destroy everything except the foodstuffs, but archaeology shows that many storerooms that contained provisions were burnt. Josephus implies that all the murders took place in the palace, but the northern palace is too small for an assembly of almost a thousand people.[41] More important, the speeches Josephus puts into the mouth of the rebel leader Eleazar ben Yair are incongruous to say the least. Imagine a Jewish revolutionary leader justifying suicide by appealing to the example of the Brahmins of India! It is highly unlikely that there was time for such speeches or that the rebels acted with such unanimity.

As we have seen, the Jewish revolt was not a reaction to an unmistakable threat or provocation by the state. In the fall of 66, as the result of the social tensions between rich and poor, between city and country, and between Jew and gentile; of the impoverishment of large sections of the economy; of religious speculations about the imminent arrival of the end time and the messianic redeemer; of nationalist stirrings against foreign rule; of the incompetent and insensitive administration of the procurators—the Jews of Palestine went to war against the Roman empire.

The war was characterized, as we have seen, by internecine fighting. The fighting was not only between revolutionary groups but also between the revolutionaries and large segments of the populace. Josephus is surely correct that many Jews opposed the war. Moreover, the number of people enrolled in the revolutionary parties was quite small. Many Jews had no desire to participate in the struggle. It was one thing to riot against the procurator, quite another to rebel against the Roman empire. Wealthy and poor alike were afraid that war would mean the loss of everything they had, and since the Romans had not done anything intolerable, there was no compelling reason to go to war. This attitude was widespread. Aside from Jerusalem, only Gamla was the site of fierce fighting. Galilee, Perea (the Transjordan), the coast, Idumea—all these saw some anti-Roman activity, but all were quickly and easily pacified immediately upon the arrival of the Roman forces. Jerusalem was the seat of the rebellion; where it began, where it ended and the stronghold of the vast majority of the combatants.

The causes for the failure of the war are not hard to see. The war began with little advance planning, the revolutionaries were badly divided, and the timing was off. Had they rebelled a few years earlier while the Romans were fighting the Parthians, they might have been able to succeed at least to the point of exacting various concessions from the Romans in return for their surrender. Had they waited two years beyond 66 A.D.—after Nero's assassination in 68 A.D.—their odds would have been immeasurably better. At that time the empire was in chaos; the succession was vigorously disputed; Gaul had risen in revolt. This would have been a perfect moment for revolt, but for the Jews it came too late.

A new   The destruction of the Temple did not mean the end of Judaism,
beginning   however.[42] The theological and religious crisis it caused seems to have been much less severe than that experienced in the aftermath of the Babylonian destruction of the First Temple in 586 B.C., perhaps because the Judaism of the Second Temple period had created new institutions and ideologies that prepared it for a time when the Temple and the sacrificial cult would no longer exist. By the time the Second Temple was destroyed, the Temple itself had been supplemented by synagogues, the priests had been supplemented by scholars, the sacrificial cult had been supplemented by prayer and the study of the Torah, and reliance on the intermediation of the Temple priesthood had been supplemented by a piety that emphasized the observance of the commandments of the Torah by every Jew.

In short, the path to the future was already clearly marked. The sufferings of this world would be compensated by rewards in the hereafter. The disgrace of seeing Rome triumph over the God of Israel and destroy the Temple would be effaced by the glory of the new kingdom to be established by God for his people in the end time. The cessation of the sacrificial cult did not mean estrangement from God, since God could be worshipped through good deeds, prayer, the observance of the commandments and the study of the Torah. Synagogues could take the place of the Temple, and rabbis could take the place of the priests. These were the responses of the Jews to the catastrophe of 70 A.D. and were greatly elaborated during the following centuries.

Thus, for all of the destruction caused by the events of 70, in many important respects the post-70 period does not mark a radical break with the past. But in other respects the post-70 period is discontinuous with the past. The period from the Maccabees to the destruction of the Temple was marked by religious and social ferment, but after 70 the ferment all but disappeared. Within a generation the Jews ceased to write (or at least ceased to preserve) apocalypses, and desisted from their detailed speculations about God's control of human events in the present and the future. The Pharisees, Sadducees, Essenes, Sicarii, Zealots, etc., are no longer living realities in Jewish society. They are mentioned by sources of the second and third centuries only as figures of the Second Temple period. Instead of sectarian diversity, the post-70 period is characterized by a peculiar homogeneity. The only group to appear in our documentation is that of the *rabbis*, as a result of which the post-70 period is often called the rabbinic period.

The origins of the rabbinic group are most obscure. They were led by Rabban Gamaliel, a scion of a prominent Pharisaic family, a fact that implies that the heirs of the Pharisees of the Second Temple period were the dominant element in this new group. Various features shared by the Pharisees and the rabbis also imply some intimate link between them, but there is no indication that all Pharisees became rabbis or that all rabbis were the descendants of Pharisees.

The absence of other organized groups does not, of course, mean that all Jews everywhere instantly became pious followers of the rabbis. The contrary was the case. In Second Temple times most Jews did not belong to any sect or group, but were content to serve God in their own folk way. This pattern continued in the rabbinic period as well, as the rabbinic texts themselves make abundantly clear. But in the end the masses recognized the rabbis as the leaders and shapers of Judaism. The rabbis were heirs to the legacy of Second Temple Judaism, but through their distinctive literature and patterns of religion they gave Judaism a new form of expression that would endure to our own day. The destruction of the Temple thus marked not only an end but also a beginning.

Endnotes

Notes to pages 1-9

I. The Patriarchal Age

1. The viewpoint is illustrated very well by the second chapter of William F. Albright's *Yahweh and the Gods of Canaan* (Garden City, NY: Doubleday, 1968), entitled "The Patriarchal Background of Israel's Faith." Its fullest expression is perhaps the discussion in John Bright, *A History of Israel* (Philadelphia: Westminster, 3rd ed., 1981), pp. 67-102.

2. See especially Ephraim A. Speiser, *Genesis*, Anchor Bible (Garden City, NY: Doubleday, 1964).

3. Albright, *From the Stone Age to Christianity* (Garden City, NY: Anchor/Doubleday, 2nd ed., 1957), p. 241.

4. Albright, *The Biblical Period from Abraham to Ezra* (New York: Torchbooks/Harper & Row, 1963), p. 5.

5. G. Ernest Wright, *Biblical Archaeology* (Philadelphia: Westminster, rev. ed., 1962), p. 40.

6. Wright, *Biblical Archaeology* (see endnote 5), p. 50, note 5.

7. See William G. Dever, "Palestine in the Second Millennium BCE: The Archaeological Picture," in *Israelite and Judaean History*, ed. John M. Hayes and J. Maxwell Miller (Philadelphia: Westminster, 1977), pp. 70-120, especially pp. 99-101.

8. The most forceful and complete statement of this position is probably that of Roland de Vaux (*The Early History of Israel*, transl. David Smith [Philadelphia: Westminster, 1978], pp. 161-287).

9. See citations in endnote 20.

10. Speiser, *Genesis* (see endnote 2), passim; Cyrus H. Gordon, "Biblical Customs and the Nuzu Tablets," *Biblical Archaeologist Reader 2*, ed. Campbell and Freedman (Garden City, NY: Anchor/Doubleday, 1964), pp. 21-33.

11. Speiser, *Genesis* (see endnote 2), pp. 120-121; Gordon, "Biblical Customs" (see endnote 10), pp. 22-23.

12. Speiser, *Genesis* (see endnote 2), p. xi; for Speiser's full discussion, see "The Wife-Sister Motif in the Patriarchal Narratives," in *Biblical and Other Studies*, ed. A. Altmann (Cambridge, MA: Harvard Univ. Press, 1963), pp. 15-28; also in *Oriental and Biblical Studies*, ed. Jacob J. Finkelstein and M. Greenberg (Philadelphia: Univ. of Pennsylvania, 1967), pp. 62-82.

13. See especially the studies of Dever, "The Beginning of the Middle Bronze Age in Syria-Palestine," in *Magnalia Dei; The Mighty Acts of God. Essays on the Bible and Archaeology in Memory of G. Ernest Wright*, ed. Frank M. Cross et al. (Garden City, NY: Doubleday, 1976), pp. 3-38; "The 'Middle Bronze I' Period in Syria and Palestine," in *Near Eastern Archaeology in the Twentieth Century. Essays in Honor of Nelson Glueck*, ed. J.A. Sanders (Garden City, NY: Doubleday, 1970), pp. 132-163; "New Vistas in the EB IV ('MB I') Horizon in Syria and Palestine," *BASOR* 237 (1980), pp. 35-64.

14. See the cautious conclusions of Dever ("Palestine in the Second Millennium" [see endnote 7], pp. 117-120).

15. This has been shown in several studies by M.B. Rowton, including the following: "Autonomy and Nomadism in Western Asia," *Orientalia* 42 (1973), pp. 247-258; "Urban Autonomy in a Nomadic Environment," *JNES* 32 (1973), pp. 201-215; "Dimorphic Structure and the Problem of the 'Apirû-'Ibrim," *JNES* 35 (1976), pp. 13-20.

16. See J.T. Luke, *Pastoralism and Politics in the Mari Period: A Re-Examination of the Character and Political Significance of the Major West Semitic Tribal Groups on the Middle Euphrates, c. 1828-1753 B.C.* (Ph.D. dissertation, Univ. of Michigan [Ann Arbor, MI: University Microfilms, 1965]); V.H. Matthews, *Pastoral Nomadism in the Mari Kingdom ca. 1830-1760 B.C.*, ASOR Dissertation Series (Cambridge, MA: ASOR, 1978).

17. See the literature cited in Dever, "Palestine in the Second Millennium" (see endnote 7), pp. 102-111.

18. The two studies that were most effective in calling attention to the problems with the early second-millennium hypothesis were Thomas L. Thompson, *The Historicity of the Patriarchal Narratives, ZAW* supp. 133 (Berlin: de Gruyter, 1974), and John Van Seters, *Abraham in History and Tradition* (New Haven, CT: Yale Univ. Press, 1975). See also Nahum Sarna, "Abraham in History," *BAR*, Dec. 1977, pp. 5-9.

19. Cf. Barry L. Eichler, "Nuzi," *IDB*, supp. vol., pp. 635-636.

20. Cf. Van Seters, *Abraham in History* (see endnote 18), pp. 40-42, and especially Thompson, *Historicity of the Patriarchal Narratives* (see endnote 18), pp. 22-36, for complete citation of the extra-biblical materials. In the Bible, "Abiram" is the name of a Reubenite who participated in the revolt against Moses in the wilderness (Numbers 16:1) and of the firstborn son of Hiel the Bethelite, who founded Israelite Jericho in the ninth century B.C. (1 Kings 16:34).

21. Compare the name "Ahiram" and its shortened form "Hiram." In the Bible it is mentioned as the name of: a son of Benjamin, a clan of Benjaminites (Numbers 26:38), the Phoenician king contemporary with David and Solomon (2 Samuel 5:11; 1 Kings 5) and the craftsman who supervised the building of Solomon's Temple (1 Kings 7:13). It appears in Phoenician inscriptions as the name of a tenth-century B.C. king of Byblos and an eighth-century B.C. king of Tyre. See also Thompson, *Historicity of the Patriarchal Narratives* (see endnote 18), pp. 29-31, and Van Seters, *Abraham in History* (see endnote 18), p. 41.

22. Cf. Herbert B. Huffmon, *Amorite Personal Names in the Mari Texts* (Baltimore, MD: Johns Hopkins Press, 1965), pp. 63-86.

23. Cf. Frauke Gröndahl, *Die Personennamen der Texte aus Ugarit*, Studia Pohl 1 (Rome: Pontifical Biblical Institute, 1967), pp. 41-42.

24. As a place name in Palestine, "Jacob-'el," to be discussed below, and as a personal name at Ugarit, *ia-qub-ba'l* = *ya'qub-ba'l*, "Jacob-Baal." Cf. Gröndahl, *Personennamen* (see endnote 23), p. 41.

25. Martin Noth, *Die israelitischen Personennamen im Rahmen der gemeinsemitischen Namengebung, Beiträge zur Wissenschaft vom Alten and Neuen Testament* 3/10 (Stuttgart, Ger.: W. Kohlhammer, 1928; reprint Hildesheim, W. Ger.: Georg Olms, 1966), pp. 45-46. See further, Thompson, *Historicity of the Patriarchal Narratives* (see endnote 18), pp. 43-50.

26. Van Seters, *Abraham in History* (see endnote 18), pp. 68-71; cf. Thompson, *Historicity of the Patriarchal Narratives* (see endnote 18), pp. 252-269.

27. Van Seters, *Abraham in History* (see endnote 18), pp. 71-76.

28. Cf. Thompson, *Historicity of the Patriarchal Narratives* (see endnote 18), pp. 243-248.

29. Noth, *The History of Israel*, transl. P.R. Ackroyd (New York: Harper & Row, 1960), pp. 53-84.

30. According to Hermann Gunkel, the critical time in the formation of the patriarchal traditions was the preliterary, oral stage, when the individual units of tradition were expressed in particular genres or forms (*Gattungen*). Thus the history of the traditions can best be studied through the identification of these units by reference to the forms in which they are preserved (form criticism) and the investigation of the manner in which these units were combined into larger narratives. See *The Legends of Genesis: The Biblical Saga and History* [1901], transl. W.R. Carruth (New York: Schocken, 1964).

31. Noth, *A History of Pentateuchal Traditions* [1948], transl. B.W. Anderson (Englewood Cliffs, NJ: Prentice-Hall, 1972).

32. This is, of course, the biblical tradition, but there are many reasons to doubt it. In working through the materials for my commentaries for *I Samuel* and *II Samuel*, Anchor Bible (Garden City, NY: Doubleday, 1980, 1984), I came to the conclusion previously reached by others that it was David who combined Judah with Israel for the first time. See, for example, James W. Flanagan, "Judah in All Israel," in *No Famine in the Land: Studies in Honor of John L. McKenzie*, ed. Flanagan and A.W. Robinson (Missoula, MT: Scholars Press, 1975), pp. 101-116.

33. Noth, *History of Israel* (see endnote 29), p. 123. Other proponents of the history of traditions method have not been as negative as Noth. According to de Vaux (*Early History* [see endnote 8], p. 180), whose work represents the best attempt to exploit both tradition-historical and archaeological methods, "It is true that the patriarchal tradition was only given its definitive form in the perspective of 'all Israel' after the conquest and settlement in the Promised Land .... However complicated this development may have been, and however obscure it may still be, we should not be

justified in concluding that the traditions have no historical value at all, since without evidence it would be wrong to claim that the Israelites had no knowledge at all of their own origins."

34. Cf. the comments by Frank M. Cross in "The Epic Tradition of Early Israel: Epic Narrative and the Reconstruction of Early Israelite Institutions," in *The Poet and the Historian. Essays in Literary and Historical Biblical Criticism*, ed. Richard E. Friedman, Harvard Semitic Studies (Chico, CA: Scholars Press, 1983), pp. 13-40, especially pp. 24-25.

35. Robert A. Oden, "Jacob as Father, Husband, and Nephew: Kinship Studies and the Patriarchal Narratives," *JBL* 102 (1983), pp. 189-205. See also Mara Donaldson, "Kinship Theory in the Patriarchal Narratives: The Case of the Barren Wife," *JAAR* 49 (1981), pp. 77-87; Terry J. Prewitt, "Kinship Structures and the Genesis Genealogies," *JNES* 40 (1981), pp. 87-98.

36. Robert Wilson, *Genealogy and History in the Biblical World*, Yale Near Eastern Researches 7 (New Haven, CT: Yale Univ. Press, 1977).

37. For a convenient summary of the meaning of the terminology "linear" and "segmented," see Wilson, "The Old Testament Genealogies in Recent Research," *JBL* 94 (1975), pp. 169-189, especially p. 179.

38. Donaldson ("Kinship Theory" [see endnote 35]) shows that the marriages of the patriarchs are a series of alliances progressing towards the ideal or "correct" marriage relationship. In the present state of our knowledge about ancient Israelite kinship reckoning, we cannot be sure she is correct in her interpretation of the relationships between the first two patriarchs and their wives (cf. Oden, "Jacob as Father" [see endnote 35], pp. 198-199). Nevertheless, her study demonstrates the necessity of the trigenerational scheme to the success of the story.

39. See the discussion of Gerhard von Rad, *Genesis: A Commentary*, transl. John H. Marks, Old Testament Library (Philadelphia: Westminster, rev. ed., 1972), p. 257.

40. Here Oden ("Jacob as Father" [see endnote 35], p. 198) follows Claude Lévi-Strauss (*The Elementary Structures of Kinship* [Boston: Beacon, rev. ed., 1969]) and Robin Fox (*Kinship and Marriage: An Anthropological Perspective* [Harmondsworth, UK: Penguin, 1967]).

41. Oden, "Jacob as Father" (see endnote 35), p. 199.

42. Oden, "Jacob as Father," p. 202.

43. See the discussion of genealogical form and social function in Wilson, *Genealogy and History* (see endnote 36), pp. 46-54.

44. See especially Noth, *History of Pentateuchal Traditions* (see endnote 31), pp. 94-98.

45. As shown by Donaldson and Oden; cf. endnote 35.

46. Cf. Prewitt, "Kinship Structures" (see endnote 35), pp. 97-98.

47. This refers to a time before Machir had been replaced by Manasseh and reduced to the status of a Manassite clan (cf. de Vaux, *Early History* [see endnote 8], pp. 651-652) and before Gilead had been replaced by Gad south of the Jabbok and the name Gilead generalized to include all of Transjordan (pp. 571-572, 574-576).

48. On the complex problems involved in the dating of the battle described in Judges 5, see chap. III of this volume and de Vaux, *Early History* (see endnote 8), pp. 789-796.

49. *ANET*, pp. 376-378.

50. The emphasis in recent research on the sociological conditions out of which the community emerged has begun to lead to excellent results. It has created a tendency, however, to overlook the importance of the emergence of an ethnic identity. A valuable balance to this tendency is provided by Baruch Halpern in *The Emergence of Israel in Canaan*, SBL Monograph Series 29 (Chico, CA: Scholars Press, 1983), especially pp. 90, 100.

51. For an overview of this subject, see the introduction to *Ethnic Groups and Boundaries*, ed. Frederick Barth (Boston: Little, Brown, 1969).

52. They are sentence names composed of a prefixed verb form and a divine name. See in general, Noth, *Die israelitischen Personennamen* (see endnote 25), pp. 27-31, and, for discussion of this pattern in Amorite and Ugaritic names, see the studies of Huffmon and Gröndahl cited in endnotes 22 and 23. In "Jacob," "Isaac" and "Joseph," the divine element (*-'el*, "El") is omitted according to a common method of shortening names. The longer forms of these three names may have been "Jacob-El," "Isaac-El" and "Joseph-El." The meanings of these names will be discussed below.

53. Jacob J. Finkelstein, "The Genealogy of the Hammurapi Dynasty," *JCS* 20 (1966), pp. 95-118, especially pp. 97-98.

54. See endnote 20.

55. As pointed out first by Hugo Gressmann ("Sage und Geschichte in den Patriarchenerzählungen," *ZAW* 30 [1910], pp. 1-34, especially p. 2 and note 4), the best parallels to the longer form of the name "Abraham," occur in Aramaic. See also de Vaux (*Early History* [see endnote 8], pp. 197-198 and notes 73 and 74), who cites evidence for a similar phenomenon in Ugaritic and Phoenician; his examples, however, are not precisely parallel.

56. Cf. Noth (*History of Pentateuchal Traditions* [see endnote 31], pp. 109-110), who points out that the association with Hebron is absent in the materials found in both the early literary sources, J and E.

57. James A. Montgomery, *Arabia and the Bible* (Philadelphia: Univ. of Pennsylvania, 1934), p. 45.

58. We cannot be certain that at this earlier, northern stage of the tradition the grandfather of Israel was called Abram or Abraham, although it is probable. There seems to have been a place in southern Judah called "the Field of Abram" in the late tenth century B.C. (J. Simons, *Handbook for the*

Study of Egyptian Topographical Lists Relating to Western Asia [Leiden: Brill, 1937], xxxiv/71-72 and pp. 183-184). This raises the possibility that Abraham was the name of a patriarchal figure from the south who entered the tradition together with the association with Hebron. The biblical account itself, however, gives no hint that Abraham originally had another name (apart from the dialectical variant "Abram"), and it seems safest to assume that the name was an original component of the tradition.

59. Yohanan Aharoni, *The Archaeology of the Land of Israel*, transl. Anson F. Rainey (Philadelphia: Westminster, 1982), p. 168.

60. Aharoni, *Archaeology of the Land of Israel* (see endnote 59), pp. 162-173.

61. Cf. Noth, *Die israelitischen Personennamen* (see endnote 25), p. 210.

62. It is possible that the transferral of the Isaac tradition to Beersheba was partly the result of the historical movement of people from the northern hills into the Negev. Note, for example, the prominent role played by Simeon and Levi, the patriarchs of the tribes of southwestern Judah and the northern Negev, in the story of the rape of Dinah at Shechem (Genesis 34). Cf. Noth, *History of Israel* (see endnote 29), pp. 71 and 76, note 1. Contrast de Vaux, *Early History* (see endnote 8), pp. 532-533.

63. See Thompson, *Historicity of the Patriarchal Narratives* (see endnote 18), pp. 45-48.

64. For the citations, see Simons, *Handbook* (see endnote 58), lists 1a and 1b/102 (Thutmosis III), 23/9 (Rameses II) and 27/104 (Rameses III), and most recently, Shmuel Ahituv, *Canaanite Toponyms in Ancient Egyptian Documents* (Jerusalem: Magnes, 1984), p. 200. Cf. *ANET*, p. 242.

65. Cf. Shmuel Yeivin ("The Short List of the Towns in Palestine and Syria Captured by Thutmosis III During His First Campaign," *Eretz Israel* 3 [Jerusalem: IES, 1954], pp. 32-38, especially p. 36), who proposes an identification with Tel Melat, west of Gezer, which is often associated with the biblical city of Gibbethon.

66. Both of these cities are mentioned in the same part of the Thutmosis list, as are a number of nearby places east of the Jordan in the Yarmuk region. See H. Wolfgang Helck, *Die Beziehungen Ägyptens zu Vorderasien im 3. und 2. Jahrtausen v. Chr,* Ägyptologische Abhandlungen 5 (Weisbaden, W. Ger.: Otto Harrassowitz, 1962), p. 128.

67. This was taken for granted by Albright ("A Third Revision of the Early Chronology of Western Asia," *BASOR* 88 [1942], pp. 28-36, especially p. 36, note 39).

68. Noth, *History of Israel* (see endnote 29), p. 71, note 2.

69. See, for example, Victor Maag, "Der Hirte Israel," *Schweizerische Theologische Umschau* 28 (1958), pp. 2-28; Horst Seebass, *Der Erzvater Israel*, ZAW supp. 98 (Berlin: A. Topelmann, 1966), pp. 1-5, 25-34.

70. Cf. Siegfried Herrmann, *A History of Israel in Old Testament Times*, transl. John Bowden (Philadelphia: Fortress, 1981), p. 51. Recent proponents of this idea in one form or another include Albert de Pury ("Genèse xxxiv et l'histoire," *RB* 76 [1969], pp. 5-49, especially pp. 39-48) and André Lemaire ("Asriel, šr'l, Israel et l'origine de la confédération israelite," *VT* 23 [1973], pp. 239-243).

71. Cf. endnote 92.

72. Cf. de Vaux, *Early History* (see endnote 8), pp. 642-643.

73. Noth, *Die israelitischen Personennamen* (see endnote 25), p. 212; de Vaux, *Early History* (see endnote 8), p. 313.

74. Theodor H. Gaster, *Myth, Legend, and Custom in the Old Testament*, 2 vols. (New York: Torchbooks/Harper & Row, 1975), vol. 1, pp. 217-218; Thompson and Irvin, "The Joseph and Moses Narratives," in Hayes and Miller, *Israelite and Judaean History* (see endnote 7), pp. 185-188.

75. *ANET*, pp. 23-25.

76. Thompson and Irvin, "The Joseph and Moses Narratives" (see endnote 74), pp. 188-190.

77. Seven years of famine are described in an Egyptian text of the Ptolemaic period (perhaps the end of the second century B.C.), which claims to derive from King Djoser of the Third Dynasty (c. 2650 B.C.); see *ANET*, pp. 31-32. Tablet VI of the Akkadian Gilgamesh epic speaks of "seven years of husks"; see *ANET*, pp. 85. The autobiographical inscription of Idri-mi, king of the Syrian city of Alalakh in the 16th century B.C., refers to two unfavorable periods, each lasting seven years; see *ANET*, pp. 557-558. There is a prediction of seven/eight years of drought in the Ugaritic myth of Aqht; see *ANET*, p. 153.

78. See Donald B. Redford, *A Study of the Biblical Story of Joseph*, *VT* supp 20 (Leiden: Brill, 1970).

79. Cf. *ANET*, p. 445 and note 10.

80. See de Vaux, *Early History* (see endnote 8), pp. 301-302.

81. Herrman Ranke, *Die ägyptischen Personnamen*, 3 vols. (Glückstadt, W. Ger.: J.J. Augustin, 1935), vol. 1, p. 14, names 13-17, and p. 15, name 3.

82. H. Hamada, "Stela of Putiphar," *Annales du Service des Antiquitës de l'Égypte* 39 (1939), pp. 273-276 and plate 39.

83. Ranke, *Die ägyptischen Personennamen* (see endnote 81), pp. 409-412.

84. Helck, *Die Beziehungen Ägyptens* (see endnote 66), pp. 77-81, 342-369; Jozef M.A. Janssen, "Fonctionnaires sémites au service de l'Égypte," *Chronique d'Égypte* 26 (1951), pp. 50-62; Albright, "Northwest-Semitic Names in a List of Egyptian Slaves from the Eighteenth Century B.C.," *JAOS* 74 (1954), pp. 222-233; Georges Posener, "Les asiatiques en Égypte sous les XII and XIII dynasties," *Syria* 34 (1957), pp. 145-163.

85. *ANET*, p. 260.

86. See Alan H. Gardiner, *Egypt of the Pharaohs* (Oxford, 1961), p. 282.

87. *ANET*, p. 259 (transl. John A. Wilson). The text

is a model letter from a scribal school.

88. See Gardiner, *Ancient Egyptian Onomastica*, 3 vols. (London: Oxford Univ. Press, 1947), pp. 191-193 (no. 265). In the present state of our knowledge, we cannot be sure that the equation of the toponym in the Egyptian texts with the name of the Israelite tribe is linguistically valid. Albright associated the name of an Asiatic female slave in 18th-century B.C. Egypt with the tribal name ("Northwest Semitic Names" [see endnote 84], p. 229-231 and note 51). The sibilant of the slave name (š̌=*š) is different from that of the geographical term (š̌=*t or *š) in the Egyptian texts. It seems to follow that the geographical term can have had nothing to do with the Israelite tribe (cf. Kenneth A. Kitchen, *Ancient Orient and the Old Testament* [Chicago: Inter-Varsity Press, 1966], pp. 70-71 and note 53). But it is not certain that Albright's association of the slave and tribal names is correct. The sibilant in the tribal name "Asher" remains unidentified. Thus, despite Kitchen's objections, Shmuel Yeivin is justified in maintaining the possibility of a connection between the Egyptian toponym and the biblical tribal name ("The Israelite Settlement in Galilee and the Wars with Jabin of Hazor," in *Mélanges bibliques rédigés en l'honneur de André Robert*, Travaux de l'Institut Catholique de Paris 4 [Paris: Bloud and Gay, 1957], pp. 95-104, especially pp. 98-99).

89. See Noth, *The Old Testament World*, transl. V.I. Gruhn (Philadelphia: Fortress, 1966), pp. 55-58. Cf. Noth, *History of Israel* (see endnote 29), pp. 56, 60, 67 and note 1, and the comments by de Vaux, *Early History* (see endnote 8), p. 665.

90. Noth, *Old Testament World* (see endnote 89), p. 72; in *History of Israel* (see endnote 29), pp. 62-63.

91. On "Manasseh," cf. Noth, *Die israelitischen Personennamen* (see endnote 25), p. 222.

92. This is confirmed by the survey of Ephraim currently underway (Israel Finkelstein, "Shiloh Yields Some, But Not All, of Its Secrets," *BAR*, Jan./Feb. 1986, pp. 22-41, especially p. 35). Cf. the demographic statistics cited by Lawrence E. Stager, in "The Archaeology of the Family in Ancient Israel," *BASOR* 260 (1985), pp. 1-36, especially p. 3.

93. The importance of the contrast between the mountains and the plains to the history of this period was first stressed by Albrecht Alt. See "The Settlement of the Israelites in Palestine," in *Essays on Old Testament History and Religion* (Garden City, NY: Anchor/Doubleday, 1968), pp. 173-221, especially pp. 188-204.

94. Giorgio Buccellati, *Cities and Nations of Ancient Syria*, Studi Semitici 26 (Rome: Ist. di Studi del Vicino Oriente, 1967).

II. Israel in Egypt

1. On wet-nurse contacts, see Brevard S. Childs, "The Birth of Moses," *JBL* 84 (1965), pp. 109-122. On the name "Moses," see Alan H. Gardiner, "The Egyptian Origin of Some English Personal Names," *JAOS* 56 (1936), pp. 192-194; J. Černý, "The Greek Etymology of the Name of Moses," *ASAE* 51 (1951), pp. 349-354; Jaroslav G. Griffiths, "The Egyptian Derivation of the Name Moses," *JNES* 12 (1953), pp. 225-231.

2. See Nahum M. Sarna, *Exploring Exodus* (New York: Schocken Books, 1986), pp. 39-42.

3. On the plagues, see Moshe Greenberg, "Plagues of Egypt," *Encyclopedia Judaica*, vol. 13, pp. 604-613; Ziony Zevit, "The Priestly Redaction and Interpretation of the Plagues Narrative in Exodus," *JQR* 66 (1976), pp. 193-211; Sarna, *Exploring Exodus* (see endnote 2), pp. 63-80.

4. For the problems and different approaches, see C. De Wit, *The Date and Route of the Exodus* (London: Tyndale, 1960); L.T. Wood, "The Date of the Exodus," in *New Perspectives on the Old Testament*, ed. J.B. Wane (Waco, TX: Word Books, 1970), pp. 66-87; B.K. Waltke, "Palestinian Artifactual Evidence Supporting the Early Date for the Exodus," *BS* 129 (1972), pp. 33-47; John J. Bimson, *Redating the Exodus and Conquest*, JSOT supp., series 5 (Leiden: Brill, 1978).

5. On the "patriarchal period," see Cyrus H. Gordon, *The Ancient Near East* (New York: Norton, 1965), pp. 113-133; Thomas L. Thompson, *The Historicity of the Patriarchal Narratives* (Berlin: de Gruyter, 1974); John A. Van Seters, *Abraham in History and Tradition* (New Haven, CT: Yale Univ. Press, 1975); Roland de Vaux, *The Early History of Israel*, transl. D. Smith (Philadelphia: Westminster, 1978), pp. 257-266; John Bright, *A History of Israel* (Philadelphia: Westminster, 3rd ed., 1981), pp. 83-87.

6. *Antiq.* 14.2.

7. *Seder Olam* 3:2.

8. For a summary of the chronological problems, see Roland K. Harrison, *Introduction to the Old Testament* (Grand Rapids, MI: Eerdmans, 1969), pp. 164-176, 308-325.

9. See Charles F. Burney, *Notes on the Hebrew Text of the Book of Kings* (New York: KTAV, 1970), p. 60.

10. For surveys of theories on these issues, see Manfred Weippert, *The Settlement of the Israelite Tribes in Palestine: A Critical Survey of the Recent Scholarly Debate*, transl. J.D. Mardin (Naperville, IL: A.R. Allenson, 1971); de Vaux, *Early History* (see endnote 5), pp. 359-392.

11. On the Hyksos, see Van Seters, *The Hyksos: A New Investigation* (New Haven, CT: Yale Univ. Press, 1966); Donald B. Redford, "The Hyksos Invasion in History and Tradition," *Orientalia* 39 (1970), pp. 1-51; William C. Hayes, "Egypt from the Death of Ammenemes III to Seqenenre II," in *CAH*,

vol. 2, part 1, pp. 54-64; T.G.H. James, "Egypt: From the Expulsion of the Hyksos to Amenophis I," in *CAH*, vol. 2, part 1, pp. 289-312; Yohanan Aharoni, *The Land of the Bible: A Historical Geography*, rev. and enlarged, transl. and ed. Anson F. Rainey (Philadelphia: Westminster, 1979), pp. 147-150.

12. Pierre Montet, *Everyday Life in Egypt in the Days of Ramesses the Great*, transl. A.R.M. Hyslop and M.S. Drower (London: E. Arnold, 1958); R.O. Faulkner, "Egypt from the Inception of the Nineteenth Dynasty to the Death of Ramesses II," in *CAH*, vol. 2, part 2, pp. 225-232.

13. *ANET*, pp. 376-378.

14. William F. Albright, "The Amarna Letters from Palestine," in *CAH*, vol. 2, part 2, pp. 98-116; Cyril Aldred, "Egypt: The Amarna Period and the End of the Eighteenth Dynasty," in *CAH*, vol. 2, part 2, pp. 49-97; Aharoni, *Land of the Bible* (see endnote 11), pp. 169-176.

15. Lawrence E. Stager, "The Archaeology of the Family in Ancient Israel," *BASOR* 260 (1985), pp. 1-35.

16. H.J. Franken, "Palestine in the Time of the Nineteenth Dynasty: Archaeological Evidence," in *CAH*, vol. 2, part 2, pp. 331-337.

17. *ANET*, p. 259.

18. On brick quota, see Kenneth H. Kitchen, "From the Brick Fields of Egypt," *THB* (1976), pp. 77ff. On brick making, see S. Clarke and R. Englebach, *Ancient Egyptian Masonry: The Building Craft* (London: Oxford Univ. Press, 1930); Kitchen, "From the Brick Fields of Egypt," pp. 136-147; A. Spenser, *Brick Architecture in Ancient Egypt* (Warminster, UK: Aris and Phillips, 1979); Sarna, *Exploring Exodus* (see endnote 2), pp. 22-24.

19. Adolf Erman, *The Ancient Egyptians: A Sourcebook of Their Writings* (New York: Torchbooks/Harper & Row, 1966), p. 124; Kitchen, *Ancient Orient and the Old Testament* (Downers Grove, IL: Intervarsity Press, 1975), pp. 156-157.

20. *ANET*, p. 441; Miriam Lichtheim, *Ancient Egyptian Literature* (Berkeley: Univ. of California Press), p. 151.

21. *ANET*, pp. 6-7.

22. *ANET*, p. 445; Lichtheim, *Ancient Egyptian Literature* (see endnote 20), p. 141.

23. On this route, see Gardiner, "The Ancient Road Between Egypt and Palestine," *JEA* 6 (1920), pp. 99-116; Eliezer D. Oren, "The Overland Route Between Egypt and Canaan in the Early Bronze Age," *IEJ* 23 (1973), pp, 198-205; Aharoni, *Land of the Bible* (see endnote 11), pp. 45-52.

24. Trude Dothan, "Gaza Sands Yield Lost Outpost of the Egyptian Empire," *National Geographic* (Dec. 1982), pp. 739-768.

25. On these peoples, see Richard D. Barnett, "The Sea Peoples," in *CAH*, vol. 2, part 2, pp. 359-378; de Vaux, *Early History* (see endnote 5), pp. 501-516.

26. For discussion of the issues and theories, see Menashe Har-El, *The Sinai Journeys: The Route of the Exodus in the Light of the Historical Geography of the Sinai Peninsula* (Tel Aviv: Am Oved, 1973), de Vaux, *Early History* (see endnote 5), pp. 376-388; Aharoni, *Land of the Bible* (see endnote 11), pp. 195-200; Bright, *History of Israel* (see endnote 5), pp. 124-129.

27. Beno Rothenberg, *God's Wilderness* (Nashville, TN: Thomas Nelson, 1962); de Vaux, *Early History* (see endnote 5), pp. 426-439.

28. Deuteronomy 33:2, Judges 5:4-5 and Habakkuk 3:3 are taken as referring to Sinai and connected with Moses' stay in Midian (Exodus 2:15, 3:1), which is located in northwest Arabia on the east side of the Gulf of Akabah.

29. Frederick S. Bodenheimer, "The Manna of Sinai," *BA* 10 (1947), pp. 2-6; M. Bates, "Insects in the Diet," *American Scholar* 24 (1959-1960), pp. 46-49; Sarna, *Exploring Exodus* (see endnote 2), pp. 116-120.

30. Sarna, *Exploring Exodus* (see endnote 2), pp. 120-126.

31. There is an extensive literature on the covenant. See George E. Mendenhall, *Law and Covenant in Israel and Ancient Near East* (Pittsburgh, PA: Biblical Colloquium, 1955); Dennis J. McCarthy, *Treaty and Covenant: A Study in Form in the Ancient Oriental Documents and in the Old Testament* (Rome: Pontifical Biblical Institute, 1963); Delbert R. Hillers, *Covenant: The History of a Biblical Idea* (Baltimore, MD: Johns Hopkins Press, 1960); K. Baltzer, *The Covenant Formulary*, transl. David E. Green (Philadelphia: Fortress, 1971); Moshe Weinfeld, "B'rith," in *TDOT*, vol. 2, pp. 253-259; de Vaux, *Early History* (see endnote 5), pp. 439-452; Sarna, *Exploring Exodus* (see endnote 2), pp. 130-157.

32. *ANET*, pp. 199, 201.

33. On the golden calf narrative, see Julius Lewy, "The Story of the Golden Calf Reanalysed," *VT* 9 (1959), pp. 318-322; F.C. Fensham, "The Burning of the Golden Calf and Ugarit," *IEJ* 16 (1966), pp. 191-193; Moses Aberbach and Leivy Smolar, "Aaron, Jereboam and the Golden Calf," *JBL* 86 (1967), pp. 129-140; Samuel E. Loewenstamm, "The Making and Destruction of the Golden Calf," *Biblica* 48 (1967), pp. 481-490; Hanan Ch. Brichto, "The Worship of the Golden Calf: A Literary Analysis of a Fable on Idolatry," *HUCA* 54 (1983), pp. 1-44; Sarna, *Exploring Exodus* (see endnote 2), pp. 215-220.

34. This view has been developed by Julius Wellhausen, *Prolegomena to the History of Ancient Israel*; Archibald R.S. Kennedy, "Tabernacle," *HDB*, vol. 4, pp. 653-668; Immanuel Benzinger, "Tabernacle," *Encyclopedia Biblica*, vol. 4, pp. 4871-4875.

35. Rothenberg, letter in *BAR*, June 1975, p. 11.

36. For the historical view, see Frank M. Cross, "The Tabernacle: A Study from an Archaeological and Historical Approach," *BA* 10 (1947), pp. 45-68; "The Priestly Tabernacle in the Light of Recent Research," in *Temples and High Places in Biblical Times*, ed. A. Biran (Jerusalem: Hebrew Union College, 1981), pp. 321-322; Harrison, *Introduction*

to the *Old Testament* (see endnote 8), pp. 403-408; Sarna, *Exploring Exodus* (see endnote 2), pp. 190-200.

37. For an examination of the traditions, see de Vaux, *Early History* (see endnote 5), pp. 551-564.

38. See Rothenberg, *God's Wilderness* (see endnote 27), pp. 46, 55, 117-170.

39. Rudolph Cohen, "Did I Excavate Kadesh-Barnea?" *BAR*, May/June 1981, pp. 20-33.

40. For an analysis of the story of the spies, see de Vaux, *Early History* (see endnote 5), pp. 523-526.

41. On this campaign, see de Vaux, *Early History* (see endnote 5), pp. 564-567.

42. On these campaigns, see Aharoni, *Land of the Bible* (see endnote 11), pp. 200-209.

43. *ANET*, pp. 328-329; see Aharoni, *Land of the Bible* (see endnote 11), pp. 144-147.

44. On this inscription, see Jacob Hoftizer and Gerrit van der Kooij, *Aramaic Texts from Deir 'Alla* (Leiden: Brill, 1976); Baruch A. Levine, "The Deir 'Allah Plaster Inscriptions," *JAOS* 101 (1981), pp. 195-205; JoAnn Hackett, *The Balaam Text* (Chico, CA: Scholars Press, 1984); André Lemaire, "Fragments from the Book of Balaam at Deir Alla," *BAR*, Sept./Oct. 1985, pp. 26-39.

45. J. Alberto Soggin, *A History of Ancient Israel* (Philadelphia: Westminster, 1984), pp. 110-111.

46. See Hayim Tadmor, "The Decline of Empires in Western Asia ca. 1200 B.C.E.," in *Symposia*, ed. Frank M. Cross (Cambridge, MA: ASOR, 1974), pp. 1-4.

47. See Yigael Yadin, "The Transition from a Semi-Nomadic to a Sedentary Society in the Twelfth Century B.C.E.," in Cross, *Symposia* (see endnote 46), pp. 57-68.

48. On the literary sources and the wars of conquest, see Abraham Malamat, "Israelite Conduct of War in the Conquest of Canaan," in Cross, *Symposia* (see endnote 46), pp. 35-55.

III. The Settlement in Canaan

1. Yigael Yadin, "Biblical Archaeology Today: The Archaeological Aspect," *Biblical Archaeology Today* (Jerusalem: IES, 1985), p. 22.

2. Yadin, "Is the Biblical Account of the Israelite Conquest of Canaan Historically Reliable?" *BAR*, Mar./Apr. 1982, p. 17; Abraham Malamat, "How Inferior Israelite Forces Conquered Fortified Canaanite Cities," *BAR*, Mar./Apr. 1982, p. 25.

3. Malamat, "How Inferior Israelite Forces" (see endnote 2), p. 26.

4. Malamat, "How Inferior Israelite Forces," p. 26.

5. Malamat, "How Inferior Israelite Forces," p. 27.

6. Joseph A. Callaway, "'Ai," *EAEHL*, vol. 1, p. 52.

7. Yadin, "Is the Biblical Account" (see endnote 2), p. 18.

8. Yadin, "Is the Biblical Account," p. 18.

9. Yadin, "Is the Biblical Account," p. 19.

10. Malamat, "How Inferior Israelite Forces" (see endnote 2), p. 27.

11. Malamat, "How Inferior Israelite Forces," p. 27.

12. Yadin, "Is the Biblical Account" (see endnote 2), p. 19.

13. Malamat, "How Inferior Israelite Forces" (see endnote 2), p. 26.

14. See Malamat's map, ibid, p. 30.

15. William H. Stiebing, Jr., "When Was the Age of the Patriarchs?—of Amorites, Canaanites, and Archaeology," *BAR*, June 1975, pp. 17-21.

16. Malamat, "How Inferior Israelite Forces" (see endnote 2), p. 28.

17. See Yadin, "The Transition from a Semi-Nomadic to a Sedentary Society in the Twelfth Century B.C.E.," in *Symposia*, ed. Frank M. Cross (Cambridge, MA: ASOR, 1979), pp. 57-68.

18. Cited by Malamat, in "How Inferior Israelite Forces" (see endnote 2), p. 31.

19. Malamat, "How Inferior Israelite Forces," p. 33.

20. See Kathleen M. Kenyon and Thomas A. Holland, *Excavations at Jericho III* (Plates) (London: British School of Archaeology in Jerusalem, 1981), pl. 236. This master section of the north side of trench I shows dramatically the successive layers of mudbrick walls that collapsed down the slope of the mound.

21. Kenyon, *Archaeology in the Holy Land* (New York: Praeger, 1960), pp. 210-211.

22. See Paul W. Lapp, "The Importance of Dating," *BAR*, Mar. 1977, pp. 13-32.

23. Kenyon, *Archaeology in the Holy Land* (see endnote 21), p. 210.

24. Yadin, "Is the Biblical Account" (see endnote 2), pp. 22.

25. Yadin, "Is the Biblical Account," pp. 22.

26. John Garstang, *Joshua, Judges* (London: Constable, 1931), p. 356.

27. William F. Albright, "The Israelite Conquest of Canaan in the Light of Archaeology," *BASOR* 74 (1939), pp. 15-16; Louis-Hugues Vincent, "Les fouilles d'et-Tell 'Ai," *RB* 46 (1937), p. 256.

28. Callaway, "The 1964 'Ai (et-Tell) Excavations," *BASOR* 178 (1965), pp. 39-40.

29. Yadin, "Is the Biblical Account" (see endnote 2), p. 23.

30. Malamat, "How Inferior Israelite Forces" (see endnote 2), p. 33.

31. Malamat, "How Inferior Israelite Forces," p. 33.

32. Malamat, "How Inferior Israelite Forces," p. 34.

33. James B. Pritchard, *Gibeon Where the Sun Stood Still* (Princeton: Princeton Univ. Press, 1962), p. 136.

34. Von Carel J.H. Vriezen, "Hirbet Kefire-eine Oberflächenuntersuchung," *Sonderdruck aus Zeitschrift des Deutschen Palästina-Vereins*, Bd 91 (1975), pp. 135-158.

35. Malamat, "How Inferior Israelite Forces" (see endnote 2), p. 34.

36. J. Alberto Soggin, *Joshua* (Philadelphia: Westminster, 1972), p. 130.

37. Soggin, *Joshua* (see endnote 36), p. 131.

38. Soggin, *Joshua*, p. 131.

39. J. Maxwell Miller, "The Israelite Occupation of Canaan," in *Israelite and Judaean History*, ed. John H. Hayes and Miller (Philadelphia: Westminster, 1977), p. 261.

40. John A. Wilson, transl., "Hymn of Victory of Mer-ne-Ptah (The Israel Stele)," in *ANET*, p. 378.

41. J. Wilson, transl., "The War Against the Peoples of the Sea," in *ANET*, pp. 262-263.

42. Miller, "Israelite Occupation" (see endnote 39), p. 272.

43. Moshe Kochavi, "Israelite Settlement in Canaan in the Light of Archaeological Surveys," in *Biblical Archaeology Today* (see endnote 1), p. 55.

44. Yadin, *Hazor: The Rediscovery of a Great Citadel of the Bible* (New York: Random House, 1975), pp. 143-145.

45. Yadin, "Is the Biblical Account" (see endnote 2), p. 23.

46. Yadin, "Is the Biblical Account," p. 22.

47. Yadin, "Is the Biblical Account," p. 23.

48. Yadin, "Is the Biblical Account," p. 23.

49. Yadin, "Is the Biblical Account," p. 19.

50. Albrecht Alt, "Settlement of the Israelites in Palestine," in *Essays on Old Testament History and Religion*, ed. Alt, transl. R.A. Wilson (Garden City, NY: Doubleday, 1968), pp. 175-221.

51. Alt, "Settlement of the Israelites" (see endnote 50), pp. 199-201.

52. Alt, "Settlement of the Israelites," pp. 216-221.

53. Manfred Weippert, *The Settlement of the Israelite Tribes in Palestine* (London: SCM Press, 1971), pp. 5-6, cited by Yadin in "Is the Biblical Account" (see endnote 2), p. 17.

54. Yadin, "Is the Bibical Account," pp. 17-18.

55. Malamat, "How Inferior Israelite Forces" (see endnote 2), p. 34.

56. Weippert, *Settlement of the Israelite Tribes* (see endnote 53), pp. 5-6.

57. Kochavi, "Israelite Settlement" (see endnote 43), p. 56.

58. Lawrence E. Stager, "Highland Village Life in Palestine Some Three Thousand Years Ago," *The Oriental Notes and News* 69 (1981), p. 1.

59. George E. Mendenhall, "The Hebrew Conquest of Palestine," *BA* 25 (1961), pp. 66-87; Norman K. Gottwald, *The Tribes of Yahweh* (Maryknoll, NY: Orbis Books, 1979), pp. 210-219.

60. Gottwald, "Were the Early Israelites Pastoral Nomads?" *BAR*, June 1978, pp. 2-7.

61. Bernhard W. Anderson, "Mendenhall Disavows Paternity," *BR*, Summer 1986, p. 43.

62. Anderson, "Mendenhall Disavows Paternity" (see endnote 61), p. 47.

63. P. Kyle McCarter, "A Major New Introduction to the Bible," *BR*, Summer 1986, p. 43.

64. McCarter, "A Major New Introduction" (see endnote 63), p. 43.

65. McCarter, "A Major New Introduction," p. 44.

66. Anderson, "Mendenhall Disavows" (see endnote 61), p. 48.

67. Kochavi, "Israelite Settlement" (see endnote 43), pp. 55-56.

68. Kochavi, "Israelite Settlement," p. 56.

69. Stager, "Highland Village Life" (see endnote 58), p. 1.

70. Stager, "Highland Village Life," p. 1.

71. Joseph C. Wampler, "Some Cisterns and Silos," in *Tell en-Nasbeh* I, ed. C.C. McCown (Berkeley, CA: Palestine Institute of the Pacific School of Religion, 1947), p. 127.

72. Callaway, *The Early Bronze Age Citadel and Lower City at Ai (et-Tell)* (Cambridge, MA: ASOR, 1980). See fig. 2 for the location of contour 840 and fig. 145 for a plan of the Iron Age I terrace.

73. Kochavi, "Israelite Settlement" (see endnote 43), p. 55.

74. Kochavi, "Israelite Settlement," p. 56.

75. Kochavi, "Israelite Settlement," p. 58.

76. Kochavi, "Israelite Settlement," p. 58.

77. Yohanan Aharoni, "The Israelite Occupation of Canaan," *BAR*, May/June 1982, p. 18.

78. Miller and Hayes, *A History of Ancient Israel and Judah* (Philadelphia: Westminster, 1986), p. 78.

79. Baruch Halpern, *The Emergence of Israel in Canaan* (Chico, CA: Scholars Press, 1983), p. 47.

80. Stager, "Merneptah, Israel and Sea Peoples," in *Eretz Israel* 18 (Jerusalem: IES, 1985), p. 56.

81. Stager, "Merneptah" (see endnote 80), p. 61.

82. Stager, "Merneptah," p. 60.

83. Stager, "Merneptah," p. 60.

84. Miller and Hayes, *History of Ancient Israel* (see endnote 78), p. 97.

85. Miller and Hayes, *History of Ancient Israel*, p. 97.

86. Miller and Hayes, *History of Ancient Israel*, p. 97.

87. Halpern, *Emergence of Israel* (see endnote 79), p. 47.

88. C.A.O. van Nieuwenhuijze, "The Near Eastern Village: A Profile," *Middle East Journal* 16 (1962), p. 300.

89. Stager, "Highland Villages and Early Israel," unpublished paper (1980), part 2, p. 38.

90. Gottwald, *Tribes of Yahweh* (see endnote 59), p. 285.

91. Gottwald, *Tribes of Yahweh*, p. 258.

92. C.H.J. de Geus, *The Tribes of Israel* (Amsterdam: Van Gorcum, Assen, 1976), p. 138.

93. Miller and Hayes, *History of Ancient Israel* (see endnote 78), p. 92.

94. Miller and Hayes, *History of Ancient Israel*, p. 97.

95. Miller and Hayes, *History of Ancient Israel*, p. 97.

96. Miller and Hayes, *History of Ancient Israel*, p. 97.

97. Miller and Hayes, *History of Ancient Israel*, p. 97.

98. Miller and Hayes, *History of Ancient Israel*, pp. 99-100.

99. These offering stands have not yet been published.

100. Ze'ev Meshel, "Did Yahweh Have a Consort?" *BAR*, Mar./Apr. 1979, pp. 29-30; André Lemaire,

"Who or What Was Yahweh's Asherah?" *BAR*, Nov./ Dec. 1984, pp. 42-51; William G. Dever, "Asherah, Consort of Yahweh? New Evidence from Kuntillet 'Ajrud," *BASOR* 255 (1984), pp. 21-37.

101. Meshel, "Did Yahweh Have a Consort?" (see endnote 100), p. 32.

102. Meshel, "Did Yahweh Have a Consort?" p. 32.

103. Lemaire, "Who or What" (see endnote 100), pp. 42ff.

104. Miller and Hayes, *History of Ancient Israel* (see endnote 78), pp. 111-112.

105. Miller and Hayes, *History of Ancient Israel*, pp. 111-112.

IV. The United Monarchy

1. William E. Evans, "An Historical Reconstruction of the Emergence of Israelite Kingship and the Reign of Saul," in William W. Hallo et al., *Scripture in Context II* (Winona Lake, IN: Eisenbrauns, 1983), pp. 61-78, especially p. 77.

2. See lately, Trude Dothan, "The Philistines Reconsidered," in *Biblical Archaeology Today* (Jerusalem: IES, 1985), pp. 165-176.

3. *ANET*, pp. 262-263.

4. Cf. Franco Pintore, "Sérèn, tarwanis, tyrannos," in *Studi orientalistici in ricordo di F. Pintore*, ed. Onofrio Carruba et al., *Studia mediterranea* 4 (Padua, Italy, 1983), pp. 285-322.

5. James D. Muhly, "How Iron Technology Changed the Ancient World and Gave the Philistines a Military Edge," *BAR*, Nov./Dec. 1982, pp. 40-54.

6. Cf. A.D.H. Mayes, "The Period of Judges and the Rise of the Monarchy," in *Israelite and Judaean History*, ed. John H. Hayes and J. Maxwell Miller (Philadelphia: Westminster, 1977), pp. 285-331, especially p. 325. Nahash's way of treating the Israelites (cf. Frank Moore Cross, "The Ammonite Oppression of the Tribes of Gad and Ruben . . . ," in *History, Historiography and Interpretation*, ed. Hayim Tadmor and Moshe Weinfeld [Jerusalem: Magnes Press, 1983], pp. 148-158) is attested in Assyria (cf. Albert Kirk Grayson, *Assyrian Royal Inscriptions I* [Wiesbaden, W. Ger.: Harrassowitz, 1972], sec. 530 [especially note 177]; vol. 2 [1976], sec. 549).

7. Cf. the essay of Volkmar Fritz, "Die Deutungen des Königtums Sauls in den Überlieferungen von seiner Entstehung, I Sam 9-11," *ZAW* 88 (1976), pp. 346-362.

8. For a possible later date of this expedition, cf. Diana Edelman, "Saul's Rescue of Jabesh-Gilead (I Sam 11:1-11)," *ZAW* 96 (1984), pp. 195-209.

9. This number seems to be accepted by J. Alberto Soggin, *A History of Ancient Israel* (Philadelphia: Westminster, 1984), pp. 49-50.

10. Cf. Joseph Blenkinsopp, "The Quest of the Historical Saul," in *No Famine in the Land, Studies*

in *Honor of John L. McKenzie*, ed. J.W. Flanagan and A.W. Robinson (Missoula, MT: Scholars Press, 1975), pp. 75-99.

11. Cf. David M. Gunn, *The Fate of King Saul*, *JSOT* supp., Series 14 (Sheffield, UK, 1980).

12. Cf., for instance, André Caquot, "L'histoire de David dans les livres de Samuel," *Annuaire du Collège de France* 74 (1974), pp. 419-429; ibid., 75 (1975), pp. 423-426; ibid., 76 (1976), pp. 451-460; ibid., 77 (1977), pp. 523-530; ibid., 78 (1978), pp. 559-570; ibid., 79 (1979), pp. 465-477; ibid., 80 (1980), pp. 555-565.

13. See W. Lee Humphreys, "The Rise and Fall of King Saul," *JSOT* 18 (1980), pp. 74-90; "From Tragic Hero to Villain: A Study of the Figure of Saul and the Development of I Samuel," *JSOT* 22 (1982), pp. 95-117.

14. Cf. P. Kyle McCarter, Jr., "The Apology of David," *JBL* 99 (1980), pp. 485-504. On this literary genre in Assyria, see Tadmor, "Autobiographical Apology in the Royal Assyrian Literature," in Tadmor and Weinfeld, *History, Historiography* (see endnote 6), pp. 36-57.

15. See Moshe Kochavi, "An Ostracon of the Period of the Judges from 'Izbet Sartah," *Tel Aviv* 4 (1977), pp. 1-13; Kochavi and Aaron Demsky, "An Israelite Village from the Days of the Judges," *BAR*, Sept./Oct. 1978, pp. 19-30; Israel Finkelstein, *The 'Izbet Sartah Excavations and the Israelite Settlement in the Hill Country*, thesis, Tel Aviv, 1983.

16. See "Philistine Temple Discovered Within Tel Aviv City Limits," *BAR*, June 1975, pp. 1, 6-9; Amihai Mazar, *Excavations at Tell Qasile I, The Philistine Sanctuary*, Qedem 12 (Jerusalem, Hebrew Univ., 1980); Dothan, *The Philistines and Their Material Culture* (New Haven, CT: Yale Univ. Press, 1982); "What We Know About the Philistines," *BAR*, July/Aug. 1982, pp. 20-44; Muhly, "How Iron Technology Changed" (see endnote 5), pp. 40-54; Ze'ev Herzog, "Tel Gerisa," *IEJ* 33 (1983), pp. 121-123.

17. "Did the Philistines Destroy the Israelite Sanctuary at Shiloh? The Archaeological Evidence," *BAR*, June 1975, pp. 3-5; I. Finkelstein and Zvi Lederman, "Shiloh, 1983," *IEJ* 33 (1983), pp. 267-268. See also, on the destruction of Ai: Joseph A. Callaway, "A Visit with Ahilud," *BAR* Sept./Oct. 1983, pp. 42-53.

18. Cf. Amnon Ben-Tor, "Yoqne'am Regional Project Looks Beyond the Tell," *BAR*, Mar./Apr. 1980, pp. 30-44; Herzog, "Beer-Sheba of the Patriarchs," *BAR*, Nov./Dec. 1980, pp. 12-28; cf. also chap. III of the present volume.

19. I. Finkelstein, comment in *Biblical Archaeology Today* (see endnote 2), p. 82.

20. Mario Liverani, "Le 'origini'd'Israele projetto irrealizzabile di ricerca etnogenetica," *Rivista biblica* 28 (1980), pp. 9-31.

21. Soggin, "The Davidic-Solomonic Kingdom," in Hayes and Miller, *Israelite and Judaean History* (see endnote 6), pp. 332-380; "The History of Israel— A Study in Some Questions of Method," *Eretz-Israel*

14 (Jerusalem: IES, 1978), pp. 44-51; "Il punto fermo nella storia d'Israele," in *Atti del I convegno sulla storia del l'antico Vicino Oriente, Roma 1976* (Rome, 1978), pp. 71-81; *History of Ancient Israel* (see endnote 9), pp. 19-40.

22. Soggin, "Davidic-Solomonic Kingdom" (see endnote 21), p. 332.

23. Ziklag is probably to be located at Tell esh-Shari'a. Cf. Eliezer D. Oren, "Ziklag—A Biblical City on the Edge of the Negev," *BA* 45 (1982), pp. 155-166, especially p. 163.

24. For the location of Mahanaim at Tulul edh-Dhahab, cf. André Lemaire, "Galaad et Makir," *VT* 31 (1981), pp. 39-61, especially pp. 53-54.

25. On the problem of David's possible responsibility, cf. James C. Vanderkam, "Davidic Complicity in the Deaths of Abner and Eshbaal: A Historical and Redactional Study," *JBL* 99 (1980), pp. 521-539.

26. Cf. N.L. Tidwell, "The Philistine Incursions into the Valley of Rephaim," in *Studies in the Historical Books of the O.T.*, ed. John A. Emerton, *VT* supp. 30 (Leiden: Brill, 1980), pp. 190-212.

27. Cf. Jon D. Levenson and Baruch Halpern, "The Political Import of David's Marriages," *JBL* 99 (1980), pp. 507-518.

28. Cf. Édouard Lipiński, "Aram et Israel du Xe au VIIIe siècle av. n. è," *Acta Antiqua* 27 (1979), pp. 49-102.

29. However, Gordon J. Wenham ("Were David's Sons Priests," *ZAW* 87 [1975], pp. 79-82) proposes to read *sknym* instead of *khnym*.

30. For a literary analysis of these traditions, cf. Francois Langlamet, "David et la maison de Saül," *RB* 86 (1979), pp. 194-213, 385-436, 481-513.

31. Cf. Henri Cazelles, "David's Monarchy and the Gibeonite Claim," *PEQ* 87 (1955), pp. 165-175.

32. Cf. Lemaire, "Vers l'histoire de la rédaction des livres des Rois," *ZAW* 98 (1986), pp. 221-236.

33. Cf. Niels P. Lemche, "David's Rise," *JSOT* 10 (1978), pp. 2-25.

34. On the problem of Nathan's personality, cf. Ilse von Loewenclau, "Der Prophet Nathan im Zwielicht von theologischer Deutung und Historie," in *Werden und Wirken des Alten Testaments, Festschrift C. Westermann*, ed. R. Albertz et al. (Neukirchen: Neukirchener Verlag/Göttingen, W. Ger.: Vandenhoeck und Ruprecht, 1980), pp. 202-215.

35. Cf. Tomoo Ishida, "Solomon's Succession to the Throne of David—Political Analysis," in *Studies in the Period of David and Solomon*, ed. Ishida (Tokyo: Yamakawa-Shuppansha, 1982), pp. 175-187.

36. Cf. Herbert Donner, "The Interdependence of Internal Affairs and Foreign Policy During the Davidic-Solomonic Period (With Special Regard to the Phoenician Coast)," in *Studies in the Period* (see endnote 35), pp. 205-214.

37. Cf. Abraham Malamat, "A Political Look at the Kingdom of David and Solomon and Its Relations with Egypt," in *Studies in the Period* (see endnote

35), pp. 189-204; *Das davidische und salomonische Königsreich und seine Beziehungen zu Ägypten und Syrien, Zur Entstehung eines Grossreichs*, Österreichische Akademie der Wissenshaften, Philosophisch-Historische Klasse, Sitzungsberichte 407 (1983); "The Monarchy of David and Solomon," in *Recent Archaeology in the Land of Israel*, ed. Hershel Shanks and Benjamin Mazar (Washington, DC: BAS/Jerusalem: IES, 1984), pp. 161-172. In a late critical study Giovanni Garbini ("L'impero di David," in *Annali della Scuola Normale superiore di Pisa, Classe di Lettere e Filosofia*, Serie III, 13/1 [1983], pp. 1-20) thinks that David's kingdom was much smaller than usually thought and that the Hebrew writer used texts concerning originally the eighth and not the tenth century B.C.; accordingly, he would have confused the Phoenician kings Hiram II and Hiram I. But such a conjecture seems improbable in the historical context of the eighth century B.C.

38. Yohanan Aharoni, "The Building Activities of David and Solomon," *IEJ* 24 (1974), pp. 13-16; see also Shanks, "King David as Builder," *BAR*, Mar. 1975, p. 13.

39. Cf. already Soggin, *History of Ancient Israel* (see endnote 9), p. 40.

40. Cf. Siegfried Herrmann, "King David's State," in *In the Shelter of Elyon, Essays on Ancient Palestinian Life and Literature in Honor of G.W. Ahlström*, ed. W. Boyd Barrick and John R. Spencer, *JSOT* supp. 31 (Sheffield, UK, 1984), pp. 261-275.

41. Egypt was then practically divided between the kingdoms of Tanis and Thebes.

42. Cf. Malamat, "The First Peace Treaty Between Israel and Egypt," *BAR*, Sept./Oct. 1979, pp. 58-61; "A Political Look" (see endnote 37), especially pp. 197-201. Kenneth A. Kitchen, *The Third Intermediate Period in Egypt (1100-650 B.C.)* (Warminster, UK: Aris and Phillips, 2nd ed., 1986), pp. 280-283.

43. Cf. William G. Dever, "Further Excavations at Gezer, 1967-1971," *BA* 34 (1971), p. 110.

44. See endnote 42.

45. This is contrary to Amenhotep III's assertion that "From of old, the daughter of an Egyptian king has not been given in marriage to anyone"; cf. Alan R. Schulman, "Diplomatic Marriage in the Egyptian New Kingdom," *JNES* 38 (1979), pp. 177-193, especially p. 179. cf. also Kitchen, *Third Intermediate Period* (see endnote 42), pp. 282-283.

46. Cf. 1 Kings 11:1,5,7. Since Rehoboam was 41 years old when he became king, the marriage of Solomon with Naamah must have taken place during David's reign.

47. Cf. E.W. Heaton, *Solomon's New Men, The Emergence of Ancient Israel as a National State* (London: Thames and Hudson, 1974).

48. This mention of Zadok and Abiathar is probably a later addition taken from 2 Samuel 8:17.

49. Cf. Trygve N.D. Mettinger, *Solomonic State Officials* (Lund, Sweden: Gleerup, 1971).

50. Cf. Aharoni, "The Solomonic Districts," *Tel Aviv* 3 (1976), pp. 5-15; Hartmut N. Rösel, "Zu den

'Gauen' Salomons," *ZDPV* 100 (1986), pp. 84-90. However there is some confusion between districts 1, 3 and 4, especially about the Land of Hepher. Cf. Lemaire, "Le 'pays de Hepher' et les 'filles de Zelophehad' à la lumière des ostraca de Samarie," *Semitica* 22 (1972), pp. 13-20; *Inscriptions hébraiques I, Les ostraca* (Paris: Cerf, 1977), pp. 287-289.

51. Cf. Moshe Elat, "The Monarchy and the Development of Trade in Ancient Israel," in *State and Temple Economy in the Ancient Near East II*, ed. Lipiński (Leuven, Belg.: Dept. Oriëntalistiek, 1979), pp. 527-546.

52. On the problem of the identification of Ophir, cf. Vassilios Christidès, "L'énigme d'Ophir," *RB* 77 (1970), pp. 240-246; Lois Berkowitz, "Has the U.S. Geological Survey Found King Solomon's Gold Mines?" *BAR*, Sept. 1977, pp. 1, 28-33. By comparison with the ancient Egyptian texts, the most probable solution still seems Somalia-Ethiopia.

53. On the change of defense strategy under Solomon, see Chris Hauer, "Economics of National Security in Solomonic Israel," *JSOT* 18 (1980), pp. 63-73.

54. Cf. the essay of Yutaka Ikeda, "Solomon's Trade in Horses and Chariots in Its International Setting," in *Studies of the Period* (see endnote 35), pp. 215-238.

55. Cf. G.W. Ahlström, *Royal Administration and National Religion* (Leiden: Brill, 1982). For this motive in Assyria, see Sylvie Lackenbacher, *Le roi bâtisseur, les récits de contruction assyriens des origines à Téglatphalasar III* (Paris: Ed. Recherche sur les civilisations, A.D.P.F., 1982).

56. There is a dispute about a possible origin of this copper from the Timna Valley in the Aravah rift. See Beno Rothenberg, *Timna, Valley of the Biblical Copper Mines* (London: Thames and Hudson, 1972); published in U.S. as *Were These King Solomon's Mines? Excavations in the Timna Valley* (New York, 1972); "Nelson Glueck and King Solomon, A Romance That Ended," *BAR*, Mar. 1975, p. 1, 10-12, 14. Suzanne F. Singer, "From These Hills . . . . ," *BAR*, June 1978, pp. 11-25; John J. Bimson, "King Solomon's Mines? A Reassessment of Finds in the Aravah," *THB* 32 (1981), pp. 123-149.

57. Cf. Soggin, "Compulsory Labor under David and Solomon," in *Studies in the Period* (see endnote 35), pp. 259-267.

58. Cf. lately Julio C. Trebolle Barrera, *Salomon y Jeroboan* (Valencia, Spain: Institución San Jerónimo, 1980), especially pp. 364-366.

59. Actually "Hadad" sounds more like an Aramean name, and Hadad originally could well have been an Aramean. In the Hebrew text of the Bible, there are several confusions between "Aram" and "Edom," and the Edomites seem to have been independent, with their own king, only about the year 845 B.C. (cf. 2 Kings 8:20-22). So Solomon's political power over Aramean countries did not last very long—if it ever existed: see Lemaire, "Hadad

l'édomite ou Hadad l'araméen?" *BN* 1987.

60. For a literary criticism of these texts, see Helga Weippert, "Die Ätiologie des Nordreiches und seines Königshauses (1 Reg 11:29-40)," *ZAW* 95 (1983), pp. 344-375.

61. The Masoretic text has "Molech," but the context indicates that we must read "Milkom."

62. Probably the Mount of Scandal or Mount of Perdition (*har hammashit*).

63. For a general history of redaction of the Book of Kings, see Lemaire, "Vers l'histoire de la rédaction" (see endnote 32), pp. 221-236.

64. Cf. Hugh Williamson, *1 and 2 Chronicles*, New Century Bible Commentary (Grand Rapids, MI: Eerdmans, 1982), pp. 229-230.

65. Cf. Donald B. Redford, "The Relations Between Egypt and Israel from El-Amarna to the Babylonian Conquest," in *Biblical Archaeology Today* (see endnote 2), pp. 192-205.

66. Cf. Alberto R. Green, "Solomon and Siamun: A Synchronism Between Early Dynastic Israel and the Twenty-First Dynasty of Egypt," *JBL* 97 (1978), pp. 353-367.

67. Cf. Cazelles, "Administration salomonienne et terminologie administrative égyptienne," *Comptes Rendus du GLECS* 17 (1973), pp. 23-25.

68. Cf. Redford, "Studies in Relations Between Palestine and Egypt During the First Millennium B.C., I, The Taxation System of Solomon," in *Studies on the Ancient Palestinian World Presented to F.V. Winnett*, ed. Wevers and Redford (Toronto: Univ. of Toronto Press, 1972), pp. 141-156.

69. Cf. Green, "Israelite Influence at Shishak's Court," *BASOR* 233 (1979), pp. 59-62.

70. Cf. Ahlström, *Royal Administration* (see endnote 55), p. 33.

71. For the Egyptian list of conquered towns, see *ANET*, pp. 263-264; B. Mazar, "The Campaign of Pharaoh Shishak to Palestine," in *Congrès de Strasbourg, VT* supp. 4 (Leiden: Brill, 1957), pp. 57-66; Aharoni, *The Land of the Bible: A Historical Geography*, rev. and enlarged, transl. and ed. A.F. Rainey (Philadelphia: Westminster, 1979), pp. 323-330.

72. Cf. Donner, "Israel und Tyrus im Zeitalter Davids und Salomos," *JNSL* 10 (1982), pp. 43-52; Green, "David's Relations with Hiram: Biblical and Josephan Evidence for Tyrian Chronology," in *The Word of the Lord Shall Go Forth, Essays in Honor of D.N. Freedman* (Winona Lake, IN: Eisenbrauns, 1983), pp. 373-397; Kitchen, *Third Intermediate Period* (see endnote 42), pp. 432-447.

73. Cf. Garbini, "Gli 'Annali di Tiro' et la storiografia fenicia," in *I Fenici, storia e religone* (Naples: Instituto Universitario Orientale, 1980), pp. 71-86; Lemaire, "Les écrits phéniciens," in A. Barucq et al., *Ecrits de l'Orient ancien et sources bibliques*, PBSB AT 2 (Paris: Desclée, 1986), pp. 213-239, especially pp. 217-219.

74. *Apion* 1.113; cf. H. St.J. Thackeray, *Josephus I, The Life Against Apion*, Loeb Classical Library (London: Heinemann, 1966), p. 209.

75. *Apion* 1.117-119; Thackeray, *Josephus I* (see endnote 74), p. 211.

76. Cf. Lemaire, "Les Phéniciens et le commerce entre la Mer Rouge et la Mer Méditerranée," *Studia Phoenicia V* (Leuven, Belg.: Peeters, 1987).

77. Cf. Israel Eph'al, *The Ancient Arabs* (Jerusalem: Magnes Press, 1984), pp. 28ff.; Garbini, "I Sabei del Nord come problema storico," in *Studi in onore di F. Gabrieli*, ed. R. Traini (Rome: Universita di Roma, 1984), pp. 373-380.

78. Cf. Hannelis Schulte, *Die Entstehung der Geschichtsschreibung im Alten Israel*, BZAW (Berlin: de Gruyter, 1972). According to John Van Seters ("Histories and Historians of the Ancient Near East," *Orientalia* 50 [1981], pp. 137-185, especially p. 185), "Dtr [Deuteronomist] stands at the beginnning of historiography," but this is probably too simplistic a view; see Lemaire, "Vers l'histoire de le rédaction" (see endnote 32).

79. Cf. Werner H. Schmidt, "A Theologian of the Solomonic Era? A Plea for the Yahwist," in *Studies in the Period* (see endnote 35), pp. 55-73.

80. Cf. Lemaire, *Les écoles et la formation de la Bible dans l'ancien Israël*, Orbis Biblicus Orientalis 39 (Freiburg: Editions Universitaires/Göttingen, W. Ger.: Vandenhoeck und Ruprecht, 1981), especially pp. 46-50.

81. Dever, "Monumental Architecture in Ancient Israel in the Period of the United Monarchy," in *Studies in the Period* (see endnote 35), pp. 269-306; cf. also Volkmar Fritz, "Salomo," *MDOG* 117 (1985), pp. 47-67.

82. Ernest-Marie Laperrousaz, "A-t-on dégagé l'angle sud-est du 'temple de Salomon'?" *Syria* 50 (1973), pp. 355-399; "Angle sud-est du 'temple de Salomon' ou vestiges de l'Accra des Séleucides'? Un faux problème," *Syria* 52 (1975), pp. 241-259; "Après le 'temple de Salomon,' la *bamah* de Tel Dan: l'utilisation de pierres à bossage phénicien dans la Palestine pré-exilique," *Syria* 59 (1982), pp. 223-237; "A propos des murs d'enceinte antiques de la colline occidentale du temple de Jérusalem," *REJ* 141 (1982), pp. 443-458; "King Solomon's Wall Still Supports the Temple Mount," *BAR*, May/June 1987, pp. 34-44.

83. Cf. Yigal Shiloh, *Excavations at the City of David I, 1978-1982*, Qedem 19 (Jerusalem: Hebrew Univ., 1984), especially p. 27; "Jérusalem, la Ville de David (1978-1981)," *RB* 91 (1984), pp. 420-431, especially pp. 428-429.

84. Yadin, "Solomon's City Wall and Gate at Gezer," *IEJ* 8 (1958), pp. 82-86; "Yadin's Popular Book on Hazor Now Available," *BAR*, Sept. 1975, pp. 14-17, 32; David Ussishkin, "Was the 'Solomonic' City Gate at Megiddo Built by King Solomon?" *BASOR* 239 (1980), pp. 1-18; Yadin, "A Rejoinder," *BASOR* 239 (1980), pp. 19-23; Valerie M. Fargo, "Is the Solomonic City Gate at Megiddo Really Solomonic?" *BAR*, Sept./Oct. 1983, pp. 8-13; cf. also D. Milson, "The Design of the Royal Gates at Megiddo, Hazor and Gezer," *ZDPV* 102 (1986), pp. 87-92.

85. Cf. Rudolph Cohen, "The Iron Age Fortresses in the Central Negev," *BASOR* 236 (1980), pp. 61-79; "Excavations at Kadesh-Barnea 1976-1978," *BA* 44 (1981), pp. 93-107; "Did I Excavate Kadesh-Barnea?" *BAR*, May/June 1981, pp. 20-33. Herzog et al., "The Israelite Fortress at Arad," *BASOR* 254 (1984), pp. 1-34, especially pp. 6-8; Cohen, "The Fortresses King Solomon Built to Protect His Southern Border," *BAR*, May/June 1985, pp. 56-70. However the precise dating and interpretation of the Iron Age installations in the Negev is still disputed; cf. Finkelstein, "The Iron Age 'Fortresses' of the Negev—Sedentarization of Desert Nomads," in *Eretz-Israel* 18 (Jerusalem: IES, 1985), pp. 366-379 (= *Tel Aviv* 11 [1984], pp. 189-209).

86. Cf. Ussishkin, "King Solomon's Palaces," *Biblical Archaeologist Reader IV* (Sheffield, UK, 1983), pp. 227-247; Shiloh, *The Proto-Aeolic Capital and Israelite Ashlar Masonry*, Qedem 11 (Jerusalem: Hebrew Univ., 1979). (However a Phoenician origin is not impossible.) B. Gregori, "Considerazioni sui palazzi 'hilani' del periodo salomonico a Megiddo," *Vicino Oriente* 5 (1982), pp. 85-101.

87. Aharoni, *The Archaeology of the Land of Israel* (Philadelphia: Westminster, 1982), especially p. 239.

88. John Bright, *A History of Israel* (Philadelphia: Westminster, 3rd ed., 1981), p. 217.

89. Cf. Winfried Theil, "Soziale Wandlungen in der frühen Königszeit Alt-Israels," in *Gesellschaft und Kultur im alten Vorderasien*, ed. H. Klengel (Berlin: Akademie Verlag, 1982), pp. 235-246.

90. Cf. Tadmor, "Traditional Institutions and the Monarchy: Social and Political Tensions in the Time of David and Solomon," in *Studies in the Period* (see endnote 35), pp. 239-257.

91. On the distinction between Israel and Judah, see Lipiński, "Judah et 'Tout Israël': Analogies et contrastes," in *The Land of Israel: Cross-Roads of Civilizations*, ed. Lipiński, OLA 19 (Leuven, Belg.: Peeters, 1985), pp. 93-112.

V. The Divided Monarchy

1. The definitive publication of Shishak's victory monument at the temple of Karnak is George R. Hughes and Charles F. Nims, *The Bubastite Portal*, vol. 3 of *Reliefs and Inscriptions at Karnak* (Chicago: Univ. of Chicago Press, 1954). Benjamin Mazar's study, *The Campaign of Pharaoh Shishak to Palestine* (*VT* supp. 4 [Leiden: Brill, 1957], pp. 57-66), solves the problems with regard to the arrangement of the names of cities conquered by the Egyptian king, as far as they have survived on the monument.

2. The chronology of the kings of Judah and Israel followed in this chapter is based on Edwin R. Thiele's *The Mysterious Numbers of the Hebrew Kings* (Grand Rapids, MI: Zondervan, rev. ed., 1983). The only exception is with regard to Hezekiah for

whom a co-regency with his father Ahaz is assumed to have taken place; see Siegfried H. Horn, "The Chronology of King Hezekiah's Reign," *AUSS* 2 (1964), pp. 40-52, and Edmund A. Parker, "A Note on the Chronology of 2 Kings 17:1," *AUSS* 6 (1968), pp. 129-133.

Other chronological schemes may differ by a few years for the individual kings. For example, "The Chronology of the Divided Monarchy of Israel" by William F. Albright (*BASOR* 100 [1945], pp. 16-22) provides dates that differ in some cases by as much as nine years from those of Thiele. However, all deviations from the scheme used in this chapter are minor since several astronomically fixed Assyrian dates are locked in by synchronisms with the chronology of the Hebrew kings. For example, the Assyrian records of Shalmaneser III mention that King Ahab of Israel took part in the battle of Karkar in 853 B.C., and state that 12 years later, in 841 B.C., King Jehu of Israel paid tribute to Shalmaneser. Hence, any chronological scheme of the Hebrew kings must allow that Ahab was reigning in 853 B.C. and Jehu in 841 B.C. Other absolutely fixed dates are a military campaign of Sennacherib against Hezekiah in 701 B.C. and that of Nebuchadnezzar II against Jehoiachin in 597 B.C.

3. On the excavations of Shechem, see G. Ernest Wright, *Shechem: The Biography of a Biblical City* (New York: McGraw-Hill, 1965); "Shechem," *EAEHL*, vol. 4, pp. 1083-1094.

4. On the excavations of Tell el-Far'ah, see Roland de Vaux, "Tell el-Far'a," *EAEHL*, vol. 2, pp. 395-404.

5. For example, the following cities conquered by Shishak, and mentioned on his victory monument at Karnak (see also endnote 1), are clearly cities of the northern kingdom of Israel (the numbers and spelling of the names are those used in Hughes and Nims, *Bubastite Portal* [see endnote 1]): Taanach (14), Shunem (15), Bethshan (16), Rehob (17), Megiddo (27). See B. Mazar, *Campaign of Pharaoh Shishak* (see endnote 1), p. 60.

6. Robert S. Lamon and Geoffrey M. Shipton, *Megiddo I* (Chicago: Univ. of Chicago Press, 1939), pp. 60-61.

7. Amihai Mazar, "Bronze Bull Found in Israelite 'High Place' from the Time of the Judges," *BAR*, Sept./Oct. 1983, pp. 34-40.

8. The large platform on which the open-air sanctuary at Dan was probably located was found during the excavations at Tel Dan. John C.H. Laughlin, "The Remarkable Discoveries at Tel Dan," *BAR*, Sept./Oct. 1981, pp. 30-34; Avraham Biran, "Tel Dan: Five Years Later," *BA* 43 (1980), pp. 172-176. Nothing similar has so far come to light during the excavations at Bethel; see James L. Kelso, "Bethel," *EAEHL*, vol. 1, pp. 190-193.

9. This military campaign is a historical enigma. It seems that the Hebrew word *kûsh*, usually translated "Ethiopian," was sometimes used in the Bible to designate Arab tribes. Edward Ullendorff considers the mention of *kûsh* in some texts to be

an "early pointer of South Arabian migrations to [African] Ethiopia," *Ethiopia and the Bible* (London: The British Academy, 1968), pp. 7-8. See also "Zerah," *IDB*, vol. 4, pp. 953-954.

10. Ze'ev Meshel, "Did Yahweh Have a Consort?" *BAR*, Mar./Apr. 1979, pp. 24-35. André Lemaire ("Who or What Was Yahweh's Asherah?" *BAR*, Nov./Dec. 1984, pp. 42-51) argues that the Asherah of the Kuntillet 'Ajrud texts does not refer to the Phoenician goddess by that name but to a cult symbol. William G. Dever, on the other hand ("Asherah, Consort of Yahweh," *BASOR* 255 [1984], pp. 21-37), defends the view that a goddess is referred to in the Kuntillet 'Ajrud texts, a view held also by the writer of this chapter.

11. This is apparent from the chronological statements in 1 Kings 16:15 and 23, which assign the seven days of Zimri's reign to Asa's 27th year and Omri's accession to the throne—as sole ruler—to Asa's 31st year.

12. On the excavations of Samaria, see Nahman Avigad, "Samaria," *EAEHL*, vol. 4, pp. 1032-1050.

13. Horn, "Why the Moabite Stone Was Blown to Pieces," *BAR*, May/June 1986, pp. 50-61.

14. A list of the more or less legible 63 ostraca at Samaria, together with transcriptions and translations of their texts, as well as commentaries on their names is given by David Diringer, *Le iscrizioni antico-ebraiche palestinesi* (Florence, Italy: Felice le Monnier, 1934), pp. 21-68. The personal names are also dealt with by Martin Noth, *Die israelitischen Personennamen im Rahmen der gemein-semitischen Namengebung* (Stuttgart, Ger.: W. Kohlhammer, 1928; reprint Hildesheim, W. Ger.: Georg Olms, 1966); André Lemaire, *Inscriptions hébraiques I, Les Ostraca* (Paris: Cerf, 1977), pp. 25-81.

15. John W. Crowfoot and Grace M. Crowfoot, *Early Ivories from Samaria* (London: Palestine Exploration Fund, 1938); Richard D. Barnett, *Ancient Ivories in the Middle East* (Jerusalem: Hebrew Univ., 1982); Hershel Shanks, "Ancient Ivory," *BAR*, Sept./Oct. 1985, pp. 40-53.

16. On the chronological correctness of the year 853 B.C. for the battle of Karkar, see Thiele, *The Mysterious Numbers* (see endnote 2), pp. 72-76.

17. *ANET*, pp. 278b-279a.

18. Horn, "Why the Moabite Stone" (see endnote 13), p. 59.

19. Sela, the capital of ancient Edom has not been identified with certainty. For a long time it was identified with Petra in southern Transjordan because the Hebrew *sela'*, "rock," has the same meaning as the Greek *petra*, but excavations have shown that the earliest occupation at ancient Petra dates from the very end of the eighth century B.C. ([Crystal-M. Bennett], "Notes and News," *PEQ* 98 [1966], pp. 123-126; "Fouilles d'Umm el-Biyara," *RB* 73 [1966], pp. 372-403). It is, therefore, not yet certain where the Sela of King Amaziah, who reigned in the first half of the eighth century B.C., was located.

20. *ANEP*. Nos. 351-355 and pp. 290-291.

21. Manfred Weippert, "Jehu," *Reallexikon der Assyriologie* 5 (1976-1980), p. 275-276, and the literature listed there.

22. Alan R. Millard and Hayim Tadmor, "Adad-nirari III in Syria," *Iraq* 35 (1973), pp. 57-64; Tadmor, "The Historical Inscriptions of Adad-nirari III," *Iraq* 35 (1973), pp. 141-150.

23. Albright, "The Discovery of an Aramaic Inscription Relating to King Uzziah," *BASOR* 44 (1931), pp. 8-10 and illustration.

24. Nelson Glueck, "The Third Season of Excavation of Tell el-Kheleifeh," *BASOR* 79 (1940), pp. 13-15 and fig. 9, with Albright's note 9 on p. 15; Larry G. Herr, *The Scripts of Ancient Northwest Semitic Seals* (Missoula, MT: Scholars Press, 1978), p. 163.

25. *ANET*, p. 282a. It is interesting to find King Ahaz referred to in the Assyrian inscription by his fuller name—Jehoahaz (*Ia-ú-(??)ha-zi*). It seems that Ahaz dropped the divine component of his name Jeho- (*Yahu-*) when he turned from the worship of Yahweh to that of foreign gods, among which the Bible mentions specifically Baal (2 Chronicles 28:2).

26. *ANET*, p. 283a.

27. Pekah counted his regnal years from the time of Menahem's accession to the throne; Pekah may have been related either to Jehu's dynasty or to King Shallum, and therefore ignored the two rulers immediately preceding him by including their 12 years of reign as part of his own. Another possible explanation of the problems posed by Pekah's chronological data may be that he ruled over an insignificant part of the country and did not recognize Menahem and Pekahiah as legitimate rulers. Whatever his reasons for usurping their regnal years may have been, it is quite certain that he enjoyed a sole reign of only about eight years.

28. Emil Forrer, *Die Provinzeinteilung des assyrischen Reiches* (Leipzig, E. Ger.: J.C. Hinrichs'sche Buchhandlung, 1921), pp. 60-61.

29. *ANET*, p. 284a.

30. An enormous and probably exaggerated amount of tribute, ten talents of gold (about 660 pounds) and a thousand (the numeral is uncertain here) talents of silver (about 66 tons) was paid by Hoshea to Tiglath-pileser III, according to the Assyrian king's annals (*ANET*, p. 284a). The tribute paid to his successor, Shalmaneser V, is mentioned only in the Bible, since no annals of Shalmaneser V have so far come to light.

31. The Hebrew text of 2 Kings 17:4 seems to indicate that *Sô'* was the name of the king of Egypt with whom Hoshea formed an alliance. However, no Egyptian king of such a name is known from Egyptian or other sources to have reigned at that time. The most plausible solution to this problem is the suggestion of Hans Goedicke, that *Sô'* stands for the name of the capital city of Egypt which was Saïs during that time (Egyptian *S Ǝ w*, Coptic *Sai* or *Sa* and Assyrian *Sai*). Hence 2 Kings 17:4 should

be read as Hoshea "sent messengers to Saïs, to the king of Egypt"; Goedicke, "The End of 'So, King of Egypt,' " *BASOR* 171 (1963), pp. 64-66.

32. *ANET*, pp. 284a-285b.

33. On the question of whether Samaria was conquered by Shalmaneser V in 723 B.C. or by Sargon in 722 B.C., see Thiele, *The Mysterious Numbers* (see endnote 2), pp. 163-172. While Thiele, on chronological grounds, comes to the conclusion that Samaria's capture and destruction occurred in 723 B.C., Hayim Tadmor's detailed reexamination of Sargon's military campaigns leads him to similar conclusions. See his article, "The Campaigns of Sargon II of Assur," *JCS* 121 (1958), pp. 22-42, 77-100. The fall of Samaria is discussed especially on pp. 33-40. Tadmor accepts the statement of the Babylonian Chronicle, which attributes the destruction of Samaria to Shalmaneser V. According to Tadmor's reconstruction of the events, Samaria was conquered during the last months of Shalmaneser's life, but the deportation of the population was carried out by his successor, Sargon II in 722. On the basis of the two evidences—chronological and historical—I have adopted the date 723/722 B.C. for the end of both King Hoshea's reign and the kingdom of Israel.

34. Yohanan Aharoni, "The Horned Altar of Beersheba," *BA* 37 (1974), pp. 2-6.

35. This is Norman H. Snaith's translation in *Documents from Old Testament Times*, ed. D. Winton Thomas (New York: Harper & Row, 1958; Torchbooks, 1961), p. 210. For a picture of the inscription, see *ANEP*, No. 275. On ancient water tunnels in general, including that of Hezekiah, see Dan Cole, "How Water Tunnels Worked," *BAR*, Mar./ Apr. 1980, pp. 8-29; Hershel Shanks, *The City of David* (Washington, DC: BAS, 1973), pp. 47-74.

36. *ANET*, p. 287a.

37. A good summary of the three invasions of Sargon II against the country of the Philistines is provided in the article by Tadmor, "Philistia Under Assyrian Rule," *BA* 29 (1966), pp. 90-95.

38. Tadmor, "Philistia" (see endnote 37), pp. 90 and 93, figs. 9 and 10.

39. For the particular portion of the 11th year of Sargon's Annals and that of the Display Inscription, see *ANET*, p. 286a-b. The fragments of the victory stele found at Ashdod during the excavations of the ancient city are depicted in Tadmor, "Philistia" (see endnote 37), p. 95, fig. 11.

40. *ANET*, p. 287a.

41. The Assyrian invasion took place in Hezekiah's 14th regnal year as sole ruler according to the biblical record (2 Kings 18:13). The Assyrian inscriptions date this same event in the year 701 B.C. Since the year 701 B.C. happened to fall 15 years before Hezekiah's death, which occurred in 686 B.C., his sickness, which also occurred 15 years before his death (2 Kings 20:6), therefore must have taken place in the same year as Sennacherib's invasion. However the question is: Did Hezekiah's sickness and healing come before or after the

Assyrian invasion? The story of it, told in 2 Kings 20, follows the account of the Assyrian invasion, thus giving the impression that Hezekiah's sickness came after it. However, the fact that Isaiah in promising Hezekiah healing also made the prediction that Jerusalem would not fall to the Assyrians (2 Kings 20:6) implies that the king's sickness seems to have preceded Sennacherib's invasion.

42. *ANET*, pp. 287a-288b.

43. In these pages, I have told the story on the assumption that there were two distinctive and different campaigns of Sennacherib against Hezekiah, of which only one is mentioned in the Assyrian records. The biblical records can be, and have been, interpreted in two ways: The majority of biblical historians believe that they all refer only to the campaign of 701 B.C., while a minority has defended the view that they refer to two campaigns, one carried out in 701 B.C. and a second one after Taharka's accession to the throne, in 689 or later. On the one-campaign theory, see Harold W. Rowley, "Hezekiah's Reform and Rebellion," *BJRL* 44 (1962), pp. 395-431, which presents a full listing of literature up to the time of writing. For the two-campaign theory, see Albright, "New Light From Egypt on the Chronology and History of Israel and Judah," *BASOR* 130 (1953), pp. 8-11; Horn, "Did Sennacherib Campaign Once or Twice Against Hezekiah?" *AUSS* 4 (1966), pp. 1-28; John Bright, *A History of Israel* (Philadelphia: Westminster, 2nd ed., 1972), pp. 296-308.

In recent years several items of evidence have come to light that strongly support the two-campaign theory. This evidence, consisting of new Assyrian and Egyptian texts and the reinterpretation of known texts, is conveniently collected and discussed by William H. Shea in "Sennacherib's Second Palestinian Campaign," *JBL* 104 (1985), pp. 401-418. Randall W. Younker presented at the ASOR meetings at Anaheim, California, in November 1985, an unpublished paper titled "Archaeological Evidence for Sennacherib's Second Campaign Against Judah," in which he showed from the published excavation reports of several ancient cities of Judah that they were destroyed twice within a few years' interval at the end of the eighth and the beginning of the seventh centuries B.C.

44. David Ussishkin, *The Conquest of Lachish by Sennacherib* (Tel Aviv: Tel Aviv Univ., Inst. of Archaeology, 1982). This book contains new photographs of the Lachish reliefs by Avraham Hay, new drawings of the reliefs by Judith Dekel and reconstructions of the Assyrian siege by Gert le Grange; see Shanks, "Destruction of Judean Fortress Portrayed in Dramatic Eighth-Century B.C. Pictures," *BAR*, Mar./Apr. 1984, pp. 48-65.

45. The Bible gives the number of casualties in the Assyrian army as 185,000 (2 Kings 19:35; Isaiah 37:36). That this figure is unrealistically high has been recognized by many commentators in the past. Although no exact figures of the size of the

Assyrian expeditionary forces exist, the highest figure ever given for any Assyrian army is 120,000 men, with whom Shalmaneser III fought against Damascus (*ANET*, p. 280a).

It is possible that the figures in the Bible usually rendered as 185,000 could be read in a different way. Second Kings 19:35 literally reads "hundred eighty and five thousand." That this number has been rendered 185,000 by all modern translators is due to the Septuagint tradition, and also because the number 180, the smaller number, precedes the larger one, 5,000. However, exceptions to the normal procedure, that the larger number precedes the smaller one, are found in Hebrew literature. First Kings 4:32, for example, states that Solomon composed "five and thousand" songs, which is regularly rendered 1,005. By analogy it should be permissible to read the number of slain Assyrians as 5,180 instead of 185,000. It is conceivable that the death of more than 5,000 soldiers in one night as the result of the outbreak of a mysterious disease could result in such a panic that a sudden return of the surviving forces became necessary, the more so since ancient man was always inclined to see the hand of a divine power in such an ordeal and to consider it a punishment.

46. Herodotus, *History* 2.141.

47. Robert H. Charles, "The Martyrdom of Isaiah," in *The Apocrypha and Pseudepigrapha of the Old Testament* (Oxford: Clarendon Press, 1913), vol. 2, pp. 155-162.

48. *ANET*, pp. 291a, 294a.

49. *ANET*, p. 301a.

50. Many historians consider the statement of the Chronicler suspect and believe that the activities attributed to Josiah, when he was still a teenager, in reality took place after the finding of the book of the law when Josiah had reached the age of 25.

51. Aharoni, "Arad," *EAEHL*, vol. 1, pp. 84-86.

52. Kathleen M. Kenyon, *Digging Up Jerusalem* (New York: Praeger, 1974), pp. 137-144, plates 56-61; *Jerusalem: Excavating 3,000 Years of History* (New York: McGraw-Hill, 1967), p. 101, figs. 8-10.

53. Diringer, "Early Hebrew Inscriptions," in Olga Tufnell, *Lachish III: The Iron Age* (London: Oxford Univ. Press, 1953), pp. 331-339.

54. Avigad, "Jerahmeel & Baruch," *BA* 42 (1979), pp. 114-118; *Hebrew Bullae from the Time of Jeremiah: Remnants of a Burnt Archive* (Jerusalem: IES, 1986), pp. 27-29, Nos. 8 and 9.

55. Donald J. Wiseman, *Chronicles of Chaldean Kings* (London: British Museum, 1956), pp. 67, 69.

56. *Apion* 1.19.

57. Wiseman, *Chronicles* (see endnote 55), p. 71.

58. The events described in this paragraph are based primarily on 2 Kings 24:1-6 and 2 Chronicles 36:5-8. Additional information regarding Jehoiakim's death is furnished by Jeremiah 22:18-19 and 36:30. The extant Babylonian records are silent about these events.

Since the surrender of Jehoiachin to Nebuchadnezzar after a reign of three months occurred in

March 597 B.C., according to the Babylonian Chronicle, the death of his father Jehoiakim must have taken place in December 598 B.C., and his death may have been the result of harsh treatment received at the hands of the marauding hostile forces of neighboring nations and Babylonian garrison troops (2 Kings 24:2). These armed forces may have acted with Nebuchadnezzar's permission or even on his orders so that the Chronicler felt justified in describing as acts of Nebuchadnezzar himself the capture of King Jehoiakim, his being put in fetters to be sent to Babylon—which was not carried out because of his death—and the carrying away of temple vessels.

59. Wiseman, *Chronicles* (see endnote 55), p. 73.

60. Albright, "King Joiachin in Exile," *BA* 5 (1942), pp. 49-51.; translations of three tablets can be found in *ANET*, p. 308b.

61. *Antiq.* 10.108.

62. A peaceful expedition of Psamtik II to the land Kharu (Syria-Palestine) in 591 B.C. is attested in a demotic papyrus of the John Rylands Library in Manchester, England. This royal visit may have served to conclude alliances with the dissatisfied Babylonian vassals of Palestine and Syria. See Henry R. Hall, in *CAH*, III, pp. 300-301; Anthony Spalinger, "Psammetichus II," in *Lexikon der Ägyptologie*, vol. 4, cols. 1169-1172.

63. Ostraca 1-18 from Lachish, discovered in 1935, were published in Harry Torczyner, *Lachish I: The Lachish Letters* (London: Oxford Univ. Press, 1938). Ostraca 19-21, discovered in 1938 were published by Diringer, "Early Hebrew Inscriptions" (see endnote 53), pp. 338-339. Translations of 8 of the 21 ostraca by Albright can also be found in *ANET*, pp. 322a-b.

64. For a different interpretation of the letters as having been sent from Lachish, see Yigael Yadin, "The Lachish Letters—Originals or Copies and Drafts?" in *Recent Archaeology in the Land of Israel*, ed. Shanks and B. Mazar (Washington, DC: BAS/Jerusalem: IES, 1984), pp. 179-186.

65. The dates used here are based on the assumption that the civil calendar employed throughout the history of the kingdom of Judah was a fall-to-fall calendar with the year beginning on Tishri 1 (Thiele, *The Mysterious Numbers* [see endnote 2], pp. 183-184). Scholars who assume that the civil year during the latter part of the history of Judah began just as that of the Babylonians in the spring—with Nisan 1—reach different dates. See David Noel Freedman, "The Chronology of Israel and the Ancient Near East," in *The Bible and the Ancient Near East*, ed. Wright (Garden City, NY: Doubleday, 1961), pp. 211-213; Lemaire, "Les formules de datation dans Ezéchiel à la lumière de données épigraphiques récentes," in *Ezekiel and his Book*, ed. J. Lust (Leuven, Belg.: Univ. Press, 1986), pp. 359-366.

66. Avigad, *Discovering Jerusalem* (Nashville, TN: Thomas Nelson, 1983), pp. 46-54, figs. 28-32 and color pictures nos. 12-14 on pp. 37-39.

67. Magen Broshi, "Naṣbeh, Tell en-," *EAEHL*, vol. 3, pp. 912-918.

68. Ruth Hestrin and Michal Dayagi-Mendels, *Inscribed Seals* (Jerusalem: Israel Museum, 1979), p. 20.

69. Herr, "The Servant of Baalis," *BA* 48 (1985), pp. 169-172.

VI. Exile and Return

1. On the economic dimensions of Gedaliah's governorship, note Jeremiah 40:10, "As for me I will dwell at Mizpah, to stand for you before the Chaldeans who will come to us; but as for you, gather wine and summer fruits and oil, and store them in your vessels, and dwell in your cities that you have taken." A recent study by J.N. Graham utilizing seal impressions (including a seal of "Gedaliah who is over the household") and other archaeological data, argues that Gedaliah was established as governor to oversee a state-managed agrarian system to generate tribute for the Babylonians and also contribute to the local welfare. It is further argued that the "vinedressers and plowmen" of 2 Kings 25:12 and Jeremiah 52:16 were technical terms for those in compulsory service in state industries. Graham, "Vinedressers and Plowmen," *BA* 47 (1984), pp. 55-58.

2. Jehoiachin was viewed by many in Jerusalem as the legitimate king, as the oracle of the prophet Hananiah ben Azzur of Gibeon (Jeremiah 28:1-4) and other sources demonstrate. For Jeremiah's alternative, and apparently minority, opinion, see Jeremiah 22:24-30. On this subject, see especially Martin Noth, "The Jerusalem Catastrophe of 587 B.C. and Its Significance for Israel," in *The Laws in the Pentateuch and Other Studies* (Edinburgh: Oliver & Boyd, 1966), pp. 260-280, especially pp. 265-280.

3. See Peter R. Ackroyd, "The Temple Vessels—A Continuity Theme," in *Studies in the Religion of Ancient Israel*, VT supp. 23 (Leiden: Brill, 1972), pp. 166-181.

4. The Chronicler was followed in this interpretation by the author of 1 Esdras, who cites only one deportation at the time of the destruction of Jerusalem, with reference to the removal of the sacred Temple vessels and without reference to the exile of Zedekiah (1 Esdras 1:52-58). Josephus, writing at a later time and conflating all of the biblical traditions (including 1 Esdras), gives the three exiles of 2 Kings and Jeremiah (*Antiq.* 10.101, 149-150, 181-182) and includes as well a fourth deportation not mentioned in the Bible: the removal of 3,000 Jews to Babylonia on the occasion of the death of Jehoiakim and the accession of Jehoiachin (*Antiq.* 10.98).

5. There are several texts from Sargon II referring to this deportation. See *ANET*, pp. 284-285; D.J.

Wiseman, "Records of Assyria and Babylonia," in *Documents from Old Testament Times*, ed. D. Winton Thomas (New York: Torchbooks/Harper & Row, 1961), p. 60.

6. As first suggested by A. von Hoonacker, *Une communauté judéo-araméenne à Élephantine en Égypte. Schweich Lectures, 1914* (London: British Academy, 1915).

7. Bustenay Oded, "Judah and the Exile," in *Israelite and Judaean History*, ed. John H. Hayes and J. Maxwell Miller (Philadelphia: Westminster, 1977), p. 483.

8. On the Murashu texts, see especially Elias J. Bickerman, "The Babylonian Captivity," in *CHJ*, vol. 1, pp. 345-348; Michael D. Coogan, "Life in the Diaspora: Jews at Nippur in the Fifth Century," *BA* 37 (1974), pp. 6-12.

9. William F. Albright, "The Seal of Eliakim and the Latest Preexilic History of Judah," *JBL* 51 (1932), pp. 77-106.

10. Albright, "King Jehoiachin in Exile," *BA* 5 (1942), p. 54.

11. An interesting scenario is presented by James D. Newsome, Jr., *By the Waters of Babylon: An Introduction to the History and Theology of the Exile* (Atlanta: John Knox, 1979), pp. 92-97.

12. See endnote 23.

13. *Antiq.* 12.388f., 63-73.

14. *Antiq.* 11.302.347

15. See Paul W. Lapp, "The Second and Third Campaigns at 'Arâq el-'Emir," *BASOR* 171 (1963), pp. 8-38; "The Qasr al-'Abd: A Proposed Reconstruction," *BASOR* 171 (1963), pp. 39-45.

16. Ackroyd, *The New Clarendon Bible, Old Testament*, vol. 4, *Israel under Babylon and Persia* (London: Oxford Univ. Press, 1970), pp. 26-27.

17. For a survey of conflicting opinions, see Ackroyd, *Exile and Restoration: A Study of Hebrew Thought of the Sixth Century, B.C.* (London: SCM Press, 1968), pp. 32-35.

18. Cf., for example, Norman K. Gottwald (*The Hebrew Bible: A Socio-Literary Introduction* [Philadelphia: Fortress, 1985], p. 427) and Yehezkel Kaufmann (*History of the Religion of Israel*, 4/1-2, *The Babylonian Captivity and Deutero-Isaiah* [New York: Union of American Hebrew Congregations, 1970], pp. 41-43), who argue against and for synagogal origins in Babylonia on the basis of differing criteria of what the synagogue was.

19. Walther Zimmerli, *Ezekiel*, Hermeneia: A Critical and Historical Commentary on the Bible (Philadelphia: Fortress, 1979), pp. 115-116.

20. See especially Bickerman, "Babylonian Captivity" (see endnote 8), pp. 355-357; Coogan, "Life in the Diaspora" (see endnote 8), pp. 11-12.

21. Nahman Avigad, "Seals of Exiles," *IEJ* 15 (1965), pp. 228-230.

22. Eliezer Oren, "Migdol, Where Jeremiah Prophesied After Babylonian Destruction, Found in Nile Delta," *BAR*, forthcoming.

23. See Bezalel Porten, *Archives from Elephantine: The Life of an Ancient Jewish Military Colony* (Berkeley: Univ. of California, 1968); "Aramaic Papyri and Parchments: A New Look," *BA* 42 (1979), pp. 74-104; "The Jews in Egypt," in *CHJ*, vol. 1, pp. 372-400. A publishing history of the Elephantine materials is found in Porten's studies.

24. Porten, "Jews in Egypt" (see endnote 23), pp. 392 and 379, respectively.

25. T. Fish, "The Cyrus Cylinder," in *Documents from Old Testament* (see endnote 5), p. 93.

26. This was the position of Albrecht Alt, which I have followed in the main. Alt contended that Samaritan hegemony over Judah, up to the time of Nehemiah, provides the background of Samaritan-Judean hostilities during the Persian period. "Die Rolle Samarias bei der Enstehung des Judentums," in *Kleine Schriften zur Geschichte des Volkes Israel* (Munich: Becksche Verlag, 1953), vol. 2, pp. 316-337; "Judas Nachbarn zur Zeit Nehemiah," ibid, pp. 338-345. Recent epigraphic discoveries necessitate the updating of Alt's work but have not altered his major conclusions. For a summary and defense of Alt's positions, see Sean McEvenue, "The Political Structure in Judah from Cyrus to Nehemiah," *CBQ* 43 (1981), pp. 353-364.

27. The editor of the materials in Ezra 1-2 has telescoped the careers of Sheshbazzar and Zerubbabel, suggesting they were contemporaries. This view is followed by some historians (e.g., George Widengren, "The Jewish Community Under the Persians," in *Israelite and Judaean History* [see endnote 7], p. 520). I suggest that Zerubbabel's contingent came to Jerusalem at a slightly later time.

28. Ephraim Stern, "The Persian Empire and the Political and Social History of Palestine in the Persian Period," in *CHJ*, vol. 1, pp. 71-72.

29. See especially Frank Moore Cross, "A Reconstruction of the Judean Restoration," *JBL* 94 (1975), pp. 4-18, 279; also in *Interpretation* 29 (1975), pp. 187-203. Shemaryahu Talmon, "Ezra and Nehemiah," in *IDB*, supp. vol., pp. 317-328.

30. See Widengren, "Problems in Reconstructing Jewish History in the Persian Period: The Chronological Order of Ezra and Nehemiah," in *Israelite and Judaean History* (see endnote 7), pp. 503-509.

31. Stern, *Material Culture of the Land of the Bible in the Persian Period, 538-332 B.C.* (Warminster, UK: Aris and Phillips/Jerusalem: IES, 1982).

32. Stern, *Material Culture* (see endnote 31), pp. 236-237.

33. In his memoirs, Nehemiah mentions "the former governors who were before me" as having laid heavy burdens on the people in exactions of food, wine and taxes and as having had subofficials who acted in a heavy-handed manner (Nehemiah 5:15). Alt suggested that this was a reference to the governors of Samaria who had administered the Judean territory in the period between Zerubbabel and Nehemiah (see endnote 26). Avigad, on the other hand, claims that Judean seal impressions and bullae of the Persian period bear witness to the existence of Jewish governors during this time, of

whom three—Elnathan, Yeho'ezer and Ahzai—are known by name: *Bullae and Seals from a Post-Exilic Judean Archive*, Qedem 4 (Jerusalem: Hebrw Univ., 1976). Eric M. Meyers has carried Avigad's position even further, and has argued that Elnathan, the first of Avigad's three Jewish governors, was the son-in-law of Zerubbabel. E. Meyers, "The Shelomith Seal and the Judean Restoration: Some Additional Considerations," in *Eretz Israel* 18 (Jerusalem: IES, 1985), pp. 33*-38*. The dating and interpretation of these data remain problematic, however. See, for example, Stern, *Material Culture* (see endnote 31), pp. 237-239; "The Persian Empire" (see endnote 28), p. 72.

34. Stern, *Material Culture* (see endnote 31), pp. 245-248. See also Stern's summary in "The Persian Empire" (see endnote 28), pp. 82-86.

35. See Avigad, *Discovering Jerusalem* (Nashville, TN: Thomas Nelson, 1983), pp. 61-63; Kathleen M. Kenyon, *Jerusalem: Excavating 3,000 Years of History* (New York: Praeger, 1974), pp. 172-187.

36. Others see this story as alluding to the Persians' punitive actions in suppressing a revolt in the satrapy of Abar Nahara during the time of Artaxerxes III (Ochus as he is surnamed by modern authorities) (358-336 B.C.). Specifically, in 351/350 B.C. a rebellion led by Tennes, king of Sidon, was put down by Ochus's general Bagoas. The memory of Bagoas's campaign in Syria-Palestine may be preserved in the apocryphal Book of Judith (Holofernes representing Bagoas). See Dan Barag, "The Effects of the Tennes Rebellion on Palestine," *BASOR* 183 (1966), pp. 6-12.

37. Cross, "Aspects of Samaritan and Jewish History in Late Persian and Hellenistic Times," *HTR* 59 (1966), pp. 201-211; "Papyri of the Fourth Century B.C. from Dâliyeh: A Preliminary Report on their Discovery and Significance," in *New Directions in Biblical Archaeology*, ed. David Noel Freedman and Jonas C. Greenfield (Garden City, NY: Doubleday, 1969), pp. 45-69.

38. James D. Purvis, *The Samaritan Pentateuch and the Origin of the Samaritan Sect*, Harvard Semitic Monographs 2 (Cambridge, MA: Harvard Univ. Press, 1968), pp. 104-109.

39. Purvis, "The Samaritan Problem: A Case Study in Jewish Sectarianism in the Roman Era," in *Traditions in Transformation: Turning Points in Biblical Faith*, ed. Baruch Halpern and Jon Levenson (Winona Lake, IN: Eisenbrauns, 1982), pp. 323-350.

VII. The Age of Hellenism

1. See, for example, William W. Tarn, *Hellenistic Civilisation* (London: Arnold, 1952); Arthur D. Nock, *Conversion* (Oxford: Clarendon, 1933); Arnaldo Momigliano, *Alien Wisdom* (Cambridge, UK: Cambridge Univ. Press, 1975); Félix M. Abel, "Hellénisme et orientalisme en Palestine au déclin

de la periode séleucide," *RB* 53 (1946), pp. 385-402.

2. Arnold H.M. Jones, *The Cities of the Eastern Roman Provinces* (Oxford: Clarendon, 1971), pp. 226-294; Victor Tcherikover, *Hellenistic Civilization and the Jews* (Philadelphia: Jewish Publication Society, 1959), pp. 90-116; Shimon Appelbaum, "Hellenistic Cities of Palestine—New Dimensions," in *The Seleucid Period in Palestine*, ed. Bezalel Bar Kokhba (Tel Aviv: Hakibbutz Hameuchad, 1980), pp. 277-288 (in Hebrew).

3. John Bright, *A History of Israel* (Philadelphia: Westminster, 3rd ed., 1981), pp. 360-402; Elias Bickerman, "The Edict of Cyrus in Ezra I," in *Studies in Jewish and Christian History*, I (Leiden: Brill, 1976), pp. 72-108; Frank Moore Cross, "A Reconstruction of the Judean Restoration," *JBL* 94 (1975), pp. 4-18; Ephraim Stern and Hayim Tadmor, "The Persian Period," in *The History of Eretz Israel*, II, ed. Israel Ephal (Jerusalem: Keter, 1984), pp. 225-307 (in Hebrew). For the more general picture, see Albert T. Olmstead, *History of the Persian Empire* (Chicago: Univ. of Chicago Press, 1948); John M. Cook, *The Persian Empire* (London: J.M. Dent, 1983); Richard N. Frye, *The Heritage of Persia* (London: Weidenfeld & Nicolson, 1966); Morton Smith, *Palestinian Parties and Politics that Shaped the Old Testament* (New York: Columbia Univ. Press, 1971).

4. Ya'akov Meshorer, *Ancient Jewish Coinage*, I (New York: Amphora, 1982), pp. 13-34; Uriel Rappaport, "The Coins of Jerusalem at the End of Persian Rule and the Beginning of the Hellenistic Period," in *Jerusalem in the Second Temple Period: Schalit Memorial Volume*, ed. Aaron Oppenheimer et al. (Jerusalem: Ben Zvi Institute, 1981), pp. 11-21 (in Hebrew).

5. Tcherikover, *Hellenistic Civilization* (see endnote 2), pp. 117-151; Eugene Taeubler, "Jerusalem 201 to 199 B.C.E.," *JQR* 37 (1946-47), pp. 1-30, 125-137, 249-263.

6. Bickerman, *From Ezra to the Last of the Maccabees* (New York: Schocken, 1962) and *The God of the Maccabees* (Leiden, 1979); Martin Hengel, *Judaism and Hellenism*, 2 vols. (Philadelphia: Fortress, 1974); John J. Collins, "Jewish Apocalyptic Against Its Hellenistic Near Eastern Environment," *BASOR* 220 (1975), pp. 27-36.

7. Tcherikover, *Hellenistic Civilization* (see endnote 2), pp. 152-174; Fergus Millar, "The Background to the Maccabean Revolution: Reflections on Martin Hengel's 'Judaism and Hellenism'," *JJS* 29 (1978), pp. 1-21; Samuel Sandmel, "Hellenism and Judaism," in *Great Confrontations in Jewish History*, ed. Stanley Wagner and Allen Breck (Denver: Center for Jewish Studies, Univ. of Denver, 1977), pp. 21-38; Paul Hanson, "Jewish Apocalyptic Against Its Near Eastern Environment," *RB* 78 (1971), pp. 31-58.

8. Robert Gordis, *The Wisdom of Koheleth* (London: East and West, 1950), pp. xii-xvii, and *Koheleth—The Man and His World* (New York: Jewish

Theological Seminary, 1951), pp. 8-57; Hengel, *Judaism and Hellenism* (see endnote 6), pp. 115-130.

9. Hengel, *Judaism and Hellenism* (see endnote 6), pp. 131-153; Gerson D. Cohen, "The Song of Songs and the Jewish Religious Mentality," in *The Samuel Friedland Lectures 1960-1966* (New York: Jewish Theological Seminary, 1966), pp. 1-22; M. Rozler, "The Song of Songs Against the Background of Greek-Hellenistic Eastern Poetry, *Eshkolot* 1 (1954), pp. 33-48 (in Hebrew). However, see also Marvin Pope, *Song of Songs*, Anchor Bible (Garden City, NY: Doubleday, 1977), pp. 22-33. For the Hellenistic background to the maxim of Simeon the righteous at the beginning of the Ethics of the Fathers, see Judah Goldin, "The Three Pillars of Simeon the Righteous," *PAAJR* 27 (1958), pp. 43-58.

10. Bickerman, "La charte séleucide de Jerusalem," *REJ* 100 (1935), pp. 4-35, and "Une proclamation séleucide relative au temple de Jerusalem," *Syria* 25 (1946-48), pp. 67-85; Albrecht Alt, "Zu Antiochos' III Erlass für Jerusalem," *ZAW* 57 (1939), pp. 282-285; Hengel, *Judaism and Hellenism* (see endnote 6), pp. 271-272.

11. *Antiq.* 12.160-234; Tcherikover, *Hellenistic Civilization* (see endnote 2), pp. 126-142; Benjamin Mazar, *Canaan and Israel—Historical Studies* (Jerusalem: Bialik, 1980), pp. 270-290 (in Hebrew); Menahem Stern, "Notes on the Story of Joseph Son of Tobias," *Tarbiz* 32 (1963), pp. 35-47 (in Hebrew).

12. Tcherikover, *Hellenistic Civilization* (see endnote 2), pp. 160-169.

13. Bar Kokhba, "The Status and Origin of the Akra Garrison Before Antiochus' Decrees," *Zion* 36 (1971), pp. 32-47 (in Hebrew); Jonathan Goldstein, *I Maccabees*, Anchor Bible (Garden City, NY: Doubleday, 1976), pp. 213-219; Willis A. Shotwell, "The Problem of the Syrian Akra," *BASOR* 176 (1964), pp. 10-19; Bickerman, *God of the Maccabees* (see endnote 6), pp. 42-53.

14. Bickerman, *God of the Maccabees* (see endnote 6), pp. 76-92, and *From Ezra* (see endnote 6), pp. 93-111. Hengel, *Judaism and Hellenism* (see endnote 6), pp. 208-303.

15. Goldstein, *I Maccabees* (see endnote 13), pp. 104-160.

16. Tcherikover, *Hellenistic Civilization* (see endnote 2), pp. 175-203.

17. For a detailed description of these battles, see Bar Kokhba, *The Battles of the Hasmoneans: The Times of Judas Maccabaeus* (Jerusalem: Ben Zvi Institute, 1980) (in Hebrew).

18. Tcherikover, *Hellenistic Civilization* (see endnote 2), pp. 211-220.

19. The reason for an eight-day festival has been explained in different ways by various sources. Second Maccabees 1:9 claims that the holiday was originally a postponed Sukkot festival; *Megillat Ta'anit* notes that the purification process lasted eight days. The Babylonian Talmud (*Shabbat* 21b) speaks of the miracle of the cruse of oil, and eight-day festivals of light in midwinter were well known

in antiquity generally and to the Jews no less (*B 'Avoda Zara* 8a); this custom may have influenced the nature of the Hannukah festival. Finally 2 Chronicles 29:17 mentions an eight-day celebration of rededication after the Temple had been cleansed by Hezekiah.

20. Bar Kokhba, *Battles of the Hasmoneans* (see endnote 17), pp. 225-263.

21. The attempts to shed light on this elusive group have been many and varied; see, for example, Tcherikover, *Hellenistic Civilization* (see endnote 2), pp. 187ff.; Hengel, *Judaism and Hellenism* (see endnote 6), pp. 175-180; Otto Plöger, *Theocracy and Eschatology* (Oxford: Blackwell, 1968), pp. 44-52.

22. Bar Kokhba, *Battles of the Hasmoneans* (see endnote 17), pp. 265-307.

23. On reactions to this synthesis of the political and religious realms, see Hengel, James H. Charlesworth, Doron Mendels, "The Polemical Character of 'On Kingship' in the Temple Scroll: An Attempt at Dating 11Q Temple," *JJS* 37 (1986), pp. 28-38.

24. *Antiq.* 13.254-283.

25. *Antiq.* 13.318-319.

26. *Antiq.* 13.320-397; M. Stern, "Judaea and Her Neighbors in the Days of Alexander Jannaeus," *Jerusalem Cathedra* 1 (Jerusalem: Ben Zvi Institute, 1981), pp. 22-46.

27. Goldstein, *I Maccabees* (see endnote 13), pp. 4-26.

28. *Antiq.* 13.397.

29. See *Apion* 2.71-142; Leon Poliakov, *The History of Antisemitism* (London: Vanguard, 1965), pp. 3-16.

30. Johanan Levi, *Studies in Jewish Hellenism* (Jerusalem: Bialik, 1960), pp. 60-78 (in Hebrew).

31. Lee Levine, "The Political Struggle Between Pharisees and Sadducees in the Hasmonean Period," *Jerusalem in the Second Temple Period* (see endnote 4), pp. 61-83.

32. This assumption of Pharisaic oppposition has been made by almost all scholars; see, for example, Yigael Yadin, "Pesher Nahum (4Q Pnahum) Reconsidered," *IEJ* 21 (1971), pp. 1-12. Against this commonly held assumption, see Chaim Rabin, "Alexander Jannai and the Pharisees," *JJS* 7 (1956), pp. 3-11.

33. *Antiq.* 13.408-415. Rabbinic sources confirm this sequence of events, focusing on the political activity of Simeon ben Shetah in the first third of the first century B.C. Levine, "Political Struggle" (see endnote 31), pp. 61-83; Israel Ephron, "Simeon Ben Shetah and King Yannai," in *Gedaliah Alon Memorial Volume*, ed. Menahem Dorman et al. (Tel Aviv: Hakibbutz Hameuchad, 1970), pp. 69-132 (in Hebrew).

34. Bickerman, *The Maccabees* (New York: Schocken, 1947), pp. 85-97.

35. Meshorer, *Jewish Coins of the Second Temple Period* (Jerusalem: 'Am Hassefer, 1967) and *Ancient Jewish Coinage* (see endnote 4), pp. 35-47. On Hasmonean coinage, see also Rappaport, "The

Emergence of Hasmonean Coinage," *AJS* 1 (1976), pp. 171-186.

36. Suzanne F. Singer, "The Winter Palaces of Jericho," *BAR*, June 1977, p. 1. Ehud Netzer, "The Hasmonean and Herodian Winter Palaces at Jericho," *IEJ* 25 (1975), pp. 89-100; "The Winter Palaces of the Judaean Kings at Jericho at the End of the Second Temple Period," *BASOR* 228 (1977), pp. 1-13; "Ancient Ritual Baths (Miqvaot) in Jericho," in *Jerusalem Cathedra* 2, ed. Levine (Jerusalem: Ben Zvi Institute, 1982), pp. 106-119.

37. Nahman Avigad, *Funerary Monuments from the Qidron Valley* (Jerusalem: Bialik, 1954), pp. 37-38 (in Hebrew); Levi Y. Rahmani, "Jason's Tomb," *IEJ* 17 (1967), pp. 61-100; *EAEHL*, vol. 3, pp. 782-792; John P. Peters and Hermann Thiersch, *Painted Tombs in the Necropolis of Marissa* (London: Palestine Exploration Fund, 1905).

38. So, for example, the following: Eupolemos, Numerius, Antiochus, Jason, Antipater, Apollonius, Alexander, Dositheus, Diodorus, Lysimmachus, Pausanias, Josephus, Mennaeus, Theodorus, Sopatrus, Straton, Theodotus, Aeneas, Aristobulus, Amyntas, Sosipater, Philip (1 Maccabees 8:17, 12:16, 14:22; *Antiq.* 13.260; 14.241, 247-248, 306-307).

39. M. Stern, *Greek and Latin Authors on Jews and Judaism*, 3 vols. (Jerusalem: Israel Academy for the Humanities and Sciences, 1974), vol. 1, pp. 27-29, 37-40.

40. B *Ketubot* 82b.

41. Markham Geller, "New Sources for the Origin of the Rabbinic Ketubah," *HUCA* 49 (1978), pp. 227-245.

42. Goldin, "A Philosophical Session in a Tannaitic Academy," *Traditio* 21 (1965), pp. 1-21.

43. Bickerman, "La chaine de la tradition pharisienne," *RB* 49 (1952), pp. 44-54; David Daube, "Rabbinic Methods of Interpretation and Hellenistic Rhetoric," *HUCA* 22 (1949), pp. 239-264. See also Saul Lieberman, *Hellenism in Jewish Palestine* (New York, 1962), pp. 47-68; Bickerman, *From Ezra* (see endnote 6), pp. 148-165; M. Smith, "Palestinian Judaism in the First Century," in *Israel: Its Role in Civilization*, ed. Moshe Davis (New York: Jewish Theological Seminary, 1956), pp. 67-81.

44. Shaye J.D. Cohen, "Patriarchs and Scholarchs," *PAAJR* 48 (1981), pp. 57-85.

45. D. Winston, "Iranian Components in the Bible, Apocrypha and Qumran," *History of Religion* 5 (1966), pp. 183-216. Shaul Shaked, "Qumran and Iran," *Israel Oriental Studies* 202 (1972), pp. 433-446; "Iranian Influence on Judaism: First Century B.C.E. to Second Century C.E.," in *CHJ*, pp. 308-325.

46. Bruno W. Dombrowski, "היחד in 1QS and τὸ κοινόν: An Instance of Early Greek and Jewish Synthesis," *HTR* 59 (1966), pp. 293-307; Hans Bardthe, "Die Rechtsstellung der Qumran-Gemeinde," *Die Theologische Literaturzeitung* 86 (1961), pp. 93-104.

47. Jerome Murphy-O'Connor, "The Essenes and

Their History," *RB* 81 (1974), pp. 215-244.

48. Hengel, *Judaism and Hellenism* (see endnote 6), pp. 228-247.

49. Avigad, *Discovering Jerusalem* (Nashville, TN: Thomas Nelson, 1983), pp. 64-81; Ruth Amiran and Avraham Eitan, "Excavations in the Courtyard of the Citadel, Jerusalem, 1968-1969 (Preliminary Report)," *IEJ* 20 (1970), pp. 9-17. See also Kathleen Kenyon, *Digging Up Jerusalem* (New York: Praeger, 1974), pp. 188-204.

50. Jan Simons, *Jerusalem in the Old Testament* (Leiden: Brill, 1952), pp. 226-281.

51. Levine, "Political Struggle" (see endnote 31), pp. 61-83.

52. *Antiq.* 14.64-71.

53. B. Mazar, *The Mountain of the Lord* (Garden City, NY: Doubleday, 1975).

54. *Apion* 1.186-189.

55. 1 Maccabees 12.

56. *Antiq.* 121.160-166.

57. Ben Sira 50.

58. 2 Maccabees 4.

59. 1 Maccabees 14:47.

60. Shmuel Safrai and M. Stern, *The Jewish People in the First Century*, II (Assen, Neth.: Van Gorcum, 1976), pp. 876-906.

61. See Levine, "The Second Temple Synagogue: The Formative Years," in *The Synagogue in Late Antiquity*, ed. Levine (Durham, NC: Jewish Theological Seminary and ASOR, 1987).

62. Marcel Simon, *Jewish Sects at the Time of Jesus* (Philadelphia: Fortress, 1967), pp. 1-16.

63. Smith, "The Dead Sea Sect in Relation to Ancient Judaism," *NTS* 7 (1960), pp. 347-360; *Palestinian Parties and Politics* (see endnote 3), pp. 57-81, 126-147. Klaus Koch, "Ezra and the Origins of Judaism," *JSS* 19 (1974), pp. 173-197.

64. Avot de Rabbi Nathan, A, IV.

65. *Antiq.* 13.371-373.

66. *Antiq.* 13.62-73.

67. Avot de Rabbi Nathan, A, IV.

68. *Antiq.* 13.297.

69. *Antiq.* 13.410-415.

70. *Antiq.* 13.298.

71. *War* 2.166.

72. Ellis Rivkin, "Pharisaism and the Crisis of the Individual in the Greco-Roman World," *JQR* 61 (1970), pp. 27-53; Levine, "Political Struggle" (see endnote 31), pp. 61ff.

73. *War* 2.165.

74. On the Sadducees, see Abraham Geiger, *The Bible and its Translations* (Jerusalem, 1949), pp. 69-102 (in Hebrew); Finkelstein, *The Pharisees*, 3 vols. (Philadelphia: Jewish Publication Society, 3rd ed., 1962), vol. 2, pp. 637-753; Jacob Lauterbach, *Rabbinic Essays* (Cincinnati: Hebrew Union College, 1951), pp. 23-83, and most comprehensively, Rudolf Leszynsky, *Die Sadduzäer* (Berlin: Mayer & Müller, 1912); Jean Le Moyne, *Les Sadducéens* (Paris, 1972). See also, Alexander Guttman, *Rabbinic Judaism in the Making* (Detroit: Wayne State Univ. Press, 1970), pp. 136-176, where the major

controversies between the sects are explicated.

75. Ralph Marcus, "The Pharisees in the Light of Modern Scholarship," *JR* 32 (1952), pp. 155-164; Gedaliah Alon, *Jews, Judaism and the Classical World* (Jerusalem: Magnes, 1977), pp. 18-47; M. Smith, "Palestinian Judaism" (see endnote 43), pp. 67-81; Levine, "On the Political Involvement of the Pharisees under Herod and the Procurators," *Cathedra* 8 (1978), pp. 12-28 (in Hebrew); Jacob Neusner, *From Politics to Piety* (Englewood Cliffs, NJ: Prentice-Hall, 1973).

76. Finkelstein, *Pharisees* (see endnote 74), pp. 73ff.; Fritz Baer, *Israel Among the Nations* (Jerusalem, 1955) (in Hebrew).

77. See Neusner, *The Rabbinic Traditions About the Pharisees*, 3 vols. (Leiden: Brill, 1971), pp. 301-319.

78. A point hotly debated among scholars. For a maximalist position, see Alon, *Jews, Judaism* (see endnote 75), p. 22 and note 11; Neil J. McEleney, "Orthodoxy in Judaism of the First Christian Century," *JSJ* 4 (1973), pp. 19-42. For a minimalist position, see Smith, "Palestinian Judaism" (see endnote 43), pp.67-81; David Aune, "Orthodoxy in First Century Judaism? A Response to N.J. McEleney," *JSJ* 7 (1976), pp. 1-10.

79. *War* 2.119-166.

80. Publications on the Dead Sea sect and scrolls are legion. A classic introductory work in this field remains that of Cross, *The Ancient Library of Qumran and Modern Biblical Studies* (Garden City, NY: Doubleday, 1958). The best single volume on the archaeology of Qumran remains that of Roland de Vaux, *Archaeology and the Dead Sea Scrolls* (Oxford: Clarendon, 1973).

81. Shemaryahu Talmon, "The Calendar-Reckoning of the Sect from the Judaean Desert," *Scripta Hierosolymitana* 4 (1958), pp. 162-199.

82. This point is meticulously documented in the magisterial work of Abraham Schalit, *King Herod* (Jerusalem, 1960) (in Hebrew); see also Levine, "Roman Rule in Judea from 63 B.C.E. to 70 C.E.," *The History of Eretz Israel*, vol. 4, ed. M. Stern (Jerusalem: Keter, 1984), pp. 11-25 (in Hebrew).

VIII. Roman Domination

Bibliographical Note: In recent years the history of the latter part of the Second Temple period has been surveyed in several large-scale and reliable works in English: Emil Schürer, *The History of the Jewish People in the Age of Jesus Christ*, rev., ed. Geza Vérmes et al., 3 vols. (Edinburgh: T. & T. Clark, 1973-1986). A fourth volume is scheduled to appear in 1987; *Compendia Rerum Judaicarum ad Novum Testamentum Sec. I: The Jewish People in the First Century*, ed. Samuel Safrai and Menahem Stern, 2 vols. (Philadelphia: Fortress, 1974-1976); and *The World History of the Jewish People, Vol. 6: The Hellenistic Age*, ed. Abraham Schalit (New Brunswick, NJ: Rutgers Univ. Press, 1972); *The World History of the Jewish People, Vol. 7: The Herodian Period*, ed. Zvi Baras (New Brunswick, NJ: Rutgers Univ. Press, 1975); E. Mary Smallwood, *The Jews Under Roman Rule* (Leiden: Brill, 1976, reprinted 1981). Interested readers are referred to these works for complete and detailed references to the ancient evidence and to modern scholarship.

In this chapter I provide only minimal bibliographical annotation. Further bibliography can be obtained from the two useful volumes of Louis H. Feldman, *Josephus and Modern Scholarship 1937-1980* (Berlin: de Gruyter, 1984), and *Josephus: A Supplementary Bibliography* (New York: Garland, 1986). Because of the centrality of Josephus to all modern discussions, Feldman's bibliography covers virtually all aspects of Jewish history of the later Second Temple period. Quotations from Josephus are taken from the Loeb Classical Library edition, edited by H. St. J. Thackeray, R. Marcus, A. Wikgren and L.H. Feldman (London: Heinemann/Cambridge, MA: Harvard Univ. Press, 1926-1965, frequently reprinted; 9 volumes).

1. The precise legal status of Judea in this period is obscure.

2. See Menahem Stern, "The Relations between Judea and Rome During the Reign of John Hyrcanus," *Zion* 26 (1961), pp. 1-22 (in Hebrew); A.N. Sherwin-White, *Roman Foreign Policy in the East, 168 B.C. to A.D. 1* (Norman: Univ. of Oklahoma, 1984); Erich S. Gruen, *The Hellenistic World and the Coming of Rome*, 2 vols. (Berkeley: Univ. of California, 1984).

3. The standard modern biography is by Abraham Schalit, *König Herodes* (Berlin: de Gruyter, 1968).

4. The phrase is from Pliny the Elder, *Natural History* 5.70; see Stern, *Greek and Latin Authors on Jews and Judaism*, 3 vols. (Jerusalem: Israel Academy of Humanities and Sciences, 1974-1984), vol. 1, p. 471, no. 204. For discussion of pagan statements about the glory of Jerusalem, see the article by Stern in *Jerusalem in the Second Temple Period: Abraham Schalit Memorial Volume*, ed. A. Oppenheimer et al. (Jerusalem: Ben Zvi Institute, 1981), pp. 257-270 (in Hebrew).

5. See the symposium on "Herod's Building Projects" in *The Jerusalem Cathedra* 1, pp. 48-80 (with contributions by Ehud Netzer, Lee Levine, Magen Broshi and Yoram Tsafrir) (Jerusalem: Ben Zvi Institute, 1981).

6. *War* 1.33.8.665.

7. *Antiq.* 17.8.1.191-192.

8. On Herod's genealogy, see *Antiq.* 14.1.3.8-10; 14.7.3.121 and 14.15.2.403; cf. Eusebius, *History of the Church* 1.7.11-14. Jews who disliked Herod fastened upon his less-than-perfect pedigree to justify their dislike; Jews who liked Herod were quite willing to overlook his origins; cf. Mishnah *Sotah* 7:8 regarding Agrippa.

9. Richard A. Horsley and John S. Hanson, *Bandits, Prophets, and Messiahs: Popular Movements in the*

Time of Jesus (New York: Winston-Seabury, 1985).

10. D.C. Braund, Rome and the Friendly King: The Character of Client Kingship (London: Croom Helm, 1984).

11. See, generally, Jean-Pierre Lémonon, Pilate et le gouvernement de la Judée (Paris: Gabalda, 1981); Daniel R. Schwartz, "Josephus and Philo on Pontius Pilate," in Josephus Flavius, Historian of Eretz Israel (Jerusalem: Ben Zvi Institute, 1983), pp. 217-236 (in Hebrew).

12. In Books 14 and 16 of the Antiquities, Josephus quotes a series of edicts, laws and letters that bestow special privileges upon the Jews in order to allow them to practice their religion. On politeumata, see Aryeh Kasher, The Jews in Hellenistic and Roman Egypt (Tübingen, W. Ger.: Mohr-Siebeck, 1985).

13. See Emil Schürer, History of the Jewish People in the Age of Jesus Christ, ed. Vérmes et al., (Edinburgh: T & T Clark, 1973), vol. 1, p. 397.

14. The argument of the following paragraphs is developed at much greater length in Shaye J.D. Cohen, From the Maccabees to the Mishnah (Philadelphia: Westminster, 1987).

15. Lee I. Levine, ed., Ancient Synagogues Revealed, (Jerusalem: IES, 1981); Hershel Shanks, Judaism in Stone: The Archaeology of Ancient Synagogues (Washington, DC: BAS, 1978).

16. Recent scholarship has questioned the usefulness of this concept, but this is not the place to enter that debate. I mean by "popular religion" not the religion of an economic or social class, but the religion of the people who were not members or followers of one of the "virtuoso" or "pietistic" groups discussed below.

17. Eric M. Meyers, Jewish Ossuaries: Reburial and Rebirth (Rome: Biblical Institute, 1971), and Pau Figueras, Decorated Jewish Ossuaries (Leiden: Brill, 1983).

18. See Morton Smith, Jesus the Magician (San Francisco: Harper & Row, 1978); compare Daniel J. Harrington, "The Jewishness of Jesus," BR, Spring 1987, pp. 32-41.

19. The best general survey is that of Schürer, History of the Jewish People (see endnote 13); Marcel Simon, Jewish Sects at the Time of Jesus (Philadelphia: Fortress, 1967), is out of date.

20. Antiq. 18.1.3-5.15.17.19-20.

21. This definition is based on Bryan Wilson, Patterns of Sectarianism (London: Heinemann, 1967), and Joseph Blenkinsopp, "Interpretation and the Tendency to Sectarianism," in Jewish and Christian Self-Definition, Vol. 2: Aspects of Judaism in the Graeco-Roman Period, ed. E.P. Sanders et al. (Philadelphia: Fortress, 1981), pp. 1-26.

22. See Daniel R. Schwartz, "Josephus and Nicolaus on the Pharisees," Journal for the Study of Judaism in the Persian, Hellenistic and Roman Periods 14 (1983), pp. 157-171.

23. This discussion of early Christianity has been abridged from Cohen, From the Maccabees to the Mishnah (see endnote 14), pp. 166-168.

24. Antiq. 20.9.7.219-222. This is the first securely attested instance of a government "make-work" project. See Gabriella Giglioni, Lavori pubblici e occupazione nell'antichità classica (Bologna, Italy, 1974), pp. 171ff, with the comments of Lionel Casson, Bulletin of the American Society of Papyrologists 15 (1978), pp. 50-51.

25. On these social tensions see Cohen, Josephus in Galilee and Rome (Leiden: Brill, 1979), pp. 206-221; Sean Freyne, Galilee from Alexander the Great to Hadrian (Notre Dame, IN: Univ. of Notre Dame, 1980), part II; Peter A. Brunt, "Josephus on Social Conflicts in Roman Judaea," Klio 59 (1977), pp. 149-153.

26. War 6.5.4.312. The Roman historian Tacitus reports the same information; see Stern, Greek and Latin Authors (see endnote 4), vol. 1, p. 31, no. 281.

27. See especially H. Kreissig, Die sozialen Zusammenhänge des judäischen Krieges (Berlin, 1970); Tessa Rajak, Josephus: The Historian and His Society (London: Duckworth, 1983), chap. 5.

28. Tacitus, Histories 4.54.2. On native revolts see Stephen L. Dyson, "Native Revolts in the Roman Empire," Historia 20 (1971), pp. 239-274, and "Native Revolt Patterns in the Roman Empire," in Aufstieg und Niedergang der römischen Welt II 3, ed. H. Temporini (Berlin: de Gruyter, 1975), pp. 138-175. On the patterns of social revolutions see Crane Brinton, The Anatomy of Revolution (New York, 1959). Compare the French and Russian revolutions.

29. Josephus tells his story in The Jewish War 3.8.340-408.

30. War 2.17.3.411. For studies of War, see Louis H. Feldman, Josephus: A Supplementary Bibliography (New York: Garland, 1986). A useful and accessible study is David Rhoads, Israel in Revolution (Philadelphia: Fortress, 1976).

31. Cohen, Josephus in Galilee (see endnote 25), pp. 152-160.

32. The Rabban Yohanan ben Zakkai tale appears in four different versions; they are conveniently available in Jacob Neusner, Development of a Legend (Leiden: Brill, 1970). The bibliography on these stories is immense: see Horst Moehring, "Joseph ben Matthia and Flavius Josephus," in Aufstieg und Niedergang der römischen Welt II 21.2, ed. W. Haase (Berlin: de Gruyter, 1984), pp. 864-944, especially pp. 917-944, and Cohen, "Josephus, Jeremiah, and Polybius," History and Theory 21 (1982), pp. 366-381.

33. See especially Smith, "Zealots and Sicarii: Their Origins and Relation," HTR 64 (1971), pp. 1-19.

34. Ever since the Persian period, the priests of the Temple had been in the habit of praying for the welfare of the reigning monarch; see Ezra 6:10. In addition, upon his accession to office the high priest took an oath of loyalty to the state; see Antiq. 11.8.3.318.

35. For a defense of this view, see Cohen, Josephus in Galilee (see endnote 25), pp. 181-206; for another

interpretation, see Rajak, *Josephus* (see endnote 27), pp. 65-103.

36. The fact that the Idumeans were invited to participate in the war, as well as the fact that they willingly accepted the invitation, shows that their conversion to Judaism during the reign of John Hyrcanus was sincere and real. The Idumean Herod was a "half-Jew" only because he was disliked. See endnote 8.

37. The question of Titus's motives and actions has been much debated. See the discussion in Stern, *Greek and Latin Authors* (see endnote 4), vol. 2, pp. 64-67, no. 282. See also Zvi Yavetz, "Reflections on Titus and Josephus," *Greek, Roman and Byzantine Studies* 16 (1975), pp. 411-432.

38. Josephus does not explicitly state John's fate. On the subsequent history of the sacred vessels, see Hans Lewy, "The Fate of the Sacred Vessels After the Destruction of the Second Temple," in *Studies in Jewish Hellenism* (Jerusalem: Bialik), pp. 255-258.

39. The translation is from Naphtali Lewis and Meyer Reinhold, *Roman Civilization Sourcebook II: The Empire* (New York: Harper & Row, 1966), p. 92.

40. Stern, *Greek and Latin Authors* (see endnote 4), vol. 2, p. 373, no. 430. The standard discussion of the *fiscus Judaicus* is Victor Tcherikover, *Corpus Papyrorum Judaicarum,* 3 vols. (Cambridge, MA: Harvard Univ. Press, 1957-1964), vol. 2, pp. 110-116.

41. D.J. Ladouceur, "Masada: A Consideration of the Literary Evidence," *Greek, Roman and Byzantine Studies* 21 (1980), pp. 245-260; Stern, "The Suicide of Eleazar ben Yair and His Men at Masada," *Zion* 147 (1982), pp. 367-397 (in Hebrew); Cohen, "Masada: Literary Tradition, Archaeological Remains, and the Credibility of Josephus," *JJS* 33 (1982), pp. 385-405. These three articles provide correction to Yigael Yadin, *Masada* (New York: Random House, 1966).

42. A full discussion of all the aspects of this question obviously is outside the scope of this essay. Here is some bibliography: W.D. Davies, *The Setting of the Sermon on the Mount* (Cambridge, UK: Cambridge Univ. Press, 1964), pp. 259-286; Neusner, "The Formation of Rabbinic Judaism: Yavneh (Jamnia) from A.D. 70 to 100," in *Aufstieg und Niedergang der römischen Welt* II 19.2, ed. Temporini and Haase (Berlin: de Gruyter, 1979), pp. 3-42; Neusner, *Eliezer ben Hyrcanus* (Leiden: Brill, 1973); Cohen, "The Significance of Yavneh: Pharisees, Rabbis, and the End of Jewish Sectarianism," *HUCA* 55 (1984), pp. 27-53; Baruch M. Bokser, "Rabbinic Responses to Catastrophe: From Continuity to Discontinuity," *PAAJR* 50 (1983), pp. 37-61.

Index